The
Alaska Almanac®

Facts About Alaska

25th Anniversary Edition

Alaska Northwest Books™

First edition published 1976
Twenty-fifth edition 2001
Previously published as FACTS ABOUT ALASKA: The ALASKA ALMANAC®

ISBN 0-88240-550-0
ISSN 0270-5370
Key title: The Alaska Almanac

Cover illustration: Mindy Dwyer
Cover and interior design: Elizabeth Watson
Editor: Don Graydon
Compiler: Nancy Gates
Yearly Highlights: Maureen Clark
Page composition/editorial assistance: Fay L. Bartels
Maps: Gray Mouse Graphics

Alaska Northwest Books™
An imprint of Graphic Arts Center Publishing
P.O. Box 10306, Portland, OR 97296-0306
(503) 226-2402
www.gacpc.com

Printed in the United States of America

To Our Readers

Alaska Northwest Books™ once again welcomes the wisdom,
wit and wackiness of Mr. Whitekeys to this, our
25th anniversary edition of *The Alaska Almanac*®.
Thousands of visitors and Alaskans alike enjoy his
Alaska-based comedy, songs and dance showcased
at Anchorage's Fly By Night Club. Originator of the
infamous "Whale Fat Follies," Mr. Whitekeys brings
his distinctive insights on Northland life—from
moose nuggets to politics—to the pages of
The Alaska Almanac®.

Contents

Fast Facts About Alaska

Motto: North to the Future.

Nickname: The Last Frontier.

Capital: Juneau.

Purchased from Russia: 1867.

Organized as a territory: 1912.

Entered the Union: Jan. 3, 1959, as the 49th state.

Governor: Tony Knowles.

Land area: 570,374 square miles, or about 365 million acres. The largest state in the country, Alaska is one-fifth the size of the combined Lower 48 states.

Population: 626,932.

Median age of residents: 30.1.

Per capita personal income: $28,523 in 1999, 17th in the nation.

Area per person: About 0.9 square mile for each person; New York state has 0.003 square mile per person.

Largest city in population: Anchorage, 260,283.

Highest temperature: 100°F, at Fort Yukon, 1915.

Lowest temperature: –80°F, at Prospect Creek Camp, 1971.

Heaviest annual snowfall: 974.5 inches, at Thompson Pass, near Valdez, winter of 1952–53.

Largest newspaper: *Anchorage Daily News,* paid circulation of 85,707 on Sundays.

Most popular park: Klondike Gold Rush National Historical Park, in Skagway, visited by 697,000 people in 2000.

North America's tallest mountain: Mount McKinley at 20,320 feet.

Nation's farthest-north city: Barrow, 350 miles north of the Arctic Circle.

World's busiest seaplane base: Anchorage's Lake Hood; handles more than 1,000 takeoffs and landings on a peak summer day.

North America's longest highway tunnel: Anton Anderson Memorial Tunnel, 2.5 miles long, on the Portage Glacier Highway.

Nation's largest contiguous state park: Wood–Tikchik State Park, with 1.6 million acres of wilderness.

North America's biggest earthquake: The Good Friday earthquake of March 27, 1964, with a magnitude rated at 9.2.

North America's second-greatest tide range: 38.9 feet near Anchorage in Upper Cook Inlet.

Nation's greatest concentration of glaciers: About 29,000 square miles—5 percent of the state—is covered by glaciers.

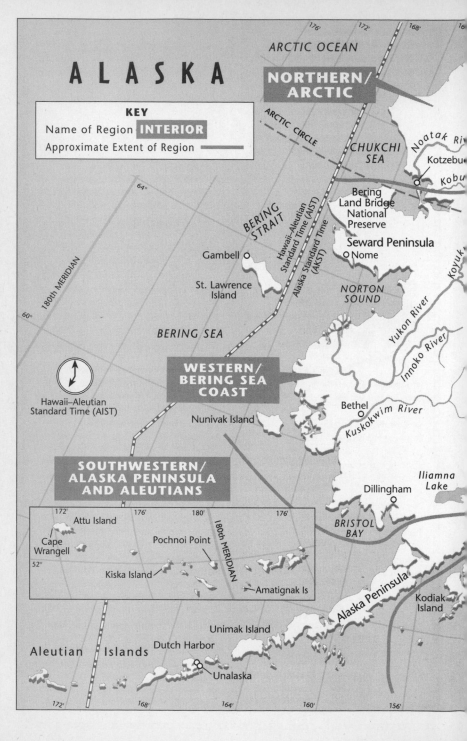

ALASKA

KEY
Name of Region: **INTERIOR**
Approximate Extent of Region ━━━━━

ARCTIC OCEAN

NORTHERN/ ARCTIC

ARCTIC CIRCLE

CHUKCHI SEA

Noatak Ri

Kotzebu

Kobu

64°

Bering Land Bridge National Preserve

Seward Peninsula

Bering–Aleutian Standard Time (AIST)

Alaska Standard Time (AKST)

BERING STRAIT

Gambell

St. Lawrence Island

Nome

60°

180th MERIDIAN

NORTON SOUND

Yukon River

Koyuk

Innoko River

BERING SEA

WESTERN/ BERING SEA COAST

Bethel

Kuskokwim River

Hawaii–Aleutian Standard Time (AIST)

Nunivak Island

Iliamna Lake

Dillingham

SOUTHWESTERN/ ALASKA PENINSULA AND ALEUTIANS

BRISTOL BAY

172°   176°   180°   176°

Attu Island

Cape Wrangell

52°

Pochnoi Point

180th MERIDIAN

Kiska Island

Amatignak Is

Alaska Peninsula

Kodiak Island

Unimak Island

Aleutian   Islands

Dutch Harbor

Unalaska

172°   168°   164°   160°   156°

176°   172°   168°   16

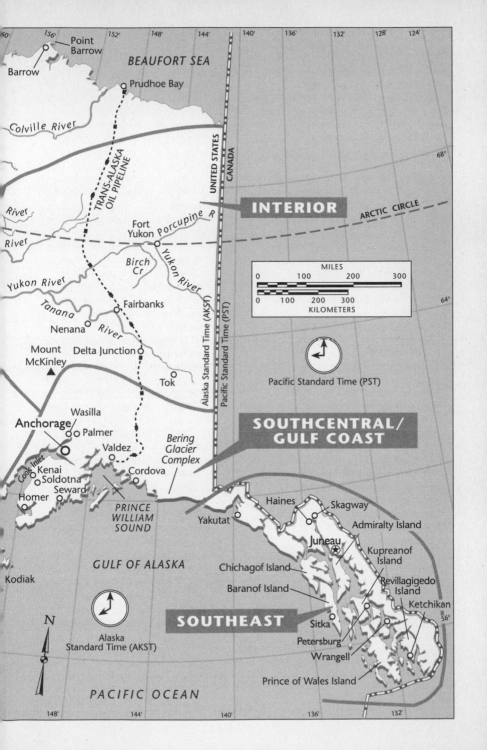

BEAUFORT SEA

156'   152'   148'   140'   136'   132'   128'   124'

Point Barrow
Barrow
Prudhoe Bay
Colville River
TRANS-ALASKA OIL PIPELINE
UNITED STATES
CANADA

INTERIOR

ARCTIC CIRCLE

68°

Fort Yukon
Porcupine R
Yukon River
Birch Cr
River
River
Yukon River
Tanana
River
Fairbanks
Nenana
Mount McKinley
Delta Junction
Tok

Alaska Standard Time (AKST)
Pacific Standard Time (PST)

64°

MILES
0   100   200   300
0   100   200   300
KILOMETERS

Pacific Standard Time (PST)

Wasilla
Anchorage
Palmer
Valdez
Kenai
Soldotna
Seward
Homer
Cook Inlet

Bering Glacier Complex

SOUTHCENTRAL/ GULF COAST

Cordova

PRINCE WILLIAM SOUND

Haines
Skagway
Yakutat
Admiralty Island
Juneau
Kupreanof Island
Chichagof Island
Revillagigedo Island
Baranof Island
Ketchikan

GULF OF ALASKA

Kodiak

N

Alaska Standard Time (AKST)

SOUTHEAST

Sitka
Petersburg
Wrangell
Prince of Wales Island

56°

PACIFIC OCEAN

148'   144'   140'   136'   132'

7

Acknowledgments

This 25th edition of The Alaska Almanac® has been compiled and updated from information supplied by many helpful state and federal offices, publications, consultants, organizations, experts and individuals. The editors gratefully acknowledge:

Joan Antonson, Deputy State Historic Preservation Officer / State Historian

Kevin Banks, Alaska Department of Natural Resources

Scott Banks, Alaska Railroad

Ed Bovy, Bureau of Land Management

Roger Burnside, Alaska Department of Natural Resources

Joan Cahill, Alaska Permanent Fund Corp.

Francis Dun, Bureau of Indian Affairs

Deborah Erikson, Alaska Division of Public Health

Justin Frodella, Alaska Department of Community and Economic Development

Kathy Frost, Alaska Dog Mushers Association

Rich Harris, National Park Service

Mike Heatwole, Alyeska Pipeline Service Co.

Thomas Jensen, Alaska Communications Systems

Lana Johnson, Alaska Permanent Fund Corp.

Bruce Kato, Alaska State Museum

Bob King, Office of the Governor

Kerwin Krause, Alaska Department of Natural Resources

Karen Lipson, Alaska Department of Education

Jon Lyman, Alaska Department of Fish and Game

Steve McGroarty, Alaska Department of Natural Resources

Steve McMains, Alaska Oil and Gas Conservation Commission

Linda Mickle, Alaska Marine Highway System

Harold Moeser, Alaska Department of Transportation

Rachael Moreland, Alaska Forest Association

Linda Nelson, Alaska Heritage Tours

Nancy Perry, Anchorage Fur Rendezvous

Jim Potdevin, Alaska Marine Highway System

Toby Pyle, Hostelling International

John Quinley, National Park Service

William Roche, Alaska Department of Revenue

Melody Roos, Alaska Agricultural Statistics Service

Julie Rowe, U.S. Forest Service

Stanley Senner, National Audubon Society

Joette Storm, Federal Aviation Administration

Dick Swainback, Alaska Department of Community and Economic Development

David Szumigala, Alaska Department of Natural Resources

Judy Weske, Alaska Department of Community and Economic Development

Petty Officer Roger Wetherell, U.S. Coast Guard

Polly Wheeler, Alaska Department of Fish and Game

Natasha Willows, Inuit Circumpolar Conference (Canada)

Tim Wolfton, Alyeska Pipeline Service Co.

Mr. Whitekeys wishes to gratefully acknowledge the off-center contributions of the *Anchorage Daily News,* Jenny Haggar, The Blue J., Anna B. Castillo, the *Seward Phoenix-Log,* Ralph Ashley, Karen Laing, Fred Janvrin, Heather Brock, Rich Owens, Max Lowe, Joe Senungetuk and Mike Wiedmer.

AGRICULTURE

Agriculture in Alaska ranges from backyard gardens to 3,000-acre farms. Extremes of weather and a short growing season challenge cultivation in the state, but certain crops—notably potatoes and carrots—thrive in the cool soil temperatures. Overall, climate is not the greatest impediment to Alaska farming. More significant hurdles are high production costs and competition from the Lower 48.

Alaska's traditional farming is concentrated in two regions: the Matanuska Valley, northeast of Anchorage, which in 1999 contributed 57 percent of the state's farm production value, and the Tanana Valley, surrounding Fairbanks, which was responsible for 33 percent.

An estimated 15 million to 18 million acres in Alaska are believed to be arable, but only 910,000 acres—less than one-half of 1 percent of the state—are currently considered land in farms. In 1999, crops covered 31,000 acres; the balance was in pasture and uncleared land.

Total market value of Alaska's agricultural products in 1999 was $50 million. Feed crops accounted for $3 million of total market receipts, and vegetables (including potatoes) were $4.4 million of the total.

Aquaculture now accounts for the largest portion of the Alaska market basket, at $21.4 million. Shellfish farming and finfish ranching make up these market receipts.

Greenhouse and nursery industries—a substantial portion of the state's agricultural picture—amounted to $13.4 million, or 26 percent of total cash receipts for 1999.

More than 96 percent of the barley grown in 2000 was harvested in the Tanana Valley. Total production netted 102,500 bushels, yielding 31.1 bushels an acre. Production value for the 2000 barley crop was roughly $369,000, down from the 1999 crop of $581,000. Harvest of oats yielded 23.3 bushels an acre for a total of 7,000 bushels at an estimated value of $22,000. This reflects a decrease from 55,100 bushels valued at $152,000 in 1999.

Another Alaska agriculture enterprise is the raising of reindeer. Officials estimate there are a total of 19,000 head in 23 herds throughout Alaska. Most of the reindeer are located on the Seward Peninsula and Nunivak Island, where they contribute significantly to the local economies. Among the by-products of reindeer is the powder made from clipped antler, most of which is exported to the Far East, where it is believed to be an aphrodisiac. Sales related to reindeer were valued at $540,000 in 1999, down from $562,000 in 1998.

Milk production in 2000 totaled 1.52 million gallons, a decrease of 34,884 gallons from 1999. Dairy products brought in $2.72 million in 2000. Economic stresses continue to reduce the number of farmers involved in this capital-intensive industry. In 1988, 2,100 cows produced nearly 3.57 million gallons of milk. By 1999, the number of cows had decreased to 900. Only 10 dairies were operating in the state on Jan. 1, 2000.

The small vegetable gardens of the Russian fur traders are believed to constitute the first Alaska agriculture. Gold-rush days saw growing interest in local farming possibilities, but it wasn't until 1935 that there was a concerted effort to introduce commercial growing. President Franklin Roosevelt's New Deal resettlement plan transplanted 200 farm families from the Midwest to the Matanuska Valley, where they were to create a food source for the territory.

Although most produce comes from Outside, local farmers still supply the Anchorage area with some fresh produce and dairy products. The growing season averages 117 days; there are some days with more than 19 hours of sunlight in the summer (which helps produce giant-size vegetables).

Crops	Volume	Acres Harvested	2000 Value
Hay	94 tons	18,000	$3.74 million
Potatoes	154,000 cwt	840	$2.76 million
Barley, for grain	102,500 bushels	3,300	$369,000
Oats, for grain	7,000 bushels	300	$22,000

The Tanana Valley growing season is shorter than that of the Matanuska Valley, with about 106 frost-free days. Because growing-season temperatures are warmer in the Tanana Valley, many experts consider the area to have greater agricultural potential. Barley and oats are raised for grain and hay. Most Alaska-grown grain is used for domestic livestock feed. All are spring varieties since few winter types survive the cold.

Beef, pork, hay, eggs and fresh produce are produced throughout the Railbelt region and are easily transported to major markets. (The Railbelt is the region linked by the Alaska Railroad, from Seward north to Fairbanks.) Umnak and Unalaska Islands in the Aleutian Islands provide grazing area for nearly 1,300 sheep, down from 27,000 in 1970.

Across Alaska, the pressure of urban development is reducing the number of acres available for farming. At the same time, the state is attempting to increase the number of farms through sales of agriculture tracts. Many Alaskans rely on farming to supplement other income. In 2000, there were 580 farms with annual sales of $1,000 or more.

Since 1978, state land sales have placed more than 165,000 acres of potential agricultural land into private ownership. Most of this acreage is in the Delta Junction area, south of Fairbanks, where tracts of up to 3,200 acres were sold by lottery for grain farming.

The Nenana area southwest of Fairbanks is among those under consideration for future agricultural development.

Additional information is available from the Alaska Agricultural Statistics Service, P.O. Box 799, Palmer 99645; (907) 745-4272; www.usda.gov/nass.

Total Acreage of Alaska Cropland by Region

Region	Percent	Acres
Tanana Valley	58.3	18,260
Matanuska Valley	34.3	10,760
Kenai Peninsula	7.1	2,220
Southeast and Southwestern Alaska	0.3	100

Alaskans now rank number one in the U.S. in both per-capita ownership of computers and Internet access. You can now connect to a site that claims, "You might be a REAL Alaskan if people admiring your earthtone carpet suddenly realize that it really IS the earth!!"

AIR TRAVEL Alaska is the flyingest state in the Union; the only practical way to reach many areas of rural Alaska is by airplane. According to the Federal Aviation Administration, Alaska Region, in January 2001 there were 10,016 registered pilots and 8,053 registered aircraft. Alaska has approximately six times as many pilots per capita and 14 times as many airplanes per capita as the rest of the United States.

From its inception in 1946 through 2001, the federal airport improvement program provided $1.2 billion for airport development throughout the state.

By the 1930s, the airplane had replaced the dog team as carrier of U.S. mail to many Alaska villages. Photo courtesy Carmen Jefford Fisher. From *Winging It!* by Jack Jefford.

These federal funds provided for more than 1,000 projects. Grants totaling $90 million were distributed to state and local airport sponsors by the FAA Alaskan Region in 2000.

According to the FAA, Alaska has 325 airports, plus 1,100 recorded landing areas and 103 seaplane bases. Additionally, pilots land on many of the thousands of lakes and gravel bars across the state where no constructed facility exists. Of the seaplane bases, Lake Hood in Anchorage is the largest and busiest in the world. On a yearly basis, an average of 234 takeoffs and landings occur daily, and more than 1,000 on a peak summer day.

Merrill Field in Anchorage recorded 170,754 flight operations during 2000. Ted Stevens Anchorage International Airport saw more than five million passengers pass through in 2000.

Ted Stevens Anchorage International is the No. 1 airport in the United States for cargo traffic, based on all-cargo aircraft landed weights. In fiscal 2000, 3.6 billion pounds of cargo moved through the airport. Operating revenue for fiscal 2000 was more than $56 million. The airport counted 38,144 revenue landings of cargo aircraft during the fiscal year, up from 26,674 in 1996.

Pilots who wish to fly their own planes to Alaska should have the latest federal government flight information publication, *Alaska Supplement.* Travel and safety information is available from the Federal Aviation Administration, 222 W. Seventh Ave., No. 14, Anchorage 99513-7587; www.faa.gov/capstone; and http://akweathercams.faa.gov.

Air taxi operators are found in most Alaska communities, and aircraft can be chartered to fly you to a wilderness spot and pick you up later at a prearranged time and location. Most charter operators charge an hourly rate, either per plane load or per passenger (sometimes with a minimum passenger requirement); others may charge on a per-mile basis.

NUGGETS

June 13, 1988, was the day of the momentous Nome–Provideniya Friendship Flight One by Alaska Airlines. A group of 82 politicians, Natives and members of the media made the 45-minute flight across Bering Strait to the Soviet Union to promote goodwill, re-establish family ties and, for some, to see once more the land they left so long ago. —1989 *The ALASKA ALMANAC®*

Alaska's Largest Air Cargo Carriers
(Ranked by 2000 Revenue Cargo Ton-Miles in Alaska)

Current Ranking	Company Name, Location	2000 Revenue Cargo Ton-Miles	Employees in Alaska	Year Estab.
1.	Alaska Airlines Cargo	$66,801,138	1,600	1932
2.	Northern Air Cargo	16,375,805	260	1956
3.	Danzas Corp., AEI	10,200,000	31	1972
4.	Air Cargo Express	9,544,839	215	1995
5.	ERA Aviation	5,846,712	650	1948

Source: *Alaska Journal of Commerce*

Flightseeing trips to area attractions are often available at a fixed price per passenger. Charter fares range from $140 to $175 per person (four-person and up minimum) for a short flightseeing trip, to $350 an hour for an eight-passenger Cessna 404.

A wide range of aircraft is used for charter and scheduled passenger service in Alaska. The larger interstate airlines—Alaska, Continental, Delta, Northwest and United—use jets (Douglas DC-8, DC-10, Boeing 727, 737, 757, 767). Prop jets and single- or twin-engine prop planes on wheels, skis and floats are used for most intrastate travel. A few of these types of aircraft flown in Alaska are: 19-passenger de Havilland Twin Otter, 10-passenger Britten-Norman Islander, 7-passenger Grumman Goose (amphibious), DC-3, 4-passenger Cessna 185, 9-passenger twin-engine Piper Navajo Chieftain, 5- to 8-passenger de Havilland Beaver, 3- to 4-passenger Cessna 180, 5- to 6-passenger Cessna 206 and single-passenger Piper Super Cub.

International Service. Several international carriers provide cargo or passenger service in Alaska through the Anchorage gateway. The list includes Air China, Alaska Airlines (to Russia and Mexico), Asiana, Cathay, China Airlines, ERA Aviation, Federal Express, Korean Air, Nippon Cargo Airlines, Northwest Airlines, Singapore Airlines, United Airlines and United Parcel Service.

Interstate Service. U.S. carriers providing interstate passenger service: Alaska Airlines, Continental Airlines, Delta Air Lines, ERA Aviation, Northwest Airlines, Peninsula Airways, Southcentral Air and United Airlines. These carriers also provide freight service between Anchorage and Seattle. For commercial passenger information, consult city phone directories, chambers of commerce or your travel agent.

ALASKA–CANADA BOUNDARY
In 1825, Russia, in possession of Alaska, and Great Britain, in possession of Canada, established the original boundary between Alaska and Canada. The demarcation was to begin at 54°40' north latitude, just north of the mouth of Portland Canal, follow the canal to 56° north latitude, then traverse the mountain summits parallel to the coast as far as 141° west longitude. From there it would conform with that meridian north to the Arctic Ocean. The boundary line along the mountain summits in southeastern Alaska was never to be farther inland than 10 leagues—about 30 miles.

After purchasing Alaska in 1867, the United States found that the wording about the boundary line was interpreted differently by the Canadians. They felt the measurements should be made inland from the mouths of bays, while Americans argued the measurements should be made from the heads of the bays. In 1903, an international tribunal upheld the American interpretation of the treaty, providing

Alaska the 1,538-mile-long border it has with Canada today. The southeastern Alaska border is 891 miles long, and 181 miles of that border is over water. If the Canadians had won their argument they would have had access to the sea, and Haines, Dyea and Skagway now would be in Canada.

A 20-foot-wide vista—a swath of land 10 feet on each side of the boundary between southeastern Alaska, British Columbia and Yukon Territory—was surveyed and cleared between 1904 and 1914. Portions of the 710-mile-long land portion of the boundary were again cleared in 1925, 1948, 1978 and 1982 by the International Boundary Commission. Monument and vista maintenance in 1978 and 1982 was conducted by the Canadian section of the commission and by the U.S. section in 1983, 1984 and 1985.

The Alaska-Canada border along the 141st meridian was surveyed and cleared between 1904 and 1920. Astronomical observations were made to find the meridian's intersection with the Yukon River; then, under the direction of the International Boundary Commission, engineers and surveyors of the U.S. Coast and Geodetic Survey and the Canadian Department of the Interior worked together north and south from the Yukon. The straight-line vista extends from Demarcation Point on the Arctic Ocean south to Mount St. Elias in the Wrangell Mountains (from there the border cuts east to encompass southeastern Alaska). This part of the border stretches for 647 miles in one of the world's longest straight lines, as well as the world's longest unguarded border.

Monuments are the actual markers of the boundary and are located so they tie in with survey networks of both the United States and Canada. Along the Alaska boundary most monuments are 2¹/₂-foot-high cones of aluminum-bronze set in concrete bases or occasionally cemented into rock. A large pair of concrete monuments with a pebbled finish marks major boundary road crossings. Because the boundary is not just a line but in fact a vertical plane

RV travel on the Alaska Highway and its spur roads continues to increase with road improvements. Photo by Tricia Brown.

dividing land and sky between the two nations, bronze plates mark tunnel and bridge crossings. Along the meridian, 191 monuments are placed, beginning 200 feet from the Arctic Ocean and ending at the south side of Logan Glacier.

ALASKA HIGHWAY (SEE ALSO Highways) The Alaska Highway runs 1,488 miles through Canada and Alaska from Milepost 0 at Dawson Creek, British Columbia, through Yukon Territory to Fairbanks, Alaska. Until this overland link between Alaska and the Lower 48 was built in 1942, travel to and from Alaska was primarily by water.

History. The highway was built to relieve Alaska from the hazards of shipping by water and to supply a land route for equipment during World War II.

By agreement between the governments of Canada and the United States, the highway was built in eight months by the U.S. Army Corps of Engineers and was dedicated in November 1942. Crews worked south from Delta Junction, Alaska, north and south from Whitehorse, Yukon, and north from Dawson Creek, British Columbia.

The building of the highway was recognized as one of the greatest engineering feats of the 20th century. Two major sections of the highway were connected on Sept. 23, 1942, at Contact Creek, Milepost 588.1, where the

35th Engineer Combat Regiment working west from Fort Nelson met the 340th Engineer General Service Regiment working east from Whitehorse. The last link in the highway was completed Nov. 20, 1942, when the 97th Engineer General Service Regiment, heading east from Tanacross, met the 18th Engineer Combat Regiment, coming northwest from Kluane Lake, at Milepost 1200.9. A ceremony commemorating the event was held at Soldiers Summit on Kluane Lake, and the first truck to negotiate the entire highway left that day from Soldiers Summit and arrived in Fairbanks the next day.

After World War II, the Alaska Highway was turned over to civilian contractors for widening and graveling, replacing log bridges with steel and rerouting at many points. Road improvements on the Alaska Highway continue today.

Preparation for Driving the Alaska Highway. Make sure your vehicle and tires are in good condition before starting out. A widely available item to include is clear plastic headlight covers to protect your headlights from flying rocks and gravel.

You might also consider a wire-mesh screen across the front of your vehicle to protect paint, grille and radiator from flying rocks. For those hauling trailers, a piece of quarter-inch plywood fitted over the front of your trailer offers protection from rocks and gravel.

You'll find well-stocked auto shops in the North, but may wish to carry your own emergency items: flares; first-aid kit; mosquito repellent; trailer bearings; good bumper jack with lug wrench; a simple set of tools, such as hammer, screwdrivers, pliers, wire, crescent wrenches, socket and/or open-end wrenches, pry bar; electrician's tape; small assortment of nuts and bolts; fan belt; one or two spare tires (two spares for traveling any remote road); and any parts for your vehicle that might not be available along the way.

Include an extra few gallons of gas and water, especially for remote roads. You may wish to carry a can of brake, power steering and automatic transmission fluids.

Along the Alaska Highway, dust is at its worst during dry spells, following heavy rain (which disturbs the road surface) and in construction areas. If you encounter much dust, check your air filter frequently. To help keep dust out of your vehicle, try to keep air pressure in the car by closing all windows and turning on the fan. Filtered heating and air-conditioning ducts in a vehicle bring in much less dust than open windows or vents.

Mosquito netting placed over the heater/fresh-air intake and flow-through ventilation will help eliminate dust.

Alaska welcomes over 1.1 million visitors each year, but one of the most popular bumper stickers in the state reads, "If it's tourist season, why can't we shoot 'em?"

ALCOHOLIC BEVERAGES The
legal age for possession, purchase and

consumption of alcoholic beverages is 21 in Alaska. Under-age drinkers may lose their driver's licenses for 90 days.

Any business that serves or distributes alcoholic beverages must be licensed by the state. The number of different types of licenses issued is limited by the population in a geographic area. Generally one license of each type may be issued for each 3,000 persons or fraction thereof. Licensed premises include bars, some restaurants and clubs. Packaged liquor, beer and wine are sold by licensed package stores. Licenses are renewed biennially.

Recreational site licenses, caterer's permits and special events permits allow the holder of a permit or license to sell at special events, and allow nonprofit fraternal, civic or patriotic organizations to serve beer and wine at certain activities.

State law allows liquor outlets to operate from 8 A.M. to 5 A.M., but provides that local governments may impose tighter restrictions.

Dozens of communities have banned possession and/or sale and importation of alcoholic beverages (knowingly bringing, sending or transporting alcoholic beverages into the community). Others have banned the sale of all alcoholic beverages. Contact the Alcoholic Beverage Control Board at (907) 269-0350 for a current list or check www.abc.revenue.state.ak.us.

ALYESKA (SEE ALSO Skiing) Pronounced Al-YES-ka, this Aleut word means "the great land" and was one of the original names of Alaska. Mount Alyeska, a 3,939-foot peak in the Chugach Mountains south of Anchorage, is the site of the state's largest ski resort.

AMPHIBIANS In Alaska, there are three species of salamander, two species of frog and one species of toad. In the salamander order, there are the rough-skinned newt, long-toed salamander and northwestern salamander. In the frog and toad order, there are the boreal toad, wood frog and spotted frog. The northern limit of each species may be the latitude at which the larvae fail to complete their

development in one summer. While some species of salamander can overwinter as larvae in temperate southeastern Alaska, the shallow ponds of central Alaska freeze solid during the winter. All these amphibians are found primarily in southeastern Alaska, except for the wood frog, *Rana sylvatica,* which with its shortened larval period is found widespread throughout the state and north of the Brooks Range.

ANCHORAGE (SEE ALSO Regions of Alaska) Anchorage is located on a broad peninsula in Cook Inlet, defined by Knik Arm and Turnagain Arm, and bordered to the east by the Chugach Mountains. Anchorage and the Kenai Peninsula make up the region Alaskans call Southcentral, a region milder in climate than the Interior, with average temperatures of 15°F in January and 58°F in July, and an average snowfall of about 70 inches a year.

Anchorage's daylight has a daily maximum of 19 hours, 21 minutes in summer and reaches a minimum of 5 hours, 28 minutes in winter.

Anchorage's population was 1,856 in 1920, and remained at a few thousand until after World War II. In 1994, Anchorage, Alaska's most populous city, broke the quarter-million mark for the first time; in 2001 it was home to 260,283 people (about 42 percent of the state's population).

Anchorage suffered millions of dollars in damage in a devastating earthquake on March 27, 1964, originally measured at 8.6 on the Richter scale but later upgraded to a magnitude of 9.2—the strongest ever recorded in North America. (SEE ALSO Earthquakes)

Sometimes called the "Air Crossroads of the World," Anchorage is a gateway for international travelers. Surrounded by dense spruce, birch and aspen forests, it is just a step away from wilderness and multiple recreational opportunities. Anchorage also serves as a jump-off point for tourists—heading 200 miles north to

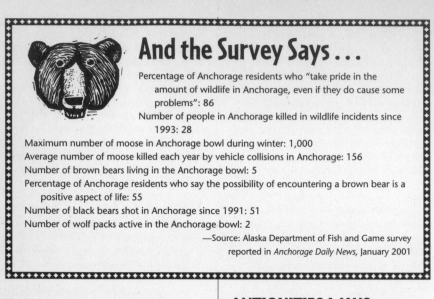

And the Survey Says...

Percentage of Anchorage residents who "take pride in the amount of wildlife in Anchorage, even if they do cause some problems": 86

Number of people in Anchorage killed in wildlife incidents since 1993: 28

Maximum number of moose in Anchorage bowl during winter: 1,000

Average number of moose killed each year by vehicle collisions in Anchorage: 156

Number of brown bears living in the Anchorage bowl: 5

Percentage of Anchorage residents who say the possibility of encountering a brown bear is a positive aspect of life: 55

Number of black bears shot in Anchorage since 1991: 51

Number of wolf packs active in the Anchorage bowl: 2

—Source: Alaska Department of Fish and Game survey reported in *Anchorage Daily News,* January 2001

---

visit Denali National Park and Mount McKinley, North America's highest mountain; or south 52 miles to view Portage Glacier, one of the state's most-visited sights; or even to one of Alaska's Bush locations for hunting, fishing, skiing, hiking, nature photography or sightseeing.

Although bear and moose may occasionally wander the city's highways and byways, Anchorage offers many of the attractions of any large metropolis, such as art galleries, museums, libraries, cultural diversity, music—including a symphony orchestra, opera and dance—and theaters big enough to stage productions by national touring companies. Anchorage has more than 200 churches and 96 schools, including the University of Alaska Anchorage and Alaska Pacific University. Restaurants offer everything from fine dining and ethnic cuisine to fast food. Accommodations are offered at more than 140 hotels, motels and inns, and at 134 bed-and-breakfasts. Anchorage has more than 6,000 hotel/motel rooms.

Contact the Anchorage Convention and Visitors Bureau for a free visitor's guide, maps and additional information: 524 W. Fourth Ave., Anchorage 99501; (800) 478-1255; www.anchorage.net.

ANTIQUITIES LAWS (See also

National Historic Places) State and federal laws prohibit excavation or removal of historic and prehistoric cultural materials without a permit. Nearly all 50 states have historic preservation laws; Alaska's extends even to tidal lands, making it illegal to pick up artifacts on the beach while beachcombing.

It sometimes is difficult to distinguish between historic sites and abandoned property. Old gold-mining towns and cabins, as well as areas such as the Chilkoot and Iditarod Trails, should always be considered historic sites or private property. Also, cabins that appear to be abandoned may be seasonally used trapping cabins; the structure and possessions are vital to the owner.

Alaska law prohibits the disturbance of fossils, including prehistoric animals such as mammoths.

ARCHAEOLOGY (See also Bering Land

Bridge) Alaska has a long and rich archaeological history. The first human migrants to North and South America some 40,000 to 15,000 years ago came first to Alaska, crossing over the now-submerged Bering Land Bridge that connected Siberia to Alaska in the Ice Age.

Some of the oldest archaeological

materials that demonstrate human occupation of Alaska come from Trail Creeks Cave north of Nome, where a 15,000-year-old cracked bison leg bone and bone point were found. Better evidence can be found for human occupation from 11,000 years ago. Small hunting tools have been found throughout Alaska, probably belonging to nomadic hunting and gathering peoples. The archaeological record becomes more complicated about 4,000 years ago, when it reveals cultural patterns characteristic of Alaska Native groups still extant at the time of contact with Europeans.

In 1993, the presence of what may be the oldest documented site of human habitation in North America was discovered. Called the Mesa Site, it is located about 150 miles north of the Arctic Circle in the foothills of the Brooks Range. The 11,700-year-old hunting site is perched atop a 200-foot mesa overlooking the surrounding plain. It probably was used for 2,000 years as a hunters' lookout for prey such as caribou.

There is still much to discover about Alaska's prehistory. Many archaeological sites are small, representing the camps of wandering hunters and gatherers; some sites, especially along the coast where rich natural resources allowed people to become more sedentary and established, are large and deep. Where permafrost occurs, preservation of even the most perishable organic materials offers a wealth of information on life in the past. There are several thousand known archaeological sites in the state. One of the most famous is the 500-year-old Utkeaviq Site at Barrow, where a "frozen family" was unearthed from Mound 44 in the Birnirk archaeological site during 1982–83.

Archaeological excavations, or digs, are almost always confined to the summer months. The University of Alaska in both Fairbanks and Anchorage frequently sponsors digs, as do several state and federal agencies. Recent excavations have taken place near Unalaska, Tok, Kodiak, Fairbanks, Prince William Sound, Point Franklin, Sitka and on the Kenai Peninsula.

Participants, who will be required to pay a fee, are invited to take part in a dig on Afognak Island. Inquire with the Afognak Native Corp., P.O. Box 1277, Kodiak 99615; (800) 770-6014; www.afognak.com.

Tourists are invited to dig for free at a 10,000-year-old site near Unalaska. For information call Rick Knecht or Belinda Sunderland, (907) 581-5150; www.aleutians.org.

Additional information about projects is available from the Alaska Office of History and Archaeology, www.dnr.state. ak.us/parks/oha.

NUGGETS

The lower jawbone of a mastodon that lived 100,000 years ago was uncovered in June 1989. Found by dredge operators at a sand and gravel pit just outside of Fairbanks, the 25-pound bone is believed to have come from a 20-year-old female. The upper jawbone of another mastodon was found last year in about the same location. Both pieces have been given to the University of Alaska Fairbanks. —1990 The ALASKA ALMANAC®

ARCTIC CIRCLE (SEE ALSO Daylight Hours) The Arctic Circle (SEE map, pages 6–7) is the latitude at which the sun does not set for one day at summer solstice and does not rise for one day at winter solstice. The latitude, which varies slightly from year to year, is approximately 66°34' north from the equator and circumscribes the northern frigid zone.

A solstice occurs when the sun is at its greatest distance from the celestial equator. On the day of summer solstice, June 20 or 21, the sun does not set at the Arctic Circle, and because of refraction of sunlight, it appears not to set for four days. Farther north, at Barrow (the

And the Winners Are . . .

The Arctic Winter Games, March 5–11, 2000, were held at Whitehorse, Yukon Territory. Among the Alaskan winners:

One-foot High Kick: Junior women, Bronze: Amy Allen. Junior men, Silver: Andrew Constantine. Senior women, Silver: Noel Gould. Senior women, Bronze: Nicole Johnston. Senior men, Gold: Bradley Weyiouanna. Senior men, Silver: Phil Blanchett (tied with Elias Irwin, NWT). Senior men, Bronze: George Melton

Triple Jump: Junior men, Gold: Andrew Constantine. Junior men, Bronze: William Brown. Senior women, Silver: Nicole Johnston

Arm Pull: Junior men, Gold: Andrew Constantine. Senior women, Gold: Nicole Johnston

Kneel Jump: Junior women, Bronze: Jenna Ring. Senior women, Gold: Nicole Johnston. Senior women, Silver: Noel Gould

One-Hand Reach: Senior men, Silver: Gary Hull. Senior men, Bronze: Bradley Weyiouanna (tied with Jimmy Merkosat)

All-Around: Junior women, Silver: Jenna Ring. Junior men, Gold: Andrew Constantine

Dene Games: Snow Snake, Silver: Maxim Dolchok. Stick Pull, Silver: Daniel Amidon. Hand Games, Bronze: Alaska

Alaska High Kick: Junior women, Silver: Jenna Ring. Senior women, Gold: Nicole Johnston. Senior men, Gold: George Melton. Senior men, Bronze: Bradley Weyiouanna

Russian Sledge Jump: Senior women, Gold: Emily Frantz

Airplane: Senior men, Bronze: Bradley Weyiouanna

Two-Foot High Kick: Junior women, Silver: Jenna Ring. Junior men, Gold: Andrew Constantine. Senior men, Silver: Phil Blanchett

—Source: *Anchorage Daily News*

northernmost community in the United States), the sun does not set from May 10 to August 2.

At winter solstice, December 21 or 22, the sun does not rise for one day at the Arctic Circle. At Barrow, it does not rise for 67 days.

ARCTIC WINTER GAMES

The Arctic Winter Games are held every two years in mid-March for northern athletes from Alaska, northern Alberta, Greenland, Northwest Territories, Yukon Territory and Russia. The first games were held in 1970 in Yellowknife, Northwest Territories, and have since been held in Fairbanks and Whitehorse, Yukon. Greenland and Nunavut will host the games in March 2002.

In 2000, 316 athletes, coaches and support staff from Alaska participated in the games. Competition includes alpine skiing, arctic sports (traditional Inuit and Dene games), badminton, basketball, curling, cross-country skiing, dog mushing, figure skating, gymnastics, hockey, short track speed skating, ski biathlon, snowboarding, snowshoeing, indoor soccer, volleyball and wrestling. Cultural events and performances encourage participation by people of all ages. Information: www.awg.ca.

AURORA BOREALIS The

northern lights—the aurora borealis—is produced by charged electrons and protons striking gas particles in the earth's upper atmosphere. The electrons and protons are released through sunspot activity on the sun and emanate into space. A few drift the one- to two-day course to Earth, where they are pulled to the most northern and southern latitudes by the planet's magnetic forces.

The color of the aurora borealis varies, depending on how hard the gas particles are being struck. Auroras can range from simple arcs to draperylike forms in green, red, blue and purple. The lights occur in a pattern rather than as a solid glow because electric current sheets flowing through gases create V-shaped potential double layers. Electrons near the center of the current sheet move faster, hit the atmosphere harder and cause the different intensities of light observed in the aurora.

Displays take place as low as 40 miles above the Earth's surface, but usually begin about 68 miles above and extend hundreds of miles into space. They concentrate in two bands roughly centered above the Arctic Circle and Antarctic Circle (the latter known as the aurora australis) that are about 2,500 miles in diameter. In northern latitudes the greatest occurrence of auroral displays is in the spring and fall months, because of the tilt of the planet in relationship to the sun's plane. Displays may occur on dark nights throughout the winter.

If sunspot activity is particularly intense and the denser-than-usual solar wind heads to Earth, the resulting auroras can be so great that they cover all but the tropical latitudes.

Some observers claim that the northern lights make a sound similar to the rustle of taffeta, but scientists say the displays cannot be heard in the audible frequency range.

Residents of Fairbanks, located on the 65th parallel, see the aurora borealis an average of 240 nights a year. The University of Alaska Fairbanks issues weekly aurora forecasts in winter. Additional information and forecasts can be found at www.geo.mtu.edu/weather/aurora.

Photographing the Aurora Borealis. To capture the northern lights on film, you will need a 35mm camera that has adjustable f-stop and shutter speed, a sturdy tripod, a locking-type cable release (some 35mm cameras have both *time* and *bulb* settings, but most have *bulb* only, which calls for use of the locking-type cable release) and an f3.5 lens (or faster).

f-stop	ASA 200	ASA 400
f1.2	3 sec.	2 sec.
f1.4	5	3
f1.8	7	4
f 2	20	10
f2.8	40	20
f3.5	60	30

It is best to photograph the lights on a night when they are not moving too rapidly. And as a general rule, photos improve if you manage to include recognizable subjects in the foreground— trees and lighted cabins are favorites of many photographers. Set up your camera at least 75 feet back from the foreground objects to make sure that both the foreground and aurora are in sharp focus.

Normal and wide-angle lenses are best. Try to keep your exposures under a minute—a 10- to 30-second exposure is generally best. The lens openings and exposure times are only a starting point, since the amount of light generated by the aurora is inconsistent. (For best results, bracket widely.)

Ektachrome 200 and 400 color film can be push-processed in the home darkroom or by most custom-color labs, allowing use

In Alaska it is legal to shoot bear, but waking a sleeping bear for the purpose of taking a photograph is prohibited.

of higher ASA ratings (800, 1200 or even 1600 on the 400 ASA film, for example). Kodak will push-process film if you include an ESP-1 envelope with your standard film-processing mailer. (Consult your local camera store for details.)

A few notes of caution: Protect the camera from low temperatures until you are ready to make your exposures. Some newer cameras have electrically controlled shutters that will not function properly at low temperatures.

Wind the film slowly to reduce the possibility of static electricity, which can lead to streaks on the film. Grounding the camera when rewinding can help prevent the static-electricity problem. (To ground the camera, hold it against a water pipe, drain pipe, metal fence post or other grounded object.) Follow the basic rules and experiment with exposures.

The first photographs to show the aurora borealis in its entirety were published in early 1982. These historic photographs were taken from satellite-mounted cameras specially adapted to filter unwanted light from the sunlit portion of the earth, which is a million times brighter than the aurora. From space, the aurora has the appearance of a nearly perfect circle.

BAIDARKA
The *baidarka* (also spelled bidarka or bidarkee), or Aleut kayak, is a portable decked boat made of skins (usually seal) stretched over wood frames. The *baidarka* (a Russian term for the skin boats) was widely used by Aleuts and Alaska coastal Natives for transportation and hunting in areas associated with Russian influence. *Baidarkas* were the only form of kayak commonly built with three hatchways, and generally had a forked bow.

BALEEN
(See ALSO Baskets; Whales) Baleen (often mistakenly called whale "bone") hangs from the upper jaw of baleen whales in long, fringed, bonelike strips. Baleen whales, such as humpback, bowhead, minke and gray, feed by taking in seawater and filtering small fish, plankton and the tiny, shrimplike creatures called krill through the baleen. Baleen is made of

Three-hatch *baidarka*, about 1909. Photo by J. E. Thwaites, courtesy Anchorage Museum of History and Art. From *Baidarka* by George Dyson.

keratin, a substance found in human fingernails. The outer edge of baleen is hard; the inside edges of the baleen plates form a fringe of coarse bristles that resembles matted goat hair.

The number of plates along an adult humpback's jaw, the largest of the baleen whales, varies from 600 to 800 (300 to 400 a side); the roof of the mouth is empty of plates. The bowhead whale has 600 plates, some of which reach 14 feet or more in length. Baleen varies in thickness and texture. Baleen from humpback whales is coarse; sei whales have finely textured baleen.

Baleen was once used for corset stays, Venetian blinds, hairbrushes and buggy whips. It is no longer of significant commercial use, although Alaska Natives use brownish black bowhead baleen to craft fine baskets and model ships to sell.

BARABARA
Pronounced buh-RAH-buh-ruh, this traditional Aleut or Eskimo dwelling is built of sod supported by driftwood or whale ribs.

BARANOV, ALEXANDER
(See ALSO Sitka) Alexander Andreyevich Baranov (1747–1819), sometimes called "Lord of Alaska," was manager of the Russian-American fur-trading company and the first governor of Russian Alaska.

A failed Siberian fur businessman, Baranov seemed an unlikely choice for overseeing the expansion of the Russian

American empire when he arrived at Kodiak in 1790. But his aggressiveness and tough political skills proved indispensable. Within seven years, he had eliminated all competitors and secured the entire south Alaska coast, from the Aleutian Islands to Yakutat, for the Russian-American Company.

Learning to handle a *baidarka* and navigate a seagoing sloop, he established Fort St. Michael at remote Sitka Bay in 1799 and in 1804 reestablished the post following its destruction by Tlingit warriors.

Baranov was a pragmatic ruler. He encouraged marriage between European men and Native women. The settlement's need for clerks and artisans led him to require basic schooling for all children. Lacking military support to exclude British and American ships from Alaska waters, he cultivated cordial relations with foreign captains. By the time he retired in 1818, Russian influence in the North Pacific stretched from Siberia to Fort Ross in northern California.

Baranov died of fever aboard ship en route to St. Petersburg in 1819.

BARROW (SEE ALSO Museums; Native Peoples; Regions of Alaska) Situated 350 miles north of the Arctic Circle, Barrow is the northernmost city in the United States and the largest Inupiat Eskimo community in the world.

Barrow was called Utqiagvik by its Inupiat founders. Because of its key location at the junction of the Chukchi and Beaufort Seas, Barrow became an important whaling site. The town remains a center of subsistence whaling and harvesting of other land and water species.

More than 4,500 people live in this polar environment, unconnected to any other community by road. Within the 21-square-mile city limits, however, are 28 miles of roadway covering three distinct areas of settlement: the traditional Inupiat community of Barrow, the former Naval Arctic Research Laboratory, and portions of the former Distant Early Warning (DEW) Line station.

Barrow is the seat of government of the

NUGGETS

The farthest north supermarket, in Barrow, was constructed on stilts to prevent snow build-up, at a cost of $4 million.

—1980 *The ALASKA ALMANAC*®

North Slope Borough, and serves as a regional center for the 89,000-square-mile borough. It is also the corporate headquarters for the Arctic Slope Regional Corp. and the Ukpeagvik Inupiat Corp., which were established under the Native Claims Settlement Act.

Barrow has a strong and growing tourist industry. Visitors are attracted by everything from traditional whaling celebrations to polar bear watching, northern lights and the midnight sun. A monument across from the airport is dedicated to Will Rogers and Wiley Post, who were killed in a 1935 airplane crash 15 miles south of Barrow.

BASEBALL Six teams make up the Alaska Baseball League: Fairbanks Goldpanners, Anchorage Bucs, Hawaiian Island Movers, Anchorage Glacier Pilots, Kenai Peninsula Oilers and Mat–Su Miners.

Baseball season opens in June and runs through the end of July. Each team plays a round-robin schedule with the other Alaska teams in addition to scheduling games with visiting Lower 48 teams.

The Anchorage Bucs began playing during the 1981 season. They defeated Team USA in 1991, defeated the Moscow Red Devils in 1992 and won the Alaska League championship several times. In 1993, the Bucs were recognized as America's No. 1 summer collegiate team.

The Anchorage Glacier Pilots are entering their 31st year. This semipro team drafts collegiate athletes from all over the

United States. More than 80 former players have gone on to play in the major leagues. The Pilots consistently finish in the top seven at the annual National Baseball Congress Championships in Wichita, Kansas.

The caliber of play in Alaska is some of the best nationwide at the amateur level. Major league scouts rate Alaska baseball at A to AA, visiting each season to check out talent for possible recruitment.

The list of major league players who were once on Alaska teams is impressive, and includes stars Tom Seaver, Mark McGwire, Chris Chambliss and Dave Winfield. Some 20 former Bucs playing in the majors include Wally Joyner, Mike McFarlane, Bobby Jones and Jeff Kent.

Information on the Alaska Baseball League is at www.goldpanner.com/abl.

BASKETS (See also Baleen; Native Arts and Crafts)

Native basketry varies greatly according to materials locally available. Athabascan Indians of the Interior, for example, weave baskets from willow root gathered in late spring. The roots are steamed and heated over a fire to loosen the outer bark. Weavers then separate the material into fine strips by pulling the roots through their teeth.

Eskimo grass baskets are made in river delta areas of Southwestern Alaska from Bristol Bay north to Norton Sound and from Nunivak Island east to interior Eskimo river villages. Weavers use very fine grass harvested in fall. A coil basketry technique is followed, using coils from an eighth to three-quarters of an inch wide. Seal gut, traditionally dyed with berries (today with commercial dyes), is often interwoven into the baskets.

Baleen, a glossy, hard material that extends in slats from the upper jaw of some types of whales, is also used for baskets. Baleen basketry originated about 1905 when Charles D. Brower, trader for a whaling company at Point Barrow, suggested, after the decline of the whalebone (baleen) industry for women's corsets, that local Eskimo men make the baskets as a source of income. The baskets

Tlingit spruce-root basket. From *Indian Baskets of the Pacific Northwest and Alaska* by Allen Lobb, Art Wolfe and Barbara Paxson.

were not produced in any number until 1916. The weave and shape of the baskets were copied from the split-willow Athabascan baskets acquired in trade. A decorative "knob" of ivory is often added. Later, baleen baskets were also made in Point Hope and Wainwright.

Most birch-bark baskets are made by Athabascan Indians, although a few Eskimos also produce them. Baskets are shaped as simple cylinders, or canoe shapes, held together with spruce root lashings. Sometimes the birch bark is cut into thin strips and woven into diamond or checkerboard patterns. Birch bark is usually collected in spring and early summer; large pieces free of knots are preferred. Birch-bark baskets traditionally were used as cooking vessels. Food was placed in them and hot stones added. Birch-bark baby carriers also are still made, chiefly for collectors.

Among the finest of Alaska baskets are the tiny, intricately woven Aleut baskets made of rye grass, which in the Aleutians is abundant, pliable and very tough. The three main styles of Aleut baskets—Attu, Atka and Unalaska—are named after the islands where the styles originated. Although the small baskets are the best known, Aleuts also traditionally made large, coarsely woven baskets for utilitarian purposes.

Tlingit, Haida and Tsimshian Indians

make baskets of spruce roots and cedar bark. South of Frederick Sound, basket material usually consists of strands split from the inner bark of red cedar. To the north of the sound, spruce roots are used. Maidenhair ferns are sometimes interwoven into spruce root baskets to form patterns resembling embroidery. A large spruce root basket may take months to complete.

Examples of Alaska Native basketry may be viewed in many museums, including the University of Alaska Museum, Fairbanks; the Anchorage Museum of History and Art, Anchorage; the Sheldon Jackson Museum, Sitka; and the Alaska State Museum, Juneau.

Prices for Native baskets vary greatly. A fine-weave, coiled beach grass basket may cost from $100 to $700; birch-bark baskets may range from $35 to $200; willow root trays may cost $800; finely woven Aleut baskets may cost $200 to $800; cedar-bark baskets may range from $30 to $80; and baleen baskets range in price from $800 to more than $2,400 for medium-size baskets. These prices are approximate and are based on the weave, material used, size and decoration added, such as beads, embroidery or ivory.

BEADWORK (SEE ALSO Native Arts and Crafts; Parka) Eskimo and Indian women create a variety of handsomely beaded items. Before contact with Europeans, Indian women sometimes carved beads of willow wood or made them from seeds of certain shrubs and trees. Glass seed beads became available to Alaska's Athabascan Indians in the mid-19th century, although some types of larger trade beads were in use earlier. Beads quickly became a coveted trade item. The *Cornaline d'aleppo*, an opaque red bead with a white center, and the faceted Russian blue beads were among the most popular types.

The introduction of small glass beads sparked changes in beadwork style and design. More colors were available and the smaller, more easily maneuvered beads made it possible to work out delicate floral patterns impossible with larger trade beads.

Historically, beads were sewn directly onto leather garments or other items with the overlay stitch. Contemporary beadwork is often done on a separate piece of felt that is not visible once the beads are stitched in place.

Alaska's Athabascan beadworkers sometimes use paper patterns, often combining several motifs and tracing their outline on the surface to be worked. The most common designs include flowers, leaves and berries, some in very stylized form. Many patterns are drawn simply from the sewer's environment. Since the gold rush, magazines, graphic art, advertising and patriotic motifs have inspired Athabascan beadworkers, although stylized floral designs are still the most popular.

Designs vary regionally as do the ways in which they are applied to garments or footgear. Skilled practitioners execute beadwork so distinctive it can be recognized at a glance.

BEARS (SEE ALSO Mammals; McNeil River State Game Sanctuary) Three species of bear inhabit Alaska: the black, the brown/grizzly and the polar bear. Most of Alaska can be considered bear country, and for those wishing to spend time in Alaska's great outdoors, bear country becomes "beware" country. Sows are extremely aggressive if their young are around, and bears will guard a moose kill against all passersby. Bear behavior should always be considered unpredictable. Bear scat or a large concentration of flies in one area are signs for hikers to watch for and retreat

It was recently reported that a person is statistically more likely to be killed by a bear in Alaska than to be run over by a taxi in New York City.

Brown/grizzly bears range throughout much of Alaska. From *Alaska's Bears* by Bill Sherwonit (text) and Tom Walker (photographs).

from. The Alaska Department of Fish and Game publishes *The Bears and You*, recommended reading for hikers and campers.

Black Bears. Black bears are usually jet black or brown with a brown-yellow muzzle, and weigh from 100 to 200 pounds as adults. The brown color phase can sometimes be confused with grizzlies but black bears are generally smaller and lack the grizzly's distinct shoulder hump. Black bear habitat covers three-fourths of Alaska, with high concentrations found in the Southeast, Prince William Sound and the coastal mountains and lowlands of Southcentral Alaska. Low to moderate densities are found in Interior and Western Alaska. Their range is semi-open forests, and though omnivorous, their diet consists mainly of vegetation due to the difficulty of getting meat or fish. Black bears often spend their lives within five miles of their birthplace and will frequently return to their home range if transplanted. They easily climb trees; both cubs and adults use trees as a place of escape. Cubs are generally born in late January or February weighing 8 to 10 ounces. Average litter size is two cubs, but three or four cubs in a litter is not unusual. Black bears den in winter for up to six months but are not true hibernators. Their body temperature remains high and they awaken easily—even in midwinter.

Brown/Grizzly Bears. Fur colors of brown/grizzly bears vary from blond to black with shades of brown and gray in between. As adults, they can weigh over 1,000 pounds, but are usually smaller; size depends on sex, age, time of year and geographic location. Coastal bears, referred to as "browns" or "brownies," are the largest living omnivorous land mammals in the world and grow larger than Interior "grizzlies." Browns or grizzlies are found in most of Alaska except for islands in the extreme southeastern part of the state.

The lowest populations are found in the northern Interior and the Arctic. Their range is wherever food is abundant, but the bears prefer open tundra and grasslands. Diet consists of a wide variety of plants and animals, including their own kind, and humans under some circumstances. In their realm, grizzlies are king and fear no other animal except humans with a firearm. While attacks on people are the exception, the results can be tragic. These bears are also tremendously strong and have been seen carrying—off the ground—an 800-pound moose. One to two hairless cubs are usually born in late January or February weighing 8 to 10 ounces, and sows have been known to adopt orphaned cubs. Time of year and duration of denning varies with the location and physical condition of the bear, and can be up to six months of the year. Dens are frequently on hillsides or on mountain slopes.

Polar Bears. The only areas on a polar bear not covered with heavy, white fur are its eyes and large, black nose. The bear, seemingly aware that his nose gives him away to prey, will hold a paw up to hide it when hunting. An adult polar bear weighs 1,500 pounds or more and has a long neck with a proportionately small head. Their habitat is the Canadian–eastern Alaska Arctic and the western Alaska Arctic–eastern Russia, the latter being home to the world's largest polar bears. Their range is the arctic ice cap, and they are more numerous toward the southern edge of the ice pack. Occasionally polar bears will come ashore, but generally stay near the coast. While ashore they eat some vegetation, but their diet consists primarily of ringed seals, walrus, stranded whales, birds and fish. Cannibalism of cubs and young bears by older males is not unusual. Polar bears are strong swimmers; reports exist of swimming bears found 50 miles from the nearest land or ice. When swimming, they use their front paws for propulsion and trail their rear paws. Mother bears have been seen with a cub hanging onto their tail, towing it through the water. Cubs are born in December with two being the common litter size. They weigh about a pound at birth and remain with their mother for

about 28 months. Usually only pregnant sows den up, for an average of six months in the winter. Polar bears need stable, cold areas for denning, and dens in Alaska have been found 30 miles inland, along the coast, on offshore islands, on shorefast ice and on drifting sea ice.

BERING, VITUS
Vitus Jonassen Bering (1681–1741) is credited as the first European to discover Alaska. A Danish captain serving Russia under the crown of Peter the Great, Bering was in command of an expedition to find out if the continents of Asia and America were connected and to claim new lands for Russia.

He piloted his first expedition in 1728 through the strait that now bears his name, concluding that Asia and America were not joined. On that voyage, however, he never saw the fog-shrouded Alaska mainland. The expedition was considered a failure.

In June 1741, Bering set sail again as captain of the ill-fated *St. Peter*. Also on board was the German naturalist Georg Steller; the Steller sea lion and Steller's jay owe their names to his field work on the journey. A second ship piloted by Aleksei Chirikov accompanied the *St. Peter*.

During the voyage, Bering and Chirikov lost contact in foul weather, never to meet again. In July both ships sighted southern Alaska. On July 16, Steller led a landing party on what is now Kayak Island at Cape St. Elias, just east of Prince William Sound.

Short of food and weakened with scurvy, Bering was anxious to set sail for Kamchatka before winter. Against the advice of Steller, the explorer sailed for home. In heavy seas the *St. Peter* ran aground on a rocky island off the Siberian coast, since known as Bering Island. Twenty sailors, including Bering, died of scurvy. The remaining sailors survived by eating fish and seals, eventually built a boat from the wreckage of the *St. Peter*, and returned to Russia.

Bering's voyage not only laid the basis for Russian claims to Alaska but also opened the fur trade. His crews brought back many pelts, among them 800 sea otter skins. By the late 1700s, the Russian fur

Are You Free for Lunch?

In 1987, Larry Hadselford, camp cook at El Camp Gold Mine near Ketchikan, got more than he bargained for when he walked to the camp outhouse.

"Was just about to sit down and I hear this noise," he said. "Then I turn around and I'm looking straight into a bear's eyes."

The black bear's head was sticking up through the seat hole. It was not known how the bear crawled into the privy. Four men at the camp shoved the outhouse over, freeing the animal, who promptly ran away into the woods.   —1988 *The ALASKA ALMANAC®*

Spanish Exploration

When residents think of explorers who came to Alaska, they usually think of Captain Cook. But Britain was not the only country to explore northern waters. For 30 years after Vitus Bering's 1741 voyage, Russians dominated the area. Then European countries began to make inroads. In 1773 and on several other occasions, Spain sent explorers to Alaska to document Russian activities, make land claims and search for a Northwest Passage. Spain withdrew from the region in 1795 when it surrendered a plot of land at Nootka Sound to the British. However the Spanish legacy is still evident in such place names as Valdez, Cordova, Revillagigedo and Malaspina.

trade had become the richest fur enterprise in the world, setting the stage for the extinction of the Steller's sea cow by 1768 and the near-extinction of the sea otter in the 1820s.

BERING LAND BRIDGE The

Bering Land Bridge was formed when the glaciers of the Wisconsin period flowed across the northern cap of the earth. Millions of cubic miles of water from the earth's oceans were bound in these glaciers, causing the ocean levels to lower by more than 300 feet. Between 40,000 and 15,000 years ago, the lowered sea levels exposed a 1,000-mile-wide corridor of dry land connecting North America with Asia. Now known as the Bering Land Bridge, it enabled the migration of plants and animals, including humans, between the old world and the new world.

When the glaciers retreated the water returned to the sea, covering the bridge and creating the Bering Strait between Alaska and Siberia. Recognizing the need to preserve the area's unique paleontological and archaeological resources, the U. S. Congress created in 1980 the Bering Land Bridge National Preserve, managed by the National Park Service. The preserve occupies 2.7 million acres of the Seward Peninsula in northwest Alaska.

Visitors will find extensive lava flows and maar lakes formed by ash and steam explosions, sandy beaches, tundra and Serpentine Hot Springs, which is considered one of the preserve's highlights. Located in a valley of granite spires called tors, the hot springs attract those who come to bathe, hike, relax and observe wildlife.

More than 400 species of plants have been found in the preserve. The Bering Land Bridge preserve also has a rich and diversified bird life. Animals found here include musk oxen, bears, moose, wolves, wolverines, reindeer, caribou, foxes and other smaller species.

Depending on the season, access is possible only by aircraft (special permit required for helicopter), boat, dogsled, foot, skis or snowmobile. Recreational options include camping, backpacking, hiking, photography, wildlife viewing and coastal boating.

Federal Highway access ends 400 miles from Bering Land Bridge National Preserve, but the information superhighway leads right to it. The preserve's Web site, www.nps.gov/bela, gives a detailed look at the region.

BERRIES Wild berries abound in Alaska,

with the circumboreal lingonberry/lowbush cranberry *(Vaccinium vitisidaea)* being the most widespread. Blueberries of one species or another grow in most of the state. Some 50 other species of wild fruit are found in Alaska including strawberries, raspberries, cloudberries, salmonberries, crowberries, nagoonberries and crab apples. High-bush cranberries (which are not really cranberries) can be found on bushes even

Fresh Blueberry Sauce

Most recipes for blueberry sauce start by cooking the berries with water. I find this dilutes the flavor, and add water only if the berries aren't very juicy.

2 cups blueberries	1 teaspoon cornstarch
1/4 cup sugar	1 tablespoon lemon juice

Mix the blueberries, sugar and cornstarch in a heavy saucepan and place over medium-low heat. Add the lemon juice and stir gently while the sugar dissolves and the berries gradually release their juice. (Add 1 tablespoon of water only if necessary to get them started.) Simmer very gently until the sauce thickens slightly, about 5 minutes, then adjust the flavor and consistency with additional sugar, lemon juice or water. Cultivated berries generally require a bit more lemon than their wild cousins. Makes about 1 1/2 cups.

For Blueberry Ripple Ice Cream: Sieve blueberry sauce to remove skins. Swirl the puree into softened vanilla ice cream, and refreeze until firm.

—Sarah Eppenbach, *Baked Alaska: Recipes for Sweet Comforts from the North Country*

---

in the dead of winter; the frozen berries provide a refreshing treat to the hiker.

The fruit of the wild rose, or rose hip, is not strictly a berry but is an ideal source of vitamin C for Bush dweller and city resident alike. A few hips will provide as much of the vitamin as a medium-size orange. The farther north the hips are found, the richer they are in vitamin C.

Lingonberry/Lowbush Cranberry (*Vaccinium vitisidae*). **From** *Alaska Wild Berry Guide and Cookbook*.

Alaska does have one poisonous berry, the baneberry. Sometimes called doll's eyes or chinaberries, baneberries may be white or scarlet in color. As few as six berries can induce violent symptoms of poisoning in an adult.

BILLIKEN
This smiling ivory figure with a pointed head, though long a popular Northland souvenir, is not an Eskimo invention. The billiken was patented in 1908 by Florence Pretz of Kansas City.

A small, seated, Buddha-like figure, the original billiken was manufactured by the Billiken Co. of Chicago and sold as a good luck charm. Thousands of these figurines were sold during the 1909 Alaska-Yukon-Pacific Exposition in Seattle.

Billikens vanished soon afterward from most Lower 48 shops; however, someone had brought them to Nome, and the Eskimos of King Island, Little Diomede and Wales began carving replicas of the billikens from walrus ivory and walrus teeth.

A popular notion contends that rubbing a billiken's tummy brings good fortune.

BIRDS
The Alaska state office of the National Audubon Society acknowledges 462 naturally occurring bird species in Alaska. If unsubstantiated sightings are included, the species total increases.

Millions of ducks, geese and swans wing north to breeding grounds each spring. Millions of seabirds congregate in nesting colonies on exposed cliffs along Alaska's coastline, particularly on the Aleutian Islands and on islands in the Bering Sea.

Migratory birds reach Alaska from many corners of the world. Arctic terns travel up to 22,000 miles on their round trip each year from Antarctica. Others come from South America, Hawaii, the South Pacific islands and Asia.

Each May one of the world's largest concentrations of shorebirds funnels through the Copper River Delta near Cordova. Waterfowl such as trumpeter swans and the world's entire population of dusky Canada geese breed here.

More than 100 species of birds can be spotted in the Seward area.

Other key waterfowl habitats include the Yukon–Kuskokwim Delta, Yukon Flats, Innoko Flats and Minto Lakes. During migration, huge flocks gather at Egegik, Port Heiden, Port Moller, Izembek Bay, Chickaloon Flats, Susitna Flats and Stikine Flats.

Raptors, led by the bald eagle, range throughout the state. The largest gathering of eagles in the world takes place in Alaska each year between October and February. In 1982, the Alaska Chilkat Bald Eagle Preserve was set aside to protect the 3,000-plus eagles that assemble at the site along the Chilkat River near Haines.

Alaska has three subspecies of peregrine falcon: arctic, American and Peale's. Arctic and American peregrine falcons join the Eskimo curlew, the Steller's and spectacled eider and short-tailed albatross on the endangered or threatened species list for

Arctic tern near the Mendenhall Glacier, Juneau. From *Alaska's Birds* by Robert H. Armstrong.

the state. The Aleutian Canada goose was removed in 2001.

Following is a list of some geographically restricted birds whose origins are in Siberia or Asia, as well as a few of the state's more well-known species:

- **Aleutian Tern.** Breeds in coastal areas, marshes, islands, lagoons, rivers and inshore marine waters. Nests in Alaska on the ground in matted, dry grass. Casual sightings in southeastern Alaska in spring and summer, and in northern Alaska in summer.

Arctic Tern. Breeds in tidal flats, beaches, glacial moraines, rivers, lakes and marshes. Nests in colonies or scattered pairs on sand, gravel, moss or in rocks. The arctic tern winters in Antarctica, bypassing the Lower 48 in its 20,000-mile round-trip migration. Common sightings in southeastern, southcoastal and western Alaska in spring, summer and fall, and in southwestern Alaska in spring and fall.

Arctic Warbler. Nests on the ground in grass or moss in willow thickets. Common sightings in the Alaska Range, the Seward Peninsula and the Brooks Range in spring, summer and fall.

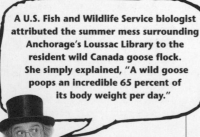

A U.S. Fish and Wildlife Service biologist attributed the summer mess surrounding Anchorage's Loussac Library to the resident wild Canada goose flock. She simply explained, "A wild goose poops an incredible 65 percent of its body weight per day."

Bald Eagle. Found in coniferous forests, deciduous woodlands, rivers and streams, beaches and tidal flats, rocky shores and reefs. Nests in old-growth timber along the coast and larger mainland rivers. In treeless areas, nests on cliffs or on the ground. There are more bald eagles in Alaska than in all the other states combined, and sightings commonly occur in southeastern, southcoastal and southwestern Alaska year-round.

Bluethroat. Nests on the ground in shrub thickets in the uplands and the foothills of western and northern Alaska. Casual sightings in southwestern Alaska in spring and fall.

Emperor Goose. Nests near water in grassy marsh habitat on islands or banks or in large tussocks. The bulk of the world's population nests in the Yukon–Kuskokwim Delta, with a few others nesting farther north to Kotzebue Sound and a few more in eastern Siberia. Rarely is an emperor goose seen east or south of Kodiak. Common sightings in southwestern Alaska in spring, fall and winter, and in western Alaska in spring, summer and fall.

Horned Puffin. Nests on sea islands in rock crevices or in burrows among boulders, on sea cliffs and on grassy slopes. Breeds inshore, in marine waters and on islands. Common sightings in southwestern and western Alaska in spring, summer and fall.

Pacific Loon. Breeds on lakes in coniferous forests or on tundra lakes, and nests on projecting points or small islands. Folklore credits the loon with magical powers and several legends abound. Common sightings in southeastern and southcentral Alaska in spring, fall and winter, and in southwestern, central, western and northern Alaska in spring, summer and fall.

Red-faced Cormorant. Habitat includes inshore marine waters. Nests in colonies on ledges of sea cliffs, small piles of rocks and shelves on volcanic cinder cones. In North America this bird appears only in Alaska. Common sightings in southcoastal and southwestern Alaska year-round.

Red-legged Kittiwake. Breeds in the Pribilof Islands, and on Buldir and Bogoslof islands in the Aleutians. Nests on cliff ledges and cliff points. Common sightings near breeding areas in southwestern Alaska in summer.

Whiskered Auklet. A small gray diving seabird with white whiskers. It nests only in the Aleutians, particularly at the eastern end of Unalaska Island and on nearby Baby Islands.

White Wagtail. Found in open areas with short vegetation usually along the Seward Peninsula coast. Nests near or on the ground in crevices or niches in old buildings. Casual sightings in central Alaska in spring, and in southwestern Alaska in spring and summer.

About 10 million swans, geese and ducks also nest in Alaska each year, making the state critical habitat for many of the continent's waterfowl. In North America some species and subspecies use Alaska as exclusive nesting grounds, while more than

NUGGETS

Firefighters came to the aid of ducks and geese arriving in Fairbanks on April 20, 1998, transforming an unusually dry Creamer's Field Migratory Waterfowl Refuge into a watery haven. About 150,000 gallons of water, donated by Golden Heart Utilities, poured onto the field. —1998 *The ALASKA ALMANAC*®

half the North American population of other species nests in the state.

Five chapters of the National Audubon Society are based in Alaska: the Anchorage Audubon Society (P.O. Box 101161, Anchorage 99510), the Juneau Audubon Society (P.O. Box 021725, Juneau 99802), the Arctic Audubon Society (P.O. Box 82098, Fairbanks 99708), the Kodiak Audubon Society (P.O. Box 1756, Kodiak 99615) and the Prince William Sound Audubon Society (P.O. Box 2725, Cordova

99574). These local chapters coordinate some of the more than 20 annual Christmas bird counts around the state. The Fairbanks Bird Club (P.O. Box 81791, Fairbanks 99708) conducts the annual Christmas count for that area. The Alaska State Office of the National Audubon Society is located at 308 G St., Suite 217, Anchorage 99501.

Bird-watchers gather during the first week of May for the Copper River Delta Shorebird Festival in Cordova and the Kachemak Bay Shorebird Festival in

No Kiddin', No Lie

Just before April Fools Day in 1987, a flying fish collided with an Alaska Airlines jet. It was no joke. The flight of a Boeing 737 was delayed for about an hour while the plane was inspected for damage. The fish was dropped by a bald eagle as the Boeing 737 approached. The plane was taking off from the Juneau airport and about 400 feet past the runway's end, the jet crossed the flight path of the bald eagle, fish in talons. A mechanic was dispatched to the plane's next stop in Yakutat to check over the plane. The eagle escaped injury.
—1988 *The ALASKA ALMANAC®*

Homer. Ketchikan holds an annual rufous hummingbird festival. The Bald Eagle Festival is held in Haines each November.

BLANKET TOSS As effective as a trampoline, the blanket toss (or *nalukataq*) features a walrus-hide blanket grasped by a number of people in a circle. They toss a person on the blanket as high as possible for as long as that person can remain upright. Every true Eskimo festival and many non-Native occasions include the blanket toss, which originally was used to allow Eskimo hunters to spot game such as walrus and seal in the distance. Depending on the skill of the person being tossed and the number of tossers, a medium-weight person might typically go 20 feet in the air.

BOATING (SEE ALSO Baidarka; Cruises; Ferries) Travel by boat is an important means of transportation in Alaska where highways serve only about one-third of the state. Until the advent of the airplane, boats often were the only way to reach many parts of Alaska. Most of Alaska's supplies still arrive by water and in Southeast—where precipitous terrain and numerous islands make road building impossible—water travel is essential.

In January 2001, vessel registration was transferred from the U.S. Coast Guard to the Alaska Division of Motor Vehicles. The department reported that there were 25,343 vessels registered in the state as of December 2000.

Moorage. To accommodate the needs of this fleet, there are approximately 8,000 rental slips and 2,000 transient slips available at public small-boat harbors in Alaska. State officials say actual service capacity is somewhat greater because of the transient nature of many boats and "double parking." There are also harbors at various remote locations where no services other than moorage are provided.

Local governments have the major responsibility for operating public floats, grids, docks, launching ramps and associated small-boat harbor facilities throughout the coastal areas of the state. Moorage facilities constructed by the state are intended for boats up to a maximum of 100 feet, with a limited number of facilities for larger vessels where large boats are common. With the exception of Ketchikan,

Valdez Harbor holds pleasure craft as well as commercial fishing vessels and tour boats.
Photo by Tricia Brown.

Sitka and Juneau, there are no private marine facilities.

Recreational Boating. Alaska ranks 16th nationally in per capita ownership of recreational boats. Alaska has thousands of miles of lakes, rivers and sheltered seaways. For information about boating within national forests, parks, monuments, preserves and wildlife refuges, contact the appropriate federal agency. For travel by boat in southeastern Alaska's Inside Passage and the sheltered seaways of Southcentral Alaska's Prince William Sound—or elsewhere in Alaska's coastal waters—NOAA nautical charts, pilot guides and tidal current tables are available. (SEE Information Sources)

Sea kayakers from around the world are drawn to Alaska to paddle its sheltered waterways and challenge its open coast. Kayakers in Alaska may visit tidewater glaciers and natural hot springs, meeting whales and sea otters along the way.

Inland boaters will find hundreds of river and lake systems suitable for traveling by boat, raft, kayak or canoe. Canoe routes have been established on the Kenai Peninsula (contact Kenai National Wildlife Refuge, P.O. Box 2139, Soldotna 99669; 907-

262-7021); in Nancy Lake State Recreation Area (contact Superintendent, Mat–Su District, HC32, Box 6706, Wasilla 99687; 907-745-3975); and on rivers in the Fairbanks and Anchorage areas (contact Bureau of Land Management, 1150 University Ave., Fairbanks 99709; 907-474-2200, and 222 W. Seventh Ave., No. 13, Anchorage 99513; 907-271-5960).

Travel by water in Alaska requires extra caution. Weather changes rapidly and is often unpredictable; it's important to be prepared for the worst. Even in midsummer, Alaska waters are cold. A person falling overboard may become immobilized by the cold water in only a few minutes. And since many of Alaska's water routes are far from civilization, help may be a long way off.

Persons inexperienced in traveling Alaska's waterways might consider hiring a charter boat operator or outfitter. Guides offer local knowledge and provide all necessary equipment. For information on such services, contact the chamber of commerce or the convention and visitors bureau for an area. A listing of these agencies is given at www.dced.state.ak.us/tourism/sources/visinfo.htm.

Recreation information on both state and federal lands is available at the four Alaska Public Lands Information Centers: 605 W. Fourth Ave., Suite 105, Anchorage 99501, (907) 271-2737; 250 Cushman St.,

Suite 1A, Fairbanks 99701, (907) 456-0527; P.O. Box 359, Tok 99780, (907) 883-5667; and 50 Main St., Ketchikan 99901, (907) 228-6220. Web site: www.nps.gov/aplic.

BORE TIDE (SEE ALSO Tides) A "bore" is an abrupt rise of tidal water moving rapidly inland from the mouth of an estuary into a constricted inlet; the term derives from the Middle English word for "wave."

There are only a handful of bore tides in the world, among them Canada's Bay of Fundy and England's Severn Bore.

Cook Inlet has one of the largest fluctuating tides in the world. Maximum tidal range here approaches 40 feet. Incoming tides are further compressed in the narrowing of Knik and Turnagain Arms and tidal bores are commonly seen. One- to 2-foot bores are common but spring tides in Turnagain Arm in particular can produce spectacular bores up to 6 feet high, running at speeds of up to 10 knots. Good spots to view Turnagain's bore tides are along the Seward Highway, between 26 and 37 miles south of Anchorage. They arrive there about 2 hours and 15 minutes later than the tide book prediction for low tide at Anchorage.

BREAKUP (SEE ALSO Nenana Ice Classic)
Breakup occurs when melting snows raise the level of ice-covered streams and rivers sufficiently to cause the ice to break apart and float downstream. Breakup is one of two factors determining the open-water season for river navigation, the second being the depth of the river. Peak water conditions occur just after breakup.

The navigable season for the Kuskokwim and Yukon rivers is June 1 through Sept. 30; the Nushagak River, June 1 through Aug. 31; and the Noatak River, late May through mid-September.

Breakup is a spectacular sight-and-sound show. Massive pieces of ice crunch and pound against one another as they push their way downriver racing for the sea, creating noises not unlike many huge engines straining and grating. The spine-

tingling sound can be heard for miles. It marks the finale of winter and the arrival of spring in Alaska.

Sometimes great ice jams occur, causing the water to back up and flood inhabited areas. Flooding occurred at Fort Yukon in spring 1982, at McGrath in 1990 and at Allakaket in 1993.

BUNNY BOOTS Bunny boots, also called vapor barrier boots, are large, insulated rubber boots that protect feet from frostbite. Black bunny boots are generally rated to –20°F, while the more common white bunny boots are even warmer and have been used in the most extreme conditions, including the heights of Mount McKinley, even though they're cumbersome for climbing. They are no longer made but are still in demand. Used bunny boots can fetch $50 to $150 a pair.

BUSH Originally used to describe large expanses of wilderness beyond the fringes of civilization inhabited only by trappers and prospectors, Bush has come to stand for any part of Alaska not accessible by road. A community accessible only by air, water, sled or snow machine is considered a Bush village and anyone living there is someone from the Bush. The Bush is home to most of Alaska's Native people and to many individuals who live on homesteads, operate mines or work as guides, pilots, teachers, trappers or fishermen.

The term is also applied to the small planes and their pilots who service areas lacking roads. Bush planes are commonly equipped with floats and skis to match terrain and season. For their oftentimes courageous air service, Alaska Bush pilots have become modern frontier heroes.

BUS LINES Scheduled bus service is available in summer to and within Alaska, although buses don't run as frequently as in the Lower 48. (Local transit service is also available in some major communities.) Service may be infrequent; consult current schedules.

Alaska Direct Buslines, 125 Oklahoma St., Anchorage 99504; (907)

277-6652. Provides service to Anchorage, Dawson, Fairbanks, Whitehorse, Skagway and all points in between.

Alaska Park Connection, P.O. Box 22-1011, Anchorage 99522; (907) 245-0200 or (800) 208-0200. Provides service between Anchorage, Seward, Denali National Park and Talkeetna.

Alaska Sightseeing/Cruise West, 349 Wrangell St., Anchorage 99501; (907) 276-1305. Provides service between Anchorage, Denali National Park and Preserve, Columbia Glacier, Fairbanks, Prince William Sound and Valdez.

Eagle Custom Tours, P.O. Box 212529, Anchorage 99521; (907) 277-6228. Provides group transportation and tours throughout Alaska and the Yukon.

Fun Bus Alaska, 8150 Williwa Ave., Anchorage 99504; (907) 345-2432. Year-round charters and transfers to Alaska and the Yukon.

Gray Line of Alaska/Westours, 745 W. Fourth Ave., Suite 200, Anchorage 99501; (907) 277-5581. Provides local city sightseeing tours, travel between Anchorage, Denali National Park, Fairbanks, Kenai Peninsula, Dawson, Prudhoe Bay, Skagway, Valdez, Ketchikan, Juneau and Whitehorse.

Homer Stage Lines, 3339 Fairbanks St., Anchorage 99503; (907) 563-0800 Anchorage; (907) 224-3608 Seward; (907) 235-2252 Homer.

Princess Tours, 6441 Interstate Circle, Anchorage 99518; (800) 426-0500. Provides sightseeing excursions and tours throughout Alaska; operates several hotels.

Seward Bus Lines, 3339 Fairbanks St., Anchorage 99503; (907) 563-7711 Anchorage; (907) 224-3608 Seward. Provides daily service between Anchorage and Seward.

CABBAGE
Meet the king of Alaska's monster vegetables. Alaska's abundant summer sun, cool temperatures and rich soil make it possible for gardeners to grow colossal cold-weather vegetables, most notably cabbage. The Matanuska and Susitna valleys, north of Anchorage, are a hotbed of cabbage cultivation, where the biggest are grown not for eating but for glory and prize money. The Giant Cabbage Weigh-off is one of the highlights of the Alaska State Fair in Palmer. The winner collects a $2,000 prize. Past winners include:

2000—Barb Everingham, Wasilla, 105.6 pounds, a U.S. record.

1999—Gene Dinkel, Wasilla, 91.6 pounds.

1998—Donald Dinkel, Wasilla, 89.4 pounds.

1997—Gene Dinkel, Wasilla, 83.3 pounds.

CABIN FEVER
Cabin fever is a state of mind blamed on cold, dark,

Cabbage grows to extra-large proportions under the Midnight Sun. Photo by Roy Corral.

Coca-Cola has a toll-free hotline in Atlanta for information and complaints. When asked who calls this number, an operator replied, "People from Alaska call in the winter just to talk."

The Forest Service cabin at Paradise lake on the Kenai Peninsula. From *Alaska's Kenai Peninsula: A Traveler's Guide.* Photo by Andromeda Romano-Lax.

winter weather when people are often housebound. It is characterized by depression, preoccupation, discontent and occasionally violence, and has been described as "a 12-foot stare in a 10-foot room." Today these symptoms are known as seasonal affective disorder, or SAD.

Cabin fever is commonly thought to afflict miners and trappers spending a lonely winter in the wilderness but, in truth, these people are active and outdoors enough to remain content. It is more likely to strike the snowbound city dwellers who do not ski or mush dogs, or the disabled. The arrival of spring or a change of scene usually relieves the symptoms.

CABINS (See also Camping; National Forests; State Park System) Rustic cabins in remote Alaska places can be rented from the Forest Service, the Bureau of Land Management (BLM), the National Park Service, the Alaska State Parks and the U.S. Fish and Wildlife Service. The modest price ($15 to $65 a night per cabin) makes this one of the best vacation bargains in Alaska. Visitors should prepare for rigorous backcountry travel and be ready to seek emergency shelter should they be unable to reach their cabin.

Almost 200 Forest Service cabins are scattered through the Tongass and Chugach national forests in Southeastern and Southcentral Alaska. Some are located on salt water, others on freshwater rivers, streams or lakes. Some of the cabins can be reached by boat or trail but because of the remote locations, visitors frequently arrive by chartered aircraft.

The average cabin is 12 feet by 14 feet and is usually equipped with a table, an oil or wood stove and wooden bunks without mattresses. Most will accommodate a group of four to six. There is no electricity. Outhouses are within walking distance. Visitors need to bring food, bedding, cooking utensils and stove fuel. It's advisable to have a gas or propane stove for cooking, a lantern and insect repellent. Splitting mauls are provided on site for cutting firewood. Since firewood is scarce and often wet, visitors should carry a supply of dry wood. Reservations may be made in person or by mail. Payment must accompany the reservation. Permits for use are issued on a first-come, first-served basis, up to 180 days in advance. Length of stay for some cabins is limited.

General information on all public-use cabins is available from the Alaska Public Lands Information Centers: 605 W. Fourth Ave., Suite 105, Anchorage 99501, (907) 271-2737; P.O. Box 359, Tok 99780, (907) 883-5667; 250 Cushman St., Suite 1A, Fairbanks 99701, (907) 456-0527;

50 Main St., Ketchikan 99901, (907) 228-6220. Web site: www.nps.gov/ aplic/center.

For information on national forest cabins in Alaska, contact **Forest Service** Information Center, 101 Egan Drive, Juneau 99801, (907) 586-8751, or Southeast Alaska Visitor Center, 50 Main St., Ketchikan 99901, (907) 228-6220. Web site: www.nrrc.com.

The Forest Service recommends that visitors contact the Information Center and request Forest Service cabin information. It's a good idea to do this at least six months ahead. A booklet contains the applications for cabin use and tips on planning a stay.

The **National Park Service** has three coastal cabins, open during summer months only, in Kenai Fjords National Park. One winter-only cabin is available at Exit Glacier. For information, contact Kenai Fjords National Park, Cabin Reservations, P.O. Box 1727, Seward 99664; (907) 224-3175.

The **Bureau of Land Management** has about a dozen public-use cabins in the White Mountains National Recreation Area east of Fairbanks, used primarily by winter recreationists. Only one of the cabins is accessible during summer months. In addition one cabin near the roadside (not part of the White Mountains system) is available year-round. Cabins must be reserved prior to use and a fee is required. Contact the BLM Support Center, 1150 University Ave., Fairbanks 99709-3844; (907) 474-2250.

The **U.S. Fish and Wildlife Service** maintains public-use cabins within Kodiak National Wildlife Refuge. Contact the refuge manager, 1390 Buskin River Road, Kodiak 99615; (907) 487-2600.

Alaska State Parks offers more than 40 public-use cabins throughout the state. For reservations and information contact the Department of Natural Resources Public Information Center, 550 W. Seventh Ave., Suite 1260, Anchorage 99501-3557; (907) 269-8400; TDD (907) 269-8411; fax (907) 269-8901; www.dnr.state.ak.us/ parks/parks.htm.

CACHE Pronounced "cash," this small storage unit is built to be inaccessible to marauding animals. A cache traditionally is a miniature log cabin mounted on stilts. It is reached by a ladder that bears, dogs, foxes and other hungry or curious animals can't climb. Extra precautions include wrapping tin around the poles to prevent climbing by clawed animals and extending the floor a few feet in all directions from the top of the poles to discourage those clever enough to get that high.

Squirrels are the most notorious of Alaska's cache-crashing critters.

To be truly animal-proof, a cache should be built in a clearing well beyond the 30-foot leaping distance a squirrel can manage from a treetop.

Bush residents use the cache as a primitive food freezer for game and fish in winter. A cache may also store furs from a trapline, extra fuel and bedding. Size is determined by need. Sometimes a cache will be built between three or four straight trees growing close together.

Like *mush (marché)*, the word *cache* is borrowed from French-Canadian voyageurs.

CAMPING (SEE ALSO Boating; Cabins; Chilkoot Trail; Hiking; National Forests; National Parks; National Wildlife Refuges; State Park System) Numerous public and privately operated campgrounds are found along Alaska's highways. Electrical hookups and dump stations are scarce.

The dump station at Russian River campground is available for Chugach National Forest visitors. Alaska's back-country offers virtually limitless possibilities for wilderness camping. Get permission before camping on private land. If the land is publicly owned, it's worthwhile to contact the managing agency for regulations and hiking/camping conditions.

The **U.S. Forest Service** maintains 26 campgrounds in the Tongass and Chugach national forests, most with

(Continued on page 40)

Calendar of Annual Events 2002

JANUARY
Anchorage—Alaskan Sled Dog and Racing Association Sled Dog Races.
Big Lake—Klondike 300 Sled Dog Derby; Snow machine racing.
Chistochina—Copper Basin 300 Sled Dog Race.
Glennallen—Copper Basin 300 Sled Dog Race.
Juneau—State Legislature convenes.
Kenai—Tustumena 200 Sled Dog Race.
Kodiak—Russian Christmas and Starring; Russian New Year and Masquerade Ball.
Seward—Polar Bear Jump-Off Festival.
Sitka—Northwest Coast Arts Symposium.
Soldotna—Tustumena 200 Sled Dog Race; Ty Clark Memorial Sled Dog Race.
Unalaska—Russian Orthodox Christmas Eve and Starring; Russian New Year's Eve.
Valdez—Quest for Gold Sled Dog Race.
Willow—Winter Carnival.

FEBRUARY
Anchorage—Fur Rendezvous; World Championship Sled Dog Races.
Anchor Point—Snow Rondi.
Big Lake—Tesoro Iron Dog Snowmachine Race.
Chistochina—Fun Days.
Cordova—Iceworm Festival.
Dillingham—Nushagak Classic Sled Dog Race; Beaver Round-Up Festival; Western Alaska Sled Dog Championship.
Fairbanks—Iron Dog Gold Rush Classic; Yukon Quest International Sled Dog Race.
Homer—Winter Carnival.
Kenai—Peninsula Winter Games; Quilt Artist Show.
Ketchikan—Festival of the North.
Nenana—Tour de Minto Sled Dog Race.

Nome—Iron Dog Gold Rush Classic Snow Machine Race.
Seldovia—Winter Carnival.
Soldotna—Peninsula Winter Games; Ski Joring; Sled Dog Races.
Tok—Tok to Dawson Run (snow machine).
Valdez—Alaskan Local Snowboarding Championship.
Wasilla—Iditarod Days Festival; Tesoro Iron Dog Snowmachine Race.
Wrangell—Tent City Days.

MARCH
Anchorage—Iditarod Trail Sled Dog Race; International Ice Carving Competition; Tour of Anchorage Cross-Country Ski Race.
Anchor Point—Cabin Fever Variety Show.
Big Lake—Iditarod Trail Sled Dog Race.
Chatanika—Chatanika Days.
Cordova—Million Dollar Iron Dog Tour.
Eagle River—Iditarod Trail Sled Dog Race.
Fairbanks—Festival of Native Arts; North American Sled Dog Championships; Winter Carnival; World Ice Art Championship.
Homer—Kachemak Bay Marathon Ski; Snomads' Fun Run; Winter King Salmon Tournament.
Kenai—Alaska Native Art Show; Central Peninsula Writers' Night.
Kodiak—Comfish Alaska.
Nenana—Nenana Ice Classic Tripod Weekend.
Nome—Bering Sea Ice Golf Classic; Iditarod Trail Sled Dog Race; Miners and Mushers Ball; Nome–Council Sled Dog Race; Nome–Golovin Snowmachine Race.
North Pole—Winter Carnival.
Palmer—Lions Club Gun Show.
Skagway—Buckwheat Ski Classic; Windfest. *(continued)*

More Calendar of Annual Events

March *(continued)*
Soldotna—St. Patrick's Day Celebration.
Tok—Race of Champions (sled dog); Tok to Dawson Run (snow machine).
Trapper Creek—Cabin Fever Reliever.
Unalaska—USAFV Soup-off, sponsored by Unalaskans against Sexual Assault and Family Violence.
Valdez—Mayor's Cup Snowmachine Race; Ice Climbing Festival.
Wasilla—Iditarod Trail Sled Dog Race; Iditarod Days Festival.

APRIL
Anchorage—Native Youth Olympics.
Barrow—Spring Festival.
Bethel—Camai Dance Festival.
Fairbanks—Arctic Man Ski and Snow-Go Classic.
Girdwood—Alyeska Spring Carnival.
Juneau—Alaska Folk Festival.
Kenai—Alaska Native Art Show.
Kodiak—Old Harbor Whaling Festival.
Nome—Cannonball Run; Northwest Arctic Games.
Tok—Tok Trot.
Valdez—Alaska's Big Mountain Extreme Snowboard Competition.
Wrangell—Garnet Festival.

MAY
Anchor Point—Calcutta Auction; King Salmon Saltwater Tournament.
Cold Bay—Silver Salmon Derby.
Cordova—Copper River Delta Shorebird Festival.
Delta Junction—Buffalo Wallow Square Dance Festival.
Haines—Great Alaska Craftbeer and Homebrew Festival; Koot to Kat Skat Biathlon; King Salmon Derby.
Homer—Crafts Fair; Halibut Derby begins; Kachemak Bay Wooden Boat Festival; Shorebird Festival.
Juneau—Jazz and Classics Festival.
Ketchikan—Celebration of the Sea.

Kodiak—Great Alaska Rubber Duck Race; International Migratory Bird Day.
Nome—Polar Bear Memorial Day Swim in the Bering Sea; Stroke and Croak Triathlon.
Palmer—Operation Clean Sweep.
Pelican—Boardwalk Boogie.
Petersburg—Little Norway Festival; Salmon Derby.
Seward—Exit Glacier 5K and 10K Runs; Jackpot Halibut Tournament; Seward Harbor Opening Weekend.
Sitka—Salmon Derby.
Soldotna—State Parks Annual Kenai River Clean Up.
Talkeetna—Miners' Day Festival.
Unalaska—World Record Halibut Derby begins.
Valdez—Halibut Derby.
Wasilla—Mat-Su King Salmon Derby.
Wrangell—King Salmon Derby.

JUNE
Anchorage—Mayor's Midnight Sun Marathon; Blues on the Green Festival.
Anchor Point—Kids All-American Fishing Derby.
Barrow—Nalukataq Whaling Festival.
Big Lake—Regatta Water Festival.
Cordova—Alaska Salmon Runs.
Dillingham—Nushagak King Derby.
Eagle River—Highland Games.
Fairbanks—Midnight Sun Run; Midnight Sun Baseball Game; Summer Fine Arts Camp; Summer Solstice Celebration; Yukon 800 Boat Race.
Haines—King Salmon Derby; Summer Solstice Celebration.
Hyder/Stewart—International Rodeo.
Juneau—Gold Rush Days.
Kenai—Kenai River Festival.
Ketchikan—King Salmon Derby.
Kodiak—All American   *(continued)*

37

More Calendar of Annual Events

June (continued)

Soap Box Derby.

Moose Pass—Summer Solstice Festival.

Nenana—River Daze.

Nikiski—Family Fun in the Midnight Sun.

Nome—Midnight Sun Festival; River Raft Race.

North Pole—Farmers' Market; Christmas in June Parade.

Palmer—Colony Days.

Seward—Jackpot Halibut Tournament.

Sitka—Summer Music Festival; Writers' Symposium.

Soldotna—Pop Drop; Quilting on the Kenai.

Unalaska—Halibut Derby.

Valdez—Halibut Derby; Pink Salmon Derby; Prince William Sound Theatre Conference.

Wasilla—Alaska Transportation Expo and Air Show; Mat–Su Salmon Derby.

Wrangell—King Salmon Derby.

JULY

(Fourth of July celebrations take place in most towns and villages.)

Anchor Point—Homesteaders Beach Run.

Chugiak/Eagle River—Bear Paws Festival.

Delta Junction—Buffalo Barbeque; Deltana Fair.

Dillingham—Nushagak King Derby.

Fairbanks—Golden Days; Summer Arts Festival; Summer Fine Arts Camp; World Eskimo–Indian Olympics.

Girdwood—Forest Faire.

Glennallen—Brown Bear Arts Festival; Ahtna Arts and Crafts Fair.

Homer—American Legion Carnival; Concert on the Lawn; Halibut Derby; Summer Street Fair.

Kodiak—Bear Country Music Festival.

Naknek—Fishtival.

Nome—Anvil Mountain Run.

Palmer—Palmer Pride Picnic.

Petersburg—Canned Salmon Classic.

Seldovia—Salmon Shuffle.

Seward—Halibut Tournament; Mount Marathon Race.

Skagway—Ducky Derby.

Soldotna—Dog Show; Progress Days.

Sterling—Moose River Raft Race.

Sutton—Old Timers' Picnic.

Talkeetna—Moose Dropping Festival.

Unalaska—Mount Ballyhoo Run; Halibut Derby; Carl's Carnival.

Valdez—Halibut Derby; Silver Salmon Derby (July–September); Pink Salmon Derby.

Wasilla—Water Festival; Mat–Su Salmon Derby.

Willow—Volleyball Challenge.

AUGUST

Dillingham—No-See-Ums Festival.

Fairbanks—Tanana Valley State Fair.

Haines—Bald Eagle Music Festival; Southeast Alaska State Fair.

Homer—Silver Salmon Derby.

Houston—Founders' Day.

Juneau—Golden North Salmon Derby.

Ketchikan—Blueberry Arts Festival.

Kodiak—Pink Salmon Jamboree.

Ninilchik—Kenai Peninsula State Fair.

Palmer—Alaska State Fair; State Fair Parade.

Seward—Silver Salmon Derby.

Skagway—Flower and Garden Show.

Soldotna—Silver Salmon Derby; State Fair; 10K Run for Women.

Talkeetna—Bluegrass Festival.

Tok—Mainstreet Alaska Sourdough Potlatch.

Unalaska—Tundra Gold Classic; Halibut Derby.

Valdez—Silver Salmon Derby; Gold Rush Days; Halibut Derby. *(continued)*

More Calendar of Annual Events

SEPTEMBER
Anchorage—Great Alaska Quilt Show.
Chugiak/Eagle River—Outrageous Dinner and Auction.
Fairbanks—Equinox Marathon.
Homer—End of Halibut Derby; Halibut Derby Banquet.
Kenai—Lions Rubber Ducky Race; Silver Salmon Derby.
Kodiak—Silver Salmon Derby; State Fair and Rodeo.
Nome—Great Bathtub Race; Rubber Duck Race.
Skagway—Klondike Road Relay.
Soldotna—Labor Day Picnic.
Unalaska—Island Half Marathon; World Record Halibut Derby ends.
Valdez—Halibut Derby ends; Fall Dinner Cruise and Wine Tasting Auction; Silver Salmon Derby.
Wrangell—Block Party.

OCTOBER
Anchorage—Quyana Alaska; Johnson Nissan Hockey Tournament.
Homer—Octoberfest; Taste of Homer.
Kenai—Chamber of Commerce Wine Tasting.
Kodiak—Oktoberfest.
Petersburg—October ArtsFest.
Sitka—Alaska Day Festival.
Skagway—Paranormal.
Soldotna—Pie Auction.
Wasilla—Murder on the Alaska Railroad Excursion.
Wrangell—Harvest Festival.

NOVEMBER
Anchorage—Great Alaska Shootout Basketball Tournament; Crafts Emporium.
Anchor Point—Holiday Craft Fair.
Fairbanks—Athabascan Old-Time Fiddling Festival; Top of the World Classic (basketball); beginning of Winter Solstice Celebration.
Haines—Bald Eagle Festival.
Kenai—Christmas Comes to Kenai and City of Lights Parade; Potters' Guild Exhibit.
Ketchikan—Winter Arts Faire.
Petersburg—Festival of Lights.
Sitka—WhaleFest.
Soldotna—Craft Bazaars.
Tok—Tok-A-Tans Christmas Bazaar.

DECEMBER
Barrow—Christmas Festival.
Chugiak/Eagle River—Merry Merchant Munch.
Homer—"The Nutcracker."
Juneau—Gallery Walk.
Ketchikan—Festival of Lights Holiday Ball; Winter Art Walk.
Kodiak—Harbor Stars Boat Parade.
Nome—Firemen's Carnival.
North Pole—Candle Lighting Ceremony.
Palmer—Colony Christmas.
Petersburg—Julebukking.
Seward—Holiday Train.
Sitka—Christmas Boat Parade.
Soldotna—Tree Lighting Ceremony.
Talkeetna—Bachelor Society Ball and Wilderness Women Contest; Winterfest.
Wrangell—Festival of Lights and Christmas Tree Lighting.

(Continued from page 35)
tent and trailer sites and minimum facilities. Most campgrounds are available on a first-come, first-served basis. Stays are limited to 14 days except in Russian River campground where the limit is three days during the salmon run. Campground fees are $8 to $16 per night depending upon facilities, which can include fire grates, pit toilets, garbage pickup, picnic tables and water. Most campgrounds are open from Memorial Day through Labor Day, weather permitting.

For information on camping in the Chugach National Forest, contact the Forest Service Information Center, 101 Egan Drive, Juneau 99801; (907) 586-8751.

The state's Division of Forestry requires permits for open burning in most areas of Interior and Southcentral Alaska. Permits are not required if fires are in approved burn barrels or are used for signaling.

National Park Service at Denali National Park and Preserve operates seven different campgrounds along the single road into the park. The campgrounds range in cost and comfort level, and advance reservations are recommended. Private vehicle access on Denali Park Road is limited, so some campgrounds are accessible only by shuttle bus. Reservations and fee information for campsites or shuttle buses are available at (800) 622-7275. Anchorage and international callers should phone (907) 272-7275. Except for the Riley Creek Campground, most camping areas are open from mid-May to mid-September, weather permitting.

Listed in order of the closest to the park entrance, the camping areas include:

• Riley Creek Campground, near the park entrance. Offers 100 sites for RVs and tents, flush toilets, pay phone. Open year-round. Register at Visitor Center or in advance by phone.

• Morino Backpacker Campground, Mile 1.9 Denali Park Road. No vehicles allowed; chemical toilets; limit of two people per site. Self-register at the grounds.

• Savage River Campground, Mile 13. Offers 33 sites for RVs and tents; water, flush toilets. Reserve in advance.

• Sanctuary River Campground, Mile 23. Offers 7 tent sites; accessible only by shuttle bus. Chemical toilets, no water available. Reserve at Visitor Center.

• Teklanika River Campground, Mile 29. Offers 53 sites for RVs and tents; water, flush toilets. Reserve in advance or at Visitor Center.

• Igloo Creek Campground, Mile 34. No vehicles allowed. Offers 7 tent sites; accessible only by shuttle bus. Chemical toilets. Reserve at Visitor Center.

• Wonder Lake Campground, Mile 85. Offers 28 tent sites; accessible by shuttle bus only. Water, flush toilets available. Reserve in advance. Open mid-June to mid-September.

Shuttle buses depart on a regular schedule from the Visitor Center, located one mile inside the park. The center also features a bookstore, exhibits and ranger presentations on safe travel within the park, natural history, bear behavior, dog mushing and other topics. It is open daily from 7 A.M. to 8 P.M. during the peak summer season of early May to late September. Another visitor center, accessible only by shuttle bus, is located at Mile 66.

Brochures may be obtained from Denali National Park and Preserve, P.O. Box 9, Denali Park 99755, or check www.nps.gov/dena.

Glacier Bay and Katmai National Parks each offer one campground for walk-in

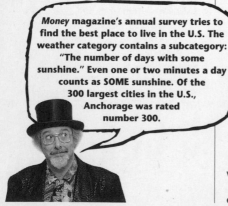

Money magazine's annual survey tries to find the best place to live in the U.S. The weather category contains a subcategory: "The number of days with some sunshine." Even one or two minutes a day counts as SOME sunshine. Of the 300 largest cities in the U.S., Anchorage was rated number 300.

Wood-Tikchik State Park's vast wilderness attracts kayakers, backpackers and anglers. From *Alaska's Accessible Wilderness* by Bill Sherwonit.

campers; Katmai requires reservations, which may be obtained in advance by calling (800) 365-2267. Backcountry camping is permitted in Denali, Glacier Bay, Katmai and Klondike Gold Rush national parks, as well as other national parks and monuments.

Alaska State Parks maintains the most extensive system of roadside campgrounds and waysides in Alaska. All are available on a first-come, first-served basis. Fees are charged and a yearly pass is offered. Contact Alaska State Parks, Public Information Center, 550 W. Seventh Ave., Suite 1260, Anchorage 99501-3557; (907) 269-8400; fax (907) 29-8901; www.dnr.state.ak.us/parks.

U.S. Fish and Wildlife Service has several wildlife refuges open to campers, although most are not accessible by highway. The Kenai National Wildlife Refuge (P.O. Box 2139, Soldotna 99669) has several campgrounds accessible from the Sterling Highway linking Homer and Anchorage. Contact Fish and Wildlife Service, 1011 E. Tudor, Anchorage 99503; (907) 786-3909; fax (907) 786-3844.

The **Bureau of Land Management** maintains 11 campgrounds in Interior Alaska. In 1994, BLM opened its first fully developed campground on the Dalton Highway at Mile 180 (5 miles north of Coldfoot). Fees vary by location. Brochures describing the campgrounds are available. Contact BLM, 222 W. Seventh Ave., No. 13, Anchorage 99513; (907) 271-5076; fax (907) 271-4596.

Alaska Public Lands Information Centers provide information on all state and federal campgrounds in Alaska, along with state and national park passes and details on wilderness camping. Visit or contact one of the following centers:

605 W. Fourth Ave., Suite 105, Anchorage 99501, (907) 271-2737; P.O. Box 359, Tok 99780, (907) 883-5667; 250 Cushman, Suite 1A, Fairbanks 99701, (907) 456-0527; 50 Main St., Ketchikan 99501, (907) 228-6220.

For a recording of state parks area conditions, call (907) 762-2278. Web site: www.nps.gov/aplic.

Since the late 1950s, the Forest Service has charged fees for using campgrounds. Some campgrounds are now "fee demonstration projects," and at least 80 percent of the money collected is returned to the administering unit for maintenance and improvements at the site. Pack Creek Bear Viewing Area charges fees from early June through mid-September. Begich–Boggs Visitors Center charges no admission, but will charge for viewing the movie *Voices from the Ice*.

Private Campgrounds. For information, contact the Alaska Campground Owners Association, P.O. Box 84884, Fairbanks 99708; (907) 883-5877.

CHAMBERS OF COMMERCE

(SEE ALSO Convention and Visitors Bureaus)

Alaska State Chamber, 217 Second St., Suite 201, Juneau 99801; (907) 586-2323; fax (907) 463-5515. P.O. Box 91896, Anchorage 99501; (907) 278-2722; fax (907) 278-6643; www.alaskachamber.com.

Anchor Point Chamber, P.O. Box 610, Anchor Point 99556; (907) 235-2600; www.xyz.net/~apcoc.

Anchorage Chamber, 441 W. Fifth Ave., Suite 300, Anchorage 99501-2309; (907) 272-2401; fax (907) 272-4117; www.anchoragechamber.org.

Barrow, City of, P.O. Box 629, Barrow 99723; (907) 852-5211.

Bethel Chamber, P.O. Box 329, Bethel 99559; (907) 543-2911; www.home. gci.net/~chamber1/bethel.

Big Lake Chamber, P.O. Box 520067, Big Lake 99652; (907) 892-6109; www.biglake-ak.com.

Chugiak/Eagle River Chamber, P.O. Box 770-353, Eagle River 99577; (907) 694-4702; fax (907) 694-1205; www.cer.org.

Copper Valley (Greater) Chamber, P.O. Box 469, Glennallen 99588; (907) 822-5555; fax (907) 822-3010.

Cordova Chamber, P.O. Box 99, Cordova 99574; (907) 424-7260; fax (907) 424-7259; www.cordovachamber.com.

Delta Junction Chamber, P.O. Box 987, Delta Junction 99737; (907) 895-5068; fax (907) 895-5141; deltacc@wildak.net.

Dillingham Chamber, P.O. Box 348, Dillingham 99576; (907) 842-5115; fax (907) 842-4097; www.nushtel.com/ ~dlgchmber.

Fairbanks (Greater) Chamber, 250 Cushman, Suite 2D, Fairbanks 99701; (907) 452-1105; fax (907) 456-6968.

Haines Chamber, P.O. Box 1449, Haines 99827; (907) 766-2202; fax (907) 766-2271; www.haineschamber.org.

Healy Chamber, P.O. Box 437, Healy 99743-0437; (907) 683-4636; fax (907) 683-2281; www.alaska.net/~denst1/ healy.chamber.html.

Homer Chamber, P.O. Box 541, Homer 99603; (907) 235-7740; (907) 235-5300; fax (907) 235-8766; www.homeralaska.org.

Juneau Chamber, 3100 Channel Drive, Suite 300, Juneau 99801; (907) 463-3488; fax (907) 463-3489; www.ptialaska. net/~juneaucc.

Kenai Chamber, 402 Overland, Kenai 99611; (907) 283-7989; fax (907) 283-7183; www.kenaichamber.org.

Ketchikan Chamber, P.O. Box 5759, Ketchikan 99901; (907) 225-3184; fax (907) 225-3187; www.ketchikan chamber.com.

Kodiak Area Chamber, P.O. Box 1485, Kodiak 99615; (907) 486-5557; fax (907) 486-7605; www.kodiak.org.

Kotzebue, City of, P.O. Box 46, Kotzebue 99752; (907) 442-3401.

Moose Pass Chamber, P.O. Box 558, Moose Pass 99631.

Nenana, City of, P.O. Box 70, Nenana 99760; (907) 832-5441.

Ninilchik Chamber, P.O. Box 39164, Ninilchik 99639; (907) 567-3571; fax (907) 567-1041.

Nome Chamber, P.O. Box 240, Nome 99762; (907) 443-3879; fax (907) 443-2742.

North Peninsula Chamber, P.O. Box 8053, Nikiski 99635; (907) 776-8369.

North Pole Community Chamber, P.O. Box 55071, North Pole 99705; (907) 488-2242; www.fairnet.org/npcc.

Palmer Chamber, P.O. Box 45, Palmer 99645; (907) 745-2880; www.palmer chamber.org.

Petersburg Chamber, P.O. Box 649, Petersburg 99833; (907) 772-3646.

Prince of Wales Chamber, P.O. Box 497, Craig 99921; (907) 826-3870; fax (907) 826-5467; www.princeofwales coc.org.

Seldovia Chamber, Drawer F-A,

Seldovia 99663; (907) 234-7612; mary@
seldovia.com.

Seward Chamber, P.O. Box 749,
Seward 99664; (907) 224-8051; (907)
224-5353; www.seward.net/chamber.

Sitka Chamber, P.O. Box 638,
Sitka 99835; (907) 747-8709; fax (907)
747-3739; www.sitka.org.

Skagway Chamber, P.O. Box 194,
Skagway 99840; (907) 983-1898; fax (907)
983-2031.

Soldotna Chamber, 44790 Sterling
Highway, Soldotna 99669; (907) 262-9814;
fax (907) 262-3566; www.soldotna
chamber.com.

Talkeetna Chamber, P.O. Box 334,
Talkeetna 99676; (907) 733-2330.

Tok Chamber, P.O. Box 389, Tok
99780; (907) 883-5775; fax (907) 883-
3682; info@tokalaskainfo.com.

**Unalaska/Port of Dutch Harbor
Chamber,** P.O. Box 920833, Dutch Harbor
99692; (907) 581-4242; veda@arctic.net.

Valdez Chamber, P.O. Box 512,
Valdez 99686; (907) 835-2330.

Wasilla (Greater) Chamber, 415 E.
Railroad Ave., Wasilla 99654; (907)
376-1299; fax (907) 373-2560; city hall fax
(907) 373-0788; www.wasillachamber.org.

Willow Chamber, P.O. Box 0183,
Willow 99688-0183; (907) 495-5858;
www.willowchamber.org.

Wrangell Chamber, P.O. Box 49,
Wrangell 99929; (907) 874-3901;
www.wrangell.com.

CHEECHAKO Pronounced chee-
CHA-ko—or chee-CHA-ker by some
old-time Alaskans—the word means
tenderfoot or greenhorn. According to
The Chinook Jargon, a 1909 dictionary of
the old trading language used by traders
from the Hudson's Bay Company in the
early 1800s, the word *cheechako* comes
from combining the Chinook Indian word
chee, meaning "new, fresh or just now,"
with the Nootka Indian word *chako,*
which means "to come, to approach
or to become."

CHILKAT BLANKET Dramatic,
bilaterally symmetrical patterns, usually in

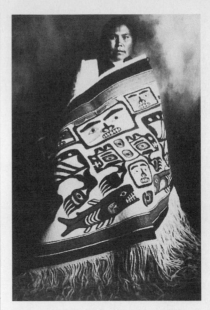

Woman in Chilkat blanket, about 1900.
Picture Alaska Art Gallery. From *The Alaska
Heritage Seafood Cookbook* by Ann Chandonnet.

black, white, yellow and blue, adorn these
heavily fringed ceremonial blankets.

The origin of the Chilkat dancing
blanket is Tsimshian Indian. Knowledge of
the weaving techniques apparently diffused
north to the Tlingit, where blanket-making
reached its highest form among the Chilkat
group. Visiting traders coined the blanket's
name during the late 19th century.

Time, technical skill and inherited
privileges were required to weave Chilkat
blankets and other ceremonial garments.
High-ranking men and women wore the
blankets as cloaks. Portions of worn
blankets, or smaller weavings, were made
into dance aprons and tunics.

Yarn for Chilkat dancing blankets was
spun primarily from the wool of the
mountain goat. Designs woven into Chilkat
blankets are geometric totemic shapes that
can be reproduced by the method known
as twining. (Early blankets are unadorned or
display geometric patterns lacking
curvilinear elements.) Often totemic crests
on painted house posts and the designs
woven into garments were quite similar.

The Chilkoot Trail remains a popular route for modern hikers. Photo by Tricia Brown.

Female weavers reused pattern boards of wood painted with a design by men.

A few weavers are producing Chilkat blankets and the related Raven's Tail robes today.

CHILKOOT TRAIL (SEE ALSO Gold; Skagway) The Chilkoot Trail, which spans 33 miles from Dyea, just north of Skagway, over Chilkoot Pass to Lake Bennett, British Columbia, was one of the established routes taken by prospectors to Yukon District goldfields during the Klondike gold rush of 1897–98. Thousands of stampeders climbed the tortuous trail over Chilkoot Pass that winter. Those who reached Lake Bennett built boats to float down the Yukon River to Dawson City.

NUGGETS

The National Park Service decided in 1993 that it must require back-country permits for hikers of the historic 33-mile Chilkoot Trail. In 1992, a total of 3,000 backpackers hiked the trail.

—1993 *The ALASKA ALMANAC*®

Today the steep and rocky Chilkoot Trail is part of Klondike Gold Rush National Historical Park and is climbed each year by approximately 3,000 backpackers.

The Chilkoot Trail begins about 9 miles from Skagway on Dyea Road. There are a dozen campgrounds along the trail and ranger stations on both the Alaska and British Columbia portions of the trail.

The trail crosses the international border at 3,739-foot Chilkoot Pass, 16.5 miles from the trailhead. Highlights of the area include Slide Cemetery near the remains of the town of Dyea; the Golden Stairs, a 45-degree climb to the summit; and numerous relics left by prospectors still visible along the trail. The trail ends at Bennett, 8 miles from the nearest roadway. For more information, contact Klondike Gold Rush National Historical Park, P.O. Box 517, Skagway 99840; www.nps.gov/klgo.

CHITONS Chitons are oval-shaped marine mollusks with shells made up of eight overlapping plates. The gumboot and the Chinese slipper chiton are favorite Alaska edible delicacies. The gumboot, named for the tough, leathery, reddish brown covering that hides its plates, is the largest chiton in the world. It is prized as traditional food by southeastern Alaska Natives.

CLIMATE (SEE ALSO Regions of Alaska; Winds) Alaska's climate zones are maritime, transition, continental and arctic. With the exception of the transition zone along Western Alaska, the zones are divided by mountain ranges that form barriers to shallow air masses and modify those deep enough to cross the ranges.

The Brooks Range inhibits southward movement of air from the Arctic Ocean, thus separating the arctic climate zone from the Interior. The Chugach, Wrangell, Aleutian and Alaska mountain ranges often limit northward air movement and dry the air before it reaches the Interior's continental zone.

Just a Little Nip in the Air?

Cold weather in Alaska doesn't usually raise eyebrows, but one January cold snap did just that. For Alaskans, the winter of '89 will not soon be forgotten. Across the state, temperatures fell, fell some more and then stayed where they fell. The official low recorded was minus 76 degrees; however, lower temperatures than that were reported at various locations within the Interior.

Caused by a massive high-pressure system, the cold settled in for three weeks. It seemed much longer, though, due to temperatures dropping on the front end of the high-pressure system and very slowly rising on the tail end.

The weather was also responsible for barometric pressure so high that aviation operations were curtailed or suspended altogether. This resulted in stranding travelers up to two weeks if they happened to be traveling via air taxi. Alaska's weather was so severe that national news programs devoted major coverage to it throughout its duration. —1990 *The ALASKA ALMANAC*®

Other meteorologic and oceanographic factors affecting Alaska's climate zones are air temperature, water temperature, cloud coverage, and wind and air pressure. The amount of moisture that air can hold in a gaseous state is highly dependent on its temperature. Warm air can contain more water vapor than cold air. Therefore precipitation as rain or snow or in other forms is likely to be heavier from warm than from cold air. Water temperatures change more slowly and much less than land temperatures. Coastal area temperatures vary less than those farther inland.

Climate Zones. The maritime climate zone includes Southeast, the Northern Gulf Coast and the Aleutian Chain. Temperatures are mild—relatively warm in the winter and cool in summer. Precipitation ranges from 50 to 200 inches annually along the coast and up to 400 inches on mountain slopes. Storms are frequently from the west and southwest, resulting in strong winds along the Aleutian Islands and the Alaska Peninsula. Amchitka Island's weather station has recorded some of the windiest weather in the state, followed by Cold Bay. Frequent storms with accompanying high winds account for rough seas and occasional waves to 50 feet

in the Gulf of Alaska, particularly in fall and winter.

The transition zone may be thought of as two separate zones. One is the area between the coastal mountains and the Alaska Range, which includes Anchorage and the Matanuska Valley. Summer temperatures are higher than those of the maritime climate zone, with colder winter temperatures and less precipitation. Temperatures however are not as extreme as in the continental zone.

Another transition zone includes the west coast from Bristol Bay to Point Hope. This area has cool summer temperatures that are somewhat colder than those of the maritime zone, and cold winter temperatures similar to the continental

(Continued on page 48)

A Fairbanks writer once claimed, "Got so cold here, my whiskey froze." That's awful darn cold. Whiskey freezes at minus 55 degrees Fahrenheit.

Average Temperatures (Fahrenheit) and Precipitation (Inches)

	ANCHORAGE	BARROW	BETHEL	COLD BAY	FAIRBANKS	HOMER	JUNEAU
January							
Temperature	14.9	−13.4	6.7	28.6	−10.1	22.7	24.2
Precipitation	0.80	0.20	0.81	2.71	0.55	2.23	3.98
February							
Temperature	18.7	−17.8	6.0	27.4	−3.6	24.7	28.4
Precipitation	0.86	0.18	0.71	2.30	0.41	1.78	3.66
March							
Temperature	25.7	−15.1	13.3	29.9	11.0	28.0	32.7
Precipitation	0.65	0.15	0.80	2.19	0.37	1.57	3.24
April							
Temperature	35.8	−2.2	23.6	33.3	30.7	35.4	39.7
Precipitation	0.63	0.20	0.65	1.90	0.28	1.27	2.83
May							
Temperature	46.6	19.3	39.9	39.6	48.6	42.8	47.0
Precipitation	0.63	0.16	0.83	2.40	0.57	1.07	3.46
June							
Temperature	54.4	34.0	50.5	45.7	59.8	49.3	53.0
Precipitation	1.02	0.36	1.29	2.13	1.29	1.00	3.02
July							
Temperature	58.4	39.3	55.0	50.5	62.5	53.4	56.0
Precipitation	1.96	0.87	2.18	2.50	1.84	1.63	4.09
August							
Temperature	56.3	37.9	52.9	51.5	56.8	53.3	55.0
Precipitation	2.31	0.97	3.65	3.71	1.82	2.56	5.10
September							
Temperature	48.4	30.5	45.2	47.7	46.5	47.6	49.4
Precipitation	2.51	0.64	2.58	4.06	1.02	2.96	6.25
October							
Temperature	36.6	13.5	29.4	39.6	25.1	37.5	42.2
Precipitation	1.86	0.51	1.48	4.45	0.81	3.41	7.64
November							
Temperature	21.2	−1.7	16.8	34.4	2.7	28.6	33.0
Precipitation	1.08	0.27	0.98	4.33	0.67	2.74	5.13
December							
Temperature	16.3	−11.2	8.5	31.0	−6.5	24.3	27.1
Precipitation	1.06	0.17	0.95	3.16	0.73	2.71	4.48
Annual							
Temperature	35.9	9.4	29.0	38.3	26.9	37.4	40.6
Precipitation	15.37	4.67	16.90	35.84	10.37	24.93	52.86
Mean Seasonal Snowfall (inches)	69.0	28.0	47.0	62.0	68.0	58.0	100.0

Average Temperatures and Precipitation (continued)

KETCHIKAN	KING SALMON	KODIAK	MCGRATH	NOME	PETERSBURG	VALDEZ	
							January
33.9	14.9	29.9	−8.7	7.0	27.6	20.5	Temperature
14.01	1.11	9.52	0.81	0.88	9.31	5.63	Precipitation
							February
38.9	14.8	30.5	−2.6	3.9	31.1	24.1	Temperature
12.36	0.82	5.67	0.74	0.56	7.85	5.08	Precipitation
							March
38.9	22.4	32.9	10.2	8.6	34.7	29.2	Temperature
12.22	1.06	5.16	0.75	0.63	7.19	4.06	Precipitation
							April
42.8	30.2	37.5	26.5	17.6	40.4	37.1	Temperature
11.93	1.07	4.47	0.73	0.67	6.94	2.89	Precipitation
							May
48.6	42.4	43.5	44.5	35.6	47.2	45.2	Temperature
9.06	1.25	6.65	0.84	0.58	5.92	2.74	Precipitation
							June
54.0	50.0	49.6	55.3	45.9	53.0	51.8	Temperature
7.36	1.54	5.72	1.56	1.14	5.00	2.64	Precipitation
							July
58.0	54.7	54.4	58.7	51.5	55.8	54.9	Temperature
7.80	2.10	3.80	2.16	2.18	5.36	3.77	Precipitation
							August
58.4	53.9	55.2	54.3	50.2	55.0	53.5	Temperature
10.60	2.96	4.03	2.87	3.20	7.57	5.73	Precipitation
							September
53.6	47.2	50.0	44.2	42.5	50.3	47.2	Temperature
13.61	2.75	7.18	2.19	2.59	11.15	7.99	Precipitation
							October
46.3	32.4	40.7	24.7	28.0	43.5	38.1	Temperature
22.55	1.98	7.85	1.24	1.38	16.83	8.23	Precipitation
							November
39.0	22.0	34.4	4.4	15.9	35.6	27.4	Temperature
17.90	1.45	6.89	1.18	1.02	11.99	6.09	Precipitation
							December
35.4	15.9	30.8	−6.0	7.3	30.5	22.9	Temperature
15.82	1.19	7.39	1.12	0.82	10.66	6.65	Precipitation
							Annual
45.5	33.5	40.8	25.5	26.2	42.1	37.7	Temperature
155.22	19.28	74.33	16.18	15.64	105.77	61.50	Precipitation
							Mean Seasonal
37.0	46.0	80.0	93.0	56.0	102.0	320.0	**Snowfall (inches)**

Climate Records

Highest temperature:
100°F, at Fort Yukon,
June 27, 1915.

Lowest temperature:
–80°F, at Prospect Creek
Camp, Jan. 23, 1971.

Most precipitation in one year:
332.29 inches, at MacLeod Harbor
(Montague Island), 1976.

Most monthly precipitation:
70.99 inches at MacLeod Harbor,
November 1976.

Most precipitation in 24 hours:
15.2 inches, in Angoon,
Oct. 12, 1982.

Least precipitation in a year:
1.61 inches, at Barrow, 1935.

Most snowfall in a season:
974.5 inches, at Thompson Pass,
1952–53.

Most monthly snowfall:
297.9 inches, at Thompson Pass,
February 1953.

Most snowfall in 24 hours:
62 inches, at Thompson Pass,
December 1955.

Least snowfall in a season:
3 inches, at Barrow, 1935–36.

Highest recorded snowpack (also
highest ever recorded in North
America): 356 inches on Wolverine
Glacier, Kenai Peninsula, after the
winter of 1976–77.

Highest recorded wind speed:
143 mph, at Dutch Harbor,
November 2000.

NUGGETS

In December 1994, deep
snow caused one city
moose to scale new
heights in Anchorage. Homeowner
Roger Pickering called Fish and
Game for help when he discovered
a moose on his roof. Biologists
chased it off, unhurt. Fresh snowfall
in March brought the season total
to 117.4 inches, marking the third-
snowiest winter on record.
—1995 *The ALASKA ALMANAC*®

(Continued from page 45)
zone. Cold winter temperatures are partly
due to the sea ice in the Chukchi and
Bering Seas.

The continental climate zone covers
the majority of Alaska except the coastal
fringes and the Arctic Slope. It has extreme
temperatures and low precipitation. There
are fewer clouds in the continental zone
than elsewhere, so there is more warming
by the sun during the long days of
summer and more cooling during the long
nights of winter. Precipitation is light
because air masses affecting the area lose
most of their moisture crossing the
mountains to the south.

The Arctic north of the Brooks Range
has cold winters, cool summers and
desertlike precipitation. Prevailing winds
are from the northeast off the arctic ice
pack, which never moves far offshore.
Summers are generally cloudy and winters
are clear and cold. The cold air allows little
precipitation and inhibits evaporation.
Because continuous permafrost prevents
the percolation of water into the soil, the
area is generally marshy with numerous
lakes. (SEE ALSO Permafrost)

The two-page chart that accompanies
this entry shows normal average monthly
temperatures and precipitation for
14 communities in Alaska. Included are
annual temperatures, precipitation and
mean seasonal snowfall. The chart is
based on data from NOAA and the Alaska
state climatologist. You may also refer to
the Web site of the National Weather
Service Forecast Office in Anchorage:
www.alaska.net/~nwsar.

COAL (SEE ALSO Minerals and Mining) About
half of the coal resource of the United

States is believed to lie in Alaska. The demonstrated coal reserve base of the state is over 6 billion short tons, identified coal resources are about 160 billion short tons, and hypothetical and speculative resource estimates range upward to 6 trillion short tons. The regions containing the most coal are northwestern Alaska, Cook Inlet–Susitna Lowland and the Nenana Trend. Geologists estimate that perhaps 80 percent of Alaska's coal underlies the 23-million-acre National Petroleum Reserve on the North Slope. Although the majority of the coals are of bituminous and subbituminous ranks, anthracite coal does occur in the Bering River and Matanuska fields. In addition to the vast resource base and wide distribution, the important selling points for Alaska coal are its extremely low sulfur content and access to the coast for shipping.

Exploration, technology and economics will ultimately determine the marketability

NUGGETS

Coal production in Alaska hit $24 million in 1984, up from $18 million in 1983. Test shipments of Alaska coal to Korean markets have been made in hopes of establishing long-term contracts. —1986 The ALASKA ALMANAC®

of Alaska's coal. Large-scale exploration programs have been conducted in most of Alaska's coalfields by private industry and state and federal governments. In December 1997, Usibelli Coal Mine Inc. purchased the Wishbone Hill Mine near Palmer. Usibelli will put Wishbone into operation depending on market demand. The company continues to produce from the Nenana coalfield. The Arctic Slope Regional Corp. is working to develop its coal reserves in northwestern Alaska.

Alaska's production of coal in 2000 was 1.5 million short tons and came exclusively from the Usibelli Coal Mine near Healy. Of that amount, one-half was burned in Interior Alaska power plants and the remainder was shipped to Korea.

CONK Alaskans apply this term to a type of bracket fungus. The platelike conks grow on dead trees. When dry and hard, conks are snapped off and painted by artists or burned as mosquito repellent.

CONSTITUTION OF ALASKA
One of the most remarkable achievements in the long battle for Alaska statehood was the creation of the state's constitution in the mid-1950s. Statehood supporters believed that a constitution would demonstrate Alaska's maturity and readiness for statehood, so in 1955 the territorial legislature appropriated $300,000 to convene a Constitutional Convention in Fairbanks.

For 73 days in 1955–56, a total of 55 elected delegates from all across the territory met in the new Student Union Building (now called Constitution Hall) on the University of Alaska campus. William A. Egan, a territorial legislator and former mayor of Valdez, who later became the first governor of the state of Alaska, was president of the convention. Under his leadership, the disparate group of Alaskans hammered out a document that is considered a model state constitution.

The National Municipal League calls the brief 14,000-word document drafted by the convention delegates "one of the best, if not the best, state constitutions ever written." By an overwhelming margin Alaskans approved the new constitution at the polls in 1956, paving the way for the creation of the 49th state in 1959.

A copy of the constitution is available on the Internet through the lieutenant governor's office at www.gov.state.ak.us/ltgov/akcon/table.html.

CONTINENTAL DIVIDE (See also

Mountains) The Continental Divide extends
into Alaska. Unlike its portions in the
Lower 48, which divide the country into
east–west watersheds, the Continental
Divide in Alaska trends through the Brooks
Range, separating watersheds that drain
north into the Arctic Ocean and west and
south into the Bering Sea.

Alaska Science Nuggets says that
geologists once regarded the Brooks Range
as a structural extension of the Rocky
Mountains. Recent thinking assumes the
range to be 35 million to 200 million years
older than the Rockies. The Alaska Range is
comparatively young—only about 5 million
years old.

CONVENTION AND VISITORS BUREAUS AND INFORMATION CENTERS

**Anchorage Convention and Visitors
Bureau,** 524 W. Fourth Ave., Anchorage
99501-2122; (907) 276-4118; fax (907)
278-5559; www.anchorage.net.

Barrow, City of, P.O. Box 629, Barrow
99723; (907) 852-5211.

Begich–Boggs Visitors Center,
P.O. Box 129, Girdwood 99587; (907)
783-2326.

**Copper Valley (Greater) Visitor
Information Center,** P.O. Box 469,
Glennallen 99588; (907) 822-5555; fax
(907) 822-3010.

**Delta Junction Visitor Information
Center,** P.O. Box 987, Delta Junction
99737; (907) 895-5069.

**Fairbanks Convention and Visitors
Bureau,** 550 First Ave., Fairbanks 99701-
4790; (800) 327-5774; fax (907) 452-4190;
www.explorefairbanks.com.

Gustavus Visitors Association,
P.O. Box 167, Gustavus 99826; (907)
697-2285.

Haines Visitor Bureau, P.O. Box 530,
Haines 99827; (907) 766-2234; fax (907)
766-3155; www.haines.ak.us.

Hyder Community Association,
P.O. Box 149, Hyder 99923; (250)
636-2708; fax (250) 636-2518.

**Juneau Convention and Visitors
Bureau,** 369 S. Franklin St., Juneau 99801;
(800) 587-2201; (907) 586-1737; fax (907)
586-1449; www.traveljuneau.com.

**Kenai Visitors and Convention
Bureau,** 11471 Kenai Spur Highway,
Kenai 99611; (907) 283-1991; fax (907)
283-2230; www.visitkenai.com.

Ketchikan Visitors Bureau, 131
Front St., Ketchikan 99901; (800) 770-
3300; (907) 225-6166; fax (907) 225-4250;
www.visit-ketchikan.com.

**Kodiak Island Convention and
Visitors Bureau,** 100 Marine Way,
Kodiak 99615; (907) 486-4782; fax (907)
486-6545; www.kodiak.org.

Kotzebue, City of, P.O. Box 46,
Kotzebue 99752; (907) 442-3401.

**Matanuska–Susitna Convention
and Visitors Bureau,** HC0-1, P.O. Box
6166 J21, Palmer 99645; (907) 746-5000;
fax (907) 746-2688; www.alaskavisit.com.

Nenana, City of, P.O. Box 70, Nenana
99760; (907) 832-5441.

**Nome Convention and Visitors
Bureau,** P.O. Box 240, Nome 99762;
(907) 443-6624; fax (907) 443-5832;
www.nomealaska.org.

Palmer Visitor Information Center,
723 S. Valley Way, Palmer 99654; (907)
745-2880.

Pelican Visitors Association, P.O.
Box 737, Pelican 99832; (907) 735-2207;
fax (907) 735-2258; pelican@ptialaska.net.

Petersburg Visitor Information,
P.O. Box 649, Petersburg 99833; (907)
772-3646; fax (907) 772-3646;
www.petersburg.org.

**Seward Visitor Information
Cache,** P.O. Box 749, Seward 99664;
(907) 224-8051.

**Sitka Convention and Visitors
Bureau,** P.O. Box 1226, Sitka 99835;
(907) 747-5940; fax (907) 747-3739;
www.sitka.org.

**Skagway Convention and Visitors
Bureau,** P.O. Box 1025, Skagway 99840;
(907) 983-2854; fax (907) 983-3854;
www.skagway.org.

Tok Main Street Visitor Center,
P.O. Box 389, Tok 99780; (907) 883-5775;
www.tokalaskainfo.com.

**Unalaska/Port of Dutch Harbor
Convention and Visitors Bureau,** P.O.

Box 545, Unalaska 99685; (877) 581-2612; (907) 581-2612; fax (907) 581-2613; www.arctic.net/~updhcvb.

Valdez Convention and Visitors Bureau, P.O. Box 1603, Valdez 99686; (800) 770-5954; (907) 835-4636; fax (907) 835-4854; www.valdezalaska.org.

Whittier (City of) Visitors Center, P.O. Box 608, Whittier 99693; (907) 472-2327; fax (907) 472-2404; cowadmin@pobox.alaska.net.

COOK, CAPTAIN JAMES

James Cook (1728–79) went to sea as an apprenticed seaman, entering the British Royal Navy at the age of 27. He rose in rank by merit and was sent on two scientific expeditions—the first to the South Pacific (1768–71) and the second to Antarctica (1772–75).

In July 1776, the British Admiralty instructed Cook to proceed to the northwest coast of North America and attempt to find the Northwest Passage, hoped-for sea link from the Pacific to the Atlantic.

The *Resolution* and *Discovery* sailed from Plymouth via Cape of Good Hope, New Zealand, Tahiti and the Hawaiian Islands, arriving at Nootka Sound on Vancouver Island on March 30, 1778.

From then until Oct. 3, Cook cruised north and west to the Arctic Ocean, sketching the chief features of the coast, practically unknown to Europeans before Cook's historic voyage. He named many features of the coast, including Turnagain Arm, where land blocked his ships and they were forced to "turn again."

Failing to find the Northwest Passage, Cook left Unalaska in the Aleutians on Oct. 27. Cook returned to Hawaii's Big Island, where he was killed by local residents on Feb. 14, 1779. His accounts of the voyage were published in 1784–85 in three volumes and a large atlas.

This pioneering navigator and explorer is commemorated in Alaska by Cook Inlet and Mount Cook. A statue of Cook stands in Anchorage, facing the Knik Arm of Cook Inlet.

A statue of Captain Cook overlooks Cook Inlet in Anchorage. Photo by Tricia Brown.

COPPERS (SEE ALSO Potlatch) Coppers

(tinnehs) are beaten copper plaques that were important symbols of wealth among the Pacific Northwest Coast Natives.

Coppers are shaped something like a keyhole or a shield, are usually 2 feet to 3 feet long and weigh approximately 40 pounds. Coppers varied in value from tribe to tribe.

Early coppers were made of ore from the Copper River area, although western traders quickly made sheet copper available. Some scholars believe that Tlingit craftsmen shaped placer copper into the desired form themselves, while

It's true—we've triple checked: The Arabic word for Popsicle is *Alaska!!* Those Arabs know! When you find something that's cold, tasteless, and cheap—people just keep comin' back for more.

others maintain that coppers were forged by Athabascans. The impressive plaques were engraved or carved in relief with totemic crests.

The value of coppers increased as they were traded or sold, and their transfer implied that a potlatch would be given by the new owner. Coppers were given names, such as "Cloud," "Point of Island" or "Killer Whale," and were spoken of in respectful terms. They were thought of as powerful and their histories were as well known as those of the noblest families.

Coppers were often broken and destroyed during public displays and distribution of wealth. Some parts of the coppers were valued nearly as much as the whole.

To this day, certain coppers that were part of museum collections for years are still valued highly by some tribes, and are displayed as symbols of wealth and prestige during marriage ceremonies and potlatches.

COST OF LIVING Determining how expensive it is to live in Alaska not only depends on whom you ask, but how. Labor economists hired by the state to track cost-of-living data rely on several indexes, each with its own methods, focus and results.

For a comparison among cities, the American Chamber of Commerce Researchers Association (ACCRA) offers valuable data as does Runzheimer International, a private research group under contract to the state. To learn how prices have changed in a particular place over time, the Consumer Price Index is a useful gauge of inflation.

One way to unlock cost-of-living data in Alaska is to look at a map of the state's roads. Where there are fewer roads and fewer people, costs are generally higher. That's contrary to other states, where cost of living tends to be higher in cities. But because transportation to and within Alaska figures into the price of everything from a can of corn to roofing material, costs tend to be far lower in urban centers like Anchorage and Fairbanks, where highways and economies of scale are factors.

Alaska has only limited agriculture and manufacturing so most goods and foods must be shipped in at added cost. Highest food costs are found in isolated communities dependent on airfreight.

Some studies overlook distinctive elements of Alaska life that play a role in cost of living. For instance, Alaska is among the few places without a state income tax. A factor unique to Alaska is the state's annual distribution from its oil wealth savings account, the Permanent Fund Dividend. In 2000 a dividend of $1,963.86 was paid to every qualified resident.

The ACCRA data, which do not include taxation or the Permanent Fund Dividend in its calculations, places Alaska cities among the most expensive in the nation. The study attempts to duplicate spending of a mid-management executive's household. It focused on three Alaska cities in the fourth quarter of 2000: Anchorage, Fairbanks and Kodiak. The ACCRA study found the cost of living in Anchorage was nearly 23 percent higher than the national average; Fairbanks was 20 percent higher and Kodiak was 29 percent higher.

The data compiled by Runzheimer International show a much smaller cost-of-living differential between Alaska and the rest of the nation. This is because Runzheimer studies the cost of

NUGGETS

Alaska has one of the highest concentrations of millionaires in the nation, as well as more than one in five people living below the poverty level. —1990 *The ALASKA ALMANAC®*

living for a family of four that earns $32,000—a lower-income group than in the ACCRA study. In addition, Runzheimer includes the effect of taxes on consumer spending.

Runzheimer found that, for 2000, consumer spending in Anchorage was about 5 percent above the national average and Fairbanks was about 8 percent higher than the national average.

Inflation. While the cost of living in Alaska may be higher than in the Lower 48, consumer prices in Alaska have increased more slowly than in the rest of the nation since the early 1980s, according to the U.S Department of Labor's Bureau of Labor Statistics. In 2000, consumer prices in Anchorage rose 1.7 percent, compared with the national average of 3.4 percent. Anchorage is the only Alaska city for which the bureau tracks consumer prices.

Food. Economists have long relied on the Cost of Food at Home study prepared by the University of Alaska Fairbanks' Cooperative Extension Service to track food prices around the state. This study has its limitations. Many grocery items that can be purchased in larger cities are not available in rural communities. In addition, the market basket of foods tracked by the university in each community is identical, despite dramatic differences in buying habits between communities. But the university's quarterly survey is the only study to offer a comparative measure among 20 Alaska communities and it has been produced consistently for many years.

The study found Fairbanks had the state's lowest food prices in September 2000. It cost $100.63 to feed a family of four at home for a week in Fairbanks. Anchorage was close behind with a cost of $100.89. Of the eight towns the university studied, Bethel had the highest food prices. It cost $162.63 to feed a family of four at home for a week in Bethel, which is located on the Yukon–Kuskokwim Delta in Southwestern Alaska.

Housing. The state Labor Department monitors housing costs by studying rental markets in 10 communities statewide. Costs vary widely depending on the local economy, vacancy rates and demographics.

In the fourth quarter of 2000, the median adjusted monthly rent was highest in Kodiak, where the cost of a two-bedroom apartment was $955. Juneau followed close behind with a monthly rent of $950. Valdez ranked third at $894. Kenai

Remembering the Pipeline Days

As of October 1975, costs of food, clothing, housing and gasoline were 15 to 40 percent higher than in the Lower 48 states.

Sample Anchorage prices back then were:

Man's haircut: $5

Woman's cut, shampoo, set: $8 to $18

Premium gas: 71.9 to 79.9 cents per gallon

Unleaded gas: 69.9 to 78.9 cents per gallon

Regular gas: 69.9 to 76.9 cents per gallon

Steak dinner (New York cut): $7.50 to $12.90

Coffee: 15 to 35 cents a cup

Tuna sandwich: $1.35 to $2.10

Deluxe hamburger: $1.90 to $2.25

Ham and eggs: $3 to $3.25

1-bedroom apartment: $150 to $325

2-bedroom apartment: $300 to $420

3-bedroom apartment: $400 to $600

Furnished apartments: Add $50

Buy 2-bedroom home: $23,000 to $65,000 ($55,154 average)

Buy 3-bedroom home: $50,000 to $78,000 ($69,119 average)

Beer (Budweiser), per case: $8.93

Beer, per glass (bar): $1 to $1.25

Wine (bottle of least expensive red): $1.75

Bourbon (Jim Beam), per fifth: $6.25

Scotch and water (bar): $1.25 to $1.50

—1976 *The ALASKA ALMANAC®*

had the cheapest monthly rent during the fourth quarter at $578.

The rental market for a three-bedroom home in the fourth quarter of 2000 was most expensive in Juneau, where such a home would have rented for $1,468. Kodiak ranked second with a monthly rent of $1,261 and Anchorage was close behind at $1,247. Petersburg in Southeast Alaska was lowest with a monthly rental of $828.

Personal income. Preliminary figures for 2000 compiled by the federal Bureau of Economic Analysis show that annual per capita personal income for Alaska was $30,064, positioning the state 16th among the states. That was up from $28,523 in 1999. The nation's per capita income in 2000 was $29,676.

For more cost-of-living information, write the Alaska Department of Labor, Research and Analysis section, P.O. Box 21149, Juneau 99802-1149. The department's cost-of-living data can be found at www.labor.state.ak.us by going to "Economic/Occupation" and clicking on "Wages" and "Cost of living."

COURTS
The Alaska court system operates at four levels: the supreme court, court of appeals, superior court and district court. The Alaska judiciary is funded by the state and administered by the supreme court.

The five-member supreme court, established by the Alaska Constitution in 1959, has final appellate jurisdiction of all actions and proceedings in lower courts. It sits monthly in Anchorage and Fairbanks, quarterly in Juneau and occasionally in other court locations.

The three-member court of appeals was established in 1980 to relieve the supreme court of some of its ever-increasing caseload.

The supreme court retained its ultimate authority in all cases, but concentrated its attention on civil appellate matters, giving authority in criminal and quasi-criminal matters to the court of appeals. The court of appeals has appellate jurisdiction in certain superior court proceedings and jurisdiction to review district court decisions. It meets regularly in Anchorage and travels occasionally to other locations.

The superior court is the trial court with original jurisdiction in all civil and criminal matters and appellate jurisdiction over all matters appealed from the district court. The superior court has exclusive jurisdiction in probate and in cases concerning minors. There are 32 superior court judges.

The district court has jurisdiction over misdemeanor violations and violations of ordinances of political subdivisions. In civil matters, the district court may hear cases for recovery of money, damages or specific personal property if the amount does not exceed $50,000.

The district court may also inquire into the cause and manner of death, as well as issue summonses, writs of habeas corpus, and search and arrest warrants. District court criminal decisions may be appealed directly to the court of appeals or the superior court. There are 17 district court judges.

Administration of the superior and district courts is divided by region into four judicial districts: First Judicial District, Southeast; Second Judicial District, Nome–Barrow–Kotzebue; Third Judicial District, Anchorage–Kodiak–Kenai; and Fourth Judicial District, Fairbanks.

District magistrates serve rural areas and help ease the workload of district courts in metropolitan areas. In criminal matters, magistrates may enter judgment of conviction upon a plea of guilty to any state misdemeanor and may try state misdemeanor cases if defendants waive their right to a district court judge. Magistrates may also hear municipal ordinance violations and state traffic infractions without the consent of the accused. In civil matters, magistrates may hear cases for recovery of money, damages or specific personal property if the amount does not exceed $7,500.

Selection of Justices, Judges and Magistrates. Supreme court justices and judges of the court of appeals, superior court and district court are appointed by the governor from candidates submitted by the Alaska Judicial Council.

The chief justice of the supreme court, selected by majority vote of the justices, serves a three-year term and may not serve consecutive terms.

Each supreme court justice and each judge of the court of appeals is subject to approval or rejection by a majority of the voters of the state on a nonpartisan ballot at the first general election held more than three years after appointment. Thereafter, each justice must participate in a retention election every 10 years. A court of appeals judge must participate every eight years.

Superior court judges are subject to approval or rejection by voters of their judicial district at the first general election held more than three years after appointment. Thereafter, it is every sixth year. District court judges must run for retention in their judicial districts in the first general election held more than two years after appointment and every fourth year thereafter.

District magistrates are appointed for an indefinite period by the presiding superior court judge of the judicial district in which they will serve.

Additional information about the court system is available at www.alaska.net/~akctib/ctinfo.htm.

Alaska State Supreme Court, 1960–2001: Justices and Tenure.
Current Justices:
Dana Fabe, 1996–
 Chief Justice, 2000–
Alexander O. Bryner, 1997–
Walter L. Carpeneti, 1998–
Robert L. Eastaugh, 1994–
Warren W. Matthews, 1977–
 Chief Justice, 1987–90; 1997–2000
Former Justices:
Harry O. Arend, 1960–65
George F. Boney, 1968–72
 Chief Justice, 1970–72
Robert Boochever, 1972–80
 Chief Justice, 1975–78
Edmond W. Burke, 1975–96

 Chief Justice, 1981–84
Allen T. Compton, 1980–98
 Chief Justice, 1996–97
Roger G. Connor, 1968–83
John H. Dimond, 1959–71
Robert C. Erwin, 1970–77
James M. Fitzgerald, 1972–75
Walter H. Hodge, 1959–60
Daniel A. Moore, Jr., 1983–96
 Chief Justice, 1992–96
Buell A. Nesbett, 1959–70
 Chief Justice, 1959–70
Jay A. Rabinowitz, 1965–77
 Chief Justice, 1972–75; 1978–81; 1984–87; 1990–92

Alaska State Court of Appeals, 1980–2001: Judges and Tenure.
Current Judges:
Robert G. Coats, 1980–
 Chief Justice, 1997–
David Mannheimer, 1990–
David C. Stewart, 1997–
Former Judges:
Alexander O. Bryner, 1980–97
 Chief Justice, 1980–97
James K. Singleton, Jr., 1980–90

CRUISES (SEE ALSO Boating; Ferries) There are many opportunities for cruising Alaska waters aboard charter boats, scheduled boat excursions or luxury cruise ships.

Charter boats are readily available in Southeast and Southcentral Alaska. Charter boat trips range from daylong fishing and sightseeing trips to overnight and longer customized trips or package tours. There is a wide range of charter boats, from simple fishing boats to sailboats, yachts and mini-class cruise ships.

NUGGETS

An estimated 75,000 cruise ship passengers visited Southeast Alaska in 1978.

—1980 *The ALASKA ALMANAC®*

Cruise-ship travel allows close-up views of Glacier Bay's tidewater glaciers. Photo by Tricia Brown.

In summer, scheduled boat excursions—from day trips to overnight cruises—are available: Ketchikan (Misty Fiords); Sitka (harbor and area tours); Bartlett Cove and Gustavus (Glacier Bay); Juneau (Lynn Canal); Valdez and Whittier (Columbia Glacier, Prince William Sound); Seward (Resurrection Bay, Kenai Fjords); Homer (Kachemak Bay); and Fairbanks (Chena and Tanana Rivers).

For details and additional information on charter boat operators and scheduled boat excursions, contact the appropriate chamber of commerce or convention and visitors bureau at www.dced.state.ak.us/tourism/sources/visinfo.htm.

From May through September, cruise lines that carry visitors to Alaska via the Inside Passage include Carnival, Princess, Holland America, Crystal Cruises, Alaska Sightseeing/Cruise West, Norwegian Cruise Line, World Explorer, Royal Caribbean, Celebrity, Clipper, Radisson Seven Seas, Japan Cruise Line, Mitsui O.S.K. and Society Expeditions. For the phone number of a particular company, contact Cruise Lines International, (212) 921-0066 or www.cruising.org. Both round-trip and one-way cruises are available, or a cruise may be sold as part of a package tour that includes air, rail and/or motorcoach transportation. (SEE Bus Lines)

Prices vary. The cost for a 7- to 11-day Inside Passage cruise ranges from $1,800 to $4,200. Booking by Feb. 14 can yield substantial savings. The cruise industry in Alaska waters continues to thrive, posting a 2 percent increase in capacity during 1999. Because of the wide variety of cruise trip options, it is wise to work with a travel agent.

DALTON HIGHWAY (SEE ALSO Highways)

The 414-mile-long Dalton Highway begins at Milepost 73.1 on the Elliott Highway.

This all-weather gravel road bridges the Yukon River, crosses the Arctic Circle at Mile 115.3, and climbs the Brooks Range. At Atigun Pass (Mile 246.8) it crosses a continental divide, the highest highway pass in Alaska (elevation 4,800 feet). Then the road passes through tundra plains before reaching the Prudhoe Bay oil fields at Deadhorse on the coast of the Arctic Ocean.

Public travel for the final eight miles may be restricted. As of 2001, the state had paved 55 miles of the Dalton Highway, with a goal of eventually paving the entire route.

The highway was named for James Dalton, a post–World War II explorer who played a large role in the development of

Pioneering Tourism

The first cruise ships to carry sightseeing passengers as well as cargo along the [Inside Passage] were lavishly fitted Pacific Coast Steamship vessels. The *Idaho* took the initial batch of tourists to view Glacier Bay in 1883, and other paddle wheelers like the S.S. *Ancon* followed in her wake; within a year, there were 1,650 people cruising up here.

—Paul and Audrey Grescoe,
Alaska: The Cruise-Lover's Guide

North Slope oil and gas industries. It was built as a haul road for supplies and to provide access to the northern half of the 800-mile trans-Alaska oil pipeline during construction. Originally called the North Slope Haul Road, it is still often referred to as the Haul Road.

The Dalton Highway is open to all vehicles and is maintained. Services are limited to Yukon Ventures (Mile 56) and Coldfoot Services (Mile 175). As of winter 1997–98, no fuel, food, lodging or automotive services were available from Fox to Coldfoot from October through March. Travelers should call (907) 273-6037 or (800) 478-7675 for current road and weather conditions.

DAYLIGHT HOURS
(See also Arctic Circle)

Maximum (at Summer Solstice, June 20 or 21)

	Sunrise	Sunset	Hours of Daylight
Adak	6:27 A.M.	11:10 P.M.	16:43 hrs
Anchorage	3:21 A.M.	10:42 P.M.	19:21 hrs
Barrow	May 10	Aug. 2	84 days continuous
Fairbanks	1:59 A.M.	11:48 P.M.	21:49 hrs
Juneau	3:51 A.M.	10:09 P.M.	18:18 hrs
Ketchikan	4:04 A.M.	9:33 P.M.	17:29 hrs

Minimum (at Winter Solstice, Dec. 21 or 22)

	Sunrise	Sunset	Hours of Daylight
Adak	10:52 A.M.	6:38 P.M.	7:46 hrs
Anchorage	10:14 A.M.	3:42 P.M.	5:28 hrs
Barrow	*	*	0:00 hrs
Fairbanks	10:59 A.M.	2:41 P.M.	3:42 hrs
Juneau	9:46 A.M.	4:07 P.M.	6:21 hrs
Ketchikan	9:12 A.M.	4:18 P.M.	7:06 hrs

*From Nov. 18 through Jan. 24—a period of 67 days—there is no daylight in Barrow.

DIAMOND WILLOW
Fungi, particularly *Valsa sordida Nitschke,* are generally thought to be the cause of diamond-shaped patterns in the wood grain of some willow trees. There are 33 varieties of willow in Alaska, at least five of which can develop diamonds. They are found throughout the state but are most plentiful in river valleys. Diamond willow, stripped of bark, is used to make lamps, walking sticks and novelty items.

DOG MUSHING
(See also Calendar of Annual Events; Iditarod Trail Sled Dog Race; Yukon Quest International Sled Dog Race) In many areas of the state where snow machines had nearly replaced the working dog team, the sled dog has returned, due in part to a rekindled appreciation of the reliability of nonmechanical transportation. In addition to working and racing dog teams, many people keep 2 to 20 sled dogs for recreational mushing.

Sled dog racing is Alaska's official state sport. Races ranging from local club meets to world championships are held throughout the winter.

Championship speed races are usually run over two or three days, with the cumulative time for the heats deciding the winner. Distances for the heats vary from about 5 to 30 miles. The size of dog teams also varies, with mushers using anywhere from 4 to 20 dogs in their teams. Since racers are not allowed to replace dogs in the team, most finish with fewer than they

57

Dog mushing is Alaska's state sport. From *Fairbanks: Alaska's Heart of Gold* by Tricia Brown (text) and Roy Corral (photographs).

started with. Attrition may be caused by anything from tender feet to sore muscles.

Sprint mushing is divided into limited and open classes. Limited class ranges from 3 to 10 dogs and from 3 to 12 miles a day. Open class racing has no limit on the number of dogs and ranges from 10 to 30 miles a day.

Long-distance racing (the Yukon Quest; the Iditarod) pits racers not only against one another but also against the elements. Sheer survival can quickly take precedence over winning when a winter storm catches a dog team in an exposed area. Stories abound of racers giving up their chance to finish "in the money" to help out another musher who has gotten into trouble. Besides the weather, long-distance racers also have to contend with moose attacks on the dogs, sudden illness, straying off the trail and sheer exhaustion. With these and other challenges to overcome, those who finish have truly persevered against the odds.

Prizes range from trophies to cash from a purse that is split among the finishers. The richest purse in sled-dog racing is the Iditarod, which paid a record total of $577,066 in 2001.

For information about dog mushing, call the Alaska Dog Mushers Association in Fairbanks, (907) 457-6874 or e-mail *Mushing* magazine at info@mushing.com.

See charts on next page for statistics on two of the biggest championship races. Other major races around the state follow.

Ty Clark Memorial Sled Dog Race, Soldotna to Hope, 100 miles. Held in January.

Copper River 300, Glennallen. Covering 300 miles over two to three days. Held in January.

Iditarod Trail Sled Dog Race. (SEE Iditarod Trail Sled Dog Race)

Junior North American Championships, Fairbanks. For children under 18. Three heats, one- to eight-dog classes. Held in March.

Junior World Championship Race, Anchorage. Three heats in three days. Held in February.

Open World Championship Sled Dog Race, Anchorage

Scheduled during Fur Rendezvous in February. Best elapsed time in three heats over three days, 25 miles each day. Purse is split among the top 15 finishers. Winners since 1990:

Year Winner	Elapsed Time (minutes:seconds)				
	Day 1	Day 2	Day 3	Total	Purse
1990 Charlie Champaine	89:00	96:13	94:01	279:14	$50,000
1991 Charlie Champaine	89:10	94:49	95:43	279:42	70,000
1992 Roxy Wright-Champaine	87:30	89:35	92:22	269:42	70,000
1993 Roxy Wright-Champaine	87:44	90:45	93:21	271:50	75,000
1994 Ross Saunderson	86:26	90:24	*	176:50	50,000
1995 Ross Saunderson	84:19	88:57	85:07	258:23	45,000
1996 Cancelled due to lack of snow					
1997 Axel Gasser	95:47	99:09	102:03	296:59	45,000
1998 Ross Sanderson	96:12	99:20	101:28	291:00	50,000
1999 Egil Ellis	84:02	90:28	88:33	263:03	20,000
2000 Egil Ellis	84:42	90:26	90:59	266:07	38,400
2001 Canceled due to lack of snow					

*Trail conditions shortened race to two heats.

Open North American Sled Dog Race Championship, Fairbanks

Held in March. Best elapsed time in three heats over three days; 20 miles on Days 1 and 2; 30 miles on Day 3. (Times have been rounded off.) In 1998, the Day 3 heat was shortened to 20 miles. Purse is split among the top 15 finishers. Winners since 1990:

Year Winner	Elapsed Time (minutes:seconds)				
	Day 1	Day 2	Day 3	Total	Purse
1990 Charlie Champaine	62:47	67:38	95:40	226:05	$45,000
1991 Ross Saunderson	60:12	63:53	97:44	221:50	46,000
1992 Roxy Wright-Champaine	66:17	65:59	94:29	226:46	52,000
1993 Roxy Wright-Champaine	64:48	64:06	95:36	224:31	58,000
1994 Ross Saunderson	*	63:16	91:12	154:28	49,000
1995 Amy Streeper	61:42	65:29	94:48	221:59	46,940
1996 Amy Streeper	68:58	63:17	90:29	222:45	32,500
1997 Neil Johnson	64:06	64:53	94:25	223:24	22,500
1998 Michi Konno	70:05	69:41	67:00	206:47	40,000
1999 Egil Ellis	**	63:07	91:46	154:52	46,300
2000 Egil Ellis	59:58	61:08	90:40	211:46	40,000
2001 Egil Ellis	58:52	59:36	88:46	207:14	50,000

*Time not counted because locked gate delayed the first three mushers.

**No first-day time as trail was clocked.

Source: Alaska Sled Dog and Racing Association

Kusko 300, Bethel to Aniak. Held in January.

Limited North American Championships, Fairbanks. Three heats over three days; one- and two-dog skijoring. Held in March.

Tok Race of Champions, Tok. Two heats in two days, 20.5 miles a day. Held in March.

Willow Winter Carnival Race, Willow. Two heats in two days, 18 miles each day. Held in January.

Women's World Championship Race, Anchorage. Three heats in three days, 12 miles each day. Held in February.

Yukon Quest International Sled Dog Race. (SEE Yukon Quest International Sled Dog Race)

EARTHQUAKES (See also Waves)

Between 1899 and mid-1996, 10 Alaska earthquakes occurred that equaled or exceeded a magnitude of 8 on the Richter scale. During the same period, more than 75 earthquakes took place that were of magnitude 7 or greater.

Alaska averages 1,000 earthquakes a year that measure 3.5 or more on the Richter scale. In May 1995 alone, the Alaska Earthquake Information Center detected and located 540 earthquakes in Alaska. The largest of these measured 5.5 and was located 16 miles southwest of Anchorage.

The West Coast/Alaska Tsunami Warning Center is responsible for warning coastal residents of Alaska, Washington, Oregon, California and British Columbia about any earthquake that could generate a tsunami, a seismic sea wave. According to the Center, Alaska's earthquake activity typically follows the same pattern from month to month, interspersed with sporadic swarms, or groups of small earthquakes, and punctuated every decade or so by a great earthquake and its aftershocks.

Alaska is the most seismic of the 50 states, and the most seismically active part of the state is the Aleutian Islands arc system. Seismicity related to this system extends into the Gulf of Alaska and northward into Interior Alaska to a point near Mount McKinley. These earthquakes are largely the result of underthrusting of the North Pacific Plate. Many earthquakes

The Joint is Jumping

Intense episodes of quakes on March 10–11 and March 13–14, 1996, alarmed residents when Akutan Volcano, one of the liveliest peaks in the Aleutian Chain, rattled the island of Akutan. As a result, ceilings cracked, scientists arrived to install seismometers and beer consumption skyrocketed on the island. More than 800 small earthquakes a day occurred on March 13 and 14. Half of the 100 residents of the town of Akutan and some seasonal cod fishery processors boarded amphibious planes for Dutch Harbor.
—1996 *The ALASKA ALMANAC*®

resulting from this underthrusting occur in Cook Inlet—particularly near Mount Iliamna and Mount Redoubt—and near Mount McKinley. North of the Alaska Range, in the central Interior, most earthquakes are of shallow origin.

The earthquake that created the highest seiche, or splash wave, ever recorded occurred on the evening of July 9, 1958, when a quake with a magnitude of 7.9 on the Richter scale rocked the Yakutat area. A landslide containing approximately 40 million cubic yards of rock plunged into Gilbert Inlet at the head of Lituya Bay. The gigantic splash resulting from the slide sent a wave 1,740 feet up the opposite mountainside, denuding it of trees and soil down to bedrock. It then fell back and swept through the length of the bay and out to sea. One fishing boat anchored in Lituya Bay at the time was lost with its crew of two; another was carried over a spit of land by the wave and soon after foundered, but

> An Anchorage builder once sent an entire harbor to Wainwright through the U.S. mail thanks to special Bush delivery rates. The cost of stamps on 6,000 concrete blocks and 4,600 bags of cement was only a fraction of any other shipping method.

Earthquake damage in downtown Anchorage, 1964. Special Collections Division, UW Libraries. From *Alaska's History* by Harry Ritter.

its crew was saved. A third boat anchored in the bay miraculously survived intact.

The most destructive earthquake to strike Alaska occurred at 5:36 P.M. on Good Friday, March 27, 1964. Registering between 8.4 and 8.6 on the Richter scale in use at the time, its equivalent moment magnitude has since been revised upward to 9.2, making it the strongest earthquake ever recorded in North America. With its primary epicenter deep beneath Miners Lake in northern Prince William Sound, the earthquake spread shock waves that were felt 700 miles away. The earthquake and seismic waves that followed killed 131 people, including 115 Alaskans. Of the 131 deaths, 119 were caused by the tsunami generated by the earthquake.

The 1964 earthquake released 10 million times more energy than the atomic bomb that devastated Hiroshima in World War II, and 80 times the energy of the San Francisco earthquake of 1906. It also moved more earth farther, both horizontally and vertically, than any other earthquake ever recorded except the 1960 Chilean earthquake. In the 69-day period after the main quake, there were 12,000 jolts of 3.5 magnitude or greater.

The highest sea wave caused by the 1964 earthquake occurred when an undersea slide near Shoup Glacier in Port Valdez triggered a wave that toppled trees 100 feet above tidewater and deposited silt and sand 220 feet above salt water.

During June 1996, the Alaska Earthquake Information Center located 567 earthquakes in or near Alaska. The largest of these was a major earthquake on June 9 with a magnitude of 7.9, the largest earthquake to have occurred in North America in more than 10 years. The earthquake was felt sharply at Adak and Atka; minor damage was reported at Adak. This quake generated minor tsunamis in Alaska and other locales in the Pacific Basin.

Through the end of June 1996, 118 aftershocks of magnitude 4 or larger were recorded and many hundreds of smaller aftershocks were observed on seismic records. The seismic energy radiated by the June 9 earthquake was about 30 times that generated by the January 1995 Northridge earthquake in California or the January 1994 Kobe, Japan, quake, both of which had magnitudes around 7.2. For comparison, the 1964 Good Friday earthquake released about

1,000 times the energy of the Northridge and Kobe quakes.

To learn more about earthquakes, visit the University of Alaska Fairbanks Web site at www.aeic.alaska.edu/seis.

ECONOMY (SEE ALSO Cost of Living; Employment) While Alaska's resource-dependent economy has been characterized by boom and bust cycles, overall growth has been positive since statehood in 1959. Setbacks, such as the recession that hit the state in 1986, often are linked to markets for raw goods. Movements in these global markets can be felt strongly in Alaska where oil, fishing, timber and mining are mainstays of the economy.

Alaska's economy expands when it's able to export goods and services. But the state faces obstacles in tapping its vast natural resources, due to long distances to markets and expensive transportation costs. And, when it comes to prices for oil and other resources, Alaska's economy is at the mercy of national and world events.

The state saw it's 13th year of uninterrupted growth in 2000, according to the Alaska Department of Labor and Workforce Development. Employment grew by 2.2 percent, twice the rate in 1999.

Oil and gas industries continued to play a key role as Alaska entered the 21st century and much of the economic growth in 2000 came from a rebound in the oil patch. Strong oil prices spurred job growth in the oil industry. Phillips Petroleum Co.'s purchase of Arco's Alaska assets averted the threat of large layoffs expected when BP Amoco announced its purchase of Arco.

Development of the Alpine and Northstar fields in 2000 kept the industry humming. Alpine began producing at the end of the year and is the state's third-largest producing oil field.

In addition to oil, Alaska's major energy companies also got serious about developing the North Slope's natural gas

reserves in 2000. They joined together to study the feasibility of a natural gas pipeline and began seismic work to look for natural gas. The extra zip in the oil industry boosted employment in both Anchorage and northern regions of the state.

Much of Alaska's job growth in 2000 occurred in the service sector, which includes health care, business services, the hospitality industry and social services. This sector grew by 2,900 jobs in 2000, accounting for nearly half of the 6,200 new jobs created in 2000.

The transportation sector saw growth in 2000 as Federal Express, Northwest Airlines and other cargo companies added flights.

The retail sector saw modest growth, even though grocery employment took a hit with the closure of the seven Alaska Marketplace stores. Alaska Marketplace was formed in 1999 when Safeway took over Carrs, the state's largest supermarket chain. Safeway sold seven of its stores to the newly formed Alaska Marketplace chain in an effort to address competitive concerns raised by state regulators. But the Alaska Marketplace stores were open only 15 months before they closed, laying off 400 workers.

Much of the job growth in the retail sector came in the restaurant business, which has grown for the past seven years.

The construction industry grew in 2000, due partly to the increased activity in the oil sector. Public projects also boosted this sector, including expansion of Ted Stevens Anchorage International Airport, construction of a new jail in Anchorage, construction of a new state courthouse in Fairbanks and $300 million in highway construction around the state.

The state's manufacturing sector saw its fifth yearly consecutive drop in employment. Lower fish harvests led to a drop in seafood processing jobs, while weak demand for timber in Asia hurt prices for Alaska timber.

The 2000 census gave a boost to government employment, after seven consecutive years of declines. The national head counts required a large temporary labor force. State and local government employment also grew moderately. Most of the growth in local government occurred in schools.

EDUCATION (SEE ALSO School Districts; Universities and Colleges)

According to the 2001–2001 Alaska Education Directory, Alaska has 506 public schools. The Bureau of Indian Affairs operated rural schools in Alaska until 1985.

The state Board of Education has seven members appointed by the governor. (In addition, two nonvoting members are appointed by the board to represent the military and public school students.) The board is responsible for setting policy for education in Alaska schools and appoints a commissioner of education to carry out its decisions. The public schools are controlled by 53 school districts, and each school district elects its own school board. There are 19 Regional Education Attendance Areas that oversee education in rural areas outside the 34 city and borough school districts.

Any student in grades kindergarten through 12 may choose to study at home through the state-operated correspondence school, the Alyeska Central School, which also serves traveling students, GED students, migrant students and students living in remote areas. Home study has been an option for Alaska students since 1939.

Several school districts also operate distance learning correspondence programs available to Alaska school-aged children.

The state Department of Education also operates the Alaska Vocational Technical Center at Seward and a number of other education programs ranging from adult basic education to literacy skills.

Alaskans between 7 and 16 years old are required to attend school. According to state regulations, a student must earn a minimum of 21 high school credits to receive a high school diploma. The state Board of Education has stipulated that four credits must be earned in language arts, three in social studies, two each in math and science, and one in physical education or health. Local school boards set the remainder of the required credits.

Since 1976 the state has provided secondary school programs to any community in which an elementary school is operated and one or more children of high school age wish to attend high school. This mandate was the result of a class action suit initiated on behalf of Molly Hootch, a high school-age student. Prior to the Molly Hootch Decree, high school-age students in villages without a secondary school attended high school outside their village. Of the 127 villages originally eligible for high school programs under the Molly Hootch Decree, only a few remain without one.

There were 8,581 teachers and administrators in the public schools and 133,351 students enrolled in K–12 in public schools in 2000–2001. The size of

In another example of our state tax dollars at work, the Talkeetna Community School offered a course called Roadkill 101. The tuition was $10. Coincidentally, Alaskans are still the second-highest per capita consumers of SPAM® in the nation.

schools in Alaska varies greatly, from a 2,300-student high school in Anchorage to one- or two-teacher, one-room schools in remote rural areas.

Nearly 62 percent of the school districts' operating fund is provided by the state, about 31 percent by local governments and about 7 percent by the federal government. Alaska's average salary for classroom teachers is among the highest in the nation, with the statewide average in 2000 at $48,165.

The Alaska Legislature passed a law in 1997 that directed the Department of Education to develop the Alaska High School Qualifying Examination. Beginning with the class of 2002, students must pass the exam to receive a high school diploma. Those students who do not pass will receive a certificate of attendance.

EMPLOYMENT (See also Economy)

Even as Alaska enters a new century, its key employment sectors—fishing, timber, mining and oil and gas—have remained the same since the 1960s.

The oil industry was seeing strong gains in employment as 2000 ended after a slump in 1999, according to the Alaska Department of Labor. Alpine, the state's third-largest oil field, went into production and work on the Northstar project shifted into high gear. An average of more than 8,000 people were employed in the oil industry during 2000.

With oil prices averaging about $23 to $25 per barrel, oil industry service providers were seeing steady employment growth.

Strong growth in the air cargo industry was also giving Alaska's economy a lift. Federal Express, United Parcel Service and Northwest Airlines were awarded routes to the People's Republic of China. That additional activity was expected to fill the gap created by United Airlines' decision to close its Anchorage air freight facility.

Residential construction activity was relatively slow, but commercial and public projects were giving a boost to construction employment, which was up 2 percent from 1999. The state's largest construction project was the expansion of the Ted

NUGGETS

If you're seriously considering a move to Alaska to seek a job, first make a visit and see it for yourself. Jobs are scarce in Alaska and housing is expensive. There are now, and will be in the foreseeable future, plenty of Alaska residents out of work and anxious to find jobs. —1978 *The ALASKA ALMANAC*®

Stevens Anchorage International Airport.

There was moderate job growth in state and local government in 2000. The Alaska Department of Labor said that growth offset the loss of federal jobs related to the privatization of the Indian Health Service.

The service sector saw growth with the opening of the new Marriott Hotel in downtown Anchorage and the expansion of other hotels around the state. In addition, the health care industry continued strong. During the 1990s, job growth in the private sector of the health care industry climbed by 30 percent, compared with 19 percent for the Alaska workforce overall. State economists attribute the growth to changes in the delivery of health care and an aging population.

The only two sectors of the economy that saw job declines were manufacturing and finance. Job losses in timber and fish processing accounted for the manufacturing declines. Wells Fargo & Co.'s purchase of National Bank of Alaska resulted in some consolidation in that sector.

Alaska's unemployment rate was 6.6 percent in 2000, relatively low by historical standards. Like much about Alaska, the state's unemployment rate fluctuates seasonally. Added jobs linked to tourism and commercial fishing drive down unemployment in summer, while decreased business activity in winter prompts rates to rise again.

Alaska Average Annual Employment 1987–2000

Employees (in thousands)

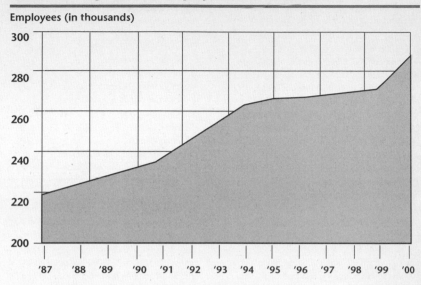

Source: Alaska Department of Labor

Alaska Employment by Month 1996–2000

Employees (In thousands)

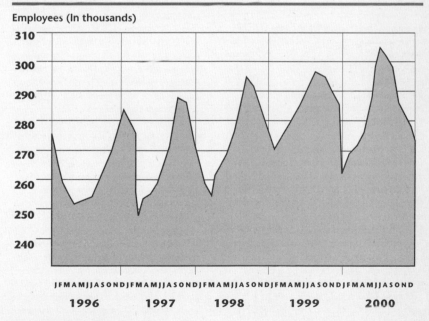

1996   1997   1998   1999   2000

Source: Alaska Department of Labor

Joblessness also varies widely depending on region; high unemployment is found in some rural areas where paying jobs are scarce and there is greater reliance on subsistence hunting and fishing.

Residents of other states hoping to find work in Alaska are strongly advised to make a visit and gauge possibilities for themselves. Consolidation in petroleum has largely meant an end to the state's fabled big-money oil jobs. In the populous Railbelt region between Seward and Fairbanks, job seekers will find housing, taxes and food costs more in line with prices in the West, a departure from just a few decades ago when Alaska prices were far higher.

Employment offices are found in most large communities. State government information is available from the Alaska Department of Labor, Alaska State Employment Service, P.O. Box 3-7000, Juneau 99802; www.jobs.state.ak.us. A Labor Department publication, Alaska Economic Trends, is an excellent monthly compilation of state workforce issues; look for it at www.labor.state.ak.us/research/research.htm.

Unemployment January 2001

Area	Percent
Statewide	7.8
Anchorage	5.0
Fairbanks North Star Borough	7.2
Juneau Borough	5.8
Kodiak Island Borough	11.4
Nome	11.3
Ketchikan Gateway Borough	10.3
Bristol Bay Borough	13.4

Source: Alaska Department of Labor

Wage and Salary Employment by Industry 2000

Industry	Percent
Government (federal, state, local)	26
Services	26
Trade	20
Transportation/Communications/ Utilities	10
Manufacturing	5
Construction	5
Oil and Mining	4
Finance/Insurance/Real Estate	4

Source: Alaska Department of Labor

ENERGY AND POWER

When it comes to power use, Alaska can be divided into three major regions, each having similar energy patterns, problems and resources: the Extended Railbelt region, the Southeast region and the Bush region. The Extended Railbelt consists of major urban areas linked by the Alaska Railroad (Seward, Anchorage and Fairbanks). The southcentral area of this region uses relatively inexpensive natural gas from Cook Inlet and hydroelectric power plants for electrical production and heating. The Fairbanks–Tanana Valley area uses primarily coal and oil to meet its electrical needs. Future electrical demand for the Extended Railbelt region will be met by a combination of hydropower and coal- and gas-fired generators.

The Southeast region relies on hydropower for much of its electrical generation. Most of the existing hydroelectric power projects in Alaska are located in the Southeast region. In the smaller communities, diesel generators are used.

The Bush region includes all communities that are remote from the major urban areas of the Extended Railbelt and Southeast regions. Electricity in Bush communities is typically provided by small diesel generators. Where wind projects are feasible, such as at Lolo Bay and Unalakleet, wind power can be a viable, fuel-saving alternative to diesel-powered generators. Bush residents rely heavily on heating oil. Wood and kerosene heaters are used to a limited extent. Natural gas is available in Barrow.

ESKIMO ICE CREAM
Also called *akutak* (the Yup'ik Eskimo word for Eskimo ice cream), this classic Native delicacy, popular throughout Alaska, is traditionally made of whipped berries, seal oil and freshly fallen snow. Sometimes shortening, raisins and sugar are added. Ingredients vary by region. One recipe uses the soopalallie berry, *Shepherdia canadensis* (also called soapberry), a bitter species that forms a frothy mass like soapsuds when beaten.

Soapberry. From *Alaska Wild Berry Guide and Cookbook.*

EXPORTS
(SEE ALSO Economy) The value of Alaska's worldwide exports declined 3.9 percent in 2000 to $2.5 billion, as a decrease in oil and mineral exports offset a slight increase in seafood exports.

The decrease in oil exports was due to a decision by North Slope oil producers to ship more crude to West Coast refineries in the United States. But officials with Alaska's Department of Community and Economic Development said that decline would have no lasting impact on the state's economy since oil is a commodity traded on the open market and the destination of the oil sold has little significance. Crude oil exports totaled $288 million in 2000, down 42 percent from 1999.

The decline in mineral exports was attributed to a short-term production decline at the Red Dog zinc and lead mine while a new, more efficient processing system was installed.

Seafood exports in 2000 totaled $1 billion, up 4.5 percent from 1999.

Japan remained Alaska's largest trading partner, accounting for more than 53 percent of the state's total exports. Exports to Japan in 2000 totaled $1.3 billion, down 1.1 percent from 1999.

Exports to Korea totaled $449 million in 2000, down nearly 8 percent from 1999. Exports to Canada dropped 18 percent to $165 million; exports to Belgium slipped 4 percent to $105 million; and exports to China declined nearly 7 percent to $103 million.

FAIRBANKS
Nicknamed "The Golden Heart City," Fairbanks is located in Alaska's Interior, 200 miles south of the Arctic Circle and 120 miles north of Denali National Park and Preserve.

Long before European explorers and trappers came to the area, Athabascan Indians lived, fished and hunted in the Tanana Valley, site of the present-day city.

Fairbanks was founded through the misadventure of Ohio trader E. T. Barnette, who never intended to establish a town on the Chena River. Barnette and his $20,000 worth of trading goods had set out from St. Michael in late August 1901, bound to establish a trading post at the village of Tanacross, where the Valdez Trail crossed the Tanana Valley. After Barnette's own stern-wheeler was wrecked, he hired Charles Adams, part-owner of the *Lavelle Young,* to take him to Tanacross. Once again Barnette ran into trouble when the 150-foot *Lavelle Young* could not ascend the Tanana past the sandy shallows called the Bates Rapids, a few miles above the mouth of the Chena River. In hopes that the Chena would meet up with the Tanana, Barnette persuaded Adams to carry him up the Chena until the boat ran into shallow water. Adams left Barnette, his party and his goods on the banks of the Chena River near what is now First Avenue and Cushman Street in Fairbanks.

Things were looking bleak for Barnette until Felix Pedro struck gold about 16 miles away on July 22, 1902. Barnette took this opportunity to expand his trading goods business and immediately dispatched Jujiro Wada, a Japanese employee, to Dawson City to spread the good news of a gold strike in the Tanana Valley. Soon the community became the new hub of the Alaska gold rush. A friend of Barnette's, Judge James Wickersham, suggested Fairbanks as the name for the new town, in honor of Indiana Senator Charles Fairbanks. In exchange, Wickersham agreed to move the seat of the District Court from Eagle to Fairbanks, thus ensuring that the town would further flourish.

By 1908, Fairbanks was the largest, busiest city in the territory, boasting electric lights, city sewer, fire and police protection, a courthouse and jail, a hospital, school, library and three newspapers.

Today Fairbanks is Alaska's second-largest city, home to just over 30,000 residents, and the service and supply center for Interior and Arctic industries. About 83,000 people live in the Fairbanks North Star Borough. Government, oil, mining, construction and tourism are important elements in the Fairbanks economy, as are Fort Wainwright, the first Army airfield in Alaska, and Eielson Air Force Base. The University of Alaska Fairbanks campus overlooks the city.

The "Unknown First Family" is a Fairbanks landmark. From *Fairbanks, Alaska's Heart of Gold* by Tricia Brown (text) and Roy Corral (photographs).

Summer temperatures average 59.5°F, often ranging into the 70s and 80s, with nearly 24 hours of daylight at the solstice (June 20 or 21), when a Midnight Sun Baseball Game is played after 10:30 P.M. with no artificial lighting. Winter temperatures range from 7.6°F to –19.2°F with the lowest-ever temperature recorded at –66°F in 1934. The winter snowfall averages 68.9 inches.

Winter attractions include the World Ice Art Championships, sled dog races and northern lights viewing. Fairbanks is considered one of the best places on earth to view the northern lights. Summer activities include the Golden Days celebration, Tanana Valley Fair (the state's oldest) and the World Eskimo–Indian Olympics held annually in July. (SEE World Eskimo–Indian Olympics)

Alaskaland Pioneer Park is a 44-acre park offering a gold-rush town, historic buildings, food, small shops, entertainment and the SS *Nenana*.

Fairbanks also offers river rafting, stern-wheeler riverboat tours, gold-rush sites and dog mushing and is a good jumping-off spot for the Alaska Railroad, Denali National Park and Preserve and remote wilderness

If you activate your computer's spell-check program for a paragraph containing the Alaska cities of Seward, Fairbanks and Naknek, the software will recommend that you change the words to Sewer, Fatbacks and Naked.

Free and Clear

U.S. District Court in Fairbanks received payment-in-full on a 52-year-old loan in November 1988. The letter, signed only with initials, explained the reason for the loan—the recipient was looking for work and was broke—and offered apologies for being so late in repaying the debt. No record of the loan has been found, and the clerk's office feels it was probably cash out of a kind-hearted employee's pocket. Nonetheless, the money would have gone a long way back then. In Fairbanks in 1936, dinner out cost $1, a hot sandwich 35 cents, and two pounds of coffee 75 cents. The money was turned over to the U.S. financial deputy in Anchorage where unexpected windfalls are processed—in this case, $15.   —1989 The ALASKA ALMANAC®

---

areas. For information, contact the Fairbanks Convention and Visitors Bureau, 550 First Ave., Fairbanks 99701-4790; (800) 327-5774; www.explorefairbanks.com.

FERRIES (SEE ALSO Boating; Cruises)

The Marine Highway System, within the state Department of Transportation and Public Facilities, provides year-round scheduled ferry service for passengers and vehicles to communities in Southeast and Southcentral Alaska and seasonal service in Southwestern Alaska. Monthly sailings in the summer connect the southeastern ferry system with Southcentral and Southwestern Alaska.

A fleet of seven ferries on the southeastern system connects Bellingham, Wash., and Prince Rupert, British Columbia, with the southeastern Alaska ports of Hyder/Stewart, Ketchikan, Metlakatla, Hollis, Petersburg, Wrangell, Kake, Sitka, Angoon, Pelican, Hoonah, Tenakee Springs, Juneau, Haines and Skagway. These southeastern communities (with the exception of Hyder, Haines and Skagway) are accessible only by boat, ferry or airplane. The seven vessels of the southeastern system are the *Aurora, Columbia, Kennicott, LeConte, Malaspina, Matanuska* and *Taku*.

With the addition of the *Kennicott* in 1998, the *Malaspina* began service as a day boat between Juneau, Skagway and Haines. Southwestern and Southcentral Alaska are served by two ferries. The *Tustumena* serves Seward, Port Lions, Kodiak, Homer and Seldovia, with limited summer service to Valdez, Chignik, False Pass, Akutan, Sand Point, King Cove, Cold Bay and Dutch Harbor. The *Bartlett* provides service between Valdez and Cordova with summer service to Whittier and year-round stops at Chenega Bay and Tatitlek.

Scheduled state ferry service to southeastern Alaska began in 1963; ferry service to Kodiak Island began in 1964. The first three ferries of the Alaska ferry fleet were the *Malaspina, Matanuska* and *Taku*.

Reservations are required for all sailings. Rates for senior citizens and for passengers with disabilities are available. Contact the Alaska Marine Highway System, 1591 Glacier Ave., Juneau 99801-1427; (800) 642-0066; (907) 465-3941; www.state.ak.us/ferry; or read the *Marine Highway News*, published May 1.

Nautical Miles Between Ports

Southeastern System

Bellingham–Ketchikan	.595
Prince Rupert–Ketchikan	91
Ketchikan–Metlakatla	16
Ketchikan–Hollis	40
Hollis–Petersburg	123
Hollis–Wrangell	100
Ketchikan–Wrangell	89
Wrangell–Petersburg	41

(continued)

The ferry Aurora, and a commercial fishing boat. Alaska Division of Tourism.

Southeastern System *(continued)*

Petersburg–Kake 65
Kake–Sitka 115
Sitka–Angoon 67
Angoon–Tenakee 35
Tenakee–Hoonah 49
Angoon–Hoonah 63
Hoonah–Juneau (Auke Bay) 48
Sitka–Hoonah 115
Hoonah–Pelican via South Pass 64
Hoonah–Juneau 48
Haines–Skagway 13
Juneau (Auke Bay)–Haines 68
Petersburg–Juneau (Auke Bay) 123
Petersburg–Sitka 156
Juneau (Auke Bay)–Sitka 132
Juneau–Yakutat 234

Southwestern System

Seward–Cordova 144
Seward–Valdez 144
Cordova–Valdez 74
Valdez–Whittier 78
Seward–Kodiak 185
Kodiak–Port Lions 48
Kodiak–Homer 136
Homer–Seldovia 17
Kodiak–Sand Point via Sitkinak Strait . .353
Yakutat–Valdez 286

Alaska State Ferry Boats

Aurora (235 feet, 14.5 knots):
250 passengers, 34 vehicles, no cabins.
Began service in 1977.
Bartlett (193 feet, 13.6 knots):
190 passengers, 29 vehicles, no cabins.
Began service in 1968.

Columbia (418 feet, 17.3 knots):
625 passengers, 134 vehicles, 91 cabins.
Began service in 1974.
Kennicott (382 feet, 16.75 knots):
500 passengers, 120 vehicles, 109 cabins.
Began service in summer 1998.
LeConte (235 feet, 14.5 knots):
250 passengers, 34 vehicles, no cabins.
Began service in 1973.
Malaspina (408 feet, 16.5 knots):
500 passengers, 88 vehicles, 73 cabins.
Began service in 1963 and was lengthened
and renovated in 1972.
Matanuska (408 feet, 16.5 knots):
500 passengers, 88 vehicles, 108 cabins.
Began service in 1963.
Taku (352 feet, 16.5 knots):
450 passengers, 69 vehicles, 44 cabins.
Began service in 1963.
Tustumena (296 feet, 13.5 knots):
210 passengers, 36 vehicles, 26 cabins.
Began service in 1964.

Embarking Passengers and Vehicles on Alaska Mainline Ferries*

Southeastern System

Year	Passengers	Vehicles
1987	326,600	83,500
1988	344,200	90,700
1989	344,400	89,800
1990	363,100	94,700
1991	368,800	95,200
1992	372,700	97,200
1993	342,600	92,600
1994	348,000	90,800
1995	332,200	88,900
1996	318,900	87,900
1997	300,600	82,400
1998	303,600	84,300
1999	323,500	88,100

Southwestern System

Year	Passengers	Vehicles
1987	52,000	16,500
1988	50,300	16,600
1989	44,200	15,700
1990	50,500	16,500
1991	36,200	12,800
1992	47,800	15,700

Southwestern System (continued)

Year	Passengers	Vehicles
1993	48,700	15,700
1994	48,500	15,200
1995	45,400	15,100
1996	46,100	14,800
1997	49,400	15,800
1998	48,300	16,500
1999	45,500	17,000

*Numbers rounded off. Mainline ports for the southeastern system are Bellingham, Prince Rupert, Ketchikan, Wrangell, Petersburg, Sitka, Juneau, Haines and Skagway. Mainline ports for the Southwestern system are Cordova, Valdez, Whittier, Homer, Seldovia, Kodiak, Seward and Port Lions.

FISHING
Commercial Fishing

Alaska's abundant and largely pristine fishing grounds have provided a harvest of more than 50 billion pounds of seafood over the past 10 years, accounting for nearly 55 percent of all domestically produced seafood.

This staggering volume is almost four times more than the next largest seafood-producing state. The Alaska Department of Fish and Game, which oversees certain Alaska commercial harvests, estimates the ex-vessel value of Alaska's commercial harvest at $883 million in 2000. That's down from $1.3 billion in 1999. Ex-vessel refers to prices paid to fishermen.

Commercial fishing's ripple effect is felt beyond the generations of coastal families that have made their living from the sea. Seafood is Alaska's largest export, representing about 40 percent of Alaska's exports.

A University of Alaska Anchorage study concluded in 1991 that the state's seafood industry was the most important private industry in Alaska, both in terms of employment and income. More than 75,000 people rely on commercial fishing or seafood processing for all or part of their income, and in many small coastal and river towns, commercial fishing is the top source of income. Cities and boroughs receive one half of the state's fisheries business tax. This is a key element of the tax base in many smaller communities.

Alaska's commercial fleet faces complex issues in the next millennium. Scientists are trying to gain a better understanding of continued declining salmon returns in Western Alaska—a region heavily dependent on salmon for income and to support subsistence life. And researchers are trying to determine if there is a link between commercial fishing and the steep decline in the Steller sea lion population in Western Alaska.

Value and Volume of Alaska Fish and Shellfish Landings

Year	Value	Volume
1990	$1.50 billion	5.9 billion lbs.
1991	$1.22 billion	5.1 billion lbs.
1992	$1.58 billion	5.6 billion lbs.
1993	$1.28 billion	6.0 billion lbs.
1994	$1.35 billion	5.8 billion lbs.
1995	$1.40 billion	5.3 billion lbs.
1996	$1.19 billion	5.0 billion lbs.
1997	$1.22 billion	4.2 billion lbs.
1998	$1.18 billion*	5.1 billion lbs.*
1999	$1.21 billion	4.9 billion lbs.
2000	$883 million	4.5 billion lbs.

Source: National Marine Fisheries Service,
     U.S. Department of Commerce
*Source: Alaska Department of Fish and Game

Salmon. Five species of Pacific salmon inhabit Alaska waters and are commercially harvested: king (also known as chinook); silver (coho); pink (humpback); red (sockeye); and chum (dog salmon).

The ex-vessel value of Alaska's commercial salmon harvest in 2000 was $275 million, down from $383 million in 1999.

The total catch of all these species of salmon in 2000 was 142 million fish. The harvest of all species except chum salmon came in lower than expected in 2000. But the chum harvest set a statewide record, with 24.3 million fish caught.

Western Alaska once again saw extremely low king and chum salmon returns in 2000. King salmon in the Yukon and Kuskokwim rivers have been classified as stocks of concern under the state's sustainable fisheries policy. Chum salmon

Anglers flock to the Kenai River for the challenge of king fishing. From *Alaska's Kenai Peninsula: A Traveler's Guide* by Andromeda Romano-Lax. Photo by Bill Sherwonit.

from the Kuskokwim, Yukon and Nome areas have also been classified as stocks of concern.

Shellfish. Alaska's commercial shellfish harvest includes king crab, Dungeness crab and Tanner crab, also known as snow crab.

The ex-vessel value of the state's shellfish harvest in 2000 dropped to $133 million from $310 million in 1999. The decline was due largely to a steep drop in the harvest of snow crab in the Bering Sea. State fishery managers reduced the harvest quota to a fraction of that in previous years after tests revealed a steep decline in the number of young crabs. The 2000 snow crab fishery was also delayed when the sea ice extended much farther south than normal, covering much of the fishing grounds until spring.

Herring. Much of Alaska's commercial herring is harvested as sac roe, a longtime delicacy in Japan where consumption has begun to taper.

The value of the 2000 herring sac roe fishery totaled $7 million, down from $17 million in 1999.

Relied on by earliest Alaska Natives for food, herring are found in commercial quantities from Dixon Entrance in Southeast as far north as Norton Sound. Traditional dried herring is still savored in some Bering Sea villages; Southeast Alaska Natives consume herring eggs.

Halibut. Alaska's commercial halibut season is federally regulated and runs from March 15 through Nov. 15. A quota program imposed in 1995 limited the number of halibut permit holders and ended "derby-style" fishing that had boats awaiting numerous openings of just 24 hours to 48 hours.

Halibut are targeted in three zones: the Bering Sea, Southeast and the Gulf of Alaska, which accounts for most of the catch. The value of the state's halibut fishery rose to $145 million in 2000 from $116 million in 1999.

Top Ten Trophy King Salmon

1. 97 lbs., 4 oz. (Kenai River, 1985)
2. 95 lbs., 10 oz. (Kenai River, 1990)
3. 92 lbs., 4 oz. (Kenai River, 1985)
4. 91 lbs., 10 oz. (Kenai River, 1988)
5. 91 lbs., 4 oz. (Kenai River, 1987)
6. 91 lbs. (Kenai River, 1995)
7. 90 lbs., 4 oz. (Kenai River, 1995)
8. 89 lbs., 3 oz. (Kenai River, 1989)
9. 89 lbs., 1 oz. (Kenai River, 1995)
10. 89 lbs. (Kenai River, 1994)

Source: Alaska Department of Fish and Game Trophy Fish Program

Ex-vessel Value of Alaska's Commercial Fisheries (in millions of dollars)

Species	1993	1994	1995	1996	1997	1998	1999	2000*
Salmon	$390	$482	$481	$365	$248	$261	$383	$272
Shellfish	356	314	265	164	161	215	310	133
Halibut	60	85	65	78	111	68	116	145
Herring	17	22	42	64	16	12	17	7
Groundfish	455	443	434	685	652	627	503	323

* Preliminary figures

Source: Alaska Department of Fish and Game, www.cf.adfg.state.ak.us

2000 Final Commercial Salmon Harvest* (in thousands of fish)

Region	King	Sockeye	Coho	Pink	Chum	Total
Southeast	230	1,220	1,950	20,250	15,850	39,500
Central (Prince William Sound, Cook Inlet, Kodiak, Chignik and Bristol Bay)	73	28,220	1,540	50,850	6,930	87,750
Arctic–Yukon–Kuskokwim	40	110	350	170	230	900
Western (Alaska Peninsula and Aleutian Islands)	10	3,960	340	3,580	1,150	9,050
Total	360	33,500	4,200	74,800	24,290	137,163

* Preliminary figures

Figures may not total exactly or match figures from other summary tables due to rounding or differing methods of calculation.

Source: Alaska Department of Fish and Game, www.cf.adfg.state.ak.us

Groundfish. Commercially harvested groundfish in Alaska include Pacific cod, rockfish, sablefish and pollock. The fisheries are regulated by the National Marine Fisheries Service.

By far the largest catch is pollock, much of it taken in the Bering Sea. Pollock is the mild white fish used to make the fish sticks and fillets found in fast-food restaurants around the world. It's also used to make surimi, the fish paste that is fashioned into imitation crab and other products.

The value of the state's groundfish harvest fell to $323 million in 2000 from $503 million in 1999, according to the Alaska Department of Fish and Game.

The groundfish fleet saw tough new restrictions in 2000, designed to keep them out of waters around Steller sea lion rookeries and haulouts. The restrictions were put into place in response to a lawsuit filed by environmentalists who think the commercial groundfish harvest is responsible for the sea lion's steep decline in Western Alaska over the past three decades.

Alaska still ranks number one in occupational fatalities. How many people remember that President Warren G. Harding died after eating tainted crab on his 1923 visit to Alaska?

Alaska State Record Trophy Fish

Species	Min. Wt.	Lbs./oz.	Year	Location	Angler
Arctic Char/					
Dolly Varden	10 lbs.	19/12.5	1991	Noatak River	Ken Ubben
Brook Trout*	3 lbs.				
Burbot	8 lbs.	24/12	1976	Lake Louise	George R. Howard
Chum Salmon	15 lbs.	32/0	1985	Caamano Point	Frederick Thynes
Coho Salmon	20 lbs.	26/0	1976	Icy Strait	Andrew Robbins
Cutthroat Trout	3 lbs.	8/6	1977	Wilson Lake	Robert Denison
Grayling	3 lbs.	4/13	1981	Ugashik	Paul F. Kanitz
Halibut	250 lbs.	459/0	1996	Unalaska Bay	Jack Tragis
King Salmon	**	97/4	1985	Kenai River	Lester Anderson
Lake Trout	20 lbs.	47/0	1970	Clarence Lake	Daniel Thorsness
Lingcod	45 lbs.	70/0	2000	Seward	Mark D. Gomez
Northern Pike	15 lbs.	38/0	1991	Innoko River	Jack Wagner
Pink Salmon	8 lbs.	12/9	1974	Moose River	Steven A. Lee
Rainbow Trout/					
Steelhead	15 lbs.	42/3	1970	Bell Island	David White
Rockfish	18 lbs.	37/2	1995	Passage Canal	Colin Gamble
Sheefish	30 lbs.	53/0	1986	Pah River	Lawrence E. Hudnall
Sockeye Salmon	12 lbs.	16/0	1974	Kenai River	Chuck Leach
Whitefish	4 lbs.	9/0	1989	Tozitna River	Al Mathews

* This species was added in 1995; no entries to date

** King salmon minimum weight for Kenai River is 75 lbs; for rest of state, 50 lbs.

Source: Alaska Department of Fish and Game Trophy Fish Program

A federal court ruling banned all trawl fishing in areas within 20 miles of places designated as critical habitat to the sea lions. The ruling closed much of the prime fishing grounds and caused turmoil in the industry. The commercial fleet was forced to make more costly and dangerous trips, farther from shore, in search of pollock. The larger vessels of the Bering Sea fleet could go farther out to sea in search of fish. But the smaller boats of the Gulf of Alaska fleet had greater difficulty finding fish.

U.S. Sen. Ted Stevens won a delay in full implementation of the court's restrictions while securing money for further study of the sea lion's decline.

Sport Fishing

The Alaska Department of Fish and Game has established five regulatory zones, each with its own sportfishing rules. Anglers are advised to consult the Alaska Sport Fishing Regulations summary for areas they plan to fish. Summaries may be obtained through the department at P.O. Box 25526, Juneau 99802-5526; sfregs@fishgame.state.ak.us; www.sf.adfg.state.ak.us/statewide/regulatio ns/2001/html/reghome.stm.

In 2000, regulations were grouped into these zones: Arctic–Yukon–Kuskokwim–Tanana–Upper Copper and Upper Susitna Rivers; Bristol Bay–Lower Kuskokwim; Alaska Peninsula–Aleutian Islands–Kodiak Island; Kenai Peninsula–Cook Inlet–Susitna drainage–Prince William Sound–Resurrection Bay; Southeast–Yakutat.

Regulations. A sportfishing license is required for residents and nonresidents 16 years of age or older. Alaska residents age 60 or older who have been resident one year or more do not need a sportfishing license as long as they remain residents. A special identification card is issued for this exemption.

Anglers rarely fish all of Alaska in a lifetime; the state has more coastline than all of the Lower 48 states and more than

100,000 lakes. Alaska's salmon sportfishing is deservedly renowned, although some urban Alaska streams have seen reductions in recent years. Conservation-minded anglers should note that while many stocks of Pacific salmon are in trouble in other states, all five species found in Alaska are at healthy levels. In general, king salmon fishing occurs in spring and ends in midsummer; sockeye, pink and chum seasons are next, followed by silver salmon in late summer and fall. Out-of-state anglers may call (907) 465-4180 for Alaska information.

Resident sportfishing licenses cost $15, valid for the calendar year issued (nonresident, $100; 1-day nonresident, $10; 3-day nonresident, $20; 7-day nonresident, $30; 14-day nonresident, $50). A resident is a person who has maintained a permanent place of abode within the state for 12 consecutive months and has continuously maintained a voting residence in the state. Military personnel on active duty permanently stationed in the state, and their dependents, can purchase a nonresident military sportfishing license ($15).

An additional stamp is required for those wishing to fish for king salmon. Cost for residents is $10. Nonresidents may purchase a king stamp that's good for the calendar year for $100. Other options are: 1-day nonresident, $10; 3-day nonresident, $20; 7-day nonresident, $30; 14-day nonresident, $50; military, $20.

Salmon in Lemon Sauce

1 red or silver salmon, filleted
1 stick butter
Juice of 1 lemon
1 tablespoon Worcestershire
2 to 3 tablespoons chopped fresh or
    dried chives

Place salmon fillets on foil and put in shallow dish. Cover tightly and bake at 450°F until milk comes to top. (Or before you bake, measure the thickest point of the fillet and allow 10 minutes cooking time per inch.) Melt butter, add lemon juice, chives and Worcestershire. Remove cover from fish, pour on sauce and finish baking uncovered, basting occasionally with sauce.

—Belva Hamilton, Cooper Landing,
Cooking Alaskan

NUGGETS

Alaska landings of salmon in 1987 were 498.4 million pounds, valued at $457.9 million—87 percent of the total U.S. landings. With surimi growing in popularity, Alaska pollock landings made a huge increase of 323 percent, to 552 million pounds.

—1989 *The ALASKA ALMANAC®*

Nearly all sporting goods stores in Alaska sell fishing licenses. They are also available by mail from the Alaska Department of Revenue, Fish and Game License Section, P.O. Box 25525, Juneau 99802-5525; (877) 934-7425; www.admin.adfg.state.ak.us/license.

FISH WHEEL The fish wheel is a handcrafted, wooden machine fastened to a river shore, propelled by current, which floats on a log raft and scoops up fish heading upstream to spawn. Widely used for subsistence salmon fishing along stretches of Alaska's largest rivers, the fish wheel provides a way of catching salmon without injuring them. Contrary to popular belief, Alaska Natives did not invent the fish wheel. Non-Natives first introduced

Fish wheel on the Tanana River. Photo by Ann Chandonnet.

the fish wheel on the Tanana River in 1904. Soon after, it appeared on the Yukon River, where it was used by both settlers and Natives. It first appeared on the Kuskokwim in 1914, when prospectors introduced it for catching salmon near Georgetown.

Today, subsistence fishing with the use of a fish wheel is allowed on the Tanana River, the Copper River and the Kuskokwim River, as well as the Yukon River and its tributaries. In 1999 there were 162 limited-entry permits for the use of fish wheels by commercial salmon fishermen on the Yukon River system—the only river where both commercial and subsistence fishermen use fish wheels. Fishing times with the wheels are regulated.

Prior to its appearance in Alaska, the fish wheel was used on the East Coast, on the Sacramento River in California and on the Columbia River in Washington and Oregon.

FURS AND TRAPPING The

major sources of harvested Alaska furs are the Yukon and Kuskokwim valleys.

The Arctic provides limited numbers of arctic fox, wolverine and wolf but the Gulf Coast areas and Southeast are more productive. Southeast Alaska is a good source of mink and otter.

Trapping is seasonal work, and most trappers work summers at fishing or other employment. Licenses are required for trapping. (SEE Hunting for license fees.) State-regulated furbearers are beaver, coyote, arctic fox (includes white or blue), red fox (includes cross, black or silver color phases), lynx, marmot, marten, mink,

muskrat, river (land) otter, squirrel (parka or ground, flying and red), weasel, wolf and wolverine. Very little harvest or use is made of parka squirrels and marmots.

Prices for raw skins are widely variable and depend on the buyer, quality, condition and size of the fur. Pelts accepted for purchase are beaver, coyote, lynx, marten, mink, muskrat, otter, red and white fox, red squirrel, weasel (ermine), wolf and wolverine.

Pelts accepted for purchase are beaver, coyote, lynx, marten, mink, muskrat, otter, red and white fox, red squirrel, weasel (ermine), wolf and wolverine.

GEOGRAPHY (SEE map, pages 6–7.

SEE ALSO Glaciers and Ice Fields; Lakes; Mountains; Populations and Zip Codes; Regions of Alaska; Rivers)

State capital: Juneau.

State population: 626,932.

Land area: 570,374 square miles, or about 365 million acres—largest state in the Union; one-fifth the size of the Lower 48. Alaska is larger than the three next largest states combined.

Area per person: About 0.9 square mile.

Diameter: East to west 2,400 miles; north to south 1,420 miles.

Coastline: 6,640 miles, point to point; as measured on the most detailed maps available, including islands, Alaska has 33,904 miles of shoreline—twice the length of the Lower 48. Estimated tidal shoreline, including islands, inlets and shoreline to head of tidewater, is 47,300 miles.

Adjacent salt water: North Pacific Ocean, Bering Sea, Chukchi Sea, Arctic Ocean.

Alaska–Canada border: 1,538 miles long: length of boundary between the Arctic Ocean and Mount St. Elias, 647 miles; Southeast border with British Columbia and Yukon Territory, 710 miles; water boundary, 181 miles.

Geographic center: 63°50' north, 152° west, about 60 miles northwest of Mount McKinley.

Northernmost point: Point Barrow, 71°23' north.

Southernmost point: Tip of Amatignak Island, Aleutian Chain, 51°13'05" north.

Easternmost and westernmost points: It all depends on how you look at it. The 180th meridian—halfway around the world from the prime meridian at Greenwich, England, and the dividing line between east and west longitudes—passes through Alaska. According to one view, Alaska has both the easternmost and westernmost spots in the country! The westernmost is Amatignak Island, 179°10' west; and the easternmost, Pochnoi Point, 179°46' east. But on the other hand, if you are facing north, east is to your right and west to your left. Therefore, the westernmost point in Alaska is Cape Wrangell, Attu Island, 172°27' east; and the easternmost point in Alaska is near Camp Point, in southeastern Alaska, 129°59' east.

Tallest mountain: Mount McKinley, 20,320 feet, and the tallest mountain in North America. Alaska has 39 mountain ranges, containing 17 of the 20 highest peaks in the United States.

Largest natural freshwater lake: Iliamna, 1,150 square miles. Alaska has more than 3 million lakes more than 20 acres in size.

Longest river: Yukon, 1,875 miles in Alaska; 2,298 total. There are more than 3,000 rivers in the state. The Yukon River ranks third in length of U.S. rivers, behind the Mississippi and Missouri rivers.

Largest island: Kodiak, in the Gulf of Alaska, 3,588 square miles. There are 1,800 named islands in the state, 1,000 of which are located in Southeast Alaska.

Largest city in population: Anchorage, population 260,283.

Largest city in area: Sitka, with 4,710 square miles, 1,816 square miles of which is water. Juneau is second, with 3,108 square miles.

GLACIERS AND ICE FIELDS

The greatest concentrations of glaciers are in the Alaska Range, Wrangell Mountains and the coastal ranges of the Chugach, Coast, Kenai and St. Elias mountains, where annual precipitation is high. All of Alaska's well-known glaciers fall within these areas. The distribution of glacier ice is shown on the map on page 78.

Glaciers cover approximately 29,000 square miles—or 5 percent—of Alaska, which is 128 times more area covered by glaciers than in the rest of the United States. There are an estimated 100,000 glaciers in Alaska, ranging from tiny cirque glaciers to huge valley glaciers.

Glaciers are formed where, over a number of years, more snow falls than melts. Alaska's glaciers fall roughly into five general categories: alpine, valley, piedmont, ice fields and ice caps. Alpine (mountain and cirque) glaciers head high on the slopes of mountains and plateaus.

The Matanuska Glacier is visible from the Richardson Highway. Photo by Tricia Brown.

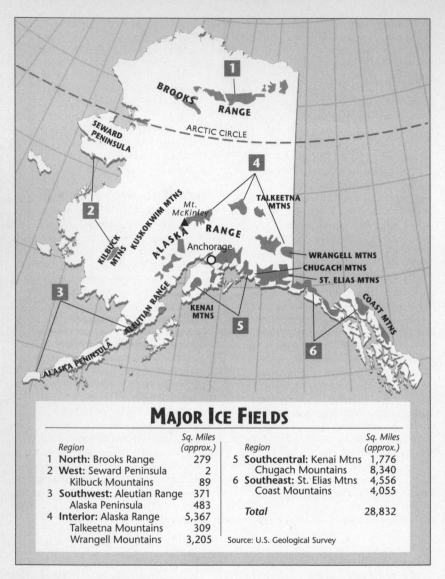

MAJOR ICE FIELDS

Region	Sq. Miles (approx.)	Region	Sq. Miles (approx.)
1 **North:** Brooks Range	279	5 **Southcentral:** Kenai Mtns	1,776
2 **West:** Seward Peninsula	2	Chugach Mountains	8,340
Kilbuck Mountains	89	6 **Southeast:** St. Elias Mtns	4,556
3 **Southwest:** Aleutian Range	371	Coast Mountains	4,055
Alaska Peninsula	483		
4 **Interior:** Alaska Range	5,367	*Total*	28,832
Talkeetna Mountains	309		
Wrangell Mountains	3,205	Source: U.S. Geological Survey	

Valley glaciers are an overflowing accumulation of ice from mountain or plateau basins. Piedmont glaciers result when one or more glaciers join to form a fan-shaped ice mass at the foot of a mountain range. Ice fields develop when large valley glaciers interconnect, leaving only the highest peaks and ridges to rise above the ice surface. Ice caps are smaller glaciers perched on plateaus.

Alaska's better-known glaciers accessible by road are Worthington (Richardson Highway), Matanuska (Glenn Highway), Exit (Seward Highway), Portage (Seward Highway) and Mendenhall (Glacier Highway). In addition, Childs and Sheridan glaciers may be reached by car from Cordova, and Valdez Glacier, also accessible by car, is only a few miles from the town of Valdez. The sediment-covered terminus of

The Quick and Living Blue

The whole front of the glacier is gashed and sculptured into a maze of shallow caves and crevasses, and a bewildering variety of novel architectural forms, clusters of glittering lance-tipped spires, gables, and obelisks, hold out standing bastions and plain mural cliffs, adorned along the top with fretted cornice and battlement, while every gorge and crevasse, groove and hollow, was filled with light, shimmering and throbbing in pale-blue tones of ineffable tenderness and beauty. The day was warm, and back on the broad melting bosom of the glacier . . . many streams were rejoicing, gurgling, ringing, singing, in frictionless channels worn down through the white disintegrated ice of the surface into the quick and living blue, in which they flowed with a grace of motion and flashing of light to be found only on the crystal hillocks and ravines of a glacier.

—John Muir, *Travels in Alaska* (1879)

Muldrow Glacier in Denali National Park and Preserve is visible at a distance along several miles of the park road.

Many spectacular glaciers in Glacier Bay National Park and Preserve, in Kenai Fjords and in Prince William Sound are visible from tour boats or by flightseeing.

Some glacier facts:

• Glacier ice often appears blue to the eye because it absorbs all the colors of the spectrum except blue, which is scattered back.

• About three-fourths of all the fresh water in Alaska is stored as glacial ice. This is many times greater than the volume of water stored in all the state's lakes, ponds, rivers and reservoirs.

• Longest tidewater glacier in North America is Hubbard, 76 miles long (heads in Canada). In 1986, the Hubbard rapidly advanced and blocked Russell Fiord near Yakutat. Later in the year, the ice dam gave way.

• Longest glacier in Alaska is Bering (including Bagley Icefield), more than 100 miles long.

• Southernmost active tidewater glacier in North America is LeConte.

• Greatest concentration of tidewater-calving glaciers is in Prince William Sound, with 20 active tidewater glaciers.

• Largest piedmont lobe glacier is

Malaspina, 850 square miles; the Malaspina Glacier complex (including tributary glaciers) is approximately 2,000 square miles in area.

• The largest glacier is the Bering Glacier complex, about 2,250 square miles in size, which includes Bagley Icefield.

• La Perouse Glacier in Glacier Bay National Park is the only calving glacier in North America that discharges icebergs directly into the open Pacific Ocean.

• There are more than 750 glacier-dammed lakes in Alaska; the largest at present is 28-square-mile Chakachamna Lake west of Anchorage.

• Variegated Glacier, at Russell Fiord in Yakutat Bay, is the most studied glacier in

Alaska has more active glaciers and ice fields than the rest of the inhabited world. We have more than half of the earthquakes in the entire USA. And we have a congressman named Don Young who once said, "That's like putting toothpaste back in the tube before it comes out." Life is still good in the Frozen North!!!

the world. The glacier, which extends 10 miles from its head to its foot, surprised scientists in 1995 by surging (a rise in forward movement) four years ahead of schedule. By the end of summer 1995, the glacier had moved hundreds of yards. Scientists attribute the surge to the movement of water underneath the glacier rather than climatic conditions.

GOLD (SEE ALSO Gold Strikes and Rushes; Minerals and Mining)

The largest gold nugget ever found in Alaska was discovered in the summer of 1998. The nugget, weighing 294 troy ounces (24.5 pounds), was found in the Ruby District of Northern Alaska. The second-largest nugget, weighing 155 troy ounces (12.9 pounds), was found Sept. 29, 1903, at the Discovery Claim on Anvil Creek, Nome District. The nugget was 7 inches long, 4 inches wide and 2 inches thick.

Four other large nuggets have been found in Alaska, one of which also came from the Discovery Claim on Anvil Creek in 1899. It was the largest Alaska nugget found up to that time, weighing 82.1 troy ounces, and was 6 1/4 inches long, 3 1/4 inches wide, 1 3/8 inches thick at one end and 1/2-inch thick at the other.

In 1914 the third-largest nugget mined, weighing 138.4 troy ounces, was found near the Discovery Claim of Hammond River in the Koyukuk–Nolan District. Three of the top five nuggets have been discovered since 1984, including one from Lower Glacier Creek, Kantisha District, in 1984, weighing 91.8 troy ounces, and the other from Ganes Creek, Innoko District, in 1986, weighing 122 troy ounces.

If you are interested in gold panning, sluicing or suction dredging in Alaska—for fun or profit—you'll have to know whose land you are on and familiarize yourself with current regulations.

Panning, sluicing, and suction dredging on private property, established mining claims and Native lands is considered trespassing unless you have the consent of the owner. On state and federal lands, contact the managing agency for current restrictions on mining. On Native-owned

NUGGETS

In 1980, the average annual price of gold peaked at $569.73 per troy ounce. Ten years earlier, gold was valued at $36.41 per troy ounce.—1983 *The ALASKA ALMANAC®*

lands, contact the tribal council of the village or the Native corporation well in advance of your visit.

You can pan for gold for a small fee by visiting one of the gold-panning resorts in Alaska. Commercial resorts rent gold pans and let you try your luck on gold-bearing creeks and streams on their property. If you want to stake a mining claim, the state Department of Natural Resources has a free booklet, *Regulation and Statutes Pertaining to Mining Rights of Alaska Lands,* obtained by calling the department offices in Juneau, (907) 465-3400, fax (907) 586-2954; or Anchorage, (907) 269-8542, fax (907) 269-8913. A general government source for information about property is www.dnr.state.ak.us.

Following are volumes (in troy ounces) and value figures for recent years of Alaska gold production.

Gold Production in Alaska, 1990–2000

Year	Vol. (in troy oz.)	Value
1990	231,700	$89.2 million
1991	243,900	$88.3 million
1992	262,530	$88.5 million
1993	191,265	$68.6 million
1994	182,100	$70.3 million
1995	141,882	$56.0 million
1996	161,565	$62.6 million
1997	590,516	$207.3 million
1998	594,111	$174.6 million
1999	509,000	$144.9 million
2000	546,000	$152.4 million

The following chart shows the fluctuation in the price of gold (1991–2000) after the gold standard was lifted in 1967. These are average annual prices and do not reflect the yearly high or low prices.

Average Annual Price of Gold, per Troy Ounce

1934 to 1967—	$ 35.00
1991—	$362.03
1992—	$337.00
1993—	$354.00
1994—	$386.00
1995—	$395.00
1996—	$387.60
1997—	$330.76
1998—	$293.88
1999—	$278.70
2000—	$279.10

Source: Alaska Division of Geological and Geophysical Survey's annual Alaska Mineral Industry reports

GOLD STRIKES AND RUSHES

1848—First Alaska gold discovery at Russian River on Kenai Peninsula

1861—Stikine River near Telegraph Creek, British Columbia; Wrangell

1872—Cassiar district in Canada (Stikine headwaters country)

1872—Near Sitka

1874—Windham Bay near Juneau

1880—Gold Creek at Juneau

1886—Fortymile discovery

1887—Yakutat areas and Lituya Bay

1893—Mastodon Creek, starting in Circle City

1895—Sunrise district on the Kenai Peninsula

1896—Klondike strike, Bonanza Creek, Yukon Territory, Canada

1896—Council (Seward Peninsula)

1898—Anvil Creek near Nome; Atlin district

1898—Hope and Sunrise on Turnagain Arm

1898—British Columbia

1899—Nome beaches

1900—Porcupine rush out of Haines

1902—Fairbanks (Felix Pedro, Upper Goldstream Valley)

1905—Kantishna Hills

1906—Innoko

1907—Ruby

1908—Iditarod

1913—Chisana

1913—Marshall

1914—Livengood

Sourdough Marriage Contract

Ten miles from the Yukon
On the banks of this lake
A partner to Koyukuk
McGillis, I take;
We have no preacher –
We have no ring –
It makes no difference
It's all the same thing.
AGGIE DALTON

I swear by my Gee-pole,
Under this tree
A faithful husband to Aggie
I always will be;
I'll love and protect her
This maiden so frail,
From the Sourdough bums
On the Koyukuk Trail.
FRANK McGILLIS

For two dollars apiece
In "cheechako" money
I unite this couple
In matrimony;
He be a rancher
She be a teacher
I do up the job
Just as well as a preacher.
FRENCH JOE

—From Ruth Allman's *Alaska Sourdough,* first published by Alaska Northwest Books in 1976. This message was carved on a birch tree during one of the early Alaskan gold stampedes.

GOLF

GOLF The Municipality of Anchorage maintains two golf courses—the Anchorage Golf Course on O'Malley Road, an 18-hole all-grass course offering views of the Chugach Range, the city and, on a clear day, Mount McKinley; and a 9-hole course (artificial turf greens) at Russian Jack Springs located at Boniface Parkway and Debarr Road. Tanglewood Lakes Golf Club offers a 9-hole all-grass course.

Two military courses are open to the public—Eagle Glen Golf Course (18 holes) at Elmendorf Air Force Base, and the 18-hole Moose Run Golf Course (the oldest golf course in Alaska) at Fort Richardson.

Palmer Municipal Golf Course (18 holes) has a driving range, clubhouse, and rental clubs and carts.

Fairbanks offers the 9-hole Fairbanks Golf and Country Club west of the downtown area, the 9-hole Chena Bend Golf Course at Fort Wainwright, and North Star Golf Club at 4.5 mile, Steese Highway, north of Fairbanks.

Mendenhall Golf Course in Juneau (9 holes) has a driving range, rental clubs and glacier views.

Every March, Kodiak holds the Pillar Mountain Golf Classic, an irreverent par-70 1-hole match up the side of 1,400-foot Pillar Mountain.

Muskeg Meadows, opened in 1998 in Wrangell, is a 9-hole, 36-acre regulation course and driving range. A tournament is held there annually in April.

During the summer months, golfers may tee off as late as 10 P.M. Die-hard golfers play in the winter using brightly painted balls. At the annual Lake Louise winter game in Wasilla, played on lake ice, golfers use orange balls that are highly visible on the snow and ice. Nome hosts the Bering Sea Ice Classic Golf Tournament in March and additional golf tournaments in September.

Alaska's northernmost golf course is in Coldfoot, featuring three holes, a driving range and rental clubs. Herds of musk-oxen are allowed to "play through."

Other golf courses can be found throughout the state, including Birch Ridge in Soldotna and Settlers Bay in Knik. An occasional private campground will offer putting greens or mini-golf for guests.

GOVERNMENT

GOVERNMENT (SEE ALSO Courts; Government Officials) Alaska is represented in the U.S. Congress by two senators and one representative. The capital of Alaska is Juneau.

A governor and lieutenant governor are elected by popular vote for four-year terms on the same ticket. The governor is given extensive powers under the constitution, overseeing 15 major departments: Administration, Commerce and Economic Development, Community and Regional Affairs, Corrections, Education, Environmental Conservation, Fish and Game, Health and Social Services, Labor, Law, Military and Veterans Affairs, Natural Resources, Public Safety, Revenue, and Transportation and Public Facilities.

The Legislature is bicameral, with 20 senators elected from a total of 20 senate districts for four-year terms, and 40 representatives from 27 election districts for 2-year terms. Under the state constitution, redistricting is done every 10 years, after the reporting of the decennial federal census. The judiciary

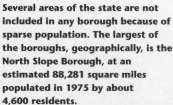

NUGGETS

Local government is by a system of organized boroughs, much like counties in other states. Several areas of the state are not included in any borough because of sparse population. The largest of the boroughs, geographically, is the North Slope Borough, at an estimated 88,281 square miles populated in 1975 by about 4,600 residents.

—1977 *The ALASKA ALMANAC*®

Governor Tony Knowles. Photo courtesy Office of the Governor.

consists of a state supreme court, court of appeals, superior court, district courts and magistrates.

Alaska is unique among the 50 states in not having most of its land mass organized into political subdivisions equivalent to the county form of government. Local government is by a system of organized boroughs, much like counties in other states. Several areas of the state are not included in any borough because of sparse population. Boroughs generally provide a more limited number of services than cities.

There are two classes of boroughs. First- and second-class boroughs have three mandatory powers: education, land use planning, and tax assessment and collection. The major difference between the two classes is in how they may acquire other powers. Both classes have separately elected borough assemblies and school boards. All boroughs may assess, levy and collect real and personal property taxes. They may also levy sales taxes.

Incorporated cities are small units of local government, serving one community. There are two classes. First-class cities, generally urban areas, have six-member councils and a separately elected mayor. Taxing authority is somewhat

broader than for second-class cities and responsibilities are broader. A first-class city that has adopted a home rule charter is called a home rule city; adoption allows the city to revise its ordinances within lawful limits. Second-class cities, generally places with fewer than 400 people, are governed by a seven-member council, one of whom serves as mayor. Taxing authority is limited. A borough and all cities located within it may unite in a single unit of government called a unified municipality.

There are 246 federally recognized tribal governments in Alaska and one community (Metlakatla, originally an Indian reservation) organized under federal law.

In 2000, there were 16 organized boroughs and unified home rule municipalities: 3 unified home rule municipalities, 5 home rule boroughs, 7 second-class boroughs.

Alaska's 149 incorporated cities include 12 home rule cities, 21 first-class cities and 116 second-class cities.

Alaska's Boroughs

Aleutians East Borough, P.O. Box 349, Sand Point 99661; (907) 383-2699; fax (907) 383-3496; www.aleutians east.org.

Municipality of Anchorage, P.O. Box 196650, Anchorage 99519; (907) 343-4431; fax (907) 343-4499; www.ci. anchorage.ak.us.

Bristol Bay Borough, P.O. Box 189, Naknek 99633; (907) 246-4224; fax (907) 246-6633; www.theborough.com.

In one of his first acts as mayor of Anchorage, George Weurch took steps to ease the restrictions on owning machine guns and grenades in the city. At the same time, a bumper sticker started appearing that read, "If guns are outlawed, only outlaws will accidentally shoot their children."

Denali Borough, P.O. Box 480, Healy 99743; (907) 683-1330; fax (907) 683-1340; www.mtaonline.net/~dbgovt/borough.html.

Fairbanks North Star Borough, P.O. Box 71267, Fairbanks, 99707; (907) 459-1000; fax (907) 459-1102; www.co.fairbanks.ak.us.

Haines Borough, P.O. Box 1209, Haines, AK 99827; (907) 766-2711; fax (907) 766-2716; www.haines.ak.us.

City and Borough of Juneau, 155 South Seward St., Juneau 99801; (907) 586-5240; fax (907) 586-5385; www.juneau.lib.ak.us; www.juneau.org.

Kenai Peninsula Borough, 144 North Binkley St., Soldotna, AK 99669; (907) 262-4441; fax (907) 262-1892; www.borough.kenai.ak.us.

Ketchikan Gateway Borough, 344 Front St., Ketchikan, 99901; (907) 228-6625; fax (907) 247-0483; www.borough.ketchikan.ak.us.

Kodiak Island Borough, 710 Mill Bay Road, Kodiak 99615; (907) 486-9300; fax (907) 486-9374; www.kib.co.kodiak.ak.us.

Lake and Peninsula Borough, P.O. Box 495, King Salmon 99613; (907) 246-3421; fax (907) 246-6602; www.bristolbay.com/~lpboro.

Matanuska-Susitna Borough, 350 East Dahlia Ave., Palmer 99645; (907) 745-4801; fax (907) 745-9845; www.co.mat-su.ak.us.

North Slope Borough, P.O. Box 69, Barrow 99723; (907) 852-2611; fax (907) 852-0337; www.co.north-slope.ak.us.

Northwest Arctic Borough, P.O. Box 1110, Kotzebue 99752; (907) 442-2500; fax (907) 442-2930; www.northwestarctic borough.org.

City and Borough of Sitka, 100 Lincoln St., Sitka 99835; (907) 747-1812; fax (907) 747-7403; www.cityof sitka.com.

City and Borough of Yakutat, P.O. Box 160, Yakutat 99689; (907) 784-3323; fax (907) 784-3281; bmanager@pti/pwescott@pti.

GOVERNMENT OFFICIALS

Russian Alaska

Emperor Paul of Russia granted the Russian-American Company an exclusive trade charter in Alaska.

Chief Manager	Dates Served
Alexander Andrevich Baranov	1799–1818
Leonti Andreanovich Hagemeiste	January–October 1818
Semen Ivanovich Yanovski	1818–1820
Matxei I. Muravief	1820–1825
Peter Egorovich Chistiakov	1825–1830
Baron Ferdinand P. von Wrangell	1830–1835
Ivan Antonovich Kupreanof	1835–1840
Adolph Karlovich Etolin	1840–1845
Michael D. Tebenkof	1845–1850
Nikolai Y. Rosenberg	1850–1853
Alexander Ilich Rudakof	1853–1854
Stephen Vasili Voevodski	1854–1859
Ivan V. Furuhelm	1859–1863
Prince Dmitri Maksoutoff	1863–1867

Territory of Alaska

United States purchased Alaska from Russia in 1867; U.S. Army was given jurisdiction over Department of Alaska.

Army Commanding Officers	Dates Served
Bvt. Maj. Gen. Jefferson C. Davis	Oct. 18, 1867–Aug. 31, 1870
Bvt. Lt. Col. George K. Brady	Sept. 1, 1870–Sept. 22, 1870
Maj. John C. Tidball	Sept. 23, 1870–Sept. 19, 1871
Maj. Harvey A. Allen	Sept. 20, 1871–Jan. 3, 1873
Maj. Joseph Stewart	Jan. 4, 1873–April 20, 1874
Capt. George R. Rodney	April 21, 1874–Aug. 16, 1874
Capt. Joseph B. Campbell	Aug. 17, 1874–June 14, 1876
Capt. John Mendenhall	June 15, 1876–March 4, 1877
Capt. Arthur Morris	March 5, 1877–June 14, 1877

U.S. Army troops left Alaska in 1877; the highest-ranking federal official left in Alaska was the U.S. collector of customs. The Department of Alaska was put under control of the U.S. Treasury Department.

U.S. Collectors of Customs	Dates Served
Montgomery P. Berry	June 14, 1877–Aug. 13, 1877
H. C. DeAhna	Aug. 14, 1877–March 26, 1878
Mottrom D. Ball	March 27, 1878–June 13, 1879

In 1879 the U.S. Navy was given jurisdiction over the Department of Alaska.

Navy Commanding Officers	Dates Served
Capt. L. A. Beardslee	June 14, 1879–Sept. 12, 1880
Comdr. Henry Glass	Sept. 13, 1880–Aug. 9, 1881
Comdr. Edward Lull	Aug. 10, 1881–Oct. 18, 1881
Comdr. Henry Glass	Oct. 19, 1881–March 12, 1882
Comdr. Frederick Pearson	March 13, 1882–Oct. 3, 1882
Comdr. Edgar C. Merriman	Oct. 4, 1882–Sept. 13, 1883
Comdr. Joseph B. Coghlan	Sept. 15, 1883–Sept. 13, 1884
Lt. Comdr. Henry E. Nichols	Sept. 14, 1884–Sept. 15, 1884

Congress provided civil government for the new District of Alaska in 1884; on Aug. 24, 1912, territorial status was given to Alaska. The U.S. president appointed territorial governors.

Presidential Appointment	Dates Served
John H. Kinkead (President Arthur)	July 4, 1884–May 7, 1885
Alfred P. Swineford (President Cleveland)	May 7, 1885–April 20, 1889
Lyman E. Knapp (President Harrison)	April 20, 1889–June 18, 1893
James Sheakley (President Cleveland)	June 18, 1893–June 23, 1897
John G. Brady (President McKinley)	June 23, 1897–March 2, 1906
Wilford B. Hoggatt (President Theodore Roosevelt)	March 2, 1906–May 20, 1909
Walter E. Clark (President Taft)	May 20, 1909–April 18, 1913
John F.A. Strong (President Wilson)	April 18, 1913–April 12, 1918
Thomas Riggs Jr. (President Wilson)	April 12, 1918–June 16, 1921
Scott C. Bone (President Harding)	June 16, 1921–Aug. 16, 1925
George A. Parks (President Coolidge)	Aug. 16, 1925–April 19, 1933
John W. Troy (President Franklin Roosevelt)	April 19, 1933–Dec. 6, 1939
Ernest Gruening (President Franklin Roosevelt)	Dec. 6, 1939–April 10, 1953
B. Frank Heintzleman (President Eisenhower)	April 10, 1953–Jan. 3, 1957
Mike Stepovich (President Eisenhower)	April 8, 1957–Aug. 9, 1958

In 1906, Congress authorized Alaska to send a voteless delegate to the House of Representatives.

Delegate to Congress	Dates Served
Frank H. Waskey	1906–1907
Thomas Cale	1907–1909
James Wickersham	1909–1917
Charles A. Sulzer	1917–contested election
James Wickersham	1918, seated as delegate
Charles A. Sulzer	1919, elected; died before taking office
George Grigsby	1919, elected in a special election
James Wickersham	1921, seated as delegate, having contested election of Grigsby
Dan A. Sutherland	1921–1930
James Wickersham	1931–1933
J. Dimond	1933–1944
E. L. Bartlett	1944–1958

Unofficial delegates to Congress to promote statehood, elected under a plan first devised by Tennessee. The Tennessee Plan delegates were not seated by Congress but did serve as lobbyists.

Senator	Dates Served
William Egan	1956–1958
Ernest Gruening	1956–1958

Representative	Dates Served
Ralph Rivers	1956–1958

State of Alaska
Alaska became a state Jan. 3, 1959, and sent two senators and one representative to the U.S. Congress.

Governor	Dates Served
William A. Egan	Jan 3. 1959–Dec. 5, 1966
Walter J. Hickel*	Dec. 5, 1966–Jan. 29, 1969
Keith H. Miller*	Jan 29, 1969–Dec. 7, 1970
William A. Egan	Dec. 7, 1970–Dec. 2, 1974
Jay S. Hammond	Dec. 2, 1974–Dec. 6, 1982
Bill Sheffield	Dec. 6, 1982–Dec. 1, 1986
Steve Cowper	Dec. 1, 1986–Dec. 3, 1990
Walter J. Hickel	Dec. 3, 1990–Dec. 5, 1994
Tony Knowles	Dec. 5, 1994–

*Hickel resigned before completing his first full term as governor to accept the position of secretary of the interior. He was succeeded by Miller.

Addresses
Gov. Tony Knowles, Office of the Governor, P.O. Box 110001, Juneau 99811-0001; www.gov.state.ak.us.

Lt. Gov. Fran Ulmer, Office of the Lieutenant Governor, P.O. Box 110015, Juneau 99811-0015.

U.S. Congressional Delegation

Senator	Dates Served
E. L. Bartlett	1958–1968
Ernest Gruening	1958–1968
Mike Gravel	1968–1980
Ted Stevens	1968–
Frank H. Murkowski	1980–

Representative	Dates Served
Ralph Rivers	1958–1966
Howard Pollock	1966–1970
Nicholas Begich	1970–1972
Donald E. Young	1972–

Addresses

Sen. Ted Stevens, U.S. Senate, 522 Hart Senate Office Bldg., Washington, D.C. 20510; (202) 224-3004; fax (907) 224-2354; senator_stevens@stevens.senate.gov; www.senate.gov/~stevens.

Sen. Frank H. Murkowski, U.S. Senate, 709 Hart Senate Office Bldg., Washington, D.C. 20510; (202) 224-6665; fax (202) 224-5301; e-mail@murkowski. senate.gov; www.senate.gov/~murkowski.

Rep. Donald E. Young, House of Representatives, 2111 Rayburn House Office Bldg., Washington, D.C. 20515; (202) 225-5765; fax (202) 225-0425; don.young@mall.house.gov; www.house.gov/donyoung.

Alaska State Legislature

During sessions, members of the legislature receive mail at the State Capitol, Juneau 99801-1182. Direct e-mail to a specific legislator by typing Senator OR Representative_First name_Lastname@ legis.state.ak.us. The legislature's Web site is www.legis.state.ak.us.

House of Representatives

District 1: Bill Williams (R)
District 2: Peggy Wilson (R)
District 3: Beth Kerftula (D)
District 4: Bill Hudson (R)
District 5: Albert Kookesh (D)
District 6: Gary Stevens (R)
District 7: Drew Scalzi (R)
District 8: Ken Lancaster (R)
District 9: Mike Chenault (R)
District 10: Joseph Green (R)
District 11: Norman Rokeberg (R)
District 12: Andrew Halcro (R)
District 13: Ethan Berkowitz (D)
District 14: Lisa Murkowski (R)
District 15: Eric Croft (D)
District 16: Gretchen Guess (D)
District 17: John Cowdery (R)
District 18: Con Bunde (R)
District 19: Kevin Meyer (R)
District 20: Brian Porter (R)
District 21: Sharon Cissna (D)
District 22: Harry Crawford (D)
District 23: Eldon Mulder (R)
District 24: Pete Kott (R)
District 25: Fred Dyson (R)
District 26: Vic Kohring (R)
District 27: Scott Ogan (R)
District 28: Beverly Masek (R)
District 29: John Davies (D)
District 30: Joe Hayes (D)
District 31: Jim Whitaker (R)
District 32: John Coghill Jr. (R)
District 33: Hugh (Bud) Fate (R)
District 34: Jeannette James (R)
District 35: John Harris (R)
District 36: Carl Morgan (R)
District 37: Reggie Joule (D)
District 38: Richard Foster (D)
District 39: Mary Kapsner (D)
District 40: Carl Moses (D)

Alaska Senate

District A: Robin Taylor (R)
District B: Kim Elton (D)
District C: Alan Austerman (R)
District D: John Torgerson (R)

NUGGETS

Gov. Walter Hickel proposes to pump 12 trillion gallons of water a year to California through a 1,700-mile plastic pipeline under the Pacific Ocean. The state could stand to make $10 million a year by selling the water.

—1991 *The ALASKA ALMANAC*®

Alaska Senate (continued)

District E: Jerry Ward (R)
District F: Drue Pearce (R)
District G: Loren Leman (R)
District H: Johnny Ellis (D)
District I: John Cowdery (R)
District J: Dave Donley (R)
District K: Bettye Davis (D)
District L: Randy Phillips (R)
District M: Rick Halford (R)
District N: Lyda Green (R)
District O: Gary Wilken (R)
District P: Pete Kelly (R)
District Q: Gene Therriault (R)
District R: Georgianna Lincoln (D)
District S: Donald Olson (D)
District T: Lyman Hoffman (D)

HIGHWAYS (SEE ALSO Alaska Highway;
Dalton Highway) As of January 1999, the
state Department of Transportation and
Public Facilities estimated total public road
mileage in Alaska at 12,666 centerline
miles, including those in national and state
parks and forests (1,640). The state also
operates 2,775˚miles of ferry routes.

Highways in Alaska range from six-lane

NUGGETS

The oil pipeline haul road,
the only major road
through the Arctic, is
closed to public use.
Commercial transportation is by air.
—1976 *The ALASKA ALMANAC*®

paved freeways to one-lane dirt and
gravel roads.

Approximately 30 percent of the roads
in the Alaska highway system are paved.
The following major highways are all or
partially gravel: Steese (Alaska Route 6),
Taylor (Alaska Route 5), Elliott (Alaska Route
2), Dalton (Alaska Route 11) and Denali
(Alaska Route 8). Alaska's relative lack of
roadway is accentuated by a comparison to
Austria, a country only one-eighteenth the
size of Alaska but with nearly twice as many
miles of road.

The newest highway in the state system,

Major Highways in Alaska

Route/ Highway	Number	Year Opened	Total Length (miles) in Alaska Paved	Gravel	Open
Alaska*	2	1942	198		All year
Copper River**	10		12	38	Apr.–Oct.
Dalton	11	1974	55	359	All year
Denali	8	1957	21.4	113	Apr.–Oct.
Edgerton	10	1923	33		All year
Elliott	2	1959	30	122	All year
George Parks	3	1971	324		All year
Haines*	7	1947	44		All year
Klondike*	2	1978	15		All year
Richardson	4	1923	363		All year
Seward/Glenn	9&1	1951	305		All year
Steese	6	1928	44	112	All year
Sterling	1	1950	138		All year
Taylor	5	1953	23	135	Apr.–Oct.
Tok Cutoff	1	1940	122		All year

*Most of the highway lies within Canada.

**Construction of the Copper River Highway, which was to link up with Chitina on the Edgerton
  Highway, was halted by the 1964 Good Friday earthquake, which damaged the
  Million Dollar Bridge.

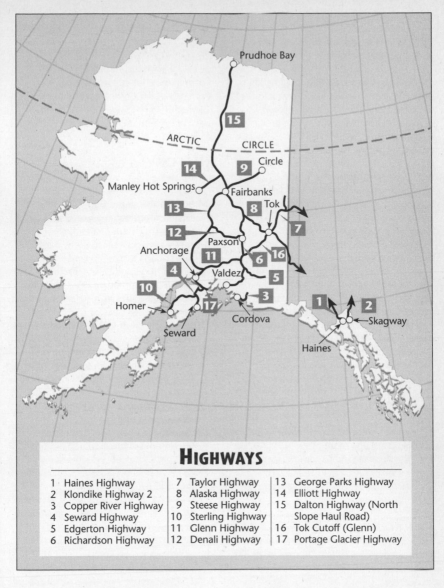

HIGHWAYS

1 Haines Highway	7 Taylor Highway	13 George Parks Highway
2 Klondike Highway 2	8 Alaska Highway	14 Elliott Highway
3 Copper River Highway	9 Steese Highway	15 Dalton Highway (North
4 Seward Highway	10 Sterling Highway	Slope Haul Road)
5 Edgerton Highway	11 Glenn Highway	16 Tok Cutoff (Glenn)
6 Richardson Highway	12 Denali Highway	17 Portage Glacier Highway

Portage Glacier Highway, connects the Seward Highway south of Anchorage with the town of Whittier on Prince William Sound. In April 2001, a toll was instituted for the highway's Anton Anderson Memorial Tunnel—at 2.5 miles long, North America's longest highway tunnel. Cars and vehicles without trailers are charged $15; RVs and vehicles with trailers pay a $40 toll.

Although cruise traffic to Alaska is growing, road traffic from Outside is on the decline. The number of visitors crossing Alaska–Canada borders dropped almost 6 percent in 2000, a figure that varied depending on the location of the border crossing.

For weather and updated road conditions, travelers may call (800)

478-7675 for a recorded message that includes avalanche warnings and weight restrictions on the Alaska highway system; also www.dot.state.ak.us.

HIKING Developed trails suitable for all ability levels may be found near Alaska's larger cities and towns. However most of Alaska's public recreation lands are wilderness. Trails are nonexistent and hikers must chart their own course using topographic maps and a compass. Using both maps and tide tables, it is also possible to hike along ocean shorelines at low tide.

Hikers in Alaska must plan for cold, wet and rapidly changing weather. Take rain gear. If staying overnight in the backcountry, carry a tent, backpacking stove, first-aid kit and emergency flares. Snow can be encountered in any season.

Plan to bring everything you need with you. Some businesses rent canoes and kayaks, but few rent personal gear such as backpacks. Backcountry guides often furnish equipment on escorted expeditions.

Bears inhabit most of Alaska. Read all bear safety information and follow safe procedures for camping and hiking in bear country. You must be completely self-sufficient and responsible for your own safety. (SEE Bears)

Information on hiking in Alaska's national parks and monuments is available from the Alaska Public Lands Information Centers: 605 W. Fourth Ave., Suite 105, Anchorage 99501, (907) 271-2737;

250 Cushman St., Suite 1A, Fairbanks 99701, (907) 456-0527; P.O. Box 359, Tok 99780, (907) 883-5667; and 50 Main St., Ketchikan 99901, (907) 228-6220; or from park headquarters for the area you're interested in. (SEE National Parks, Preserves and Monuments) The Alaska Division of Parks (SEE State Park System) has information on hiking on the lands managed by that agency.

HISTORY (SEE ALSO Gold Strikes and Rushes; Russian Alaska)

11,000–6,000 years ago—Humans inhabit southeastern, Aleutians, Interior and northwestern Arctic Alaska.

6,000 years ago—Most recent migration from Siberia across the land bridge. Earliest migration believed to have taken place up to 20,000 or more years ago.

5,000–3,000 years ago—Humans inhabit the Bering Sea Coast.

1725—Vitus Bering sent by Peter the Great to explore the North Pacific.

1741—On a later expedition, Bering and Alexei Chirikof, in separate ships, sight Alaska. Georg Steller goes ashore on Kayak Island, becoming the first European known to have set foot on Alaska soil.

1743—Russians begin concentrated hunting of sea otter, continuing until the species is almost decimated.

1772—A permanent Russian settlement is established at Unalaska.

1774–94—Explorations of Alaska waters by Juan Perez, James Cook and George Vancouver.

1784—First Russian settlement is established on Kodiak Island at Three Saints Bay.

1794—George Vancouver sights Mount McKinley.

1799—Alexander Baranov establishes the Russian post known today as Old Sitka. A trade charter is granted to the Russian-American Company.

1821—Russians prohibit trading in Alaska waters by other nations, making the Russian-American Company the sole trading firm.

The Bumper Sticker of the Year award goes to the Anchorage car that proudly claimed: "My son made the Honor Pod at the Spring Creek Correctional Center in Seward."

1824–42—Russian exploration of the mainland leads to the discovery of the Kuskokwim, Nushagak, Yukon and Koyukuk Rivers.

1837—Father Herman, last survivor of the original Russian missionaries to Alaska, dies on Spruce Island near Kodiak.

1845—The Missionary School at Sitka opens, offering the study of the Aleut, Tlingit and Eskimo languages, medicine and Latin.

1847—Fort Yukon is established by Hudson's Bay Company.

1848—American whalers first enter the Arctic Ocean through Bering Strait.

1853—Russian explorer-trappers find the first oil seeps in Cook Inlet.

1855—The U.S. Navy explores the North Pacific around the Aleutian Islands and the Bering Sea.

1859—Baron Edouard de Stoeckl, minister and *chargé d'affaires* of the Russian delegation to the United States, is given authority to negotiate the sale of Alaska.

1860—Russians estimate Native Alaskan Christians at 12,000, with 35 chapels, 9 churches, 17 schools and 3 orphanages in 43 communities.

1866—Alaska's first newspaper, *The Esquimeaux,* is published in manuscript at Libbyville.

1867—United States under President Andrew Johnson buys Alaska from Russia for $7.2 million; the treaty is signed March 30 and formal transfer takes place Oct. 18 at Sitka. Fur seal population begins to stabilize. U.S. Army is given jurisdiction over the Department of Alaska.

1869–70—The *Alaska Times,* the first newspaper to be printed in Alaska, is published in Sitka.

1872—Gold is discovered near Sitka.

1873—Frederick Schwatka conducts a military reconnaissance of Alaska's Interior.

1878—First salmon canneries established at Klawock and Old Sitka.

1882—First commercial herring fishing begins. U.S. Navy destroys the Tlingit village of Angoon.

1884—An Organic Act gives Alaska its first civil government.

1885—Lt. Henry Allen explores the Copper River.

1891—First oil claims staked in Cook Inlet area.

1897–1900—Klondike gold rush in Yukon Territory; heavy traffic through Alaska on the way to the goldfields.

1898—Gold is discovered on Nome beaches. Frank Reid shoots and kills con artist Soapy Smith in Skagway. U.S. Geological Survey begins mapping Alaska.

1902—First oil production, at Katalla. Telegraph from Eagle to Valdez is completed.

1906—Peak gold production year. Alaska is granted a nonvoting delegate to Congress. Governor's office moves from Sitka to Juneau.

1911—Copper production begins at Kennicott.

1912—Territorial status for Alaska; first territorial Legislature is convened the following year. Mount Katmai erupts.

Many children joined their parents in the gold rushes of the North. UAF Archives, Margaret Lentz Collection. From *Children of the Gold Rush* by Claire Rudolf Murphy and Jane G. Haigh.

1913—First airplane flight in Alaska, at Fairbanks. First automobile trip from Fairbanks to Valdez.

1914—President Woodrow Wilson authorizes construction of the Alaska Railroad.

1916—First bill proposing Alaska statehood is introduced in Congress. Peak copper production year.

1917—Creation of Mount McKinley National Park. Founding of Wasilla.

1918—Worldwide epidemic of Spanish flu decimates Alaska's Native population. Creation of Katmai National Monument.

1922—First pulp mill starts production at Speel River near Juneau.

1923—President Warren Harding drives spike completing the Alaska Railroad.

1930—The first "talkie" motion picture is shown in Fairbanks, featuring the Marx Brothers in *The Cocoanuts.*

1935—Matanuska Valley Project, which moves farming families to Alaska, begins. First Juneau-to-Fairbanks flight.

1936—All-time record salmon catch in Alaska—126.4 million fish. Black Rapids Glacier advances 3 miles in three months, coming within a half mile of the Richardson Highway.

1937—Nell Scott is the first woman appointed to the Alaska Legislature.

1940—Military buildup in Alaska; Fort Richardson, Elmendorf Air Force Base are established. Alaska's population includes about 32,000 Natives and 40,000 non-Native Alaskans. Pan American Airways inaugurates twice-weekly service between Seattle, Ketchikan and Juneau, using Sikorsky flying boats.

1942—Dutch Harbor is bombed and Attu and Kiska islands are occupied by Japanese forces. Alaska Highway is built—first overland connection to Lower 48.

1943—Japanese forces are driven from Alaska.

1953—Oil well is drilled near Eureka, on the Glenn Highway, marking the start of modern oil history.

1957—Kenai oil strike.

1958—Statehood measure is passed

by Congress; statehood is proclaimed officially on Jan. 3, 1959; first general election is held.

1963—State ferry service to Southeast Alaska begins.

1964—Good Friday earthquake of March 27 causes heavy damage throughout the Gulf Coast region; 131 people are killed.

1967—Fairbanks flood.

1968—Oil and gas discoveries at Prudhoe Bay on the North Slope; $900 million North Slope oil lease sale the following year; pipeline proposal follows.

1970—Federal government sets aside 500,000 acres for Chugach State Park.

1971—Congress approves Alaska Native Claims Settlement Act, granting title to 40 million acres of land and providing $962.5 million in payment to Alaska Natives.

1973—The first 1,100-mile sled dog race begins March 3, following part of an old dog team mail route blazed in 1910; it's called the Iditarod Trail Sled Dog Race.

1974—Trans-Alaska pipeline receives final approval; construction buildup begins.

1975—Population and labor force soar with construction of pipeline. Alaska gross product hits $5.8 billion—double the 1973 figure.

1976—Voters select Willow area for new capital site.

1977—Completion of the trans-Alaska oil pipeline from Prudhoe Bay to Valdez; shipment of first oil by tanker from Valdez to Puget Sound.

1978—A 200-mile offshore fishing limit goes into effect. President Jimmy Carter withdraws 56 million acres of federal lands in Alaska to create 17 new national monuments. Congress designates the Iditarod as a National Historic Trail.

1979—State of Alaska files suit to halt the withdrawal of 56 million acres of Alaska land by President Carter under the Antiquities Act.

1980—Alaska Legislature votes to repeal the state income tax and establishes Permanent Fund as a repository for one-fourth of all royalty oil revenues for future generations. Census figures show Alaska's population grew by 32.4 percent during the 1970s. The Alaska National Interest Lands Conservation Act of 1980 puts 53.7 million Alaska acres into the national wildlife refuge system, parts of 25 rivers into the national wild and scenic rivers system, 3.3 million acres into national forest lands and 43.6 million acres into national park land.

1981—Secretary of the Interior James Watt initiates plans to sell oil and gas leases on 130 million acres of Alaska's nonrestricted federal land and to open 16 offshore areas of Alaska to oil and gas development.

1982—Voters turn down authorization of funds to move the state capital from Juneau to Willow, leaving the capital at Juneau. First Permanent Fund dividend checks of $1,000 each are mailed to every six-month resident of Alaska.

1983—All Alaska, except westernmost Aleutian Islands, moves to Alaska Standard Time, one hour ahead of Pacific Standard Time. Record-breaking salmon harvest in Bristol Bay. Building permits set a record at just under $1 billion.

1984—State of Alaska celebrates its 25th birthday.

1985—Anchorage receives the U.S. bid for the 1994 Winter Olympics. Iditarod Trail Sled Dog Race is won by Libby Riddles, the first woman to win in the history of the race.

1986—Mount Augustine in lower Cook Inlet erupts. World Championship Sled Dog Race held during Fur Rendezvous is canceled for the first time for lack of snow. Iditarod Trail Sled Dog Race is again won by a woman, Susan Butcher of Manley.

1987—Iditarod Trail Sled Dog Race is won by Susan Butcher for the second consecutive year.

1988—The Iditarod Trail Sled Dog Race is won by Susan Butcher for the third year in a row. Anchorage loses its bid for the 1994 Winter Olympics to Norway.

1989—Worst oil spill in U.S. history occurs in Prince William Sound when the *Exxon Valdez* runs aground. Record-breaking cold hits entire state, lasting for weeks. Soviets visit Alaska, and the Bering Bridge Expedition crosses the Bering Strait by dogsled and skis.

1990—Valdez sets a new record for snowfall. Susan Butcher wins her fourth Iditarod Trail Sled Dog Race. Election upset as Walter J. Hickel becomes governor.

1991—Fairbanks sets a new record for snowfall. Rick Swenson claims fifth Iditarod win.

1992—Alaska celebrates 50th anniversary of the Alaska Highway. One of Alaska's oldest newspapers, the *Anchorage Times*, shuts down. Mount Spurr erupts.

1993—The Department of Fish and Game announces a plan to allow aerial hunting of wolves.

1994—Diseased herring appear in Prince William Sound for the second season. Exxon is found guilty of recklessness in the 1989 oil spill in Prince William Sound. Alaska skier Tommy Moe is a gold medalist at the Olympic Games in Norway.

1995—Two Anchorage residents are killed by a grizzly along a trail in a popular hiking area of Chugach State Park.

1996—Princess Tours' Denali Lodge burns down in March but is rebuilt by June.

State Historian Rolfe Buzzell reported that the log cabin at the Indian Valley Mine was struck by an avalanche in the 1930s. It rolled over and came to rest slightly farther down the slope. The federal government questioned whether to grant the building's current status on the National Register of Historic Places because it had been "moved from its original location."

Alaska's worst wildfire destroys
$8.8 million in homes and other
buildings.

1997—Legislature approves 71-cent tax
increase per cigarette pack. Arco Alaska
and British Petroleum announce plans
to develop two more North Slope oil
fields.

1998—Falling oil prices force state to use
budget reserve funds.

1999—BP–Amoco buys out competitor
Arco Alaska. Joe Redington Sr., "Father"
of the Iditarod Trail Sled Dog Race, dies
at his home in Knik.

2000—Alaskans vote down a statewide
cap on property taxes and a measure to
legalize marijuana. Banker and philanthropist Elmer Rasmuson dies at 91.

2001—Fifteen crewmen aboard the *Arctic
Rose* die when the 92-foot vessel sinks
in the Bering Sea on April 2. Delegates
from 62 Alaska tribes sign an agreement
formalizing tribal relations with the
state.

HOLIDAYS IN 2002

New Year's Day . . . . Jan. 1
Martin Luther King Day . . . . Jan. 21
Presidents' Day
 —holiday . . . . Feb. 18
 —traditional . . . . Feb. 22
Seward's Day* . . . . March 25
Memorial Day
 —holiday . . . . May 27
 —traditional . . . . May 30
Independence Day . . . . July 4
Labor Day . . . . Sept. 2
Alaska Day** . . . . Oct. 18
Veterans Day . . . . Nov. 11
Thanksgiving Day . . . . Nov. 28
Christmas Day . . . . Dec. 25

 *Seward's Day commemorates the signing of the
 treaty by which the United States bought Alaska
 from Russia, signed on March 30, 1867.
 **Alaska Day is the anniversary of the formal
 transfer of the territory and the raising of the U.S.
 flag at Sitka on Oct. 18, 1867.

HOMESTEADING (See also Land Use)
Until 1995, any Alaska resident of at least

one year, 18 years or older and a U.S.
citizen, had a chance to receive up to
40 acres of nonagricultural land or up
to 160 acres of agricultural land nearly
free. To receive title the homesteader was
required to pay a $10 application fee and
either survey or reimburse the state for
survey costs, brush and stake the parcel
boundary, build a dwelling, and occupy
and improve the land in certain ways within
specific time frames. This is called "proving
up" on the homestead.

The last available parcel was won in a
lottery in early 1997.

The State Homestead Act also allowed
homesteaders to purchase parcels at
fair market value without occupying or
improving the property. In this category,
some subdivision lots are left from a
1995 auction; nonresidents may purchase
these parcels.

Many of the original homesteaders were
veterans who came to Alaska during the
late 1940s and early 1950s. They had to
brush up their boundaries within 90 days
after issuance of the entry permit, complete
an approved survey of the land within
two or five years (depending on purchase
option), erect a habitable permanent
dwelling on the homestead within three
years, and live on the parcel for 25 months
within five years. If the parcel was classified
for agricultural use, homesteaders labored
mightily to clear and put into production
or cultivation 25 percent of the land
within five years.

HOOLIGAN Smelt, also known as
eulachon or candlefish, are "ooligan" in
southeastern Alaska. The Tlingit dried
these oily little fish, inserted a twisted
spruce bark wick and used them as candles.
The Tlingit caught the 9-inch fish in great
numbers, ripened them for several days to
speed the release of the oil from the flesh
and then rendered their oil in baskets or
cooking pots. The flavor and color of the
oil, or "grease," were determined by
the length of time the fish ripened. The
oil was stored in bulb kelp "jars" corked
with wooden plugs or in bentwood boxes.
Some of the oil was traded with Interior

people by packing it over timeworn paths which became known as grease trails. The Tlingit considered hooligan vital to their diet and gallons of the oil were consumed during the winter as a nutritious dip for dried foods.

Hooligan, now considered a subsistence or sport catch only, are caught by dip-netting as they travel upriver to spawn. Hooligan resemble trout in general structure and have a distinctive odor and taste. The flesh is ivory colored, extremely perishable and should be cooked or pickled the same day it is caught.

HOSPITALS AND HEALTH FACILITIES (SEE ALSO Pioneers' Homes)

Alaska has numerous hospitals, nursing homes and other health care facilities.

For a list of emergency medical services, contact the Office of Emergency Medical Services, Division of Public Health, Dept. of Health and Social Services, P.O. Box 110616, Juneau 99811-0616.

Municipal, Private and State Facilities

Anchorage: Alaska Psychiatric Institute (95 beds), 2900 Providence Drive, 99508; Alaska Regional Hospital (238 beds), 2801 DeBarr Road, P.O. Box 143889, 99514-3889; Alaska Surgery Center, Laurel St., 99508-5396; Charter North Star Behavioral Health System (74 beds), 2530 DeBarr Road, 99508; Providence Alaska Medical Center (303 beds), 3200 Providence Drive, P.O. Box 196604, 99519-6604.

Cordova: Cordova Community Medical Center (23 beds), 602 Chasa Ave., P.O. Box 160, 99574.

Fairbanks: Fairbanks Memorial Hospital (162 beds), 1650 Cowles St., 99701.

Glennallen: Cross Roads Medical Center, P.O. Box 5, 99588.

Homer: South Peninsula Hospital (40 beds), 4300 Bartlett St., 99603.

Juneau: Bartlett Regional Hospital (55 beds), 3260 Hospital Drive, 99801.

Ketchikan: Ketchikan General Hospital (92 beds), 3100 Tongass Ave., 99901.

Kodiak: Providence Kodiak Medical Center (44 beds), 1915 E. Rezanof Drive, 99615.

Palmer: Valley Hospital (36 beds), P.O. Box 1687, 515 E. Dahlia, 99645.

Petersburg: Petersburg Medical Center (27 beds), P.O. Box 589, 103 Fram St., 99833.

Seward: Providence Seward Medical Center (6 beds), P.O. Box 365, 417 First Ave., 99664.

Sitka: Sitka Community Hospital (25 beds), 209 Moller Ave., P.O. Box 500, 99835.

Soldotna: Central Peninsula General Hospital (62 beds), 250 Hospital Place, 99669.

Valdez: Valdez Community Hospital (15 beds), P.O. Box 550, 911 Meal St., 99686.

Wrangell: Wrangell Medical Center (22 beds), P.O. Box 1081, 99929.

Tribal Health Facilities

Tribal organizations oversee a variety of health facilities in villages and urban centers.

Anchorage: Alaska Native Medical Center (140 beds), 4315 Diplomacy Drive, 99508.

Barrow: Samuel Simmonds Memorial Hospital (14 beds), P.O. Box 29, 99723-0029.

Bethel: Yukon–Kuskokwim Delta Regional Hospital (50 beds), P.O. Box 287, 99559.

Dillingham: Kanakanak Hospital (15 beds), P.O. Box 130, 99576.

Fairbanks: Chief Andrew Isaac Health Center, 1408 19th Ave., 99701.

Juneau: SEARHC Medical Clinic, 3245 Hospital Drive, 99801.

Ketchikan: KIC Tribal Health Clinic, 3289 Tongass Ave., 99901.

Kodiak: Kodiak Area Native Association, 3449 Rezanof Drive E., 99615.

Kotzebue: Maniilaq Health Center (17 beds), P.O. Box 43, 99752.

Metlakatla: Annette Island Service

Unit, P.O. Box 439, 99926.

Nome: Norton Sound Regional (36 beds), P.O. Box 966, 5 Bering St., 99762.

Sitka: SEARHC Mount Edgecumbe Hospital (78 beds), 222 Tongass Drive, 99835.

Military Hospitals

Eielson Air Force Base: Eielson Air Force Base Clinic, 354 MDG/SG, 3349 Central Ave., Suite 1M07, Eielson AFB 99702-2399.

Elmendorf AFB: Headquarters Third Medical Group, 5955 Zeamer Ave., Elmendorf AFB, 99506-3700.

Fort Richardson: U.S. Army Troop Medical Clinic, 99505.

Fort Wainwright: Bassett Army Community Hospital, 99703.

Ketchikan: Coast Guard Dispensary, 1300 Stedman St., 99901.

Kodiak: USCG Integrated Support Command, Rockmore–King Medical Clinic, P.O. Box 195002, 99619-5002.

Sitka: U.S. Coast Guard Air Station, 611 Airport Road, 99835.

Nursing Homes

Anchorage: Mary Conrad Center (89 beds), 9100 Centennial Drive, 99504; Providence Extended Care Center (224 beds), 4900 Eagle St., 99503.

Fairbanks: Denali Center (90 beds), 1510 19th Ave., 99701.

Juneau: St. Ann's Care Center (44 beds), 415 Sixth St., 99801.

Ketchikan: General Hospital Long Term Care Unit (46 beds), 3100 Tongass Ave., 99901.

Seward: Wesley Rehabilitation and Care Center (66 beds), P.O. Box 430, 431 First Ave., 99664.

Soldotna: Heritage Place (45 beds), 232 Rockwell Ave., 99669.

Chemical Dependency Centers

Alaska has 17 chemical dependency treatment centers, located in Anchorage, Eagle River, Fairbanks, Juneau, Palmer, Sitka and Wasilla. For details call the Alaska State Medical Association at (907) 562-0304.

HOSTELS Alaska has Hostelling International member hostels in the following locations:

Anchorage International Hostel, 700 H St., Anchorage 99501; (907) 276-3635; fax (907) 276-7722; www.alaska.net/~hianch. Corner of Seventh and H streets.

Hostelling International, Mile 3 Oil Well Road, P.O. Box 39083, Ninilchik 99639; (907) 567-3905.

Juneau International Hostel, 614 Harris St., Juneau 99801; (907) 586-9559; juneauhostel@gci.net. Four blocks northeast of the capitol building.

Ketchikan Youth Hostel, P.O. Box 8515, Ketchikan 99901; (907) 225-3319. In the United Methodist Church, Grant and Main streets.

Sitka Youth Hostel, P.O. Box 2645, Sitka 99835; (907) 747-8661. In the United Methodist Church, Edgecumbe and Kimsham streets.

Tok International Youth Hostel, P.O. Box 532, Tok 99780; (907) 883-3745. One mile south of Mile 1322.5 of the Alaska Highway on Pringle Drive.

The hostels accept reservations by mail. Opening and closing dates, maximum length of stay and hours vary.

Hostels are available to anyone with a valid membership card issued by one of the associations affiliated with Hostelling International. Membership is open to all ages. A valid membership card, which ranges in price from $10 to $250 (life), entitles a member to use hostels.

Hostel memberships and a guide to American Youth Hostels can be purchased from the state office (Alaska Council, HI–AYH, Box 240347, Anchorage 99524; 907-243-3844; fax 907-243-8780), national office (American Youth Hostels, 733 15th St., Suite 840, Washington, D.C. 20005; 202-783-6161; fax 202-783-6171; www.hiayh.org) or from most local hostels.

HOT SPRINGS The Alaska Division of Geological and Geophysical Surveys identifies 124 geothermal areas in the state that include hot springs, fumaroles, geothermal wells or a combination of these.

Most geothermal areas (56) occur along the Aleutian volcanic arc, 19 are located in the Southeast panhandle and 49 are scattered throughout mainland Alaska. Most are inaccessible by automobile.

Only 19 of these geothermal areas have experienced any sort of development, and only six hot spring areas provide resort facilities. Resorts with swimming pools, changing rooms, restaurants and lodging are found at Chena Hot Springs (a 62-mile drive east from Fairbanks) and Circle Hot Springs (136 miles northeast by road from Fairbanks). Although not accessible by road, Bell Island Hot Springs (40 air miles northeast of Ketchikan and accessible by boat) and Melozi Hot Springs (200 air miles northwest of Fairbanks) have lodging, pool and accommodations.

Less developed is Manley Hot Springs in the small community of the same name at the end of Elliott Highway (160 miles west of Fairbanks). The hot springs are privately owned and a primitive bathhouse is used primarily by local residents. Manley Hot Springs Resort is located near the springs, but its waters are supplied from a geothermal well. The resort does have a pool, restaurant and lodging facilities. Ophir Hot Springs (about 50 miles southwest of Aniak) has a private hunting camp with accommodations and an aboveground hot pool.

There are 11 additional springs with cabins and/or bathing tubs and changing facilities. Most of these are accessible only by boat, plane, snowmobile, dog team, ATV or on foot. Among them is the community of Tenakee Springs on Chichagof Island in southeastern Alaska, which maintains an old bathhouse near the waterfront for public use. The state Marine Highway System provides ferry service to Tenakee Springs. Chief Shakes Hot Springs, near Wrangell, and White Sulfur Hot Springs and Goddard Hot Springs, both near Sitka, all have Forest Service cabins and are accessible by boat or floatplane. Tolovana Hot Springs, 45 miles northwest of Fairbanks, features two cabins and a hot tub. Reservations are required. Visitors can soak and photograph the old

Chena Hot Springs lies about an hour northeast of Fairbanks. Photo by Roy Corral.

buildings that were once an orphanage at Pilgrim Hot Springs, 60 miles from Nome, accessible by road in summer only. Also on the Seward Peninsula is Serpentine Hot Springs, a winter destination by snow-mobile from Nome.

Other springs include Baranof Hot Springs on Baranof Island. Kanuti Hot Springs is about 10 miles west of the Dalton Highway near Caribou Mountain. These springs are used primarily by skiers and mushers in the winter.

A map featuring most of the thermal areas in Alaska can be purchased for $5 from the Alaska Division of Geological and Geophysical Surveys, 794 University Ave., Suite 200, Fairbanks 99709; (907) 451-5006; fax (907) 451-5050; www.dggs.dnr.state.ak.us.

HUNTING There are 26 game management units in Alaska with a wide variety of seasons and bag limits. Current copies of *Alaska State Hunting Regulations* with maps showing game unit boundaries are available from the Alaska Department of Fish and Game (P.O. Box 25526, Juneau 99802), from Fish and Game offices and sporting goods stores throughout the state, or at www.state.ak.us.

Both male and female Dall sheep grow horns. From *Alaska's Mammals* by Dave Smith (text) and Tom Walker (photographs).

Regulations. A hunting or trapping license is required for all residents and nonresidents with the exception of Alaska residents under 16 or older than 60. A special identification card is issued for the senior citizen exemption.

A resident hunting license (valid for the calendar year) costs $25; trapping license (valid until Sept. 30 of the year following the year of issue), $15; hunting and trapping license, $39; hunting and sportfishing license, $39; hunting, trapping and sportfishing license, $53.

A nonresident (U.S. citizen) hunting license (valid for the calendar year) costs $85; hunting and sportfishing license, $185; hunting and trapping license, $250. Non-U.S. citizens pay $300 for a big-game hunting license.

Military personnel stationed in Alaska may purchase a fishing license for $15, a small-game hunting license for $25, and a small-game hunting and sportfishing license for $39. Military personnel must purchase a nonresident hunting license at full cost ($85) and pay nonresident military fees for big-game tags (one-half the nonresident rate), unless they are hunting big game on military property.

Licenses may be obtained from any designated issuing agent, via the Internet at www.admin.adfg.state.ak.us/license, or by mail from the Alaska Department of Fish and Game, Licensing Division, P.O. Box 25525, Juneau 99802; (907) 465-2376.

Big-game tags and fees are required for residents hunting musk-oxen and brown/grizzly bear and for nonresidents and noncitizens hunting any big-game animal. These nonrefundable, nontransferable, locking tags (valid for the calendar year) must be purchased prior to the taking of the animal. A tag may be used for any species for which the tag fee is of equal or less value. Fees quoted below are for each animal.

All residents (regardless of age), nonresidents and aliens intending to hunt brown/grizzly bear must purchase tags (resident, $25; nonresident, $500; alien, $650). Residents, nonresidents and aliens are also required to purchase musk-oxen tags (resident, $500 each bull taken on Nunivak Island, $25 each cow from Nelson Island or in Arctic National Wildlife Refuge; nonresident, $1,100; alien, $1,500).

Nonresident tag fees for other big game animals: deer, $150; wolf, $30; black bear, $225; elk or goat, $300; caribou, $325; moose, $400; bison, $450; sheep, $425.

Nonresident alien tag fees for other big game animals: deer, $200; wolf, $50; black bear, $300; elk or goat, $400; caribou, $425; moose, $500; bison, $650; and sheep, $550.

Nonresidents hunting brown/grizzly bear, Dall sheep or mountain goat are required to have a guide or be accompanied by an Alaska resident relative over 19 within the second degree of kinship (includes parents, children, sisters or brothers). Nonresident aliens hunting big game must have a guide. A list of registered Alaska guides is available for $5 from the Department of Commerce, Division of Occupational Licensing, Big Game Commercial Services Board, P.O. Box 11806, Juneau 99811-0806.

Residents and nonresidents 16 or older hunting waterfowl must have a signed federal migratory bird hunting stamp (duck stamp) and a signed state waterfowl conservation stamp. The Alaska duck stamp is available from agents who sell hunting licenses, by mail from the Alaska Department of Fish and Game, Licensing Section, or at www.state.ak.us.

'Aklaq'–Respected and Feared

The traditional Inupiat attached great spiritual significance to the grizzly, whom they called *aklaq*. While they considered the black bear to be somewhat of a dimwit, they respected and feared the grizzly above all other animals. If a hunter killed one, the skin became the door of his house, and whoever entered was notified of the man's bravery and skill. Considering how bears were hunted in the days before firearms, such a door was no idle boast. A hunter would stalk a bear with a stout bone-tipped spear, or wait in ambush under a cutbank. When the surprised animal would rear up to get a better look at his attacker, the man would dart under the front paws, moving in from the right (since bears are said to be left-handed) and plant his spear on the ground, angling up and inward. As the bear came down to crush the man, he impaled himself. The hunter would dive out of the way and wait for the bear to thrash out his life, and finish him with another spear if needed. . . . Once a bear was killed, there were rules of spiritual etiquette which were strictly followed . . . acts that assured that the bear's spirit would not molest the hunter, and that it would be born again.

—Nick Jans, *The Last Light Breaking*

Trophy Game. Record big game in Alaska as recorded by the Boone and Crockett Club (www.boone-crockett.org).

Black bear: Skull 14 $12/16$ inches long, 8 $14/16$ inches wide (1975).

Brown bear (coastal region): Skull 17 $15/16$ inches long, 12 $13/16$ inches wide (1952).

Grizzly bear: (Three-way tie) Skull 17 $6/16$ inches long, 9 $12/16$ inches wide (1970); skull 16 $14/16$ inches long, 10 $4/16$ inches wide (1982), skull 17 $3/16$ inches long, 9 $5/16$ inches wide (1991).

Polar bear: Skull 18 $1/2$ inches long, 11 $7/16$ inches wide (1963). It is illegal for anyone but an Alaska Eskimo, Aleut or Indian to hunt polar bear in Alaska.

Bison: Right horn 21 $2/8$ inches long, base circumference 16 inches; left horn 23 $2/8$ inches long, base circumference 15 inches; greatest spread 35 $3/8$ inches (1925).

Barren Ground caribou: Right beam 50 $6/8$ inches, 24 points; left beam 40 $1/8$ inches, 23 points (1987).

Moose (Alaska–Yukon): Right palm length 54 $4/8$ inches, width 22 $2/8$ inches; left palm length 53 $6/8$ inches, width 21 $4/8$ inches; right antler 19 points, left 15 points; greatest spread 65 $1/8$ inches (1994).

Rocky Mountain goat: Right horn 12 inches long, base circumference 6 $4/8$ inches; left horn 12 inches long, base circumference 6 $4/8$ inches (1949).

Musk-ox: Right horn 29 $7/8$ inches; left horn 29 $6/8$ inches; tip-to-tip spread 29 $5/8$ inches (1996).

Dall sheep: Right horn 48 $5/8$ inches long, base circumference 14 $5/8$ inches; left horn 47 $7/8$ inches long, base circumference 14 $3/4$ inches (1961).

The Harbor Bar and Liquor Store in Petersburg advertised, "We sell fishing equipment by the glass, bottle, case or keg."

HYPOTHERMIA (See also Windchill Factor)

Hypothermia develops when the body is exposed to cold and cannot maintain normal temperatures. In an automatic survival reaction, blood flow to the extremities is shut down in favor of preserving warmth in the vital organs. As internal temperature drops, judgment and coordination become impaired. Hypothermia leads to stupor, collapse and death. Immersion hypothermia occurs in cold water.

Hypothermia can occur at any season. To prevent hypothermia, always bring warmer clothing, even in relatively warm summer months. Dress in layers, including inner layers that give warmth even when wet. Keep your energy up by eating snacks and drinking warm beverages.

Travel outdoors with a partner, or in groups, to watch one another for early signs of hypothermia such as shivering, fatigue, stumbling, aimless wandering or irrationality.

Victims of hypothermia should be sheltered from wind and weather and brought indoors as soon as possible.

ICE (See Glaciers and Ice Fields; Icebergs; Ice Fog; Iceworms; Nenana Ice Classic)

ICEBERGS (See also Glaciers and Ice Fields)

Icebergs are formed in Alaska wherever glaciers reach salt water or a freshwater lake. Some accessible places to view icebergs include Glacier Bay, Icy Bay, Yakutat Bay, Taku Inlet, Endicott Arm, portions of northern Prince William Sound (College Fiord, Barry Arm, Columbia Bay), Mendenhall Lake and Portage Lake.

If icebergs contain little or no sediment, approximately 75 percent to 80 percent of their bulk may be underwater. The more sediment an iceberg contains, the greater its density, and an iceberg containing large amounts of sediment will float slightly beneath the surface. Glaciologists of the U.S. Geological Survey believe that some of these "black icebergs" may actually sink to the bottom of a body of water. Since salt water near the faces of glaciers may be liquid to temperatures as low as 28°F, and icebergs melt at 32°F, some of these underwater icebergs may remain unmelted indefinitely.

Alaska's icebergs are small compared to the icebergs found near Antarctica and Greenland. One of the largest icebergs ever recorded in Alaska was formed in May 1977, in Icy Bay. Glaciologists measured it at 346 feet long, 297 feet wide and 99 feet above the surface of the water.

Sea Ice.

Seawater typically freezes at –1.8°C or 28.8°F. The first indication that seawater is freezing is the appearance of *frazil*—tiny needlelike crystals of pure ice—in shallow coastal areas of low current or areas of low salinity such as near the mouths of rivers. Continued freezing turns the frazil into a soupy mass called grease ice and eventually into an ice crust approximately 4 inches thick. More freezing, wind and wave action thicken the ice and break it into ice floes ranging from a few feet to several miles across. In the Arctic Ocean, ice floes can be 10 feet thick. Most are crisscrossed with 6- to 8-foot-high walls of ice caused by the force of winds.

Sea salt that is trapped in the ice during freezing is leached out over time, making the oldest ice the least saline. Meltwater forming in ponds on multiyear-old ice during summer months is a freshwater source for native marine life.

Refreezing of meltwater ponds and the formation of new ice in the permanent ice pack (generally north of 72° north latitude) begins in mid-September. While the ice pack expands southward, new ice freezes to the coast (shorefast ice) and spreads seaward. Where the drifting ice pack grinds against the relatively stable shorefast ice, tremendous walls or ridges of ice are formed, some observed to be 100 feet thick and grounded in 60 feet of water. They are impenetrable by all but the most powerful icebreakers.

By late March the ice cover has reached its maximum extent, approximately from Port Heiden on the Alaska Peninsula in the south to the northern Pribilof Islands and northwestward to Siberia. In Cook Inlet, sea ice usually no more than 2 feet thick can extend as far south as Anchor Point and Kamishak Bay on the east and west sides of the inlet, respectively. The ice season usually lasts from mid-November to April.

The Navy began observing and forecasting sea ice conditions in 1954 during construction of defense sites along the Arctic coast. In 1969, the National Weather Service began a low-profile sea ice reconnaissance program, which expanded greatly during the summer of 1975 when, during a year of severe ice, millions of dollars of materials had to be shipped to Prudhoe Bay. Expanded commercial fisheries in the Bering Sea also heightened the problem of sea ice for crabbing and bottom fish trawling operations. In 1976, headquarters for a seven-days-a-week ice watch was established at Fairbanks; it was moved to Anchorage in 1981.

The National Weather Service operates a radio facsimile broadcast service that makes current ice analysis charts, special oceanographic charts and standard weather charts available to the public via standard radios equipped with "black box" receivers. Commercial fishing operators, particularly in the Bering Sea, use the radio-transmitted charts to steer clear of problem weather and troublesome ice formations. More information is available from the National Weather Service in Kodiak or Anchorage; www.alaska.net/~nwsar.

ICE FOG
Ice fog develops when air just above the ground becomes so cold it can no longer retain water vapor and tiny, spherical ice crystals form. Ice fog is most common in arctic and subarctic regions in winter when clear skies create an air inversion, trapping cold air at low elevations. It is most noticeable when pollutants are suspended in the air inversion.

ICEWORMS
Although often regarded as a hoax, iceworms actually exist. These small, threadlike, segmented black worms, usually less than one inch long, thrive in temperatures just above freezing. Observers as far back as the 1880s reported that at dawn or dusk, or on overcast days, the tiny worms, all belonging to the genus *Mesenchytraeus,* may literally carpet the surface of glaciers. When sunlight strikes them, ice worms burrow back down into the ice; temperatures above 75°F kill them.

The town of Cordova commemorates its own version of the iceworm each February with an Iceworm Festival when a 100-foot-long, multilegged "iceworm" leads a parade down Main Street. Other activities include an arts and crafts show, ski events, contests, dances, and honorary king and queen.

IDITAROD TRAIL SLED DOG RACE
(SEE ALSO Dog Mushing; Yukon Quest International Sled Dog Race) Two of the longest sled dog races in the world take place in Alaska: the Yukon Quest and the Iditarod. The first Iditarod Trail Sled Dog Race, conceived and organized by the late Joe Redington Sr., of Knik, and the late Dorothy Page, of Wasilla, was run in 1967 and covered only 56 miles.

The race was lengthened in 1973, and the first ever 1,100-mile sled dog race began in Anchorage on March 3, 1973, and ended April 3 in Nome. Of the 34 who started the race, 22 finished. The Iditarod has been run every year since. In 1997, the Iditarod Trail Sled Dog Race marked its 25th anniversary.

In 1976, Congress designated the Iditarod as a National Historic Trail. The

Iditarod Trail Sled Dog Race 2001 Results

Place	Musher	Days	Hrs.	Min.	Day	Arrival Time
1	Doug Swingley	9	19	55	03/14	06:55:50
2	Linwood Fiedler	10	3	58	03/14	14:58:57
3	Jeff King	10	7	19	03/14	18:19:43
4	Rick Swenson	10	15	57	03/15	02:57:28
5	Paul Gebhardt	10	20	37	03/15	07:37:05
6	John Baker	10	21	0	03/15	08:00:30
7	Rick Mackey	11	2	0	03/15	13:00:02
8	Jerry Riley	11	6	43	03/15	17:43:58
9	Sonny King	11	12	58	03/15	23:58:46
10	Dee Dee Jonrowe	11	14	33	03/16	01:33:15
11	Vern Halter	11	18	57	03/16	05:57:00
12	Ramy Brooks	11	20	47	03/16	07:47:05
13	Ramey Smyth	11	22	16	03/16	09:16:40
14	Jessica Royer	11	23	4	03/16	10:04:40
15	Jon Little	11	23	46	03/16	10:46:15
16	Ed Iten	12	0	22	03/16	11:22:45
17	Andy Moderow	12	0	44	03/16	11:44:10
18	Tim Osmar	12	1	15	03/16	12:15:00
19	Hans Gatt	12	1	46	03/16	12:46:54
20	Charlie Boulding	12	2	36	03/16	13:36:48
21	Sonny Lindner	12	6	11	03/16	17:11:28
22	Nils Hahn	12	6	37	03/16	17:37:02
23	Juan Alcina	12	6	40	03/16	17:40:01
24	Martin Buser	12	7	43	03/16	18:43:59
25	Thomas Tetz	12	7	44	03/16	18:44:17
26	Bill Cotter	12	8	14	03/16	19:14:28
27	Russell Lane	12	9	17	03/16	20:17:57
28	Daniel Govoni	12	10	38	03/16	21:38:00
29	Aaron Burmeister	12	10	39	03/16	21:39:10
30	Gwen Holdmann	12	14	24	03/17	01:24:15

official length of the Iditarod National Historic Trail System, including northern and southern routes, is 2,350 miles.

Following the old dog team mail route blazed in 1910 from Knik to Nome, the race route crosses two mountain ranges, follows the Yukon River for about 150 miles, runs through several Bush villages and crosses the pack ice of Norton Sound.

Strictly a winter trail because the ground is mostly spongy muskeg swamps, the route attracted national attention in 1925 when sled dog mushers, including the famous Leonhard Seppala, relayed 300,000 units of life-saving diphtheria serum to epidemic-threatened Nome. As the airplane and snowmobile replaced

NUGGETS

Four men with mountain bikes rode the Iditarod Trail from Anchorage to Nome in March 1989. The bikers began their trek on March 3, the day before the start of the Iditarod Trail Sled Dog Race, and finished on March 25, some 10 days after winner Joe Runyan and his team crossed the finish line. The men followed the same 1,100-mile trail the mushers take.

—1990 *The ALASKA ALMANAC®*

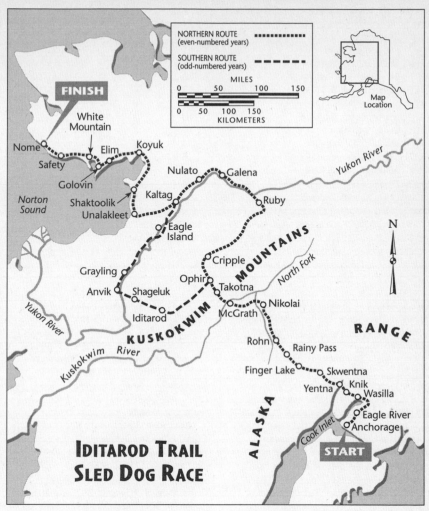

NORTHERN ROUTE (even-numbered years)

SOUTHERN ROUTE (odd-numbered years)

MILES
0   50   100   150

KILOMETERS
0   50   100   150

Map Location

N

FINISH

White Mountain

Nome
Safety
Golovin
Elim
Koyuk
Shaktoolik
Unalakleet
Kaltag
Nulato
Galena
Ruby
Eagle Island
Norton Sound
Yukon River
Cripple
Grayling
Ophir
Takotna
McGrath
Nikolai
Anvik
Shageluk
Iditarod
Rohn
Rainy Pass
Finger Lake
Skwentna
Yentna
Knik
Wasilla
Eagle River
Anchorage
Cook Inlet
START

MOUNTAINS
North Fork

RANGE

KUSKOKWIM
Kuskokwim River
Yukon River

ALASKA

IDITAROD TRAIL
SLED DOG RACE

the sled dog team, the trail fell into disuse. Thanks to Redington and Page, the trail has been assured a place in Alaska history.

The Iditarod alternates a portion of the route each year, using the northern route in even-numbered years and the southern route in odd-numbered years (see accompanying map). The Iditarod is traditionally described as 1,049 miles long (the last part of the number selected because Alaska is the 49th state), but the actual distance run each year is close to 1,100 miles.

For more information contact the Iditarod Trail committee, P.O. Box 870800, Wasilla 99687; www.iditarod.com.

> Snowmobilers breaking trail for the Iditarod Trail Sled Dog Race discovered that if they wired a can a SPAM® to their exhaust manifold, they had a perfect hot meal in 50 miles.

Winners and Times

Year	Musher	Days	Hrs.	Min.	Sec.	Prize
1989	Joe Runyan, Nenana	11	5	24	3	$50,000
1990	Susan Butcher, Manley	11	1	53	23	50,000
1991	Rick Swenson, Two Rivers	12	16	34	39	50,000
1992	Martin Buser, Big Lake	10	19	17	15	50,000
1993	Jeff King, Denali Park	10	15	38	15	50,000*
1994	Martin Buser, Big Lake	10	13	2	39	50,000**
1995	Doug Swingley, Simms, MT	9	2	42	19	52,500
1996	Jeff King, Denali Park	9	5	43	13	50,000
1997	Martin Buser, Big Lake	9	8	30	45	50,000†
1998	Jeff King, Denali Park	9	5	52	0	51,000†
1999	Doug Swingley, Lincoln, MT	9	14	31	0	60,000†
2000	Doug Swingley, Lincoln, MT	9	0	58	6	60,000†**
2001	Doug Swingley, Lincoln, MT	9	19	55	50	62,857†

*Does not include $3,000 in silver ingots for reaching the halfway checkpoint first.

**Does not include $2,500 in gold nuggets for first musher to reach Unalakleet.

†Does not include Dodge truck.

IGLOO (See also Barabara) The word igloo, meaning snowhouse, is from northern and eastern Eskimo (Inupiaq *iglu,* or "house"). The stereotypical igloo is a snow block

structure that could be built quickly as a temporary trail shelter for arctic Alaska and Canada Eskimos. Igloos are constructed in a spiral with each tier leaning inward at a greater angle. The entrance is a tunnel with a cold trap. A sleeping platform raises sleepers off the cold floor, while a vent at the top allows fresh air for ventilation and an ice window admits light.

Most Alaska indigenous dwellings were sod igloos, dome- or Quonset-shaped structures whose roof was supported with wood or whale bones and covered with insulating sod.

INFORMATION SOURCES

Agriculture. State Division of Agriculture, 1800 Glenn Hwy. Suite 12, Palmer 99645-6736; (907) 745-7200; fax (907) 745-7112; www.dnr.state.ak.us/ag.

Alaska Natives. Alaska Federation of Natives, 1577 C St., Suite 300, Anchorage 99501; www.akfednatives.org.

Boating, Canoeing and Kayaking. Alaska Department of Transportation and Public Facilities, 3132 Channel Drive, Juneau 99801-7898; (907) 465-3900; www.dot.state.ak.us; Alaska Division of Parks and Outdoor Recreation, 500 W. Seventh Ave., Anchorage 99501-3557; (907) 269-8400; fax (907) 269-8901; www.dnr.state.ak.us/parks/parks.htm.

Business. Alaska Department of Community and Economic Development, P.O. Box 110800, Juneau 99811-0801; (907) 465-2012; fax (907) 465-3767; www.dced.state.ak.us; State Chamber of Commerce, 217 Second St., Suite 201, Juneau 99801; (907) 586-2323; fax (907) 463-5515; www.alaskachamber.com.

Census Data. Alaska Department of Labor, Research and Analysis, P.O. Box 25501, Juneau 99802-5501; (907) 465-4500; fax (907) 465-2101; www.labor.state.ak.us/research/cgin/cen.htm.

Customs. U.S. Customs, 1910 Alex Holden Way, Juneau 99801; (907) 586-7211; fax (907) 586-9309.

Directory Assistance. (907) 555-1212.

Disabled Access. Challenge Alaska, P.O. Box 11065 Anchorage 99511;

(907) 344-7399; fax (907) 344-7349; www.challenge.ak.org. Outdoor recreation programs for persons with disabilities; sea kayaking, adaptive skiing.

Dog Mushing. Alaska Dog Mushers Association, P.O. Box 70622, Fairbanks 99707; (907) 457-6874; www.sleddog.org.

Education. Alaska Department of Education, 801 W. 10th St., Suite 200, Juneau 99801; (907) 465-2800; fax (907) 465-3452; www.eed.state.ak.us.

Elderly. Division of Senior Service, 3601 C St., Suite 310, Anchorage 99503-5984; (800) 478-9969; (907) 269-3666; fax (907) 269-3688; www.state.ak.us/local/akpages/admin/dss/home.htm.

Environmental Conservation. Department of Environmental Conservation, 410 Willoughby Ave., Suite 410, Juneau 99801-1795; (907) 465-5010; fax (907) 465-5097; www.state.ak.us/local/akpages/env.conserv.

Ferry System. Alaska Marine Highway; (800) 642-0066; www.state.ak.us/ferry.

Gold Panning. Alaska Miners Association, 3305 Arctic Blvd., Anchorage 99503; (907) 563-9229; fax (907) 563-9225; www.alaskaminers.org.

Health. State Department of Health and Social Services, Division of Public Health, P.O. Box 110601, Juneau 99811-0601; (907) 465-3090; fax (907) 586-1877; www.hss.state.ak.us.

Highway Information. Alaska State Troopers (for emergencies), (907) 269-5511; Alaska State Highway System, (800) 478-7675.

Historical Archives. Alaska State Archives, 141 Willoughby Ave., Juneau 99801; (907) 465-2270; fax (907) 465-2465; www.archives.state.ak.us; National Archives, 654 W. Third Ave., Anchorage 99501; (907) 271-2441; fax (907) 271-2442; www.nara.gov/regional/anchorag.html; University of Alaska Archives, 3211 Providence Drive, Anchorage 99507; (907) 786-1849; fax (907) 786-6050; ayarch@orion.alaska.edu.

Housing. Association of Alaska Housing Authorities, 4300 Boniface Pkwy., Anchorage 99504; (907) 338-3970; fax (907) 338-4904; www.alaska.net/~aaha.

Hunting and Fishing Regulations. State Department of Fish and Game, P.O. Box 25526, Juneau 99811; (907) 465-4112; www.admin.adfg.state.ak.us.

Job Opportunities. Job Service, 3301 Eagle St., Anchorage 99503; (907) 269-4800; Alaska Job Centers, 10002 Glacier Hwy., Suite 200, Juneau 99801-8569; (907) 465-4562; fax (907) 465-2984; www.jobs.state.ak.us.

Job Opportunities for People with Disabilities. ASSETS, Inc., 2330 Nichols St., Anchorage 99508; (907) 279-6617; fax (907) 274-0636; www.assetsinc.org.

Labor. State Department of Labor, P.O. Box 21149, Juneau 99802-1149; (907) 465-2700; fax (907) 465-2784; www.labor.state.ak.us.

Land. Alaska Public Lands Information Centers, 605 W. Fourth Ave., Suite 105, Anchorage 99501, (907) 271-2737; 250 Cushman St., Suite 1A, Fairbanks 99701, (907) 456-0527; P.O. Box 359, Tok 99780, (907) 883-5667; 50 Main St., Ketchikan 99901, (907) 228-6220, www.nps.gov/aplic/center; Bureau of Land Management, 222 W. Seventh Ave., Suite 13, Anchorage 99513; (907) 271-5076; fax (907) 271-4596; State Division of Lands, P.O. Box 107005, Anchorage 99510; (907) 271-5960; fax (907) 271-4596; www.ak.blm.gov.

Law. Department of Law, P.O. Box 110300, Juneau 99811-6300; (907) 465-2133; www.law.state.ak.us.

Legal Assistance. Alaska Legal Services, 1016 West Sixth Avenue, Suite 200, Anchorage 99501; (800) 478-9431; fax (907) 279-7417; www.ptialaska.net/~aklegal.

Legislature. Legislative Information Office, 716 W. Fourth Ave., Suite 200, Anchorage 99501-2133; (907) 269-0229; www.legis.state.ak.us.

Libraries. Alaska State Library, P.O. Box 110571, Juneau 99811; (907) 465-2920; www.library.state.ak.us.

Maps (topographic). U.S. Geological Survey, 4230 University Drive, Suite 201, Anchorage 99508; (907) 786-7100; www.ak.wr.usgs.gov.

Military. Department of the Air Force, Headquarters, Alaskan Air Command, 9480 Pease Dr., Elmendorf Air Force Base 99506; (907) 552-2100; fax (907) 552-8262; www.elmendorf.af.mil; Department of the Army, Headquarters, U.S. Army Alaska, 600 Richardson Dr., Suite 500, Fort Richardson 99505; (907) 384-2163; fax (907) 384-2913; www.usarak.army.mil/frapage.htm; State Department of Military and Veterans Affairs, Box 5800, Fort Richardson 99505; (907) 428-6003; fax (907) 428-6019; www.ak-prepared.com; U.S. Coast Guard, 17th Coast Guard District, P.O. Box 25517, Juneau 99802-5517; (907) 463-2025; fax (907) 463-2037.

Mines and Petroleum. Alaska Miners Association, 3305 Arctic Blvd., No. 202, Anchorage 99503; (907) 563-9229; fax (907) 563-9225; www.alaskaminers.org; State Division of Geological and Geophysical Surveys, 794 University Ave., Suite 200, Fairbanks 99707; (907) 451-5000; fax (907) 451-5050; www.dggs.dnr.state.ak.us.

Natural Resources. Department of Natural Resources, Public Information Center, 400 Willoughby Ave., Juneau 99801; (907) 465-3400; fax (907) 586-2954; www.dnr.state.ak.us/pic.

Permanent Fund Dividend. Permanent Fund, 333 Willoughby Ave., 11th Floor, State Office Bldg., Juneau 99811; (907) 465-2326; fax (907) 465-3470; www.pfd.state.ak.us.

Public Safety. Department of Public Safety, P.O. Box 111200, Juneau 99811; (907) 465-4322; fax (907) 465-4362; www.dps.state.ak.us.

Revenue. Department of Revenue, P.O. Box 110400, Juneau 99811-0400; (907) 465-2300; fax (907) 465-2389; www.revenue.state.ak.us.

River Running. Bureau of Land Management, 222 W. Seventh Ave., Suite 13, Anchorage 99513; (907) 271-5076; fax (907) 271-4596; www.ak.blm.gov; National Park Service, 2525 Gambell St., Anchorage 99503-2892; (907) 257-2687; fax (907) 456-0514; www.nps.gov; Alaska Public Lands Information Center (SEE Land).

Road Conditions. (SEE Weather)

Stranded Residents. Association for Stranded Rural Alaskans in Anchorage, 2606 C St., Suite 2B, Anchorage 99503; (907) 272-0643.

Tourism Information. Alaska Travel Industry Association, 2600 Cordova St., Suite 201, Anchorage 99503; (907) 929-2842; fax (907) 561-5733; www.alaskatia.org; Alaska Visitor Information, www.dced.state.ak.us/tourism/sources/visinfo.htm.

Veterans Affairs (SEE Military).

Weather Information. National Weather Service, Anchorage, (907) 936-2525; www.alaska.net/~nwsar; Motorist and Recreation Areas, (907) 936-2626; Marine and Boating, (907) 936-2727; General, (907) 266-5145 or (800) 472-0391.

INSIDE PASSAGE The

meandering, protected waterway that threads between the mainland and the coastal islands of Southeast Alaska and British Columbia is called the Inside Passage.

From the head of Washington's Puget Sound to the mouth of the Chilkat River near Haines, the route is about 1,000 miles long. It is a transportation corridor for fishing boats, barges, cruise ships and state ferries and a lifeline for Southeast Alaska communities inaccessible by road.

The route passes through the Tongass National Forest, the largest national forest in the United States. The spectacular scenery and wildlife found in the Inside Passage make it a popular tourist route. From the deck of a cruise ship, visitors can see misty bays, islands dense with towering spruce and hemlock trees, mountains, glaciers, bears, whales and eagles.

INUIT CIRCUMPOLAR
CONFERENCE Started in Barrow in

1977, the Inuit Circumpolar Conference brings together Inuit from Greenland, Canada, Alaska and Chukotka (Russia) to address common concerns regarding environment, human rights, health and economic development.

The ICC is prominent in national and international arenas, including the United

Nations and circumpolar initiatives such as the eight-nation Arctic Environmental Protection Strategy. In Alaska, the ICC has supported international Native-to-Native agreements on managing shared wildlife resources such as polar bears.

National offices in each of the four countries represented by the ICC carry on the work of the organization. General assemblies are held every four years at sites that rotate among the countries. The assembly in Canada in 2002 will bring together more than 1,500 Inuit from around the Arctic.

ISLANDS

Southeast Alaska contains about 1,000 of the state's 1,800 named islands, rocks and reefs; several thousand remain unnamed. The Aleutian Island chain, stretching southwest from the mainland, contains more than 200 islands.

Of the state's 10 largest islands, 6 are in southeastern Alaska. Of the remainder, Unimak is in the Aleutians, Nunivak and St. Lawrence are in the Bering Sea off the western coast of Alaska, and Kodiak is in the Gulf of Alaska (SEE map, pages 6–7). The state's 10 largest islands, according to the U.S. Geological Survey , are:

1. Kodiak, 3,588 sq. mi.
2. Prince of Wales, 2,731 sq. mi.
3. Chichagof, 2,062 sq. mi.
4. St. Lawrence, 1,780 sq. mi.
5. Admiralty, 1,709 sq. mi.
6. Baranof, 1,636 sq. mi.
7. Nunivak, 1,600 sq. mi. (estimate)
8. Unimak, 1,600 sq. mi.
9. Revillagigedo, 1,134 sq. mi.
10. Kupreanof, 1,084 sq. mi.

IVORY

Eskimos traditionally carved sea mammal ivory to make such implements as harpoon heads, dolls and ulu (fan-shaped knife) handles. For the past century, however, most carvings have been made to be sold. Etching on ivory originally was done with hand tools and the scratched designs were filled in with soot. Today power tools supplement the hand tools and carvers may color the etching with India ink, graphite, hematite or commercial coloring.

Walrus. From *Alaska's Mammals* by Dave Smith (text) and Tom Walker (photographs).

The large islands of the Bering Sea—St. Lawrence, Little Diomede and Nunivak—are home to the majority of Alaska's ivory carvers. Eskimos from King Island, renowned for their carving skill, now live in Nome. The bulk of the ivory used today comes from walrus tusks and teeth seasoned for a few months. Old walrus ivory, often mistakenly called fossil ivory, is also used. This ivory has been buried in the ground or left on beaches for years; contact with various minerals has changed it from white to tan or any of a multitude of colors. Some highly prized old ivory exhibits rays of deep blue or areas of brown and gold that shine. Most old ivory comes from ancient sites or beaches on St. Lawrence Island and is sold by the pound to non-Native buyers, generally for use in some kind of artwork.

Mastodon tusks are often unearthed in the summer by miners or found eroding on river cutbanks where they have been buried for thousands of years. Although these tusks are enormous and their colorations often beautiful, the material cannot be used efficiently because it dries and then separates into narrow ridges.

Various federal prohibitions govern the collection of old walrus, mammoth and mastodon ivory. These materials may be gathered from private or reservation lands, but may not be traded or sold if found on public lands. The taking of fresh walrus ivory is illegal for non-Natives, in accordance with the Marine Mammal Protection Act of 1972.

Walrus may be taken only by Alaska

Natives (Aleuts, Eskimos and Indians) who dwell on the coast of the North Pacific Ocean or the Arctic Ocean and rely on the animals for subsistence or for the creation and sale of Native handicrafts or clothing.

Raw walrus ivory and other parts can be sold only by an Alaska Native to an Alaska Native within Alaska, or to a registered agent for resale or transfer to an Alaska Native within the state. Only authentic Native-processed ivory articles of handicrafts or clothing may be sold or transferred to a non-Native, or sold in interstate commerce.

Beach ivory, which is found on the beach within one-quarter mile of the ocean, may be kept by anyone. This ivory must be registered by all non-Natives with the U.S. Fish and Wildlife Service (USFWS) or the National Marine Fisheries Service within 30 days of discovery. Beach-found ivory must remain in the possession of the finder even if carved or scrimshawed.

Carved or scrimshawed walrus ivory (authentic Native handicraft) or other marine mammal parts made into clothing or other authentic Native  handicrafts may be exported from the United States to a foreign country, but the exporter must first obtain a permit from the USFWS. Even visitors from the Lower 48 simply traveling through, or stopping in, Canada on their way home are required to have a USFWS export and/or transit permit. Cost is $25. Mailing the carved ivory home will avoid the need for an export/transit permit. Importation of walrus or other marine mammal parts is illegal except for scientific research purposes or for public display once a permit is granted. Because of ecological sensitivity to the use of elephant ivory, many carvers are switching to whalebone, recycled from the skeletons of harvested species.

For further information contact Division of Law Enforcement, U.S. Fish and Wildlife Service, 1011 E. Tudor Road, Anchorage 99503, (907) 786-3311; or Senior Resident, U.S. Fish and Wildlife Service, 1412 Airport Way, Fairbanks 99701, (907) 456-0255.

JADE

JADE Most Alaska jade is found near the Dall, Shungnak and Kobuk rivers, and Jade Mountain, all north of the Arctic Circle. The stones occur in various shades of green, brown, black, yellow, white and even red. The most valuable are those that are marbled black, white and green. Gem-quality jade, about one-fourth of the total mined, is used in jewelry making. Fractured jade is used for clock faces, tabletops, bookends and other items. Jade is the Alaska state gem.

JUNEAU Located on scenic Gastineau Channel, Juneau is the capital of Alaska. Established in 1880 as a mining camp, it was originally called Harrisburg after Richard Harris, who with his partner, Joseph Juneau, discovered gold and staked their claim in 1880. The camp quickly boomed.

Under Russian rule, the seat of government was at Sitka—with no official capital. In 1900 Congress moved this seat to Juneau, but Juneau did not become the capital (that is, where the legislature convenes) until 1912. In 1974, Alaskans voted to move the state capital closer to the state's population center, selecting a site between Anchorage and Fairbanks at Willow. Juneau remained the capital after funding for the transfer of government to Willow was defeated by voters in 1982. Of Southeast Alaska's 60,000 residents, half live in Juneau, Alaska's third-largest city. Juneau is accessible only by boat, ferry or plane. No roads lead into or out of town. Often called "a little San Francisco," Juneau

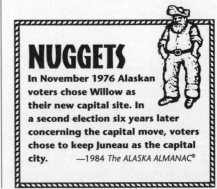

NUGGETS

In November 1976 Alaskan voters chose Willow as their new capital site. In a second election six years later concerning the capital move, voters chose to keep Juneau as the capital city. —1984 *The ALASKA ALMANAC*®

is tucked at the foot of Mount Juneau. The climate is wet and mild, with summer average daily maximum temperatures of 63°F and winter average daily minimum temperatures of 20°F. Average annual snowfall is about 92 inches in the downtown area.

Sights include the historic shopping district, the Red Dog Saloon, the State and City Museum, the Gastineau Salmon Hatchery, the State Office Building and the Governor's Mansion. Helicopter tours of the Juneau Icefield and tours to Glacier Bay National Park are popular activities, as are kayaking, fishing, hiking and Inside Passage cruises.

In the summer of 2000, a total of 632,602 cruise passengers visited Juneau. A popular attraction in Juneau is the Mount Roberts Tramway, a 2,000-foot scenic ride in a spacious gondola.

Additional information is available from the Juneau Convention and Visitors Bureau, 134 Third St., Juneau 99801; (907) 586-2201; www.traveljuneau.com. For a free Juneau travel planner, call (888) 581-2201.

Remains of the Kennecott Copper Mine.
From *Picture Journeys in Alaska's Wrangell–St. Elias* by George Herben.

KENNECOTT, KENNICOTT

Kennicott Glacier in the Wrangell Mountains was named for explorer and geologist Robert Kennicott.

The Kennecott Mines Co. was formed in 1906 to exploit the rich copper ore deposits nearby. The mining company was supposed to be named after the glacier, but the name was misspelled with a second "e" and the error stuck.

The mining town of Kennicott took its name from the glacier. The mine closed down in 1938. But the timeworn ghost town of Kennicott still stands and is a National Historic Landmark.

KODIAK (See also Islands) Kodiak, the oldest European settlement in Alaska, is located on Kodiak Island in the Gulf of Alaska, 252 air miles south of Anchorage. The 100-mile-long island, second only to Hawaii's Big Island in size in the United States, is known as Alaska's "Emerald Isle." The island and its main city are accessible only by boat, ferry or plane.

After 7,500 years of being occupied by the Alutiiq people, Kodiak Island was "discovered" by Russian explorer Stephen Glotov in 1763. The town of Kodiak served as Russian Alaska's first capital city until 1804. In 1912, Kodiak was caught in drifting ash from the eruption of Novarupta Volcano on the Alaska Peninsula, which buried the town under 18 inches of pumice. The 9.2-magnitude earthquake that struck Alaska on March 27, 1964, set off a *tsunami* (a seismic sea wave) that virtually destroyed downtown Kodiak, its fishing fleet, processing plants and more than 150 homes.

Today, more than 14,000 residents inhabit the Kodiak Island Borough. Commercial fishing is the island's main industry, with 2,600 vessels and an annual harvest exceeding $80 million—making Kodiak one of the top five commercial fishing ports in the United States. Timber activities and tourism are also important segments of the local economy.

A Rhode Island newspaper once described Homer, as "the only place in the world [where] you can stand in mud up to your knees and still have dust blow in your face."

Kodiak is home to the U.S. Coast Guard's base for North Pacific operations, the nation's largest.

The city of Kodiak has two museums, the Baranov and the Alutiiq Museum and Archaeological Repository. The Baranov Museum displays many items from the Russian era. The Alutiiq Museum chronicles the history of the indigenous Alutiiq people and the advent of the Russian fur trade. Icons, rare paintings and handmade brassworks can be seen at the Russian Orthodox Church.

It is estimated that more than 3,000 Kodiak bears, largest of the state's brown/grizzly bears, inhabit the island. Kodiak National Wildlife Refuge (accessible only by floatplane or boat) was established in 1941 to preserve the natural habitat of the bear. Bears can be observed feeding on salmon during the summer in remote parts of the refuge.

For maps, brochures, and hunting and fishing information, contact the Kodiak Island Convention and Visitors Bureau, 100 Marine Way, Kodiak 99615; (907) 486-4782; www.kodiak.org.

KUSPUK
A *kuspuk* is an Eskimo woman's parka, often made with a loosely cut back so that an infant may be carried piggyback-style. Parkas are made from seal, marmot, ground squirrel, rabbit or fox skins; traditionally, the fur lining faces

Woman in a *kuspuk,* **with her child, fishing through the ice.** Anchorage Museum of History and Art. From T*he Alaska Heritage Seafood Cookbook* by Ann Chandonnet.

inward. The ruffs are generally made of wolverine or wolf fur.

An outer shell, the *qaspeg,* is worn over a fur parka to keep it clean and to reduce wear. This outer shell is usually made of brightly colored corduroy, cotton print or velveteen-like material, and may be trimmed with rickrack.

LABOR AND EMPLOYER ORGANIZATIONS
Alaska has local branches of dozens of unions, including unions for longshoremen, carpenters, restaurant employees, pulp and paper workers, electrical workers, aerospace workers, firefighters, teachers and others. For details, consult the Alaska Labor Union Directory of the Alaska State AFL-CIO; (907) 258-6284.

LAKES
There are 94 lakes with surface areas of more than 10 square miles among Alaska's more than 3 million lakes.

According to the U.S. Geological Survey, the 10 largest natural freshwater lakes are:

1. Iliamna, 1,150 sq. mi.
2. Becharof, 458 sq. mi.
3. Teshekpuk, 315 sq. mi.
4. Naknek, 242 sq. mi.
5. Tustumena, 117 sq. mi.
6. Clark, 110 sq. mi.
7. Dall, 100 sq. mi.
8. Upper Ugashik, 75 sq. mi.
9. Lower Ugashik, 72 sq. mi.
10. Kukaklek, 72 sq. mi.

LAND USE
(SEE ALSO Highways; National Forests; National Parks; National Wild and Scenic Rivers; National Wilderness Areas; National Wildlife Refuges; Native Peoples; State Park System) At first glance it seems odd that such a huge area as Alaska has not been more heavily settled. Thousands of acres of forest and tundra, miles and miles of rivers and streams, hidden valleys, bays, coves and mountains are spread across an area so vast that it staggers the imagination. Yet more than two-thirds of the population of Alaska remains clustered around two major centers of commerce, Anchorage and Fairbanks.

Visitors flying over the state are

impressed by immense areas showing no sign of humanity. Current assessments indicate that approximately 160,000 acres of Alaska have been cleared, built on or otherwise directly altered by people, either by settlement or resource development, including mining, pipeline construction and agriculture. In comparison to the 365 million acres of land that make up the total of the state, the settled or altered area amounts to less than one-twentieth of 1 percent.

There are several reasons for this lack of development. Frozen for long periods in the Arctic, much of the land cannot support quantities of people or industry. Where the winters are "warm," the mountains, glaciers, rivers and oceans prevent easy access for commerce and trade.

In most places, the free market affects patterns of land ownership, but in Alaska all land ownership patterns until recent decades were the result of a century-long process of a single landowner, the United States government.

The Statehood Act in 1958 signaled the beginning of a dramatic shift in land ownership patterns. It authorized the state to select 104 million of the 365 million acres of land and inland waters in Alaska. (Under the Submerged Lands Act, the state has title to submerged lands under navigable inland waters.) In passing the Statehood Act, Congress cited economic independence and the need to open Alaska to economic development as the primary purposes for large Alaska land grants.

Alaska Native Claims Settlement Act.

The issue of Native claims in Alaska was resolved with the passage of the Alaska Native Claims Settlement Act (ANCSA) on Dec. 18, 1971. This act of Congress provided for the creation of Alaska Native village and regional corporations and gave Alaska Eskimos, Aleuts and Indians $962.5 million and the right to select 44 million acres from a land pool of some 115 million acres.

Immediately after the settlement act passed, and before Native lands and National Interest Lands were selected, the

Canoeists glide across Wonder Lake in Denali National Park and Preserve.
Photo by Roy Corral.

state filed to select an additional 77 million acres of land. In September 1972, the litigation initiated by the state was resolved by a settlement affirming state selection of an additional 41 million acres.

The settlement act, in addition to establishing a Joint Federal–State Land Use Planning Commission, directed the secretary of the interior to withdraw from public use up to 80 million acres of land in Alaska for study as possible national parks, wildlife refuges, national forests, and wild and scenic rivers. These were the National Interest Lands Congress was to decide upon by Dec. 18, 1978. The U.S. House of Representatives passed a bill (HR39) that would have designated 124 million acres of national parks, forests and wildlife refuges, and designated millions of acres of these and existing parks, forests and refuges as wilderness. Although a bill was reported out of committee, it failed to pass the Senate before Congress adjourned.

In November 1978, the secretary of the interior published a draft environmental impact supplement, which listed the actions that the executive branch of the federal government could take to protect federal lands in Alaska until the 96th Congress could consider the creation of new parks, wildlife refuges, wild and scenic rivers and national forests. In keeping with this objective, the secretary of the interior, under provisions of the 1976 Federal Land Policy and Management Act, withdrew about 114 million acres of land in Alaska from most public uses. On Dec. 1, 1978, President Jimmy Carter, under the authority of the 1906 Antiquities Act, designated 56 million acres of these lands as national monuments.

In February 1980, the House of Representatives passed a modified HR39.

In August 1980, the Senate passed a compromise version of the Alaska lands bill that created 106 million acres of new conservation units and affected 131 million acres in Alaska. In November 1980, the House accepted the Senate version of the Alaska National Interest Lands Conservation Act (ANILCA), which President Carter signed into law Dec. 2, 1980.

Land use in Alaska continues to be a complex subject. Distribution of land ownership from the federal government to the state of Alaska, Native village and regional corporations, and private citizens has required considerable time. Debate continues over issues such as Native sovereignty and subsistence hunting and fishing rights.

Acquiring Land for Private Use.

The easiest and fastest way to acquire land for private use is by purchase from the private sector, through real estate agencies or directly from individuals. Because of speculation, land claim conflicts and delays involving Native, state and federal groups, however, private land is considered by many people to be in short supply and often is very expensive.

Private land in Alaska, excluding land held by Native corporations, is estimated to be 2.7 million acres, but less than 1 percent of the state. Much of this land passed into private hands through the federal Homestead Acts and other public land laws, as well as land disposal programs of the state, boroughs or communities. Most private land is located along Alaska's limited road network. Compared to other categories of land, it is highly accessible and constitutes some of the prime settlement land.

All laws related to homesteading on federal land (as opposed to state land) in Alaska were repealed as of 1986. Federal land is not available for homesteading or trade and manufacturing sites. (See also Homesteading) Following are programs for the sale of state land.

Auction. Alaska has been selling land by public auction since statehood. The state may sell full surface rights, lease of surface or subsurface rights, or restricted title at an auction. There is a minimum bid of fair market value and the high bidder is the purchaser. Participants must be at least 18 years old.

Homesite. The homesite program was passed in 1977 by the state legislature. Under its provisions, each Alaska household is eligible for up to five acres. A person who has a homesite entry permit, purchase contract or patent may not apply for another homesite, and neither can any member of that person's household. The land is free, but the individual must pay the cost of the application filing fee ($10), survey and platting, and appraisal, if purchasing. Persons enrolled in this program must live on the homesite for 35 months within seven years of entry and construct a permanent, single-family dwelling on the site within five years. (This is called "proving up" on the land.) After the dwelling is completed and approved by the division, the permit holder may purchase the land at fair market value at the date of purchase. The occupancy requirement is then waived.

Remote Parcels. This remote parcel program replaced the old open-to-entry program. It permitted entry to designated areas to stake a parcel of 5, 20 or 40 acres, depending on the area, and to lease the area for five years with the option of a five-year renewal. The remote parcel program ended July 1, 1984, when it was replaced by the 1983 homesteading bill. Alaskans leasing remote parcels, but who have not yet purchased them, may obtain patent under a remote parcel lease agreement.

Lottery. One year of residency is

required to participate in the lottery program. Successful applicants are determined by a drawing and pay the appraised fair market value of the land. They repay the state over a period of up to 20 years, with interest set at the current federal land loan bank rate. Lotteries require a 5 percent down payment.

The state offered 100,000 acres of land to private ownership in each fiscal year from July 1, 1979, to July 1, 1982. Disposal levels since then have been based on an annual assessment of the demand.

On April 1, 1983, the Department of Natural Resources discontinued a program that provided Alaska residents who were registered voters a 5-percent-per-year-of-residency discount (up to $25,000) on the sale of land purchased from the state. Legislation has changed U.S. military veteran benefits. A 90-day service now qualifies the veteran. Formerly, 15-year veteran residents had been eligible for up to $37,500 on this one-time program.

Following is the amount of land owned by various entities as of 2000:

Alaska Land Ownership

Owner	Acreage (in millions)
State	90.2
U.S. Bureau of Land Management	84.7
U.S. Fish and Wildlife Service	72.4
National Park Service	52.9
Native	37.8
U.S. Forest Service	22.5
Military and other federal	2.3
Other Private (besides Native)	2.7

Source: U.S. Bureau of Land Management

Information and applications for state programs are available from the Department of Natural Resources Public Information Office (www.dnr.state.ak.us):

Northern Region, 3700 Airport Way, Fairbanks 99709-4699; (907) 451-2706.

Southcentral Region, 550 W. Seventh Ave., Suite 1260, Anchorage 99501-3557; (907) 269-8400.

Southeastern Region, 400 Willoughby Ave., Suite 400, Juneau 99801; (907) 465-3400.

LANGUAGES (See also Igloo; Masks; Native Peoples; Parka) Besides English, Alaska's languages include 20 Native American languages.

The Eskimo language group—Central Yup'ik, Siberian Yup'ik and Inupiaq—is widely spoken by many Natives in Western and Northern Alaska.

Most of these Native languages are at risk of extinction. They include Han, Haida, Eyak, Tanana, Tlingit, Dena'ina (or Tanaina), Ahtna, Ingalik, Holikachuk, Tsimshian, Koyukon, Upper Kuskokwim, Upper Tanana, Kutchin and Aleut.

MAMMALS (See also Bears; Musk-Oxen; Whales; Whaling)

Large Land Mammals

Black Bear. Highest densities are found in Southeast, Prince William Sound and Southcentral coastal mountains and lowlands. Black bears also occur in Interior and Western Alaska, but are absent from Southeast islands north of Frederick Sound (primarily Admiralty, Baranof and Chichagof) and the Kodiak archipelago. They are not commonly found west of about Naknek Lake on the Alaska Peninsula, in the Aleutian Islands or on the open tundra sloping into the Bering Sea and Arctic Ocean. (See also Bears)

Brown/Grizzly Bear. These large omnivores are found in most of Alaska except for Southeast islands south of Frederick Sound or in the Aleutians (except for Unimak Island). (See also Bears)

Polar Bear. There are two groups in Alaska's Arctic rim: an eastern group found largely in the Beaufort Sea and a western group found in the Chukchi Sea between Alaska and Siberia. The latter group are the largest polar bears in the world. Old males can exceed 1,500 pounds. (See also Bears)

American Bison. In 1928, 23 bison were transplanted from Montana to Delta Junction to restore Alaska's bison population, which had died out some 500 years before. Today, several hundred

Caribou calf. From *Caribou: Wanderer of the Tundra* by Tom Walker.

bison graze near Delta Junction; other herds range at Farewell, at Chitina and along the lower Copper River.

Barren Ground Caribou. There are at least 13 distinct caribou herds, with some overlapping ranges: Adak, Alaska Peninsula, Arctic, Beaver, Chisana, Delta, Kenai, McKinley, Mentasta, Mulchatna, Nelchina, Porcupine and Fortymile. Porcupine and Fortymile herds range into Canada. The Western Arctic herd numbers about 450,000, the state's largest. Hunters of the 50 villages along its migration route take about 20,000 caribou annually for meat.

Sitka Black-tailed Deer. These deer range the coastal rain forests of southeastern Alaska. They have been successfully transplanted to the Yakutat

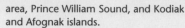

Alaska has a special class of hunting license for "blind resident hunters." The state's economy must be bad, because they don't even get a discount!

area, Prince William Sound, and Kodiak and Afognak islands.

Roosevelt Elk. Alaska's only elk occur on Raspberry and Afognak islands, the result of a 1928 transplant of 105 Roosevelt elk from the Olympic Peninsula in Washington state. Other transplant attempts have failed.

Moose. Moose occur from the Unuk River in Southeast to the Arctic Slope, but are most abundant in second-growth birch forests, on timberline plateaus and along major rivers of Southcentral and Interior. They are not found on islands in Prince William Sound or the Bering Sea, on most major islands in Southeast or on Kodiak or the Aleutians groups.

Mountain Goat. These white-coated animals are found in mountains throughout Southeast, and north and west along coastal mountains to Cook Inlet and Kenai Peninsula. They have been successfully transplanted to Kodiak and Baranof islands.

Musk-Oxen. These shaggy, long-haired mammals were eliminated from Alaska by hunters by 1865. The species was reintroduced and first transplanted to Nunivak Island, and from there to the Arctic Slope around Kavik, Seward Peninsula, Cape Thompson and Nelson Island. (SEE ALSO Musk-Oxen)

Reindeer. Introduced from Siberia just before the 20th century, reindeer roamed much of the Bering Sea Coast region but are now confined to St. George and Nunivak islands and the Seward Peninsula.

Dall Sheep. The only white, wild sheep in the world, Dall sheep are found in all major mountain ranges in Alaska except the Aleutian Range south of Iliamna Lake.

Wolf. Wolves are protected and managed as big game and valuable furbearers. Wolves are found throughout Alaska except Bering Sea islands, some Southeast and Prince William Sound islands, and the Aleutian Islands. The wolf succeeds in a variety of climates and terrains. Because some biologists believe wolves must be culled to maintain caribou herd populations, controversial wolf kills, in which wolves are hunted by air, have taken place.

Brothers of the Caribou

The year 1991 marked 100 years of reindeer herding in Alaska. In 1891, the Rev. Sheldon Jackson, who was the general agent for education in Alaska, raised private funds to bring 16 reindeer from Siberia to the Unalaska Islands in the Aleutians. In 1892, 171 more reindeer were brought to Alaska. Jackson believed that Alaska Natives were destined for starvation if they were not given some options for livelihood when wild game was scarce.

Reindeer continued to be imported from Siberia until 1902. The Alaska Natives were coached by Siberian and Lapp herders in the business of reindeer herding. By 1905, there were about 10,000 reindeer in Alaska.

Until 1937, Alaska Natives shared management and ownership of the herds with the U.S. government, Laplanders, church missions and the Lomen Co. Congress agreed in the Reindeer Act of 1937 to allow Alaska Natives sole control of reindeer on their lands.

—1992 The ALASKA ALMANAC®

Wolverine. Shy, solitary creatures, wolverines are found throughout Alaska and on some Southeast islands. They are not abundant in comparison with other furbearers.

Furbearers

Beaver. These large vegetarian rodents are found in most of mainland Alaska from the Brooks Range to the middle of the Alaska Peninsula. Abundant in some major mainland river drainages in the Southeast and on Yakutat forelands, they have also been successfully transplanted to the Kodiak area. Beaver dams are sometimes destroyed to allow salmon upstream; however, beavers can rebuild their dams quickly and usually do so on the same site.

Coyote. The coyote is a relative newcomer to Alaska, showing up shortly after the turn of the 20th century, based on reports from old-timers and records. They are not abundant statewide, but are common in Tanana, Copper, Matanuska and Susitna river drainages and on Kenai Peninsula. The coyote is found as far west as Alaska Peninsula and the north side of Bristol Bay. Coyotes are increasingly seen near Anchorage.

Fox. *Arctic* (white and blue phases): Arctic foxes are found almost entirely along the Arctic coast as far south as the northwestern shore of Bristol Bay. They have been introduced to the Pribilof and Aleutian islands, where the blue color phase, most popular with fox farmers, predominates. The white color phase occurs naturally on Saint Lawrence and Nunivak islands. *Red:* Its golden fur coveted by trappers, the red fox is found throughout Alaska except for most areas of Southeast and around Prince William Sound.

Lynx. These shy night-prowlers' main food source is the snowshoe hare. The lynx is found throughout Alaska, except on the Yukon–Kuskokwim Delta, southern Alaska Peninsula and along coastal tidelands. It is relatively scarce along the northern Gulf Coast and in southeastern Alaska.

Hoary Marmot. Present throughout most of the mountain regions of Alaska and along the Endicott Mountains east into Canada, the hoary marmot lives in the high country, especially the warm slopes near and above timberline.

Marten. The marten must have climax spruce forest to survive; its habitat ranges throughout timbered Alaska, except north of the Brooks Range, on treeless sections of the Alaska Peninsula, and on the Yukon–Kuskokwim Delta. It has been successfully introduced to Prince of Wales, Baranof, Chichagof and Afognak islands.

Muskrat. Muskrats are found in greatest numbers around lakes, ponds, rivers and marshes throughout all of mainland Alaska south of the Brooks Range except for the Alaska Peninsula west of the Ugashik lakes. They were introduced to Kodiak, Afognak and Raspberry islands. Muskrats were traditionally an important early spring subsistence food for Native Alaskans.

River Otter. A member of the weasel family, the river otter occurs throughout the state except on Aleutian Islands, Bering Sea islands and the Arctic coastal plain east of Point Lay. It is most abundant in southeastern Alaska, in Prince William Sound coastal areas and on the Yukon–Kuskokwim Delta. It is sometimes called the "land otter" to distinguish it from the sea otter.

Raccoon. The raccoon is not native to Alaska and is considered an undesirable addition because of its impact on native wild- life. It is found on the west coast of Kodiak Island, on Japonski and Baranof islands,  and on other islands off Prince of Wales Island in Southeast.

Squirrel. *Northern flying:* These small nocturnal squirrels are found in Interior, Southcentral and Southeast Alaska where coniferous forests are sufficiently dense to provide suitable habitat. *Red:* These tree squirrels inhabit spruce forests, especially along rivers, from Southeast north to the Brooks Range. They are not found on the Seward Peninsula, Yukon–Kuskokwim Delta and Alaska Peninsula south of Naknek River.

Weasel. Least weasels and short-tailed weasels are found throughout Alaska, except for the Bering Sea and Aleutian Islands. Short-tailed weasels are brown with white underparts in summer, becoming snow-white in winter (designated ermine).

Other Small Mammals

Bat. There are five common bat species in Alaska.

Northern Hare (Arctic Hare or **Tundra Hare).** This large hare inhabits western and northern coastal Alaska, weighs 12 pounds or more and measures $2^1/_2$ feet long.

Snowshoe Hare (or Varying Hare). In winter, these animals become pure white; in summer, their coats are grayish to brown. The snowshoe hare occurs throughout Alaska except for the lower portion of Alaska Peninsula, the Arctic coast and most islands; it is scarce in southeastern Alaska. Cyclic population highs and lows of hares occur roughly every 10 years. Their big hind feet, covered with coarse hair in winter, act as snowshoes for easy travel over snow.

Brown Lemming. Lemmings are found throughout Northern Alaska and the Alaska Peninsula; they are not present in Southeast, Southcentral or the Kodiak archipelago.

Collared Lemming. Resembling large meadow voles, collared lemmings range from the Brooks Range north and from the lower Kuskokwim River drainage north.

Northern Bog Lemming (some- times called lemming mice). These tiny mammals, rarely observed, are in meadows and bogs across most of Alaska.

Deer Mouse. These rodents inhabit timber and brush in southeastern Alaska.

House Mouse. Extremely adaptive, familiar house mice are found in Alaska seaports and large communities in Southcentral Alaska.

Meadow Jumping Mouse. These mice can jump 6 feet and are found in the southern third of Alaska from the Alaska Range to the Gulf of Alaska.

Collared Pika. Members of the rabbit family, pikas are found in central and southern Alaska; they are most common in the Alaska Range.

Porcupine. These slow-moving rodents prefer forests and inhabit most wooded regions of mainland Alaska.

Norway Rat. The Norway rat came to Alaska on whaling ships in the mid-1800s, thriving in Aleutian ports (the Rat Islands group is named for the Norway rats). They are now found in virtually all Alaska

If That Ain't a Bite

A Kodiak fisherman went for an unexpected dip in Kodiak Harbor in April 1987 when a 1,500-pound sea lion pulled him under water. Travis Murphy said he was working on the stern of a boat when the sea lion grabbed his buttock.

Kodiak harbormaster George McCorkle said he has seen the evidence to back up the tale. Murphy told the Associated Press the sea lion pulled him an estimated seven feet under water. He kept kicking at the animal while he was going down, and it finally let him go.

—1988 *The ALASKA ALMANAC*®

seaports, and in Anchorage and Fairbanks and other population centers with open garbage dumps.

Shrew. Seven species of shrew range in Alaska.

Meadow Vole (or Meadow Mouse). Extremely adaptive, there are seven species of meadow vole attributed to Alaska that range throughout the state.

Red-backed Vole. The red-backed vole prefers cool, damp forests and is found throughout Alaska from Southeast to Norton Sound.

Woodchuck. These large, burrowing squirrels, also called groundhogs, are found in the eastern Interior between the Yukon and Tanana rivers, from east of Fairbanks to the Alaska–Canada border.

Bushy-tailed Woodrat. Commonly called pack rats because they tend to carry off objects to their nests, woodrats are found along the mainland coast of southeastern Alaska.

Marine Mammals

Marine mammals found in Alaska waters are **dolphin** (Grampus, Pacific white-sided and Risso's); **Pacific walrus**; **porpoise** (Dall and harbor); **sea otter**; **seal** (harbor, larga, northern elephant, northern fur, Pacific bearded or oogruk, ribbon, ringed and spotted); **Steller sea lion**; and

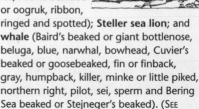

whale (Baird's beaked or giant bottlenose, beluga, blue, narwhal, bowhead, Cuvier's beaked or goosebeaked, fin or finback, gray, humpback, killer, minke or little piked, northern right, pilot, sei, sperm and Bering Sea beaked or Stejneger's beaked). (SEE Whales; Whaling)

The U.S. Fish and Wildlife Service (Department of the Interior) is responsible for the management of polar bears, sea otters and walrus in Alaska. The National Marine Fisheries Service (Department of Commerce) is responsible for the management of all other marine mammals.

MASKS (SEE ALSO Native Arts and Crafts)
Masks are integral to the cultures of the Eskimos, coastal Indians and Aleuts of Alaska.

Eskimo. Eskimo masks rank among the finest tribal art in the world. Ceremonialism and the mask-making that accompanied it were highly developed and practiced widely by the time the first Russians established trading posts in southeastern Alaska in the early 1800s.

Shaman used masks during certain ceremonies, sometimes in conjunction with wooden puppets, in ways that frightened and entertained participants. Dancers wore religious masks in festivals that honored the spirits of animals and birds to be hunted or that needed to be appeased. Each spirit was interpreted in a different mask and each mask was thought to have a spirit, or *inua*, of its own. This *inua* tied the mask to the stream of spiritual beliefs present in Eskimo religion. Not all masks were benign; some were surrealistic pieces that represented angry or dangerous spirits. Some had moving parts.

In 1996, the Anchorage Museum of History and Art held a notable exhibit, "Agayuliyararput Our Way of Making Prayer: The Living Tradition of Yup'ik Masks," to demonstrate the interest of Yup'ik people in preserving their past and carrying the vital tradition of mask-making into the future. The exhibit went on to tour the Lower 48 in 1997.

Indian. Several types of masks existed among the Tlingit and other coastal Indians of Alaska, including simple single-face masks, occasionally having an elaborately carved totemic border; a variation of the face mask with the addition of moving parts; and transformation masks, which have several faces concealed within the first.

Tlingit mask

Masked dancers were accompanied by a chorus of tribal singers who sang songs associated with the masks and reflecting the wealth of the host. Masks were the critical element in portraying the relationship of the tribe with spirits and projecting their power to spellbind their audiences.

Masks were always created to be worn, but not all members of the tribe held sufficient status or power to wear them. Ceremonial use of masks generally took place in the fall or winter, when the spirits of the other world were said to be nearby.

Northwest Coast Indian mask-makers primarily used alder, though red and yellow cedar were used at times.

Aleut. Examples of masks used on various islands of the Aleutian Chain for shamanistic and ceremonial purposes are reported as early as the mid-18th century. Some of these early masks represented animals. Many were apparently destroyed after use. Aleut legends maintain that some masks were associated with ancient inhabitants of the region.

On the Shumagin Islands, a group of cavelike chambers yielded important examples of Aleut masks late in the 19th century. A number of well-preserved masks, apparently associated with the burials of Aleut whalers, were found. All of them had once been painted. Some of them had attached ears and tooth grips. Pegs were used for inserting feathers or carved wooden appendages similar to those of Eskimo masks of southern Alaska today. Fragments of composite masks, those decorated with feathers, appendages or movable parts, have been found on Kagamil Island with earlier remains.

Early accounts of masked Aleut dances say each dance was accompanied by special songs. Most masks were apparently hidden in caves or secret places when the ceremony ended.

Today, modern Aleut mask-makers study the old traditions and reproduce masks from museum collections or create contemporary variants in clay, glass and even chrome.

McNEIL RIVER STATE GAME SANCTUARY

Photographers, naturalists, wildlife enthusiasts and researchers come to McNeil River State Game Sanctuary in Southwestern Alaska for the opportunity to view the world's largest concentration of brown bears in their natural habitat. The Alaska Department of Fish and Game manages the sanctuary's unique bear-viewing program, which allows visitors to watch the brown bears as they congregate to feed on migrating salmon. Small groups are escorted to a viewing area by a department guide and are limited to 10 visitors a day. Despite the number of bears and the presence of humans, there have been no injuries to bears or humans in the 23 years of the program.

All visitors must apply for a permit to visit the sanctuary. In 2000, almost 1,300 people applied for one of 280 permits awarded by lottery. Applications are available after Jan. 1 and due March 1 for the upcoming visitor season.

Bears and Salmon

The two are as synonymous as Alaska and winter. Both Alaska brown bears, *Ursus arctos,* and American black bears, *Ursus americanus,* catch and eat salmon, but rarely do the two species coexist on the same watercourse. Black bears enjoy exclusive use of only a few streams; most are dominated by their larger cousins. A brown bear may kill and eat any black bear it catches.

—*Alaska's Wildlife* by Tom Walker

Contact the Alaska Department of Fish and Game, Division of Wildlife Conservation, 333 Raspberry Road, Anchorage 99518-1599, Attention: McNeil River; (907) 267-2182; www.state.ak.us/adfg.

Statistics on bears in the sanctuary have been compiled since 1976:

• Most bears seen at one time at McNeil Falls—68
• Most bears seen in one day at McNeil Falls—105
• Most salmon seen caught in one day by one bear—90
• Most salmon seen caught in one year by one bear—1,012
• Most salmon seen caught in one year at McNeil Falls—15,455

MEDAL OF HEROISM By a

law enacted in 1965, the Alaska governor is authorized to award, in recognition of valorous and heroic deeds, a state medal of heroism to those who have saved a life or, at risk to their lives, have served the state or community on behalf of the health, welfare or safety of others. The heroism medal is not necessarily given every year, and may be awarded posthumously. Following are recipients and year of the award of the Alaska Medal of Heroism:

Albert Rothfuss (1965), Ketchikan. Rescued a child from drowning in Ketchikan Creek.

Randy Blake Prinzing (1968), Soldotna. Saved two lives at Scout Lake.

Nancy Davis (1971), Seattle. A flight attendant who convinced an alleged hijacker to surrender.

Jeffrey Stone (1972), Fairbanks. Saved two youths from a burning apartment.

Gilbert Pelowook (1975), Savoonga. An Alaska state trooper who aided plane crash victims on St. Lawrence Island.

Residents of Gambell (1975). Provided aid and care for plane crash victims on St. Lawrence Island.

George Jackinsky (1978), Kasilof. Rescued two persons from a burning aircraft.

Mike Hancock (1980), Lima, Ohio. Rescued a victim of a plane crash that brought down high-voltage lines.

David Graham (1983), Kenai. Rescued a person from a burning car.

Robert Larson (1983), Anchorage. An employee of the Department of Public Safety who flew through hazardous conditions to rescue survivors of the crash that took John Stimson's life.

John Stimson (1983), Cordova. A first sergeant in the Division of Fish and Wildlife Protection who died in a helicopter accident during an attempt to rescue others.

Only in Anchorage would the mayor declare an official annual "Scoop the Poop Day," when residents try to clean up six months worth of dog manure that has miraculously appeared when the snow melts in the spring.

Esther Farquhar (1984), Sitka. Tried to save other members of her family from a fire in their home; lost her life in the attempt.

Darren Olanna (1984), Nome. Died while attempting to rescue a person from a burning house.

Billy Westlock (1986), Emmonak. Rescued a youngster from the Emmonak River.

Lieutenant Commander Whiddon, Lieutenant Breithaupt, ASM2 Tunks, AD1 Saylor and **AT3 Milne (1987)**, Sitka. U.S. Coast Guard personnel rescued a man and his son from their sinking boat during high seas.

The Army and Air National Guard (1988), Gambell, Savoonga, Nome and Shishmaref. Searched for seven missing walrus hunters from Gambell.

Evans Geary, Johnny Sheldon, Jason Rutman, Jessee Ahkpuk Jr. and **Carl Hadley (1989)**, Buckland. Youths rescued two friends who, while skating on a frozen pond, had fallen through the ice.

Robert Cusack (1991), Lake Iliamna. Rescued a woman and a child who were trapped inside a floatplane that had crashed and sank in Lake Iliamna.

Clifford Comer, Robert Yerex, Gary Strebe, David Schron and **Jeffery Waite (1992)**, Air Station Kodiak. Coast Guard members rescued a four-man fishing crew in 45-knot winds and 35-foot seas.

Clyde Aketachunak (1994), Kotlik. Awarded posthumously after Aketachunak died in an attempt to save 6-year-old Jennifer Prince from drowning in Kotlik Slough.

Sgt. David Lancaster (1994), formerly of Fort Richardson, and Tom Burgess (1994), North Pole. Saved the lives of passengers on a tour bus that was involved in a head-on collision on the Parks Highway.

Eric Pentilla, Randy Oles, Walter Greaves and **Jerry Austin (1994)**. Helped rescue seven missionaries whose plane crashed in the Bering Sea when returning from Russia.

Travis Bennett (1994), North Pole. At the age of 14, waded into the Chena River to save the life of Debbie Peterson, who was drowning.

Mike Olsen, Rusty Shaub, Kevin Kramer and **George Coulter (1994)**. Rescued the survivors of an airplane crash in Taku Inlet.

METRIC CONVERSIONS (approximate)

	When you know:	You can find:	If you multiply by:
Length	inches	millimeters	25.4
	feet	centimeters	30.5
	yards	meters	0.9
	miles	kilometers	1.6
	millimeters	inches	0.04
	centimeters	inches	0.4
	meters	yards	1.1
	kilometers	miles	0.6
Temperature	degrees Fahrenheit	degrees Celsius	5/9 (after subtracting 32)
	degrees Celsius	degrees Fahrenheit	9/5 (then add 32)

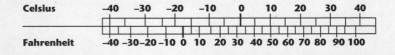

(Louis R.) Rick Gottwald (1995), Juneau. Swam to a burning boat in Juneau's Harris Harbor and saved an intoxicated man who was on board.

Rose Edgren (1995), Delta Junction. A state trooper who pushed her partner to safety when they were fired upon, shot the attacker and then administered lifesaving first aid.

Sam Hoger (1996), Eagle River. While visiting New Orleans, rescued a 10-year-old boy from drowning.

Timothy Eldridge and **Billy Luce (1997),** Anchorage. Entered an apartment on the third floor of a burning building in Anchorage, dragged the occupant to safety and doused the flames

Gene Snell (2000), Shismaref. Rescued a snow machine rider who had fallen through the ice and was clinging to his floating sled.

Rick Siangco (2000), Juneau. Fisherman and his crew rescued two fishermen whose boat had capsized in 10-foot seas near Juneau.

MICROBREWERIES As in many
parts of the United States, limited-edition stouts, ales and beers are a trend in Alaska. Many of the breweries offer dining and window observation of the brewing process. Others offer tours and samples.

Alaskan Brewing & Bottling Company, 5429 Shaune Drive, Juneau 99801.

Borealis Brewery, 349 E. Ship Creek Ave., Anchorage 99501.

Cusack's Brewpub, 598 W. Northern Lights Blvd., Anchorage 99503.

Glacier Brew House, 737 W. Fifth Ave., Anchorage 99501.

Midnight Sun Brewing Company, 7329 Arctic Blvd., Anchorage 99518.

Moose's Tooth Pub & Pizzeria, 3300 Old Seward Highway, Anchorage 99503.

Raven's Ridge, 5690 Supply Road, Fairbanks 99701.

Silver Gulch Brewing, 2195 Old Steese Hwy. N., Fairbanks 99701.

Snow Goose Restaurant/Sleeping Lady Brewing Co., 717 W. Third Ave., Anchorage 99501.

MILITARY Congress saw little need
for a strong military presence in the Territory of Alaska until the rapid escalation of World War II. Spurred by the realization that Alaska could be a strategic location both defensively and offensively, the government built and still maintains units

MILEAGE CHART

Driving Mileage Between Principal Points	Anchorage, AK	Dawson City, YT	Dawson Creek, BC	Fairbanks, AK	Haines, AK	Homer, AK	Prince Rupert, BC	Seattle, WA	Skagway, AK	Valdez, AK	Whitehorse, YT
Anchorage, AK		515	1608	358	775	226	1605	2435	832	304	724
Dawson City, YT	515		1195	393	578	741	1192	2022	435	441	327
Dawson Creek, BC	1608	1195		1486	1135	1834	706	827	992	1534	884
Fairbanks, AK	358	393	1486		653	584	1483	2313	710	284	602
Haines, AK	775	578	1135	653		1001	1132	1962	359	701	251
Homer, AK	226	741	1834	584	1001		1831	2661	1058	530	950
Prince Rupert, BC	1605	1192	706	1483	1132	1831		1033	989	1531	881
Seattle, WA	2435	2022	827	2313	1962	2661	1033		1819	2361	1711
Skagway, AK	832	435	992	710	359	1058	989	1819		758	108
Valdez, AK	304	441	1534	284	701	530	1531	2361	758		650
Whitehorse, YT	724	327	884	602	251	950	881	1711	108	650	

of the Air Force, Army, Navy and Coast Guard at dozens of installations across the state.

The Alaskan Command (ALCOM) is the senior military command in Alaska. The combined forces of ALCOM include nearly 21,000 Air Force, Army, Navy, Marine and Coast Guard personnel and reservists. At the state level are Air National Guard and Army National Guard Units.

U.S. Army. The Army is headquartered at Fort Richardson near Anchorage and the senior Army commander in Alaska, a major general, is based there. The brigade task force commander, a colonel, and his staff are located at Fort Wainwright near Fairbanks. The Army also has research facilities and training grounds at Fort Greely, near Delta Junction.

The primary element of U.S. Army Alaska is the 172nd Infantry Brigade. It is headquartered with most of its forces at Fort Wainwright. The brigade's 1st Battalion, 501st Parachute Infantry Regiment is stationed at Fort Richardson.

The 59th Signal Battalion oversees all Army communications in the state. The Northern Warfare Training Center headquartered at Fort Wainwright trains soldiers and members of other services in arctic combat and survival. The Cold Regions Test Center, at Fort Greely, tests equipment for cold-weather use.

The 68th Medical Company performs medical evacuations of military personnel and civilians. The High Altitude Rescue Team flies specially equipped Chinook helicopters in support of rescues on Mount McKinley and other peaks.

The Alaska District of the U.S. Army Corps of Engineers designs and constructs buildings, runways, roads, utilities and other facilities for the Army, Air Force and National Guard. The Corps also develops and regulates water resources and has an increasing workload in environmental restoration.

U.S. Air Force. The 11th Air Force helps maintain air superiority in Alaska and supports Alaska-based ground forces and

Captain Randy Acord, an Army Air Force engineer flight test officer in World War II, holds the prop of a twin-engine P-38 fighter at Ladd Field near Fairbanks in 1944. From *Heroes of the Horizon* by Gerry Bruder.

air forces. The largest units are the 3rd Wing at Elmendorf Air Force Base near Anchorage and the 354th Fighter Wing at Eielson Air Force Base near Fairbanks. The 3rd Wing is equipped with F–15C/D Eagles and F–15E Strike Eagles. The 3rd Wing's 517th Airlift Squadron is equipped with C–130 and C–12 aircraft and its 962nd Airborne Warning and Control Squadron flies the E–3 Sentry.

The 354th Fighter Wing uses the F–16 and OA–10 Thunderbolt II.

Remote locations of the 11th Air Force include Galena and King Salmon airports, Eareckson Air Force Station on Shemya Island and a network of 18 Air Force radar sites throughout Alaska.

Navy and Marine Corps. A small contingent of U.S. Navy officers and enlisted personnel are assigned to the Alaskan Command headquarters as staff and the U.S. Naval Forces Alaska staff. The Navy and Marine Corps have commands and detachments in Anchorage.

U.S. Coast Guard. The U.S. Coast Guard has been a part of Alaska since the mid-1800s, when it patrolled Alaska's coastline with the wooden sailing and steam ships of its predecessor, the Revenue Cutter Service. Since those early days, the service has changed names and today's fleet of ships, boats and aircraft has replaced wooden ships.

The 17th Coast Guard District encompasses the entire state of Alaska, with a coastline far longer than that of all other states combined. The Coast Guard performs its missions in Alaska with more than 1,800 active-duty members, 400 auxiliary members, 50 reservists and 140 civilian employees. The district headquarters is located in Juneau. The Air Station Kodiak is the largest in the country.

Among the Coast Guard's missions in Alaska are the enforcement of fisheries laws, search and rescue, marine safety and marine environmental protection. The service also maintains navigation aids, including six Long Range Navigation (LORAN) stations.

National Guard. The Alaska Army National Guard and the Air National Guard perform a wide range of missions, including security, search and rescue, airlift, transportation, aerial refueling, drug interdiction and youth support. Guard units also respond to emergencies or disasters.

The guard's headquarters is at Camp Denali near Anchorage. Nearly 2,000 soldiers are assigned to the Alaska Army National Guard. Most are members of the 207th Infantry Group, which has battalion headquarters at Nome, Bethel, Wasilla, Anchorage and Juneau.

The Alaska Air Guard has about 2,000 members. The 176th Wing, home of the 144th Airlift Squadron and the 210th Rescue Squadron, is at Kulis Air National Guard Base in Anchorage. The Rescue Coordination Center is located at Camp Denali. The 168th Air Refueling Wing is

NUGGETS

Clear, Alaska, was the site of one of three Ballistic Missile Early Warning System stations in 1985 (the others were in Greenland and England). Operating since 1961, the BMEW station's three 400-foot-wide, 165-foot-high radar screens scanned the skies from the North Pole to China. Designed to give the U.S. at least a 15-minute warning before the missiles hit, the BMEWs replaced the earlier Distant Early Warning (DEW) Line, which was designed to detect bombers crossing into North American air space, but was ineffective in detecting ballistic missiles.
—1986 *The ALASKA ALMANAC*®

assigned to Eielson Air Force Base. The 206th Combat Communications Squadron is at Elmendorf Air Force Base.

Military Population. Military services are a major component of Alaska's economy. The total population of the military in Alaska as of October 2000 was 20,763 service members, plus approximately 36,000 family members.

MINERALS AND MINING
(SEE ALSO Coal; Gold; Oil and Gas; Rocks and Gems)
The sum of exploration and development investment in Alaska and the value of minerals produced totaled a record $1.25 billion in 2000, exceeding $1 billion for the fifth year.

Exploration expenditures in 2000 fell to $31.2 million, down 40 percent from the $52.3 million spent in 1999. Most of this reduction was due to exploration at Pogo and Fort Knox proceeding to development.

Development expenditures increased to $137.1 million in 2000 from $33.8 million in 1999. This was due to mill optimization at Red Dog, work at Fort Knox and True North (near Fairbanks) and Pogo (near Delta), and development of Greens Creek and Kensington (near Juneau).

Total value of Alaska mineral production in 2000 increased to $1.08 billion with $979 million in metals, $62.4 million in industrial metals (such as rock, sand and gravel), and $38.9 million in coal.

Metal production accounted for 91 percent of the total 2000 production, with 669,112 tons of zinc valued at $682.5 million; 546,000 ounces of gold valued at $152.4 million; 18.2 million ounces of silver valued at $90.4 million; 123,224 tons of lead valued at $51.8 million; and 1,400 tons of copper valued at $2.3 million. Between 1999 and 2000, values of lead production declined 10 percent, and copper 23 percent.

Most of the gold in Alaska in 2000 was from the Fort Knox open-pit, hard-rock mine near Fairbanks, where almost exactly 1,000 ounces daily were produced, for a total of 362,429 ounces. About 50 placer gold mines statewide produced an additional 40,000 ounces, with seven large mines producing 75 percent of the total.

A small amount of copper was produced as a by-product at the Greens Creek gold mine.

The Usibelli Mine near Healy produced the only coal in the state in 2000, and exported 708,000 tons of the total 1.5 million tons to Korea, with the remainder firing seven power plants throughout the Alaska Interior, including a state-of-the-art, clean coal power plant.

Sealaska Corp. shipped a small amount of high-quality calcium carbonate in 2000 from the Calder limestone deposit on Prince of Wales Island, following several years of development, potentially heralding a new industry for Southeast Alaska.

Several exploration projects show promise of becoming the mines for the future. At the Kensington Mine north of Juneau all permits are in place, but modifications have been proposed to allow for profitable mining even at the depressed prices of 2000. The mine is projected to

NUGGETS

Total value of hard mineral production in Alaska amounted to $64.3 million in 1976, compared with $67.7 million in 1975. —1978 *The ALASKA ALMANAC*®

produce about 200,000 ounces of gold a year.

At Donlin Creek near Iditarod, drilling in 1998 increased the resource to 11.5 million ounces of gold, and at the Shotgun prospect 100 miles to the south, a gold resource of 1 million ounces is anticipated. In the Interior, the True North gold prospect about 8 miles from the Fort Knox Mine has a gold resource of 1.3 million ounces, the nearby Gil prospect has a resource of 450,000 ounces, and the Ryan Lode Mine to the west has a resource of more than 1 million ounces.

The Pogo gold prospect northeast of Delta Junction has a gold reserve of 5 million ounces, but unlike the low-grade Fort Knox Mine (0.024 ounces of gold per ton), Pogo has a grade 20 times that, at 0.52 ounces per ton. This rich deposit, containing more than 5.6 million ounces of gold and more projected, has created a claim-staking rush from Fairbanks to the Canadian border and beyond.

Several companies have been exploring for polymetallic deposits containing gold, silver, copper, lead and zinc along the north flank of the Alaska Range from Tok to Healy. These prospects, such as Dry Creek and Rumble Creek, resemble the Wolverine deposit in the Yukon.

About 5,500 state mining claims and 3,000 state prospecting sites were located in 2000, bringing the total active claims to about 64,000. About 550 new federal claims were staked, mainly in Southeast, with the total active federal claims numbering about 11,000.

MOSQUITOES Alaska's ubiquitous mosquito is sometimes jokingly referred to as the state bird. At least 25 species of mosquito are found in Alaska (the number may be as high as 40), the females of all species feeding on people, other mammals or birds. Males and females eat plant sugar, but only the females suck blood, which they use for egg production. The itch that follows the bite comes from an anticoagulant injected by the mosquito. No Alaska mosquitoes carry diseases.

The insects are present from April through September in many areas of the state. Out in the Bush they are often at their worst in June, tapering off in July. The mosquito menace usually passes by late August and September. From Cook Inlet south, the bugs concentrate on coastal flats and forested valleys. In the Aleutian Islands, mosquitoes are absent or present only in small numbers. The most serious mosquito infestations occur in moist areas of slow-moving or standing water, such as fields, bogs and forests of Interior Alaska, from Bristol Bay eastward.

Mosquitoes are most active at dusk and dawn; low temperatures and high winds decrease their activity. Mosquitoes can be controlled by draining their breeding areas or spraying with approved insecticides. When traveling in areas of heavy mosquito infestations, it is wise to wear protective clothing, carefully screen living areas and tents, and use a good insect repellent.

MOUNTAINS Of the 20 highest mountains in the United States, 17 are in Alaska, which has 19 peaks over 14,000 feet. (SEE MAP on pages 126–127)

MOUNT McKINLEY In the Alaska Range is the highest mountain on the North American continent. The South Peak is 20,320 feet high; the North Peak has an elevation of 19,470 feet. The mountain was named in 1896 for William McKinley of Ohio, who was the Republican candidate for president.

An earlier name had been *Denali,* an Athabascan word meaning "the high one."

The state of Alaska officially renamed the mountain Denali in 1975 and the state Geographic Names Board claims the proper name for the mountain is Denali. However, the federal Board of Geographic Names has not taken any action and congressional legislation has been introduced to retain the name McKinley in perpetuity.

Mount McKinley is within Denali National Park and Preserve. The park entrance is about 237 miles north of Anchorage and 121 miles south of Fairbanks via the George Parks Highway.

A 90-mile gravel road runs west from the highway through the park; vehicle traffic on the park road is restricted. The park is also accessible via the Alaska Railroad and by aircraft.

The mountain and its park are one of the top tourist attractions in Alaska.

(Continued on page 128)

Researchers on the northern tundra reported up to 9,000 mosquito bites per minute. At that rate, a person would lose half of his blood supply in two hours!

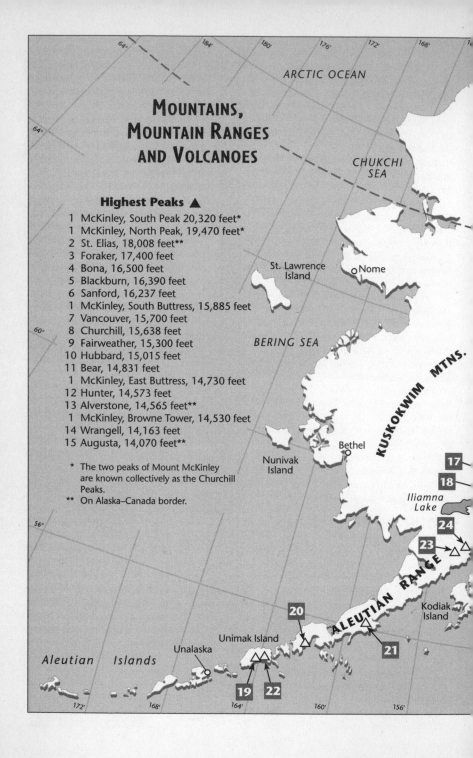

MOUNTAINS, MOUNTAIN RANGES AND VOLCANOES

Highest Peaks ▲

1 McKinley, South Peak 20,320 feet*
1 McKinley, North Peak, 19,470 feet*
2 St. Elias, 18,008 feet**
3 Foraker, 17,400 feet
4 Bona, 16,500 feet
5 Blackburn, 16,390 feet
6 Sanford, 16,237 feet
1 McKinley, South Buttress, 15,885 feet
7 Vancouver, 15,700 feet
8 Churchill, 15,638 feet
9 Fairweather, 15,300 feet
10 Hubbard, 15,015 feet
11 Bear, 14,831 feet
1 McKinley, East Buttress, 14,730 feet
12 Hunter, 14,573 feet
13 Alverstone, 14,565 feet**
1 McKinley, Browne Tower, 14,530 feet
14 Wrangell, 14,163 feet
15 Augusta, 14,070 feet**

* The two peaks of Mount McKinley
  are known collectively as the Churchill
  Peaks.
** On Alaska–Canada border.

ARCTIC OCEAN

CHUKCHI SEA

St. Lawrence Island

Nome

BERING SEA

KUSKOKWIM MTNS.

Bethel

Nunivak Island

Iliamna Lake

17
18
24
23
20
21
22
19

ALEUTIAN RANGE

Kodiak Island

Unimak Island

Unalaska

Aleutian   Islands

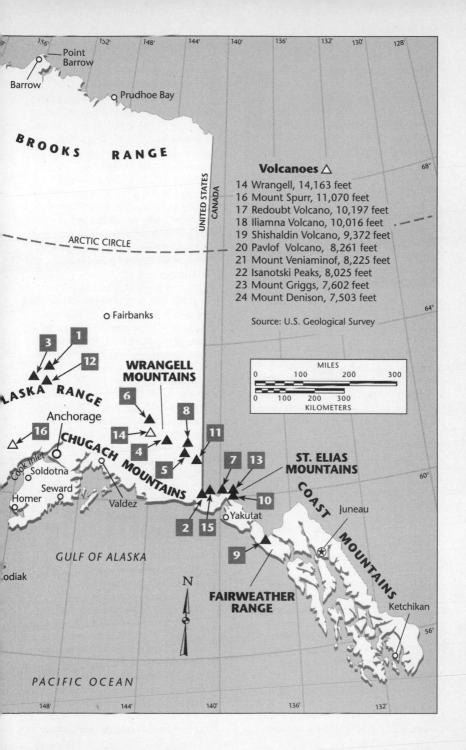

Volcanoes △
14 Wrangell, 14,163 feet
16 Mount Spurr, 11,070 feet
17 Redoubt Volcano, 10,197 feet
18 Iliamna Volcano, 10,016 feet
19 Shishaldin Volcano, 9,372 feet
20 Pavlof Volcano, 8,261 feet
21 Mount Veniaminof, 8,225 feet
22 Isanotski Peaks, 8,025 feet
23 Mount Griggs, 7,602 feet
24 Mount Denison, 7,503 feet

Source: U.S. Geological Survey

MILES
0   100   200   300

0   100   200   300
KILOMETERS

BROOKS RANGE

Point Barrow
Barrow
Prudhoe Bay

UNITED STATES
CANADA

ARCTIC CIRCLE

Fairbanks

ALASKA RANGE

WRANGELL MOUNTAINS

Anchorage
CHUGACH MOUNTAINS

Cook Inlet
Soldotna
Seward
Homer
Valdez

ST. ELIAS MOUNTAINS

Yakutat

COAST MOUNTAINS

Juneau

GULF OF ALASKA

Kodiak

N

FAIRWEATHER RANGE

Ketchikan

PACIFIC OCEAN

Photographers hope for a shot like this; McKinley is often shrouded in clouds.
Photo by Roy Corral.

(Continued from page 125)
The finest times to see McKinley up close are on summer mornings. August is best, according to statistics based on 13 summers of observation by park ranger Rick McIntyre. The mountain is rarely visible the entire day. The best view is from Eielson Visitor Center, about 66 miles from the park entrance and 33 miles northeast of the summit. The center, open from early June through the second week in September, is reached by shuttle bus provided by the park. There is a $23 bus fee for the eight-hour round trip. Discounts are available for children. Denali Park Resorts information is available by calling (907) 683-2294 or (907) 272-7275.

Eleven climbers perished on Mount McKinley in May 1992, making it the deadliest climbing season in the mountain's history. The 11 climbers, including one American mountaineering guide, died in five separate incidents on the mountain. Since 1932, when the National Park Service began keeping records of climbers attempting to reach the summit of Mount McKinley, 92 climbers have been killed on the mountain. Among the deadliest years on the mountain were 1981 and 1989,

when six mountaineers were killed each of those two years; 1967 and 1980, when eight mountaineers were killed each year; and 1992, when 11 died.

Of the 1,209 climbers taking part in the 2000 mountaineering season, 633, or 52 percent, reached the summit. Climbers came from 41 countries. From 1995 to 2000, there were 66 major search and rescue efforts and 12 fatalities.

On July 19, 2000, a park ranger, two volunteers and a pilot died in an airplane crash on McKinley. The ranger and volunteers were headed to Kahiltna Glacier to begin a patrol on the mountain. Killed were Ranger Cale Shaffer, 25; volunteers Brian Reagan, 27, and Adam Kolff, 27; and pilot Don Bowers, 52.

The Park Service spent $73,137 on search and rescue missions in 2000; military costs were $213,809. The Park Service requires climbers to register 60 days before a planned climb. In 1995, for the first time in park history, climbers were charged a $150 fee to scale the mountain.

The 2000 Denali Pro honorees were John Mislow and Andrew Swanson of the Chicago West Rib Expedition. The men assisted several expeditions that were having difficulties, helping them build camps and retrieve caches. They also helped the National Park Service with

NUGGETS

Mount McKinley was officially renamed Denali by the State of Alaska in 1975, and the state Geographic Names Board also claimed the proper name was Denali. However, the federal Board of Geographic Names did not take any action, and a congressional representative from Ohio introduced legislation in 1981 to retain the name McKinley in perpetuity.—1983 *The ALASKA ALMANAC®*

The Sourdough Expedition

In 1906 explorer Frederick Cook announced that he and a companion had conquered Mount McKinley. Cook provided detailed reports of the alleged climb, as well as a photograph of himself at the summit. He was hailed by the gullible New York press [as] a celebrity. Cook's claims did not play well in the saloons of Fairbanks where, in late 1909, a group of miners led by Tom Lloyd decided no Easterner should be first to reach Denali's summit. Thus arose the "Sourdough Expedition." Lloyd and six partners—none with climbing experience—set off in the dead of winter. Before they reached the mountain a fist fight broke out, and three turned back. The remaining four began their assault in March 1910, without ropes and carrying a 14-foot flagpole to plant at the top. In a remarkable sustained climb of 18 hours, two of the party negotiated the final 9,000-foot ascent of McKinley's north peak, planted their pole, and came down—unaware that the south peak was actually 850 feet higher. Their exploit is still considered one of mountaineering's most astonishing feats.
—Harry Ritter, *Alaska's History*

route finding, work on an electrical project, and building an igloo for storing supplies. They did not reach the summit of Mount McKinley, but rangers noted that they used good judgment and risk assessment in deciding to turn back after reaching their high camp. The Denali Pro award is presented by the National Park Service and Pigeon Mountain Industries, a climbing equipment manufacturer.

Information on climbing Mount McKinley is available at (907) 733-2231 and www.nps.gov/dena/home.

Mount McKinley Firsts

1896: Prospector William Dickey names the prominent peak Mount McKinley.

1902: Alfred H. Brooks, leader of a U.S. Geological Survey party, is the first white man to set foot on McKinley's slopes.

1903: Judge James Wickersham and four others from Fairbanks make the first attempt on the peak.

1910: The Sourdough Expedition makes an attempt; two members reach the summit of the North Peak.

1913: Hudson Stuck's expedition is the first to reach the South Peak.

1932: Bush pilot Joe Crosson makes the first glacier landing on Muldrow Glacier for the Allen Carpé Expedition.

1947: Barbara Washburn is the first woman to reach the summit.

1967: Ray Genet, Dave Johnson and Art Davidson make the first winter ascent.

1979: Mushers Joe Redington Sr. and Susan Butcher mush a team of sled dogs to the summit.

1984: Japanese explorer Naomi Uemura makes the first winter solo ascent but dies during his descent.

1988: Vern Tejas makes the first complete winter solo climb.

1991: Taras Genet, 12, the son of Ray Genet, becomes the youngest person to climb McKinley.

1995: Merrick Johnston, 12, is the youngest female climber.

1998: Korean Kim Young Sik, slightly younger than Taras Genet, sets new record as youngest male climber.

1999: Highest short-haul rescue by the National Park Service Lama helicopter is made from 19,500 feet.

2001: Galen Johnston, 11, (no relation to Merrick Johnston) holds the new record as youngest male climber.

MUKLUKS

MUKLUKS *Mukluks* are lightweight boots designed to provide warmth in extreme cold. Eskimo *mukluks* are traditionally made with *oogruk* (bearded seal) skin soles and leg uppers of caribou trimmed with fur. Athabascan *mukluks* are traditionally made of moose hide and trimmed with fur and beadwork. Hay inner soles add insulation. The *mukluks* may be either calf-height or knee-height, with a leather drawstring in a casing around the top to keep out the wind and snow.

Eskimos of long ago sewed all their own clothing, mainly from the skins of animals and seabirds. These *mukluks* were not worn in winter unless the weather was warm, for they were made from seal leather with the hair removed and *oogruk* soles. The *oogruk* was oiled very heavily to be water-resistant and no fur trim was used on the "water mukluks," as they were called. The skins of large fish, including salmon, were also used to make the water-resistant *mukluks*.

Any *mukluks* that have been exposed to water or dampness should be hung in a cool place to dry slowly; sudden heat could shrink them out of shape and make them hard and stiff.

MUKTUK This Eskimo delicacy consists of outer skin layers and attached blubber of a whale. The two species of whale from which *muktuk* is most often sliced are the bowhead and the beluga, or white whale. The outer skin layers consist of a corky protective layer, the true skin and the blubber. In the case of beluga *muktuk,* the outer layer is white, the next layer is black and the blubber is pink. It may be eaten fresh, frozen, boiled or fermented.

MUSEUMS, CULTURAL CENTERS, EXHIBITS, HISTORIC PARKS, HISTORICAL SOCIETIES AND REPOSITORIES Visiting

any of the following museums, historic sites, notable exhibits, archives or other repositories offers a look into the rich diversity of Alaska culture and history. Many of the smaller museums are open only June through September.

Information is available at www.museums.state.ak.us and www.museumsalaska.org.

Anaktuvuk Pass: Simon Paneak Memorial Museum, P.O. Box 21085, Anaktuvuk Pass 99721-0085; (907) 661-3413. Display of hunting tools and a description of the Paleo–Indian people who occupied the Mesa Site in the Brooks Range more than 11,000 years ago.

Anchorage: Alaska Aviation Heritage Museum, 4721 Aircraft Drive, Anchorage 99502; (907) 248-5325; www.home.gci. net/~aahm. On the south shore of Lake Hood. Features 30 vintage aircraft, video and a military aviation gallery. Watch takeoffs and landings from the largest floatplane base in the world.

Alaska Collection, Z. J. Loussac Library, 3600 Denali, Anchorage 99503; (907) 343-2832. Rare books, reference books, state records, microfilm of news-papers, catalogs of photographs at other archives in the state.

Alaska Experience Center, 705 W. Sixth Ave., Anchorage 99501; (907) 276-3730. "Alaska the Great Land" shows hourly on a 180-degree screen; in another exhibit, viewers "experience" a magnitude 4.5 earthquake.

Alaska Native Heritage Center, 8800 Heritage Center Drive, Anchorage 99506; (907) 330-8000; www.alaska native.net. Welcome House, contemporary culture and traditional village exhibits, theater and Native Tradition Bearers.

Alaska Public Lands Information Center, 605 W. Fourth, Anchorage 99501; (907) 271-2737; www.nps.gov/aplic/center. Displays and information on refuges, forests, parks and outdoor recreation lands in Alaska. Video programs and computers permit self-help trip-planning.

Alaska Resources Library and Information Services, 3150 C St., Anchorage 99503; (907) 272-7547; www.arlis.org. Information on archaeology, Native land claims, environmental and natural resources of Alaska, ornithology and wildlife biology, fisheries biology and cold-regions engineering.

Alaska State Troopers Museum, Sixth Avenue between C and D streets, P.O. Box 100280, Anchorage 99510-0280; (800) 770-5050; (907) 279-5050; www.alaska.net/~foast. Exhibits, memorabilia and photographs detailing Alaska law enforcement history.

Anchorage Museum of History and Art, 121 W. Seventh Ave., Anchorage 99501; (907) 343-4326; www.ci.anchorage.ak.us/services/departments/culture/museum/index.html. Alaska Gallery dioramas depict 10,000 years of Alaska history. Guided tours with docents available. "Art of the Far North" contains early engravings by artists who accompanied 18th-century explorers and features works of art from travelers, adventurers, early residents and Natives.

Elmendorf Air Force Base Wildlife Museum, 3CES/CEVP, 5312 Ninth St., Elmendorf AFB 99506; (907) 552-2436. Enter base through Boniface Parkway Gate. Habitat displays of Alaska wildlife: bear, musk-oxen, Dall sheep, small mammals, extensive displays of fish.

Fort Richardson Fish and Wildlife Center, Building 656, Fort Richardson 99505; (907) 384-0437 or 384-0823. Mounted animals and fish: moose family with calves, bear, musk-oxen, birds, wolves and sea mammals. Guided tours by military personnel who specialize in wildlife biology.

Fourth Avenue Theatre, 630 W. Fourth Ave., Anchorage 99501; (907) 257-5600; (907) 257-5650. Art deco building from the 1940s houses museum photo display of old Anchorage on the lower level. On the main level, free Alaska-theme movies on the big screen. Dinner theater during the summer. Departure point for one-hour trolley tours of Anchorage.

Heritage Library and Museum (National Bank of Alaska Heritage Library), Northern Lights and C Street, Anchorage 99503; (907) 265-2834. Native baskets, ivory and artifacts; photos, hunting implements, rare books and paintings.

Imaginarium Science Discovery Center, 737 W. Fifth Ave., Suite G, Anchorage 99501; (907) 276-3179; www.imaginarium.org. Hands-on scientific displays for children, planetarium bubble show, polar bear lair, arctic ecology. Monthly rotating exhibits.

NANA Museum of the Arctic, 100 Shore Ave., Kotzebue (c/o Tour Arctic, 1001 E. Benson Blvd., Third Floor, Anchorage 99508); (907) 265-4157. Collections reflect Eskimo ethnology and natural history of northwestern Alaska; wildlife exhibits, slide show. Cultural heritage demonstrations such as skin

> On opening night at Anchorage's most popular theater company, the leading man left at intermission to attend an Amway sales seminar. He got so wrapped up in the presentation that he forgot to return to the theater. The stunned cast muddled through, trying to replace every third line on the spur of the moment. A critic in the house never noticed that anything was wrong.

sewing, ivory carving, Eskimo dancing, Eskimo blanket toss. Winter hours by appointment.

National Archives, Alaska Region, 654 W. Third Ave., Anchorage 99501; (907) 271-2441. Historical records including photographs, maps and architectural drawings, dating from 1867 to the present. Both original records and microfilm are available for research.

Oscar Anderson House, 420 M St., Anchorage 99502; (907) 274-2336; www.customcpu.com/np/ahpi. The city's first wood-frame house, built in 1915 by Swedish immigrant Oscar Anderson, was completely restored in 1982. Swedish Christmas celebration.

Potter Section House and Historic Park, on Seward Highway, 12 miles south of Anchorage; (907) 345-5014. Alaska Railroad historic site. Chugach State Park headquarters; maps, brochures, interpretive display, rotary snowplow, railroad cars.

University of Alaska Archives and Manuscripts, Library, University of Alaska, 3211 Providence Drive, Anchorage 99508; (907) 786-1849. Historic and contemporary papers, records, photographs; some artifacts. Open by appointment to researchers. Catalog of holdings available.

Anvik: Anvik Historical Society and Museum, P.O. Box 110, Anvik 99558; (907) 663-6358. Displays history and archaeology of lower Yukon Athabascan village.

Barrow: Inupiat Heritage Center, P.O. Box 749, Barrow 99723; (800) 478-7337. Cultural collection, library, storage areas for artifacts; unusual aspects include a Traditional Room for an Elders-in-Residence program and a Skinning Room.

Bethel: Yupiit Piciryarait ("People's Lifeways") Culture Center and Museum, 420 Chief Hoffman Hwy., P.O. Box 219, Bethel 99559; (907) 543-1819. Artifacts from the region such as masks, drums, parkas, tools and a kayak.

Circle: Circle Historical Museum, Mile 127.7 Steese Highway, P.O. Box 1893, Central 99730; (907) 520-5312. Displays include a period cabin of the mining camps, the first printing press north of Juneau, equipment used in early-day mining and trapping, Yukon Quest Sled Dog Race sled display, research library with archives and photograph collection.

Copper Center: Copper Center Lodge, Drawer J, Copper Center 99673; (907) 822-3245. Historic roadhouse opened in 1898. Museum exhibits, operating fish wheel.

George I. Ashby Memorial Museum/Copper Valley Historical Society, P.O. Box 84, Copper Center 99573; (907) 822-5285. Early mining of gold and copper, church and Native artifacts. Information about the stampeders who unsuccessfully tried to take the Valdez Glacier "All-Alaska" Trail to the Klondike in 1898.

Cordova: Cordova Historical Museum, P.O. Box 391, Cordova 99574; (907) 424-6665. Exhibits of art, geology, fisheries and marine articles.

Delta Junction: Alaska Homestead and Historical Museum, Milepost 1415.4 Alaska Highway, Delta Junction 99737; (907) 895-4431. Large collection of historical farming equipment; guided tours of authentic homestead farm.

Delta Historical Society Museum/ Big Delta State Historical Park, Mile 275 Richardson Hwy., P.O. Box 1089, Delta Junction 99737; (907) 895-4555. A glimpse of life in Interior Alaska, 1904–47, the 10-acre park includes Rika's Roadhouse (built in 1910 and restored in 1986), an important waystation on the Valdez to Fairbanks Trail, sod-roofed museum, ferryman's cabin and other historic structures. Guides are in period costumes.

Sullivan Roadhouse, P.O. Box 987, Delta Junction 99737; (907) 895-5068. Visitor center and historic buildings with photos and displays depicting the winter Valdez to Fairbanks Trail.

The UA Museum in Fairbanks draws crowds for its arctic wildlife display, prehistoric mastodon tusks, hefty gold nuggets and more. Photo by Roy Corral.

Dillingham: Samuel K. Fox Museum (Dillingham Heritage Museum), corner of Seward and K Street, P.O. Box 330, Dillingham 99576; (907) 842-5115 (Chamber of Commerce). Ethno-history museum featuring Yup'ik Eskimo culture of Southwestern Alaska through contemporary and traditional arts, crafts and artifacts.

Eagle: Eagle Historical Society and Museum, P.O. Box 23, Eagle 99738; (907) 547-2325; www.eagleak.org. Restored courthouse, customs house and several Fort Egbert buildings. Daily walking tours and historical movies.

Eagle River: Alaska Museum of Natural History, 11723 Old Glenn Highway, Eagle River 99577; (907) 694-0819; www.alaskamuseum.org. Exhibits embrace geology, biology and anthropology of Southcentral Alaska; Alaska dinosaur story.

Eagle River Nature Center, 32750 Eagle River Road, Eagle River 99577; (907) 694-2108; www.ernc.org. Interpretive displays, programs, guided daily hikes, outdoor telescopes, spectacular views. Entrance to walkable section of scenic Iditarod Trail.

Eklutna Historical Park and Heritage House Museum, 16515 Centerfield Drive, Suite 201, Eagle River 99577; (907) 696-2828; www.alaskaone.com/eklutna. Located 25 miles north of Anchorage on the Glenn Highway. The park offers 30-minute tours and information about the blending of Athabascan and missionary cultures. Historic photos and objects. Unique grave monuments called spirit houses, and St. Nicholas Russian Orthodox Church.

Ester: Ester Gold Camp, P.O. Box 109, Ester 99725; (800) 676-6925; www.akvisit.com. Ester Camp was built in 1936 by the Fairbanks Exploration Company to support a large-scale gold dredge operation; reopened in 1958 as a tourist attraction and is on the National Register of Historic Places.

Fairbanks: Alaska Public Lands Information Center, 250 N. Cushman St., Fairbanks 99701; (907) 456-0527; www.nps.gov/aplic/center. Information on Alaska's state parks, national parks, national forests and wildlife refuges. Free museum featuring films on Alaska, interpretive programs, lectures, exhibits, artifacts, photographs and short video programs on each region of the state.

Dog Mushing Museum, Box 80-136, Fairbanks 99708; (907) 456-6874. Dog sleds, mushing paraphernalia.

El Dorado Gold Mine, 1975 Discovery Drive, Fairbanks 99709; (907)

479-7613. Located at Mile 1.3 Elliott Highway, just past Fox, 9 miles north of Fairbanks. Tour of a working gold mine, permafrost tunnel, sluice box, assay office, gold panning.

Fairbanks Exploration Industrial Complex, Illinois Street, Fairbanks; (907) 451-1920. Four houses for miners built in 1916 serve as an inn. Visitors may watch gold pans being manufactured and see a machine shop complex where "time stands still."

Gold Dredge No. 8, P.O. Box 81941, Fairbanks 99708; (907) 547-6058. Millions of ounces of gold have been extracted by this dredge since 1928—one of two gold dredges in Alaska open to the public. Listed in the National Register of Historic Sites. Exhibits include mastodon and woolly mammoth bones and tusks.

Interior and Arctic Alaska Aeronautical Museum, P.O. Box 70437, Fairbanks 99707; www.akpub.com/akttt/aviat.html.

Pioneer Air Museum, Box 70437, Fairbanks 99707-0437; (907) 451-0037. Located behind Civic Center at Alaskaland. Antique aircraft and stories of their Alaska pilots, with displays from 1913–48.

Pioneer Memorial Park, Alaskaland Park, Airport Way, P.O. Box 70176, Fairbanks 99707-6970; (907) 456-8579; www.akpub.com/akttt/pione.html. Photos and artifacts of Fairbanks and the Fairbanks mining district from 1902 through World War II. Also features "The Big Stampede," portraying the great gold rush to the Klondike and to Fairbanks.

Pioneers of Alaska Museum, at Alaskaland, Airport Way and Peger Road, Fairbanks 99707; (907) 451-0037. Free guided historical walking tours. Features Kitty Hensley house, Judge Wickersham house, first Presbyterian Church (1906); re-created Native village, gold-rush town and paddle-wheel riverboat.

Rasmusson Library, University of Alaska Fairbanks 99775; (907) 474-7481. Extensive Alaska and Arctic archives and photograph collection available to researchers.

SS *Nenana*/Fairbanks Historical

Preservation Foundation, at Alaskaland, 2300 Airport Way, Cabin No. 1876, Box 70552, Fairbanks 99707; (907) 456-8848. A restored river steamer, a National Historic Landmark. Compelling 300-foot diorama takes visitors on a 2,400-mile voyage through the years 1847–1932 along the Yukon River system.

University of Alaska Museum, 907 Yukon Drive, Box 756960, Fairbanks 99775-6960; (907) 474-7505; www.uaf.edu/museum/index.html. Five galleries display Alaska's history, Native culture, art, natural phenomena, wildlife, birds, geology and prehistoric past, including the mummy of a 36,000-year-old Steppe bison, and a display on the northern lights. Sculptures, totem poles, a Russian blockhouse and a nature trail; many special programs.

Girdwood: Crow Creek Mine, Mile 3.1 Crow Creek Road, Girdwood 99587; (907) 278-8060. National historic site with eight original, fully restored buildings from 1898; daily gold panning, tools.

Portage Glacier/Begich–Boggs Visitor Center, P.O. Box 129, Girdwood 99587; (907) 783-2326. Located 55 miles south of Anchorage off the Seward Highway. Exhibits on glaciers and ice caves. Theater shows 20-minute documentary "Voices from the Ice." Interpretive programs during the summer.

Haines: Alaska Indian Arts, P.O. Box 271, Haines 99827; (907) 766-2160. Workshop with totem carvers, silversmiths and printmakers. Chilkat Dancers perform several times each week during the summer.

American Bald Eagle Foundation, Haines Highway and Second Street, P.O. Box 49, Haines 99827; (907) 766-3094; www.baldeagles.org. Programs and lectures explain how birds interact with the environment.

Sheldon Museum and Cultural

Center, P.O. Box 269, Haines 99827; (907) 766-2366; www.sheldonmuseum.org. Exhibits on the Dalton Trail, the overland freight route used to Fort Selkirk in the Klondike; Tlingit culture, Chilkat blankets, pioneer history.

Homer: Pratt Museum, 3779 Bartlett St., Homer 99603; (907) 235-8635; www.prattmuseum.org. Natural and cultural history of Kenai Peninsula. Displays include Eskimo, Indian and Aleut tools and clothing dioramas, whale skeletons; marine aquarium; botanical garden.

Hoonah: Hoonah Cultural Center/ Hoonah Indian Association, P.O. Box 144, Hoonah 99829. History and culture of local Tlingit Indians; displays of Tlingit art and artifacts, totem poles, guided tours.

Hope: Hope and Sunrise Historical and Mining Museum, Second Street, P.O. Box 88, Hope 99605; (907) 782-3740; www.advenalaska.com/hope. Historic buildings; gold rush, mining and homesteading memorabilia.

Huslia: Huslia Cultural Center, P.O. Box 70, Huslia 99746. Beadwork, arts and crafts.

Juneau: Alaska State Archives, Box 6, Juneau 99811. Photographs, documents, state government records.

Alaska State Museum, 395 Whittier St., Juneau 99801-1718; (907) 465-2901; jerryh@muskox.alaska.edu. Collections on Alaska Natives, art, natural history, gold-rush days, archaeology, botany, contemporary gold-mining issues, geology and paleontology. Lectures, guided tours, workshops, films and demonstrations.

House of Wickersham (Tanana Yukon Historical Society), 123 Seventh St., Juneau 99801; (907) 586-9001. Built in 1898, the house was the residence of one of Alaska's first federal judges, James Wickersham. Educational tours and permanent collections.

Juneau–Douglas City Museum, 155 S. Seward St., Juneau 99801; (907) 586-3572; www.juneau.lib.ak.us/parksrec/museum/museum.htm. Videos and exhibits highlight Juneau's colorful history and gold-mining heritage; historic downtown walking tour.

Kake Tribal Heritage Foundation, P.O. Box 263, Juneau 99801.

Last Chance Mining Museum, 1001 Basin Road, Juneau 99802; (907) 586-5338. Historic gold-rush mining building listed on National Register of Historic Places.

Kenai: K'beq Kenaitze Indian Tribe, P.O. Box 988, Kenai 99611; (907) 283-3633. Archives of Kenai branch of Cook Inlet Athabascan Indians.

Kenai Visitors and Cultural Center, 11471 Kenai Spur Highway, P.O. Box 1991, Kenai 99611; (907) 283-1991; www.visitkenai.com. Houses all the exhibits from Fort Kenay, plus a large eagle display.

Ketchikan: Alaska Public Lands Information Center, 50 Main St., Ketchikan 99901; (907) 228-6220; www.nps.gov/aplic/center.

Saxman Totem Park and Tribal House, P.O. Box 8558, Ketchikan 99901. Historic site, 2.5 miles south of town. Park includes totems such as the famous Lincoln Pole, a carving center and Tlingit tribal house. Guided tours available.

Southeast Alaska Visitor Center, 50 Main St., Ketchikan 99901; (907) 228-6214; www.nps.gov/aplic. Exhibits and videos about public lands and mining; crystals and marble mined from southeastern Alaska; historic gold-rush photos.

Tongass Historical Museum, 629 Dock St., Ketchikan 99901; (907) 225-5600; www.city.ketchikan.ak.us/ds/tonghist/index.html. Collection of Alaskana, Northwest Coast Native materials, photo archives and maritime history displays. Summer exhibit features the historic cannery town of Loring.

Totem Heritage Center, 601 Deermount St. (mail to 629 Dock St.), Ketchikan 99901; (907) 225-5900; www.city.ketchikan.ak.us/ds/tonghert/index.html. Large collection of original Tsimshian, Haida and Tlingit totems from the surrounding islands.

Klawock: Klawock Totem Park/City of Klawock, P.O. Box 113, Klawock 99925. Historic site on west coast of Prince of Wales Island. Reached by air, private boat, state ferry. Park contains 21 totems—both replicas and originals—from the abandoned village of Tuxekan.

Kodiak: Alutiiq Musem and Archaeological Repository (Kodiak Museum), Kodiak Area Native Association, 215 Mission Road, Suite 101, Kodiak 99615; (907) 486-7004; www.alutiiqmuseum.com. Repository holds 100,000 artifacts, historic photos and archival documents about Alutiiq culture.

Baranov Museum (Erskine House)/Kodiak Historical Society, 101 Marine Way, Kodiak 99615; (907) 486-5920; www.ptialasaka.net/~baranov. Closed in February. Former Russian fur warehouse from early 1800s, oldest wooden building on the West Coast of the United States. Exhibits offer an overview of Alutiiq, Russian and early American history. National historic landmark.

> Alaska has the highest number of days without sunshine of any state in the union, and we rank number one in average annual household spending on lamps and lighting fixtures. Naknek Nick used to ask, "How many guys from Egegik does it take to screw in a light bulb? None—we don't have electricity."

Kodiak Tribal Council's Barabara, 713 Rezanof Drive, Kodiak 99615; (907) 486-4449. Authentic traditional Alutiiq dwelling (barabara) used to stage presentations by the Kodiak Alutiiq Dancers.

Veniaminov Museum, St. Herman's Russian Orthodox Theological Seminary, Mission Road, Kodiak 99615; (907) 486-3524. Archive of personal items belonging to Ivan Veniaminov (later Bishop Innocent); papers and documents, many in Russian, about Russian America and the Orthodox church in Russian America.

McCarthy: Kennecott Mine, Wrangell–St. Elias National Park, McCarthy 99588; (907) 582-5128. An abandoned copper mine with many buildings perched on steep slopes. Kennicott-McCarthy Wilderness Guides conduct historical tours of the mine and town, which ceased operating in 1938.

Metlakatla: Duncan Cottage Museum, Duncan St., P.O. Box 8, Metlakatla 99926; (907) 886-4441, ext. 232; www.tours.metlakatla.net. Tsimshian bentwood boxes, antiques, books, photographs.

Naknek: Bristol Bay Historical Museum, P.O. Box 43, Naknek 99633; (907) 246-4432. "Living history museum" features regional archaeology, history, ethnology, commercial fishing and canning.

Nenana: Alfred Starr Nenana Cultural Center, 415 Riverfront, P.O. Box 1, Nenana 99760; (907) 832-5520; www.totchaket.org. Ice Classics, boat racing, Native land claims and Episcopal Church exhibits.

Nenana Cultural Center, c/o City of Nenana, P.O. Box 270, Nenana 99760; (907) 832-5520. In log building next to salmon bake. Features Athabascan traditions linking the past to the present.

Nome: Carrie M. McLain Memorial Museum, P.O. Box 53, Nome 99762;

(907) 443-6630; www.nome100.com. Artifacts, photos and treasures; exhibits include the Nome gold rush featuring more than 6,000 gold-rush photos, Eskimo culture and the Bering Land Bridge. Videos on the history of Nome shown during the summer season.

Nome Historical Park, c/o Nome Convention and Visitors Bureau, Box 240, Nome 99762; (907) 443-5535. Contains a nonworking gold dredge and mining equipment from the gold-rush era.

Palmer: Independence Mine State Historic Park, Hatcher Pass, near Palmer 99645; (907) 745-2827. Restored gold-mine buildings, mining machinery and a visitor center in spectacular mountain setting. Recreational gold panning permitted.

Palmer Musem, 723 S. Valley Way, Palmer 99645; (907) 745-2880. Colony items, farm implements, flowers and vegetables that thrive in the North.

Petersburg: Clausen Memorial Museum, P.O. Box 708, Petersburg 99833; (907) 772-3598. Photos, Norwegian family items, cannery and fisheries items, fox farming, world's record king salmon and other artifacts from area's past.

Prince of Wales Island: Kasaan Totem Park, east side of Prince of Wales Island. Reached by charter plane or private boat. Part of a government-sponsored totem restoration program begun in 1937. Contains some examples moved from the Haida village of Old Kasaan.

Seward: Alaska SeaLife Center, P.O. Box 1329, Mile 0 Seward Highway, Seward 99664; (800) 224-2525; (907) 224-6300; www.alaskasealife.org. Live marine mammals and seabirds in habitat exhibits. Aquarium, research center and rehab center for marine mammals and seabirds.

Chugach Heritage Center, Railroad Depot, Seward 99664; (907) 224-5065. Storytelling, dancing, slides and videos, master artists at work, exhibits about Chugach peoples.

Marine Education Center, Third and Railway, P.O. Box 730, Seward 99664; (907) 224-5261. Interpretive displays about northern seas, Resurrection Bay, marine animals; live saltwater tanks; movies feature whales, salmon and other marine subjects. Operated by the University of Alaska.

Sitka: Isabel Miller Museum/Sitka Historical Society, 330 Harbor Drive, Sitka 99835; (907) 747-6455; www.sitka.org/historicalmuseum. In the Centennial Building near the cruise ship lightering dock, exhibits include Tlingit baskets and carvings; the New Archangel Russian dancers and Noow Tlien Native dancers perform; research library of manuscripts and photographs.

Russian Bishop's House, P.O. Box 738, Sitka 99835; (907) 747-6281; www.nps.gov/sitk. Located on Lincoln Street, a restored residence built in 1842 with private chapel. One of only four Russian log structures remaining in North America. Both a unit of the Sitka National Historical Park and a National Historic Landmark. Exhibits describe Russian America.

Sheldon Jackson Museum, 104 College Drive, Sitka 99835-7657; (907) 747-8981; www.museums.state.ak.us/sjhome.html. On the campus of Sheldon Jackson College, Alaska's oldest museum has exhibits of Tlingit artifacts, clothing, beadwork, art and carvings.

Sitka National Historical Park Visitor Center, 106 Metlakatla, Sitka 99835; (907) 747-6281; www.nps.gov/sitk. Tlingit history, totems, artifacts. Totem pole collection contains both original pieces collected 1901–03 and copies of originals.

Southeast Alaska Indian Cultural Center, 106 Metlakatla, Sitka 99835; (907) 747-8061. Housed in the Sitka National Park Visitor Center; visitors may talk to Native artists at work: beadworkers, carvers, printmakers, silversmiths.

Skagway: Klondike Gold Rush National Historical Park, P.O. Box

517, Skagway 99840; (907) 983-2921; www.nps.gov/klgo. An unusual unit of this park is the Chilkoot Trail, a 33-mile trek through history, sometimes called "the longest museum in the world." Hundreds of relics such as wagon wheels and coffee pots left behind by the stampeders of '98 remain on the trail.

Mascot Saloon Museum, National Park Service, Third and Broadway, Skagway 99840; (907) 983-2921. A typical saloon of 1898.

Skagway Museum and Archives, P.O. Box 521, Skagway 99840; (907) 983-2420; www.skagway museum.org. On Broadway. Gold-rush artifacts, all once used by stampeders, and some personal belongings of notorious con man Soapy Smith. Photographs, historical records.

Soldotna: Soldotna Historical Society Museum, P.O. Box 1986, Soldotna 99669; (907) 262-3756; www.geocities.com/ soldotnamuseum. Wildlife museum and historic log village, including last territorial school (1958). Homesteading artifacts and photos.

Sutton: Alpine Historical Park, P.O. Box 266, Sutton 99674, access via Elementary School Road from Glenn Highway; (907) 745-7000. Open-air museum featuring the concrete ruins of the Sutton Coal Washery (1920–22), historical buildings, perennial gardens, and picnic and playground facilities.

Talkeetna: Talkeetna Historical Society Museum, P.O. Box 76, Talkeetna 99676; (907) 733-2487. Located one block off Main Street, the Talkeetna Townsite Historic District contains buildings reflecting a small 1917–40 gold-mining community. Museum portrays lives of gold miners, early aviators and climbers of Mount McKinley.

Tok: Alaska Public Lands Information Center, Mile 1314 Alaska Highway, P.O.

Box 359, Tok 99780; (907) 883-5667; www.nps.gov/aplic/center.

Mukluk Land, Tok Chamber of Commerce, Tok 99780; (907) 833-5887. A summer display of early mining equipment, some actually operating Alaska Road Commission machinery, old snowmobile collection and gold panning.

Tok Visitor Center, P.O. Box 389, Tok 99780; (907) 883-5887 or 883-5775. At the junction of Alaska and Glenn Highways, displays of Dall sheep, waterfowl, wolf, caribou, fossils and minerals. Open May to October.

Valdez: Oil Pipeline Terminus, Valdez 99686; (907) 835-2686. Bus tours of pipeline terminal are available daily, May to September. Reservations suggested. Entry restricted to authorized bus tours only.

Valdez Museum and Historical Archive, 217 Egan St., Valdez 99686-0008; (907) 835-2764; www.alaska.net/ ~vldzmuse/index.html. Permanent exhibits celebrate the 1898 gold-rush route across Valdez Glacier. Restored 1907 Ahrens steam fire engine, log cabin, original Cape Hinchinbrook lighthouse lens, exhibits on the 1964 earthquake, the trans-Alaska oil pipeline and 1989 *Exxon Valdez* oil spill cleanup.

Wasilla: Dorothy G. Page Museum and Old Wasilla Townsite Park, 323 Main St., Wasilla 99654; (907) 373-9071; also Wasilla–Knik–Willow Creek Historical Society. Historic buildings, including first schoolhouse (1917). Eskimo and Athabascan exhibits, gold-mining exhibits, "Flying Dentist's" office.

Iditarod Trail Sled Dog Race Headquarters and Museum, Mile 2.2 Knik Road, P.O. Box 870800, Wasilla 99687; (907) 376-5155. Memorabilia, mushing films, full-size replica of checkpoint cabin and cache; the sleds that Susan Butcher and Joe Redington Sr. used to mush to the top of Mount McKinley.

Knik Museum, Mile 13.9 Knik Road (mail to 300 N. Boundary St., Suite B), Wasilla 99687; (907) 376-2005. Restored pool hall houses exhibits about fish camps, gold mines, dog mushers.

Museum of Alaska Transportation and Industry, Mile 47 Parks Highway, Wasilla 99687-0646; (907) 376-1211; www.alaska.net/~rmorris/mati1.htm. Planes, trains, vehicles, tractors, tools. Ten acres of neat old stuff.

Wrangell: Wrangell Museum, 318 Church St., P.O. Box 1050, Wrangell 99929; (907) 874-3770; www.wrangell. com/cultural/museum.htm. Housed in Wrangell's oldest building, displays include items from Wrangell history, Tlingit artifacts and petroglyphs including the oldest known Tlingit houseposts.

MUSHROOMS More than
500 species of mushrooms grow in Alaska and while most are not common enough to be seen and collected readily by the amateur mycophile (mushroom hunter), many edible and choice species shoot up in any available patch of earth. Alaska's giant arc of mushrooms extends from Southeast's panhandle through Southcentral, the Alaska Peninsula and the Aleutian Chain and is prime mushroom habitat. Interior, Western and Northern Alaska also support mushrooms in abundance.

Mushroom seasons vary considerably according to temperature, humidity and available nutrients but most occur from June through September. In a particularly cold or dry season, the crop will be scant.

There are relatively few poisonous mushrooms considering the number of species that occur throughout Alaska. Potentially fatal mushrooms, some of which occur in populated areas, include fly agaric *(Amanita muscaria),* poison pax *(Paxillus involutus)* and false morels. Easy-to-identify edible species include hedgehogs *(Hydnum repandum)* and shaggy manes *(Coprinus comatus).* Even edible mushrooms may disagree with one's digestion; the only test for an inedible or poisonous mushroom is positive identification. If you can't identify it, don't eat it.

MUSKEG Muskegs are bogs where
little vegetation can grow except for sphagnum moss, black spruce, Sitka spruce, dwarf birch, tussocks and a few other shrubby plants. Such swampy areas cover much of Alaska. Nearly half of Alaska— 175 million acres—is classified as wetlands.

With nearly two-thirds of the nation's wetlands within its borders, Alaska boasts many of the most diverse wildlife habitats in North America. Waterfowl, muskrats, moose and many species of insect depend on wetlands for survival.

During extremely cold weather, musk-oxen stand still to conserve energy. From *Alaska's Mammals* by Dave Smith (text) and Tom Walker (photographs).

MUSK-OXEN Musk-oxen are stocky,
shaggy, long-haired mammals of the extreme northern latitudes. They remain in the open through Alaska's long winters. Their name is misleading, for they have no musk gland and are more closely related to sheep and goats than to cattle. Adult males may weigh 500 to 900 pounds, females 300 to 700 pounds. Both sexes have horns that droop down from their forehead and curve back up at the tips.

When threatened by wolves or other predators, musk-oxen form circles or lines with their young in the middle. These defensive measures did not protect them from hunters and their guns.

Musk-oxen were eliminated from Alaska in about 1865, when hunters shot and killed the last herd of 13. The species was reintroduced to the territory in the 1930s when 34 musk-oxen were purchased from Greenland and brought to the University

Rescued by an Angel

Panik the musk-ox was in trouble. The fuzzy female calf, born in the early 1990s at the Musk-ox Farm in Palmer, was hardly 10 days old when she collapsed in the field where she was staying with her mother and was taken to a veterinary clinic for intravenous feeding. The calf was thin, listless and suffering from diarrhea.

By the time she was released from the clinic, the calf had become a social outcast to her herd, and was in danger of not thriving because of loneliness. A black poodle used as a playmate didn't help. Then the farm came up with the notion of borrowing a lamb.

Angel, a two-month-old white lamb, was brought over from a dairy farm in Point McKenzie. A friendship and a healthy musk-ox began when the calf and lamb competed for the bottle. The pair nursed together, slept together, munched on weeds together and frolicked together.

"She may have survived without the lamb, but she wouldn't be as happy," veterinarian Ron Williams told the *Anchorage Daily News*.   —1993 *The ALASKA ALMANAC®*

of Alaska Fairbanks. In 1935–36, the 31 remaining musk-oxen at the university were shipped to Nunivak Island in the Bering Sea, where the herd eventually thrived. Animals from the Nunivak herd have been transplanted to areas along Alaska's western and northern coasts; at least five wild herds—approximately 3,000 musk-oxen—exist in the state.

The soft underhair of musk-oxen is called *qiviut* and grows next to the skin, protected by long guard hairs. It is shed naturally every spring. The Musk Ox Development Corp. maintains a herd in Palmer and collects *qiviut* for the Oomingmak cooperative. The hair is spun into yarn in Rhode Island and sent back to Alaska, where the cooperative arranges for knitters in villages in Western Alaska, where jobs are scarce, to knit the yarn into clothing at their own pace.

Each village keeps its own distinct signature pattern for scarves knitted from *qiviut*. Villagers also produce stoles, tunics, hats and smoke rings, circular scarves that fit around the head like a hood. About 250 women are employed as knitters.

In Southcentral Alaska musk-oxen can be viewed from May to September at the musk-oxen farm in Palmer. In the Interior look for them at the university's Research Station on Yankovich Road in Fairbanks; (907) 474-7207.

NATIONAL FORESTS (SEE ALSO
Land Use; National Parks; National Wilderness Areas; Timber) Alaska has two national forests, the Tongass and the Chugach. The Tongass occupies most of the panhandle, or southeastern portion of the state. The Chugach extends south and east of Anchorage along the Southcentral Alaska coast, encompassing most of the Prince William Sound area.

These two national forests are managed by the U.S. Forest Service for a variety of uses. They provide forest products for national and international markets, minerals, recreational opportunities, wilderness experiences and superb scenery and pristine vistas.

Nearly 200 public recreation cabins are maintained in the Tongass and Chugach national forests. They accommodate visitors from all over the world and are a vacation bargain, including a boat on some freshwater lakes. Fees for the cabins are from $15 to $65 a night. All Tongass

Wilderness Units in Tongass National Forest

Wilderness Areas Established Dec. 2, 1980, by ANILCA	Acres
Coronation Island Wilderness	19,232
Endicott River Wilderness	98,729
Kootznoowoo Wilderness* (Admiralty Island National Monument)**	955,921
Maurelle Islands Wilderness	4,937
Misty Fiords National Monument**	2,142,243
Petersburg Creek–Duncan Salt Chuck Wilderness	46,777
Russell Fiord Wilderness	348,701
South Baranof Wilderness	319,568
South Prince of Wales Wilderness	90,996
Stikine–LeConte Wilderness	448,926
Tebenkof Bay Wilderness	66,839
Tracy Arm–Fords Terror Wilderness	653,179
Warren Island Wilderness	11,181
West Chichagof–Yakobi Wilderness	264,747

Wilderness Areas Established Nov. 28, 1990, by TTRA	
Chuck River Wilderness	74,298
Karta Wilderness	39,889
Kuiu Wilderness	60,581
Pleasant–Lemesurier–Inian Islands Wilderness	23,096
South Etolin Wilderness	83,371
Total acreage	5,753,211

*Kootznoowoo Wilderness includes 18,486 acres (including 24 acres of nonnational forest land) in the Young Lake Addition established by TTRA.

**Designated monuments under ANILCA; first areas so designated in the national forest system. These wildernesses include only the public lands above mean high tide.

National Forest Lands in Alaska	Tongass	Chugach
Total acreage before ANILCA	15,555,388	4,392,646
Total acreage after ANILCA	16,954,713	5,940,040*
Wilderness acreage created	5,753,211	None created
Wilderness study	None created	2,019,999 acres

*This lands act provides for additional transfers of national forest land to Native corporations, the state and the U.S. Fish and Game Department of an estimated 296,000 acres on Afognak Island, and an estimated 242,000 acres to the Chugach Native Corporation.

and Chugach national forest cabins are reserved through the National Recreation Reservation System: (877) 444-6777; (518) 885-3639 toll free international; www.reserveusa.com.

The forests are home to some of Alaska's most magnificent wildlife. It is here that the bald eagle and large brown (grizzly) bears may be encountered in large numbers. Five species of Pacific salmon spawn in the rivers and streams of the forests and smaller mammals and waterfowl abound. The Forest Service is charged with the management of this rich habitat. The Alaska Department of Fish and Game manages the wildlife species that this habitat supports.

There are many recreational opportunities in the national forests of

Alaska including backpacking, fishing, hunting, photography, boating, nature study and camping. For information concerning recreational opportunities, contact the U.S. Forest Service office nearest the area you are visiting.

The Alaska National Interest Lands Conservation Act (ANILCA) designated approximately 5.5 million acres of wilderness divided into 14 units within the 17-million-acre Tongass National Forest. It also added three new areas to the forest: the Juneau Icefield, Kates Needle and parts of the Barbazon Range, totaling more than 1 million acres.

The Tongass Timber Reform Act (TTRA) of 1990 amended ANILCA and designated five additional wilderness areas and an addition to the existing Kootznoowoo Wilderness, as well as 12 backcountry semiprimitive roadless areas managed primarily for fish, wildlife and recreation resources. The lands bill also provided extensive additions to the Chugach National Forest.

The charts on page 141 show the effect of the Alaska Lands Act on the Tongass and Chugach national forests.

NATIONAL HISTORIC PLACES (SEE ALSO Archaeology) A "place" on the National Register of Historic Places is a district, site, building, structure or object significant for its history, architecture, archaeology or culture. The national register also includes National Historic Landmarks.

Anchorage's sewage was so clean to begin with, the city could not remove 30 percent of the organic waste as required by the EPA. The problem was solved by paying fish processors to purposely dump fish by-products so the city would have enough waste to remove.

The register is an official list of properties recognized by the federal government as worthy of preservation. Listing in the register begins with the owner's consent and includes a nomination process with reviews by the State Historic Preservation Office, the Alaska Historical Commission and the Keeper of the National Register. Limitations are not placed on a listed property. The federal government does not attach restrictive covenants to the property or seek to acquire it. Listing in the register means that a property is accorded national recognition for its significance in American history or prehistory.

Additional benefits include tax credits on income-producing properties and qualification for federal matching funds for preservation, maintenance and restoration work when such funds are available. Listed properties are guaranteed a full review process for potential adverse effects by federally funded, licensed or otherwise assisted projects. Such a review usually takes place while the project is in the planning stage. Alternatives are sought to avoid damaging or destroying the property.

Alaska has 363 sites listed in the National Register of Historic Places. For details, contact the Office of History and Archaeology, 550 W. Seventh Avenue, Suite 1310, Anchorage, AK 99501-3565; www.dnr.state.ak.us/parks/oha.

Among the sites:

Most visited site: Totem Bight State Park in Ketchikan.

Oldest standing Russian Orthodox Church: Ascension of Our Lord Chapel, Karluk.

Oldest standing building: Russian-American Company Magazin (Erskine House), National Historic Landmark, Kodiak.

Oldest standing U.S. government buildings: U.S. Army Storehouses, No. 3 and No. 4 in Portland Canal and at Hyder.

The most recent additions to the list of historic places in Alaska are:

Andrew Berg Cabin, Kenai Peninsula. For 25 years, big-game guide

'Paul Bunyan In a Cassock'

The Russian Bishop's House in Sitka is one of only four original Russian structures still standing in North America. As a missionary in 1824, Father Ivan Veniaminov began fashioning an alphabet for the Aleuts, taught brickmaking and other trades, and took farflung kayak trips for months at a time to convert an estimated 10,000 Natives to his faith. American observers referred to him as Paul Bunyan in a cassock. The manse he lived in here has been restored. . . . The 1842 structure of squared spruce logs and planks features a first-floor museum of Russian-American artifacts; the second story has been authentically returned to its early grandeur.

—Paul and Audrey Grescoe, *Alaska: The Cruise-Lover's Guide*

Andrew Berg led parties from his cabin on the north shore of Tustumena Lake, and he used the cabin until his death in 1939. The cabin is typical of those built on the Kenai Peninsula by those who chose to live alone in a largely unsettled area during the early 20th century.

Council City and Solomon River Railroad, Nome. This was the first standard-gauge railroad in Alaska. Only 35 miles of track were laid before the company ran out of money in 1906, but trains ran that length of track during the summer months from 1903 until 1913. The three steam locomotives that stand at the site where they were abandoned in 1913 are testimony to the dreams of entrepreneurs who participated in the Nome gold rush.

St. Michael the Archangel Cathedral NHL, Sitka

Harry A. Johnson Trapline Cabin, Kenai Peninsula. Harry Johnson came to Alaska in 1904 to work on the Alaska Central Railway and stayed for 60 years, earning his living with seasonal work and as a wildlife photographer. He built his log trapline cabin about 20 miles southwest of Hope in 1926 and used it seasonally until 1948.

Oscar Gill House, Anchorage. This house built in 1913 at Knik and barged across the inlet to Anchorage in 1916 is one of the city's oldest existing residences. It has Arts and Crafts-style details of a late 19th- and early 20th-century American Movement house, such as exposed rafter tails, gables with brackets supporting the overhang, and double-hung sash windows.

Thorn-Stingley House, Homer. Francis H. Thorn and his family moved to Homer after World War II. Other houses constructed in Homer during this time still stand, but few retain their original look. The Thorn-Stingley house, a nice example of a mid-20th-century bungalow, has been altered little since its construction.

Gakona Historic District, Glennallen vicinity. Gakona Roadhouse opened in 1904 to serve travelers on the Eagle and Fairbanks trails. When the trail was widened for wagons, a horse barn and blacksmith shop were added, followed by a larger log roadhouse in 1929. More development came with construction of the Alaska and Glenn highways as part of the World War II military buildup. The district has the principal buildings of each phase of the wayside stop's history.

Black Rapid Roadhouse, near Paxson. Black Rapid Roadhouse opened at least by 1904 to serve travelers on the new Valdez to Fairbanks Trail and operated until 1993.

NATIONAL PARKS, PRESERVES AND MONUMENTS
The National Park Service administers approximately 54 million acres of land in Alaska, consisting of 15 units classified as national parks, national preserves and national monuments. The Alaska National Interest Lands Conservation Act of 1980—also referred to as ANILCA (SEE Land Use)—created 10 new National Park Service units in Alaska and changed the size and status of three existing Park Service units: Denali National Park and Preserve (formerly Mount McKinley National Park); Glacier Bay National Monument, now a national park and preserve; and Katmai National Monument, now a national park and preserve. (SEE MAP, pages 146–147)

In 2000, Alaska's national parks, preserves and monuments attracted 2 million visitors.

National parks are traditionally managed to preserve scenic, wildlife and recreational values; mining, cutting of house logs, hunting and other resource exploitation are carefully regulated within park, monument and preserve boundaries, and motorized access is restricted to automobile traffic on authorized roads. However regulations for National Park Service units in Alaska recognize that these units contain lands traditionally occupied and used by Alaska Natives and rural residents for subsistence activities. To accommodate these users, management of some parks, preserves and monuments in Alaska provides for subsistence hunting, fishing and gathering activities, and the use of such motorized vehicles as snowmobiles, motorboats and airplanes where these activities are customary. National preserves permit sport hunting.

Information on parks, preserves and monuments is available at the Alaska Public Lands Information Centers: 605 W. Fourth Ave., Suite 105, Anchorage 99501, (907) 271-2737; 250 Cushman St., Suite 1A, Fairbanks 99701, (907) 451-7352; 50 Main St., Ketchikan 99501, (907) 228-6220; and P.O. Box 359, Tok 99780, (907) 883-5667. Web site for the information centers is www.nps.gov/aplic/center.

Following is a list of National Park Service parks, preserves and monuments. The U.S. Forest Service manages another two national monuments: Admiralty Island National Monument, 937,000 acres; and Misty Fiords National Monument, 2.1 million acres. Both are in Southeast Alaska and part of the National Wilderness Preservation System. (SEE ALSO National Wild and Scenic Rivers; National Wilderness Areas)

There are two NPS-affiliated areas in Alaska: the Aleutian World War II National Historic Area at Unalaska (www.nps.gov/aleu) and the Inupiat Heritage Center in Barrow.

The former was designated in 1996 to educate and inspire people about the history and the role of the Aleut people

NUGGETS

On Tuesday, Nov. 4, 1980, at 4 P.M., four hours before the Alaska polling booths closed, Alaskans had the opportunity to view President Jimmy Carter concede defeat in the presidential election, live via satellite from Washington, D.C. The early concession, coupled with Carter's unpopularity over his withdrawal of millions of acres of Alaska land under the Antiquities Act, made it no surprise that Ronald Reagan claimed an overwhelming victory in the state.
—1981 *The ALASKA ALMANAC®*

and the Aleutian Islands in World War II. The federal government does not own or manage the park, which is overseen by the Ounalashka Corp., a Native village corporation. The National Park Service provides technical assistance.

The Inupiat Heritage Center is affiliated with the New Bedford Whaling National Historic Park in New Bedford, Mass. In the 19th century, more than 2,000 whaling voyages departed New Bedford for the western Arctic. The National Park Service has helped with exhibits and other technical assistance.

National Park Service units in Alaska are:

Aniakchak National Monument and Preserve, mailing address: Katmai National Park and Preserve, P.O. Box 7, King Salmon 99613; www.nps.gov/ania. 603,000 acres. Features the Aniakchak dry caldera.

Bering Land Bridge National Preserve, National Park Service, P.O. Box 220, Nome 99762; www.nps.gov/bela. 2,785,000 acres. Lava fields, rare plants, archaeological sites, migratory waterfowl.

Cape Krusenstern National Monument, National Park Service, P.O. Box 1029, Kotzebue 99752; www.nps.gov/cakr. 660,000 acres. Archaeological sites.

Denali National Park and Preserve, National Park Service, P.O. Box 9, Denali Park 99755; www.nps.gov/dena. 6,028,000 acres. Mount McKinley, abundant wildlife.

Gates of the Arctic National Park and Preserve, National Park Service, P.O. Box 74680, Fairbanks 99707; www.nps.gov/gaar. 8,472,000 acres. Brooks Range, wild and scenic rivers, wildlife.

Glacier Bay National Park and Preserve, National Park Service, Bartlett Cove, Gustavus 99826; www.nps.gov/glba. 3,283,000 acres. Glaciers, marine wildlife.

Katmai National Park and Preserve, National Park Service, P.O. Box 7, King Salmon 99613; www.nps.gov/katm. 4,090,000 acres. Valley of Ten Thousand Smokes, brown bears.

Kenai Fjords National Park, National Park Service, P.O. Box 1727, Seward 99664; www.nps.gov/kefj. 570,000 acres. Fjords,

Harding Icefield, Exit Glacier, waterfowl, sea otters.

Klondike Gold Rush National Historical Park, National Park Service, P.O. Box 517, Skagway 99840; www.nps.gov/klgo. 2,721 acres, including 15 restored turn-of-the-century structures; Chilkoot Trail.

Kobuk Valley National Park, National Park Service, P.O. Box 1029, Kotzebue 99752; www.nps.gov/klgo. 1,750,000 acres. Archaeological sites, Great Kobuk Sand Dunes, river rafting.

Lake Clark National Park and Preserve, National Park Service, 4230 University Drive, Suite 311, Anchorage 99508; www.nps.gov/lacl. 4,044,000 acres. Backcountry recreation, fishing, scenery.

Noatak National Preserve, National Park Service, P.O. Box 1029, Kotzebue 99752; www.nps.gov/noat. 6,574,000 acres. Abundant wildlife, river floating.

Sitka National Historical Park, National Park Service, P.O. Box 738, Sitka 99835; www.nps.gov/sitk. 106 acres. Russian Bishop's House, totems, trails.

Wrangell–St. Elias National Park and Preserve, National Park Service, P.O. Box 439, Copper Center 99573; www.nps.gov/wrst. 13,188,000 acres. Rugged peaks, glaciers, expansive wilderness.

Yukon–Charley Rivers National Preserve, National Park Service, P.O. Box 167, Eagle 99738; www.nps.gov/yuch. 2,523,000 acres. Backcountry recreation, river floating.

NATIONAL PETROLEUM RESERVE (SEE ALSO Oil and Gas) In 1923,

President Warren G. Harding signed an executive order creating Naval Petroleum Reserve Number 4 (NPR-4), the last of four petroleum reserves to be placed under control of the U.S. Navy. The secretary of the Navy was charged to "explore, protect, conserve, develop, use and operate the Naval Petroleum Reserves," including NPR-4, on Alaska's North Slope. (SEE MAP, pages 146–147)

The U.S. Geological Survey (USGS) had
(Continued on page 148)

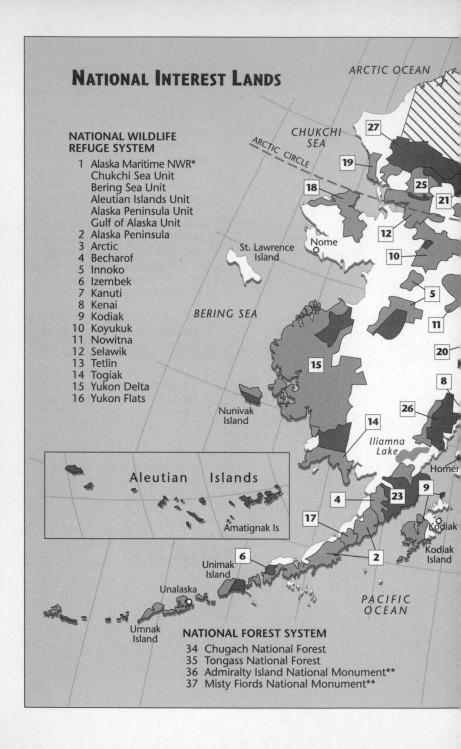

NATIONAL INTEREST LANDS

ARCTIC OCEAN

NATIONAL WILDLIFE REFUGE SYSTEM

1 Alaska Maritime NWR*
   Chukchi Sea Unit
   Bering Sea Unit
   Aleutian Islands Unit
   Alaska Peninsula Unit
   Gulf of Alaska Unit
2 Alaska Peninsula
3 Arctic
4 Becharof
5 Innoko
6 Izembek
7 Kanuti
8 Kenai
9 Kodiak
10 Koyukuk
11 Nowitna
12 Selawik
13 Tetlin
14 Togiak
15 Yukon Delta
16 Yukon Flats

CHUKCHI SEA

ARCTIC CIRCLE

St. Lawrence Island

Nome

BERING SEA

Nunivak Island

Iliamna Lake

Homer

Aleutian Islands

Amatignak Is

Unimak Island

Unalaska

Umnak Island

Kodiak

Kodiak Island

PACIFIC OCEAN

NATIONAL FOREST SYSTEM

34 Chugach National Forest
35 Tongass National Forest
36 Admiralty Island National Monument**
37 Misty Fiords National Monument**

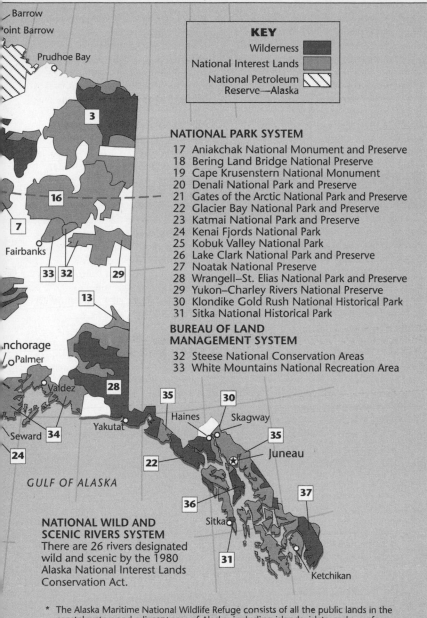

KEY

Wilderness	
National Interest Lands	
National Petroleum Reserve —Alaska	

Barrow
oint Barrow
Prudhoe Bay

3

16

7

Fairbanks

33 32

29

13

nchorage
Palmer

Valdez

28

35

30

Haines   Skagway

35

22

Juneau

Seward 34

24

GULF OF ALASKA

36

Sitka

37

31

Ketchikan

Yakutat

NATIONAL PARK SYSTEM

17 Aniakchak National Monument and Preserve
18 Bering Land Bridge National Preserve
19 Cape Krusenstern National Monument
20 Denali National Park and Preserve
21 Gates of the Arctic National Park and Preserve
22 Glacier Bay National Park and Preserve
23 Katmai National Park and Preserve
24 Kenai Fjords National Park
25 Kobuk Valley National Park
26 Lake Clark National Park and Preserve
27 Noatak National Preserve
28 Wrangell–St. Elias National Park and Preserve
29 Yukon–Charley Rivers National Preserve
30 Klondike Gold Rush National Historical Park
31 Sitka National Historical Park

BUREAU OF LAND MANAGEMENT SYSTEM

32 Steese National Conservation Areas
33 White Mountains National Recreation Area

NATIONAL WILD AND SCENIC RIVERS SYSTEM

There are 26 rivers designated wild and scenic by the 1980 Alaska National Interest Lands Conservation Act.

* The Alaska Maritime National Wildlife Refuge consists of all the public lands in the coastal waters and adjacent seas of Alaska, including islands, islets, rocks, reefs, capes and spires.

** Admiralty Island and Misty Fiords national monuments are part of the Tongass National Forest, which includes 17 other wilderness areas.

(Continued from page 145)
begun surface exploration in the area in 1901; following creation of the 23-million-acre reserve, exploration programs were conducted by the Navy. From 1944 to 1953, extensive surveys were conducted and 36 test wells were drilled. Nine oil and gas fields were discovered; the largest oil field, near Umiat, contains an estimated 70 million to 120 million barrels of recoverable oil. Active exploration was suspended in 1953.

In 1974, the Arab oil embargo, coupled with the knowledge of large petroleum reserves at nearby Prudhoe Bay, brought about renewed interest in NPR-4, and Congress directed the Navy to resume its exploration program.

In 1976, all lands within NPR-4 were redesignated the National Petroleum Reserve Alaska (NPR-A) and jurisdiction was transferred to the secretary of the interior. In 1980, Congress authorized the secretary to oversee an expeditious program of competitive leasing of oil and gas tracts in the reserve, clearing the way for private development of the area's resources.

By mid-1983, three competitive bid lease sales, involving 7.2 million acres of NPR-A, had been held. However, interest from the oil companies has lessened over the years and leases expired. Prior to 1999, the last oil lease sale was in 1984, but was canceled when no bids were entered. Currently there are 1,185 active oil and gas leases, covering nearly 2.8 million acres.

The Interior Department, through USGS, continued exploration of NPR-A into the 1980s. Past naval explorations and those conducted by USGS resulted in the discovery of oil at Umiat and Cape Simpson, and several gas fields including Walakpa, Gubic and Point Barrow. The North Slope Borough is developing reserves in the Walakpa field to provide gas for heating and electrical generation for Barrow.

Data gathered indicates NPR-A may contain recoverable reserves of 1.85 billion barrels of crude oil and 3.74 trillion cubic feet of natural gas. Such optimistic data fueled bidding in a May 1999 lease sale. Alaska's two largest oil companies at that time, BP Exploration (Alaska) and Arco Alaska won interest in 87 percent of the leases. Bidding on the 5,700-acre blocks between Teshekpuk Lake and the Colville River totaled $105 million.

In 2000, Phillips Alaska Corp. bought Arco's interest in Alaska. Those newly acquired leases in the NPR-A are currently being explored.

NATIONAL WILD AND SCENIC RIVERS (SEE ALSO Rivers) The

Alaska National Interest Lands Conservation Act (ANILCA) of 1980 gave wild and scenic river classification to 13 streams within the National Park System, six in the National Wildlife Refuge System and two in Bureau of Land Management Conservation and Recreation areas. (SEE MAP, pages 146–147) An additional five rivers are located outside designated preservation units. Twelve more rivers were designated for further study and possible wild and scenic classification.

The criteria for wild and scenic river classification covers more than just float trip possibilities. Scenic features, wilderness characteristics and recreational opportunities that would be impaired by alteration, development or impoundment are also considered.

Rivers are classified into three categories under the Wild and Scenic Rivers Act. The wild classification is most restrictive of development or incompatible uses—it stresses the wilderness aspect of the rivers. The scenic classification permits some intrusions upon the natural

> If all the 18,177,000,000 nuggets produced yearly by Alaska's 166,000 moose were stacked on top of each other, the pile would be 93,181 times as high as Mount McKinley.

Rafters prepare to launch on the Chulitna River in Denali State Park. Photo by Tricia Brown.

landscape. The recreational classification is the least restrictive category. A specified amount of land back from the river's banks is also put in protected status to ensure access, use and the preservation of aesthetic values for the public.

For those desiring to float these rivers, special consideration must be given to put-in and take-out points because most of the designated wild and scenic rivers are not accessible by road. This means that voyagers and their crafts must be flown in and picked up by charter Bush planes. Because Federal Aviation Administration regulations prohibit the lashing of canoes and kayaks to pontoons of floatplanes when carrying passengers, inflatable rafts and folding canvas or rubber kayaks are often more convenient and less expensive to transport.

Further information on rivers and river running can be obtained from the Alaska Public Lands Information Centers: 605 W. Fourth Ave., Suite 105, Anchorage 99501, (907) 271-2737; 250 Cushman St., Suite 1A, Fairbanks 99701, (907) 456-0527; 50 Main St., Ketchikan 99901, (907) 228-6220; and P.O. Box 359, Tok 99780, (907) 883-5667; www.nps.gov/aplic

Information also is available from the U.S. Fish and Wildlife Service, 1011 E. Tudor Road, Anchorage 99503, www.r7.fws.gov; and the Bureau of Land Management,

222 W. Seventh Ave., No. 13, Anchorage 99513, www.blm.gov. Information for rivers within park units or managed by the National Park Service is also available from the particular park headquarters. (SEE ALSO National Parks, Preserves and Monuments)

Rivers Within National Park Areas

Alagnak—Katmai National Preserve

Alatna—Gates of the Arctic National Park

Aniakchak—Aniakchak National Monument; Aniakchak National Preserve

Charley—Yukon–Charley Rivers National Preserve

Chilikadrotna—Lake Clark National Park and Preserve

John—Gates of the Arctic National Park and Preserve

Kobuk—Gates of the Arctic National Park and Preserve

Mulchatna—Lake Clark National Park and Preserve

Noatak—Gates of the Arctic National Park and Noatak National Preserve

North Fork Koyukuk—Gates of the Arctic National Park and Preserve

Salmon—Kobuk Valley National Park

Tinayguk—Gates of the Arctic National Park and Preserve

Tlikakila—Lake Clark National Park and Preserve

Rivers Within National Wildlife Refuges

Andreafsky—Yukon Delta NWR
Ivishak—Arctic NWR
Nowitna—Nowitna NWR
Selawik—Selawik NWR
Sheenjek—Arctic NWR
Wind—Arctic NWR

General information on rivers not listed in refuge brochures may be obtained from respective refuge offices by addressing queries to refuge managers. Addresses for refuges are given in the brochures.

Rivers Within Bureau of Land Management Units

Beaver Creek—The segment of the main stem from confluence of Bear and Champion creeks within White Mountains National Recreation Area to the Yukon Flats National Wildlife Refuge boundary.

Birch Creek—The segment of the main stem from the south side of Steese Highway downstream to the bridge at Milepost 147.

Rivers Outside of Designated Preservation Units

Alagnak—Those segments or portions of the main stem and Nonvianuk tributary lying outside and westward of Katmai National Park and Preserve.

Delta—The segment from and including all of the Tangle Lakes to a point one-half mile north of Black Rapids.

Fortymile—The main stem within Alaska, plus tributaries.

Gulkana—The main stem from the outlet of Paxson Lake to the confluence with Sourdough Creek; various segments of the west fork and middle fork.

Unalakleet—Approximately 80 miles of the main stem.

Rivers Designated for Study for Inclusion in Wild and Scenic Rivers System

Colville
Etivluk–Nigu Rivers
Kanektok
Kisaralik
Koyuk

Melozitna
Porcupine
Sheenjek (lower segment)
Situk
Squirrel
Utukok
Yukon (Rampart section)

NATIONAL WILDERNESS AREAS

(See also Cabins) Passage of the 1980 Alaska National Interest Lands Conservation Act (ANILCA) added millions of acres to the National Wilderness Preservation System. Agencies that oversee wilderness areas in Alaska include the National Park Service, U.S. Fish and Wildlife Service and U.S. Forest Service. (See map, pages 146–147)

Passage of the Tongass Timber Reform Act in 1990 designated an additional 300,000 acres of the Tongass National Forest as wilderness.

Approximate wilderness allocations to different agencies in Alaska are: U.S. Forest Service, 5.7 million acres; National Park Service, 32 million acres; U.S. Fish and Wildlife Service, 18.7 million acres.

Wilderness, according to the federal Wilderness Act of 1964, is land sufficient in size to enable the operation of natural systems without undue influence from human activities in surrounding areas and should be places in which people are visitors only. Alaska wilderness regulations follow the stipulations of the Wilderness Act as amended by the Alaska lands act.

Specifically designed to allow for Alaska conditions, the rules are considerably more lenient about transportation access, human-made structures and use of mechanized vehicles. The primary objective of a wilderness area continues to be the maintenance of the wilderness character of the land.

Some characteristics of Alaska wilderness areas:

Subsistence. Subsistence uses including hunting, fishing, trapping, berry gathering and use of timber for cabins and firewood may be allowed in some areas.

Cabins. Public recreation or safety

cabins continue to be maintained and may be replaced.

Fish. Fish habitat enhancement programs, such as construction of fish weirs, fishways and spawning channels, may be allowed.

Guides. Special-use permits for guides and outfitters are allowed.

Access. Private, state and Native lands surrounded by wilderness areas are guaranteed access through wilderness areas.

Transport. Use of fixed-wing airplanes, motorboats, and snow machines for traditional activities and for access to villages and homesites is allowed to continue.

NATIONAL WILDLIFE REFUGES
Congress has designated 16 National Wildlife Refuges in Alaska, totaling nearly 82 million acres. (See map, pages 146–147) The refuges have 10 designated wilderness areas and 6 rivers designated National Wild and Scenic Rivers. At just under 20 million acres each, both the Arctic National Wildlife Refuge and the Yukon Delta National Wildlife Refuge are among the largest wildlife refuges in the world. Refuges are managed by the U.S. Fish and Wildlife Service's Region 7 at 1011 E. Tudor Road, Anchorage 99503.

National wildlife refuges in Alaska were established to conserve fish and wildlife populations and habitats in their natural diversity. Refuges are open to the public for many noncommercial recreational and subsistence uses including wildlife observation, photography, boating, camping and hiking. Hunting, fishing and trapping are allowed in accordance with state regulations and those set by the Federal Subsistence Board.

Visitors are encouraged to contact the refuge manager for information on special closures or other special conditions. Commercial guiding, air taxi operations and other commercial uses may be authorized by special permit. Subsistence activities are permitted, as is the use of snow machines, motorboats

and nonmotorized surface transportation methods for traditional activities. With adequate snow cover, recreational snowmachining is allowed on the Kenai Refuge. Transportation in off-road vehicles, including all-terrain vehicles, motorcycles and airboats, is not permitted.

Most refuges are in remote areas—only the Kenai and Tetlin refuges are accessible from the highway system. Airplane access is allowed but helicopter access requires a permit and must be determined compatible with refuge purposes.

Refuge managers may be contacted at their field headquarters listed below or through www.r7.fws.gov.

Alaska Maritime National Wildlife Refuge, 2355 Kachemak Drive, Suite 101, Homer 99603 (4.5 million acres). Seabirds, sea lions, sea otters, harbor seals, walrus, whales.

Alaska Peninsula National Wildlife Refuge, P.O. Box 277, King Salmon 99613 (3.5 million acres). Brown bears, caribou, moose, sea otters, bald eagles, peregrine falcons, wolves, wolverines, migrating whales.

Arctic National Wildlife Refuge, 101 12th Ave., Room 236, Fairbanks 99701 (19.5 million acres). Caribou, polar bears, grizzly bears, wolves, Dall sheep, peregrine falcons, musk-oxen, snowy owls.

Becharof National Wildlife Refuge, P.O. Box 277, King Salmon 99613 (1.2 million acres). Brown bears, bald eagles, caribou, moose, salmon.

Innoko National Wildlife Refuge, P.O. Box 69, McGrath 99627 (4.25 million acres). Migratory waterfowl, beaver, lynx, marten, moose.

Izembek National Wildlife Refuge, P.O. Box 127, Cold Bay 99571 (417,000 acres). Black brant (coastal geese), brown bears.

Kanuti National Wildlife Refuge, 101 12th Ave., Room 262, Fairbanks 99701 (1.4 million acres). Waterfowl.

Kenai National Wildlife Refuge, Box 2139, Soldotna 99669 (1.9 million acres). Moose, salmon, mountain goats, Dall sheep, bears, lynx, wolves.

Kodiak National Wildlife Refuge,

1390 Buskin River Road, Kodiak 99615
(1.9 million acres). Brown bears,
black-tailed deer, bald eagles, river otters.

Koyukuk National Wildlife Refuge,
P.O. Box 287, Galena 99741 (3.5 million
acres). Wolves, bears, moose, waterfowl.

Nowitna National Wildlife Refuge,
P.O. Box 287, Galena 99741 (1.5 million
acres). Migratory waterfowl, moose, bears,
furbearers.

Selawik National Wildlife Refuge,
P.O. Box 270, Kotzebue 99752 (2.1 million
acres). Caribou, migratory birds.

Tetlin National Wildlife Refuge,
P.O. Box 779, Tok 99780 (700,053 acres).
Migratory waterfowl, Dall sheep, moose,
bears, ptarmigan.

Togiak National Wildlife Refuge,
P.O. Box 270, Dillingham 99576
(4.1 million acres). Caribou, walrus,
seabirds, moose.

**Yukon Delta National Wildlife
Refuge,** P.O. Box 346, Bethel 99559
(19.1 million acres). Migratory birds,
musk-oxen and reindeer are found on
Nunivak Island.

**Yukon Flats National Wildlife
Refuge,** 101 12th Ave., Room 264,
Fairbanks 99701 (12 million acres).
Waterfowl, moose, bears.

NATIVE ARTS AND CRAFTS

(SEE ALSO Baleen; Baskets; Beadwork; Ivory; Masks;
Native Peoples; Potlatch; Skin Sewing; Totems)
Traditional arts and crafts of Alaska's
Natives were produced for ceremonial
and utilitarian purposes. These objects
were not thought of as art in the Western
sense but as pieces and designs to fulfill
specific needs. Native art also reflected
spiritual values and the environment each
group inhabited.

Alaska Natives are known for their
ingenious use and manipulation of natural
materials to supply life's needs: Roots, bark,
grasses, wood, fur, quills, skins, feathers
and the sea's resources are still used to
produce containers, clothing, hunting
implements, ceremonial regalia and many
other items.

Today, most Native utilitarian objects
are modern adaptations using plastic, metal

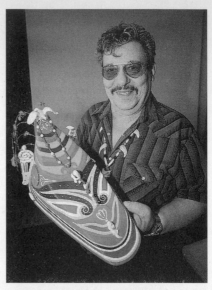

**Aleut artist Peter Lind created this
traditional-style bentwood visor.**
Photo by Ron Corral.

and glass. But many traditional Native
designs and natural materials are still
used to create ceremonial objects, and
Alaska Native arts and crafts are widely
sought by collectors, museums and tourists.
This new market has proven beneficial to
Native artists and to Native culture as it
moves from a subsistence lifestyle to a
cash economy.

The Inupiat and Yup'ik Eskimo people,
like other Alaska Native groups, are
divided geographically and linguistically.
Because their coastal environment offers
few forest resources, the Eskimo people
have learned to rely on the tundra and the
sea. The Inupiat of Northern Alaska are
known for making objects out of sea
mammal parts—especially walrus ivory,
baleen and whale bone. Their ivory carving
and scrimshaw work is world renowned.
More contemporary work in which stiff
baleen is coiled into elegant baskets is
gaining recognition.

The Yup'ik of Western Alaska also utilize
sea mammals in their art. In addition, they
rely heavily on the coastal rye grass for their
intricate coiled baskets and mat work.

Yup'ik ceremonial masks—carved primarily of driftwood, assembled and painted—are distinctive in the global tribal mask-making tradition. Both the Inupiat and Yup'ik groups produce warm, beautiful clothing using the furs and skins of land and sea mammals.

The Aleut people of the Aleutian Islands also make attractive baskets from rye grass but they use a twining technique. The Aleut are known for their traditional capes made of sea mammal gut and painted bentwood hunting hats and visors.

The Athabascan Indians of Alaska's Interior live in a region abundant with forest and river resources. They make decorative beaded clothing and other items, often on tanned, smoked moosehide; birch bark is formed into lightweight canoes, baby cradles and containers. Athabascans are also known for their skill sewing skins into clothing.

The Tlingit, Haida and Tsimshian people of southeastern Alaska are part of the Pacific Northwest Coast Indian culture, which extends down the coast of British Columbia and into Washington State. Each member of this culture is given at birth his or her own totemic crest—an animal form representing the family clan. These crests are reproduced in many art forms such as elaborate ceremonial regalia; carvings in wood, metal or stone; paintings or prints; and jewelry. The carvers of the Northwest Coast, best known for monumental totem poles, record legendary happenings and honor important people or events. Artwork adheres to a complex, formal design system and is highly stylized and dramatic. Fine Northwest Coast pieces such as carved and painted wooden hats, rattles, masks and bentwood boxes are sought worldwide by collectors and museums.

NATIVE PEOPLES Alaska's
98,000 Native people make up about 16 percent of the state's total population. Of those, the majority are Eskimo, Indian and Aleut. Although many live in widely scattered villages along the coastline and great rivers of Alaska, about 19,000 Natives lived in Anchorage as of 2000. Fairbanks had a Native population of nearly 3,000.

At the time Europeans came in contact with the Natives of Alaska in 1741, Russians estimated the Native population at 100,000. The Eskimo, Indian and Aleut people lived within well-defined regions: There was little mixing of ethnic groups. All were hunting and gathering people who did not practice agriculture.

Indian. In southeastern Alaska, the herring, salmon, deer and other plentiful foods permitted the **Haida** and **Tlingit Indians** to settle in permanent villages and develop a culture rich in art.

The **Athabascans** lived chiefly in the Interior. They migrated from one seasonal subsistence camp to another to take advantage of seasonal abundance of fish, waterfowl and other game.

Alaska's **Tsimshian Indians** moved in 1887 from their former home in British Columbia to Annette Island in Southeast Alaska, under the Rev. William Duncan, an Anglican. The Tsimshian today in Metlakatla, on Annette Island, are primarily fishermen.

Many of the Haida today live in Hydaburg on the south end of Prince of Wales Island in southeastern Alaska. It is believed they migrated to Alaska from interior Canada in the 1700s. The Haida excel at totem carving and are noted for skilled working of wood, bone, shell, stone and silver.

The Tlingit (KLINK-it) live throughout Alaska. The Tlingit, who migrated west

Alaskans are the second-highest per capita consumers of SPAM® in the nation. Winter hunters wisely take SPAM® on the polar ice pack because SPAM® *doesn't freeze!*

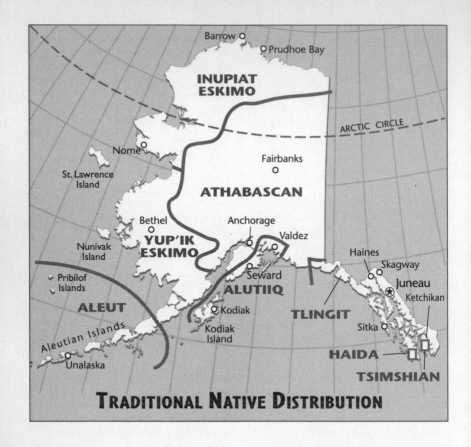

TRADITIONAL NATIVE DISTRIBUTION

from what is now Canada before the first European contact, commercially dominated the interior Canadian Indians, trading eulachon oil, copper pieces and Chilkat blankets for various furs and beaded clothing. Like the Haida and Tsimshian, Tlingit are part of the totem culture; totems provide a record of major events in family or clan history.

Athabascan Indians occupied the vast area of Alaska's Interior. They were nomadic people whose principal sources of food were caribou, moose and fish. Hard times and famines were frequent for all Athabascans except the Tanaina and Ahtna groups who lived along the Gulf of Alaska and could rely on salmon.

Eskimo. The Eskimo peoples have traditionally lived in villages along the harsh

Bering Sea and Arctic Ocean coastlines, as well as on King Island, St. Lawrence Island, Little Diomede Island and Nunivak Island. The inland Eskimos of southwestern Alaska settled along the lower reaches of Alaska's two largest rivers, the Yukon and Kuskokwim. Two major groups of Eskimos are Yup'ik (southwestern Alaska) and Inupiat (northern Alaska).

Depending on village location, Yup'ik and Inupiat Eskimos historically subsisted on traditional foods such as berries, salmon, waterfowl, ptarmigan, caribou, whales, walruses and seals. Winter dwellings were built partially underground, supported by driftwood and/or whale ribs, and covered with sod.

Aleut. The Aleut people have traditionally lived on the Alaska Peninsula and along the

Indian Bread

1 envelope dry yeast
1/4 cup very warm water
1 cup milk
1/4 cup sugar
1/4 cup shortening

1 teaspoon salt
1 egg
3 1/2 cups flour
1 cup raisins

About 6 cups cooking oil for deep-frying

Sprinkle dry yeast into warm water—110° to 115 °F—in a small bowl and let stand while mixing other ingredients. In a saucepan, over medium heat, mix milk, sugar, shortening and salt until dissolved and blended. Let mixture cool. Then add egg and yeast water and stir in flour and raisins gradually until it forms a soft dough. Place in a greased bowl and lightly grease the top of the dough. Cover and let rise until doubled in size—about 1 1/2 hours.

Place on a floured surface and knead air bubbles from dough. Pinch off small pieces and stretch them to oval shapes, being careful not to stretch them too thin. Make a hole in the center of each and place them on a clean, floured surface. Allow them to rise again until doubled in size. Heat oil in frying pan at high heat until it is bubbling hot. Deep-fry the little breads, a few at a time, turning them until both sides are golden brown. Place them on napkins or other absorbent paper to drain grease.

—Vivian James, Angoon, *Cooking Alaskan*

Aleutian Chain. When the Russians reached the Aleutians in the 1740s, practically every island was inhabited. Decimated by contact with whites, only a few Aleut settlements remain, including two established by Russians on the Pribilof Islands, St. Paul and St. George.

The Aleuts lived in permanent villages, taking advantage of sea life and land mammals for food. Their original dwellings were large, communal structures housing as many as 40 families. After Russian occupation they lived in smaller houses, many adopting the Russian-style log cabin. Today many Aleuts are commercial fishermen.

Alutiiq. The Alutiiq people lived on Kodiak Island and some coastal areas of the Kenai Peninsula and Prince William Sound. For more than two centuries, outsiders have mistakenly grouped them with the Aleut people or other Southcentral coastal groups, but the Alutiit (plural) began reclaiming their unique identity as recently as the mid-1980s. Beginning with the first

Russian attack on Kodiak in 1784, this Native group was most altered by contact with Europeans.

Rapid advances in communications, transportation and other services to remote villages have altered Native life in Alaska. Economic changes, from a subsistence to a cash economy, culminated in the passage of the Alaska Native Claims Settlement Act in 1971. It gave Alaska Natives $962.5 million and 44 million acres of land as compensation for the loss of lands historically occupied or used by their people.

Native Regional Corporations

Twelve in-state regional business corporations were formed under the 1971 Alaska Native Claims Settlement Act to manage money and land received from the government. (SEE MAP, page 157) A 13th corporation was organized for Natives residing outside Alaska.

Ahtna Inc. (Copper River Basin), P.O. Box 649, Copper Center 99588,

John Charlie, in decorated moosehide dance clothes, and his grandfather, Neil Charlie. From *Children of the Midnight Sun* by Tricia Brown (text) and Roy Corral (photographs).

or 1760 Abbott Road, Anchorage 99507.

Aleut Corp. (Aleutian Islands), 1 Aleut Plaza, 4000 Old Seward Highway, Suite 300, Anchorage 99503.

Arctic Slope Regional Corp. (Arctic Alaska), P.O. Box 129, Barrow 99723, or 301 Arctic Slope Ave., Anchorage 99518-3035.

Bering Straits Native Corp. (Seward Peninsula), P.O. Box 1008, Nome 99762.

Bristol Bay Native Corp. (Bristol Bay area), P.O. Box 310, Dillingham 99576, or P.O. Box 100220, Anchorage 99510.

Calista Corp. (Yukon–Kuskokwim Delta), 301 Calista Court, Suite A, Anchorage 99518.

Chugach Alaska Corp. (Prince William Sound), 560 E. 34th Ave., Suite 200, Anchorage 99503.

Cook Inlet Region Inc. (Cook Inlet region), 2525 C St., Anchorage 99503.

Doyon Ltd. (Interior Alaska), Doyon Place, Suite 300, Fairbanks 99701.

Koniag Inc. (Kodiak area), 4300 B St., Suite 407, Anchorage 99503, or 202 Center Ave., Suite 201, Kodiak 99615.

NANA Regional Corp. (Kobuk region), P.O. Box 49, Kotzebue 99752, or 1001 E. Benson Blvd., Anchorage 99508.

Sealaska Corp. (southeastern Alaska), One Sealaska Plaza, Suite 400, Juneau 99801.

Thirteenth Regional Corp. (outside Alaska), 951 Industry Drive, Seattle, WA 98188.

Regional Nonprofit Corporations

Aleutian–Pribilof Islands Association Inc. (Aleut Corp.), 201 E. Third Ave., Anchorage 99501.

Association of Village Council Presidents (Calista Corp.), P.O. Box 219, Bethel 99559.

Bristol Bay Native Association (Bristol Bay Native Corp.), P.O. Box 310, Dillingham 99756.

Cook Inlet Tribal Council Inc. (Cook Inlet Region Inc.), 670 W. Fireweed Lane, Suite 200, Anchorage 99503.

Copper River Native Association (Ahtna Inc.), Drawer H, Copper Center 99573.

Inupiat Community of the Arctic Slope (Arctic Slope Regional Corp.), P.O. Box 69, Barrow 99723.

Kawerak, Inc. (Bering Straits Native Corp.), P.O. Box 948, Nome 99762.

Kodiak Area Native Association (Koniag Inc.), 3449 E. Rezanof Drive, Kodiak 99615.

Maniilaq (formerly Mauneluk) Association (NANA Regional Corp.), P.O. Box 256, Kotzebue 99752.

North Pacific Rim Native Association (Chugach Alaska Corp.), 560 E. 34th Ave., Anchorage 99503.

Ounalashka Corp. (Aleut Corp.), P.O. Box 149, Unalaska 99685.

Tanana Chiefs Conference (Doyon Ltd.), 122 First Ave., Fairbanks 99701.

Other Native Organizations

Alaska Eskimo Whaling Commission, P.O. Box 570, Barrow 99723.

NATIVE REGIONAL CORPORATIONS

Alaska Federation of Natives, 1577 C St., Suite 300, Anchorage 99501.

Alaska Native Brotherhood, 320 W. Willoughby Ave., Juneau 99801.

Alaska Native Foundation, 3305 Arctic Blvd., Anchorage 99503.

Alaska Native Health Board, 4201 Tudor Centre Drive, Anchorage 99508.

Alaska Native Tribal Health Consortium, 4141 Ambassador Drive, Anchorage 99508.

Bristol Bay Area Health Corp., P.O. Box 130, Dillingham 99576.

Central Council of the Tlingit and Haida Indian Tribes of Alaska, 320 W. Willoughy Ave., Suite 300, Juneau 99801.

Eyak Corp., P.O. Box 340, Cordova 99574.

Fairbanks Native Association Inc., 911 Cushman St., Suite 206, Fairbanks 99701.

Interior Village Association, 127-1/2 Minnie St., Fairbanks 99701.

Inuit Circumpolar Conference, 401 E. Northern Lights Blvd., Anchorage 99503.

Norton Sound Health Corp., P.O. Box 966, Nome 99762.

Qawalangin (Sons of the Sea Lion), P.O. Box 334, Unalaska 99685; the federally recognized tribal government of the Unangan (Aleut) people of Unalaska.

Southeast Alaska Regional Health Corp., 3245 Hospital Drive, Juneau 99801.

Yukon–Kuskokwim Health Corp., P.O. Box 528, Bethel 99559.

Yupiktat Bista (a branch of the Association of Village Council Presidents), Bethel 99559.

NUGGETS

When Chief Walter Northway was honored in 1991 on his 115th birthday, he may have been the oldest man in the world. Yet the Athabascan patriarch couldn't officially hold the title, according to the *Guinness Book of World Records*, because a fire around the turn of the century destroyed his birth records. The Bureau of Indian Affairs listed Northway's age at 115, allowing for a five-year margin of error. —1991 *The ALASKA ALMANAC*®

Native Village Corporations

In addition to the 13 regional corporations managing money and land received as part of the Alaska Native Claims Settlement Act, eligible Native villages were required to form corporations and to choose lands made available by the settlement act. The 203 Native villages that formed village corporations eligible for land and money benefits are listed under their regional corporation.

Ahtna Inc. Cantwell, Chistochina, Chitina, Copper Center, Gakona, Gulkana, Mentasta Lake, Tazlina.

Aleut Corp. Akutan, Atka, Belkofski, False Pass, King Cove, Nelson Lagoon, Nikolski, St. George, St. Paul, Sand Point, Unalaska, Unga.

Arctic Slope Regional Corp. Anaktuvuk Pass, Atkasook, Barrow, Kaktovik, Nuiqsut, Point Hope, Point Lay, Wainwright.

Bering Straits Native Corp. Brevig Mission, Council, Golovin, Inalik/Diomede, King Island, Koyuk, Marys Igloo, Nome, St. Michael, Shaktoolik, Shishmaref, Stebbins, Teller, Unalakleet, Wales, White Mountain.

Bristol Bay Native Corp. Aleknagik, Chignik, Chignik Lagoon, Chignik Lake, Clarks Point, Dillingham, Egegik, Ekuk, Ekwok, Igiugig, Iliamna, Ivanof Bay, Kokhanok, Koliganek, Levelock, Manokotak, Naknek, Newhalen, New Stuyahok, Nondalton, Pedro Bay, Perryville, Pilot Point, Portage Creek, Port Heiden, South Naknek, Togiak, Twin Hills, Ugashik.

Calista Corp. Akiachak, Akiak, Alakanuk, Andreafsky, Aniak, Atmautluak, Bethel, Bill Moores, Chefornak, Chevak, Chuathbaluk, Chuloonwick, Crooked Creek, Eek, Emmonak, Georgetown, Goodnews Bay, Hamilton, Hooper Bay, Kasigluk, Kipnuk, Kongiganak, Kotlik, Kwethluk, Kwigillingok, Lime Village, Lower Kalskag, Marshall, Mekoryuk, Mountain Village, Napaimiute, Napakiak, Napaskiak, Newtok, Nightmute, Nunapitchuk, Ohogamiut, Oscarville, Paimiut, Pilot Station, Pitkas Point, Platinum, Quinhagak, Red Devil, Russian Mission, St. Marys, Scammon Bay, Sheldons Point, Sleetmute, Stony River, Toksook Bay, Tuluksak, Tuntutuliak, Tununak, Umkumiut, Upper Kalskag.

Chugach Natives Inc. Chenaga, Eyak, Nanwalek, Port Graham, Tatitlek.

Cook Inlet Region Inc. Chickaloon, Eklutna, Knik, Ninilchik, Seldovia, Tyonek.

Doyon Ltd. Alatna, Allakaket, Anvik, Beaver, Bettles Field, Birch Creek, Chalkyitsik, Circle, Dot Lake, Eagle, Fort Yukon, Galena, Grayling, Healy Lake, Holy Cross, Hughes, Huslia, Kaltag, Koyukuk, Manley Hot Springs, McGrath, Minto, Nenana, Nikolai, Northway, Nulato, Rampart, Ruby, Shageluk, Stevens Village, Takotna, Tanacross, Tanana, Telida.

Klukwan Inc. Klukwan.

Koniag Inc. Afognak, Akhiok, Kaguyak, Karluk, Larsen Bay, Old Harbor, Ouzinkie, Port Lions, Woody Island.

NANA Regional Corp. Ambler, Buckland, Deering, Kiana, Kivalina, Kobuk, Kotzebue, Noatak, Noorvik, Selawik, Shungnak.

Sealaska Corp. Angoon, Craig, Hoonah, Hydaburg, Kake, Kasaan, Klawock, Saxman, Yakutat.

Shee-Atika Corp. Sitka.

NENANA ICE CLASSIC (SEE ALSO Breakup) The Ice Classic is a gigantic betting pool offering $300,000 in cash prizes to the

Nenana Ice Classic, Breakup Times, 1918–2001

April	May	May
20, 1940 — 3:27 P.M.	1, 1989 — 8:14 P.M.	8, 1933 — 7:30 P.M.
20, 1998 — 4:54 P.M.	2, 1976 —10:51 A.M.	8, 1968 — 9:26 P.M.
23, 1993 — 1:01 P.M.	2, 1960 — 7:12 P.M.	8, 1986 — 9:31 P.M.
24, 1990 — 5:19 P.M.	3, 1941 — 1:50 A.M.	8, 1971 —10:50 P.M.
26, 1995 — 1:22 P.M.	3, 1919 — 2:33 P.M.	8, 2001 — 1:00 P.M.
26, 1926 — 4:03 P.M.	3, 1947 — 5:53 P.M.	9, 1923 — 2:00 P.M.
28, 1969 —12:28 P.M.	4, 1967 —11:55 A.M.	9, 1955 — 2:31 P.M.
28, 1943 — 7:22 P.M.	4, 1973 —11:59 A.M.	9, 1984 — 3:33 P.M.
29, 1939 — 1:26 P.M.	4, 1944 — 2:08 P.M.	10, 1931 — 9:23 A.M.
29, 1958 — 2:56 P.M.	4, 1970 —10:37 P.M.	10, 1972 —11:56 A.M.
29, 1953 — 3:54 P.M.	5, 1957 — 9:30 A.M.	10, 1975 — 1:49 P.M.
29, 1983 — 6:37 P.M.	5, 1961 —11:31 A.M.	10, 1982 — 5:36 P.M.
29, 1999— 9:47 P.M.	5, 1996 —12:32 P.M.	11, 1921 — 6:42 A.M.
29, 1994 —11:01 P.M.	5, 1987 — 3:11 P.M.	11, 1918 — 9:33 A.M.
30, 1997—10:28 A.M.	5, 1929 — 3:41 P.M.	11, 1920 —10:45 A.M.
30, 1936 —12:58 P.M.	5, 1946 — 4:40 P.M.	11, 1985 — 2:36 P.M.
30, 1980 — 1:16 P.M.	5, 1963 — 6:25 P.M.	11, 1924 — 3:10 P.M.
30, 1942 — 1:28 P.M.	6, 1977 —12:46 P.M.	12, 1927 — 5:42 A.M.
30, 1934 — 2:07 P.M.	6, 1974 — 3:44 P.M.	12, 1922 — 1:20 P.M.
30, 1978 — 3:18 P.M.	6, 1950 — 4:14 P.M.	12, 1952 — 5:04 P.M.
30, 1951 — 5:54 P.M.	6, 1928 — 4:25 P.M.	12, 1937 — 8:04 P.M.
30, 1979 — 6:16 P.M.	6, 1954 — 6:01 P.M.	12, 1962 —11:23 P.M.
30, 1981 — 6:44 P.M.	6, 1938 — 8:14 P.M.	13, 1948 —11:13 A.M.
May	7, 1925 — 6:32 P.M.	14, 1992 — 6:26 A.M.
1, 2000 —10:47 A.M.	7, 1965 — 7:01 P.M.	14, 1949 —12:39 P.M.
1, 1991 —12:04 A.M.	8, 1959 —11:26 A.M.	15, 1935 — 1:32 P.M.
1, 1932 —10:15 A.M.	8, 1966 —12:11 P.M.	16, 1945 — 9:41 A.M.
1, 1956 —11:24 A.M.	8, 1930 — 7:03 P.M.	20, 1964 —11:41 A.M.

lucky winner—or winners—who guess the time, to the nearest minute, of the ice breakup on the Tanana River at the town of Nenana. Official breakup time each spring is established when surging ice dislodges a four-legged "tripod" and breaks an attached line, which stops a clock set to Yukon standard time.

Tickets for the classic sell for $2 each, entitling the holder to one guess. Ice Classic officials estimate more than $7 million has been paid to lucky guessers through the years. The event was sanctioned as a state lottery by the first state legislature in one of its earliest actions in 1959.

Over the years the Ice Classic has

> Alaska made national news when Anchorage police misidentified a corpse, released the name to the media, and plunged the family into shock, grief and mourning. A friend who ran into the presumably deceased Neil Beaton said, "Neil, what are you doing here? You're supposed to be dead. Your sister's on the phone—they found your body last night."

benefited Nenana. Fifty percent of the gross proceeds goes to the winners. Nenana residents are paid salaries for ticket counting and compilation, and about 15 percent is earmarked for upkeep of the Nenana Civic Center and as donations to the local visitors center, the library and special events at the high school.

The Internal Revenue Service also gets a chunk of withholding taxes on the payroll and a bite of each winner's share. In 2000, 18 winners split the pot, giving them $18,611 each.

Breakup times for the Nenana Ice Classic from 1918 through 2001 are arranged in order of day and time of breakup (See chart, page 159).

Another pool, the Kuskokwim Ice Classic, has been a tradition in Bethel since 1924. Initially, it was said that the winner was paid 20 fish or 20 furs but stakes are considerably higher now and the winner receives 40 percent of the total ticket sales.

NEWSPAPERS AND PERIODICALS *(Rates are subject to change.)*

Alaska Angler, Box 83550, Fairbanks 99708. Monthly. Annual rate: $49.

Alaska Bar Rag, 510 L St., No. 602, Anchorage 99501. Bimonthly. Annual rate: $25.

Alaska Bush Shopper, 301 Calista Court, Suite B, Anchorage 99518. Monthly. Free.

Alaska Business Monthly, P.O. Box 241288, Anchorage 99524-1288. Monthly. Annual rate: $21.95.

Alaska Contractor, 401 W. International Airport Road, Suite 11, Anchorage 99518. Four times a year. Free.

Alaska Designs, P.O. Box 103115, Anchorage 99510-3115. Monthly (except August). Annual rate: $36 for nonmembers; free for members.

Alaska Digest, 3002 Spenard Road, No. 1, Anchorage 99503. Nine issues a year. Free.

Alaska Directory of Attorneys, 203 W. 15th Ave., Suite 102, Anchorage 99501. Biannually. Annual rate: $70.

The Alaska Geographic Society, P.O. Box 93370, Anchorage 99509. Quarterly. Annual rates: $49; outside the U.S. $59.

Alaska Guide Report, P.O. Box 20250, Anchorage 99520. Quarterly. Annual rate: $19.95.

Alaska Hunter, P.O. Box 83550, Fairbanks 99708. Monthly. Annual rate: $49.

Alaska International Trade Directory, P.O. Box 112955, Anchorage 99511-2955. Annually. Free.

Alaska Journal of Commerce, 4220 B St., Suite 210, Anchorage 99503. Weekly. Annual rate: $30.

Alaska Justice Forum, 3211 Providence Drive, Anchorage 99508. Quarterly. Free.

ALASKA magazine, 619 E. Ship Creek Ave., Suite 329, Anchorage 99501. Ten issues a year. Subscriptions: $24; outside the U.S. $30.

Alaska Media Directory, 6828 Cape Lisburne Loop, Anchorage 99504-3958. Annually. Annual rate: $88.

AlaskaMen, 205 E. Dimond Blvd., Suite 522, Anchorage 99518. Bimonthly. Subscriptions: $49.95; Mexico and Canada $54.95; Europe, Pacific Rim, Central and South America $63.

Alaska Military Weekly, 4220 B St., Suite 210, Anchorage 99503. Weekly. Free.

Alaska Miner, 3305 Arctic Blvd., Suite 202, Anchorage 99503. Monthly. Mailed to members of Alaska Miners Association.

Alaska Miners Association Handbook and Service Directory, 3305 Arctic Blvd., Suite 202, Anchorage 99503. Annually. Mailed to members of Alaska Miners Association.

Alaska Native Directory, Regional Corporation Directory, 3002 Spenard Road, Suite 1, Anchorage 99503. Updated regularly. Annual rates: Native Directory $167.50; Regional Corporation Directory $18.95–$20.95.

Alaska Pet News, P.O. Box 4083, Palmer 99645. Bimonthly. Annual rate: $18.

Alaska Post, 600 Richardson Drive, Suite 5900, Fort Richardson 99505-5900. Weekly. Free.

Alaska Sports Magazine, P.O. Box

220861, Anchorage 99522-0861. Monthly. Annual rate: $19.95.

Alaska Star, 16941 N. Eagle River Loop, Eagle River 99577. Weekly. Annual rate: $25.

Alaska Transporter, 501 W. Northern Lights Blvd., Suite 100, Anchorage 99503. Annually. Free to the trade.

Alaska Wellness Magazine, 911 W. 19th Ave., Anchorage 99503-1704. Bimonthly. Annual rate: $15.

Alaska Women Speak, P.O. Box 92842, Anchorage 99509-2842. Quarterly. Annual rate: $16.

Alaskan, 134th Public Affairs Team, P.O. Box 5800, Camp Denali, Fort Richardson 99505. Quarterly. Free to members of the Army National Guard, Air National Guard and DMVA employees.

Alaskan Bowhunters, P.O. Box 220830, Anchorage 99522-0830. Quarterly. Free to members.

Alaskan Equipment Trader, 4220 B St., Suite 210, Anchorage 99503. Monthly. Annual rate: $12.

Alaskan Snow Rider, 1801 Crescent Drive, Anchorage 99508. Monthly, September to April. Free.

Alaskan Southeaster, 9301 Glacier Highway, Suite 200, Juneau 99801. Monthly. Annual rate: $28.

Anchorage Chamber of Commerce News and Views, 441 W. Fifth Ave., Suite 300, Anchorage 99501. Monthly. Free to members.

Anchorage Daily News, P.O. Box 149001, Anchorage 99514-9001. Daily. Annual rates: Anchorage home delivery $135; second-class mail $390.

Anchorage Press, P.O. Box 241841, Anchorage 99524-1841. Weekly. Free locally. Mailed subscriptions: $30 (in state), $70 (out of state).

Anchorage Visitors Guide, 524 W. Fourth Ave., Anchorage 99501; www.anchorage.net. April and October. Free.

Arctic Sounder, P.O. Box 290, Kotzebue 99752. Weekly. Annual rates: second-class mail $45; first class $90.

Boat Broker, 1910 Alex Holden Way, Juneau 99801. Monthly. Free to Southeast communities; $10 mailed.

Bristol BayTimes, P.O. Box 1770, Dillingham 99576. Weekly. Annual rates: second-class mail $45; first class $90.

Bush Blade, P.O. Box 168, Anchor Point 99556. Monthly. Annual rate: $7.50.

Business News Alaska, P.O. Box 91830, Anchorage 99509-1830. Monthly. Annual rate: $24.

Capital City Weekly, 1910 Alex Holden Way, Juneau 99801. Weekly. Annual rates: Home delivery, free; $52 mailed.

Captn Jack's Tide & Current Almanac, P.O. Box 65119, Port Ludlow, WA 98365-0119. Annually. $14.95.

Catholic Anchor, 225 Cordova St., Anchorage 99501. Biweekly. Annual rate: $20.

The Chamber, 401 W. International Airport Road, Suite 11, Anchorage 99518. Four times a year. Free.

Chilkat Valley News, P.O. Box 630, Haines 99827. Weekly. Annual rates: $36 in Haines; $42 mailed in state.

Chugiak/Eagle River Business and Service Directory, P.O. Box 770353, Eagle River 99577. Biannually. Free.

Clarion Dispatch, P.O. Box 3009, Kenai 99611. Weekly. Free.

COAST Magazine, 702 W. 32nd Ave., Suite 203, Anchorage 99503. Monthly. Free.

Commercial Buyers Guide, P.O. Box

112955, Anchorage 99511-2955. Annually. Free.

Cordova Times, P.O Box 200, Cordova 99574. Weekly. Annual rates: second-class mail $45; first class $90.

Cuisine Scene, 702 W. 32nd Ave., Suite 203, Anchorage 99503. Biannually. Free.

Current Drift, P.O. Box 210430, Anchorage 99521-0430. Monthly. Free.

Daily Sitka Sentinel, P.O. Box 799, Sitka 99835. Monday through Friday. Annual rate: $80.

Delta Discovery, P.O. Box 1028, Bethel 99559. Weekly. Annual rate: $60.

Delta Wind, P.O. Box 986, Delta Junction 99737. Biweekly. Rate: 85 cents per issue.

Denali Summer Times, P.O. Box 40, Healy 99743. Annually. Free.

Dillingham/Southwest Alaska Visitor's Guide, P.O. Box 1770, Dillingham 99576. Annually. Free.

Dutch Harbor Fisherman, Box 920472, Dutch Harbor 99692. Weekly. Annual rates: second-class mail $45; first class $90.

Eagle Eye, P.O. Box 1429, Haines 99827. Weekly. Annual rates: $36 local; $45 second-class mail; $64 first class.

Eastside Pulse, Southside Pulse, and **Westside Pulse,** P.O. Box 92896, Anchorage 99509-2896. Monthly. Free.

Fairbanks Daily News-Miner, P.O. Box 70710, Fairbanks 99707. Daily. Annual rates: $294 Fairbanks; $306 Alaska; $334 outside Alaska.

Fairbanks Magazine, 921 Woodway, Fairbanks 99709. June through October. Rate: $2.25 per issue.

The Frontiersman, 5751 E. Mayflower Court, Wasilla 99654. Twice weekly. Annual rates: $40 Mat–Su; $65.60 Alaska; $70.60 outside Alaska.

Goldpanner, 3112 Broadway Ave., Unit 18A, Eielson AFB 99702-1895. Weekly. Free.

Great Lander Shopper, Great Lander Fairbanks, Great Lander Southeast, 3110 Spenard Road, Anchorage 99503. Monthly. Free.

Guidelines, 2207 Spenard Road, Suite 201, Anchorage 99503. Quarterly. Free to members.

Homer Alaska Tribune, 601 E. Pioneer Ave., Suite 109, Homer 99603. Weekly. Annual rate: $30.

Homer News, 3482 Landings St., Homer 99603. Weekly. Annual rate: $35 Kenai Peninsula Borough.

Hot Sheet, 1910 Alex Holden Way, Juneau 99801. Weekly. Free.

Island News, P.O. Box 19430, Thorne Bay 99919. Weekly. Annual rate: $55.

Juneau Empire, 3100 Channel Drive, Juneau 99801-7814. Monday through Friday and Sunday. Annual rate: $125.

Kaniqsirugut News, P.O. Box 966, Nome 99762. Four times a year. Free.

Ketchikan Daily News, P.O. Box 7900, Ketchikan 99901. Monday through Saturday. Annual rate: $122 local.

Kodiak Daily Mirror, 1419 Selig, Kodiak 99615. Monday through Friday. Annual rates: $96; $132 mailed in state.

The Local Paper, 516 Stedman, Ketchikan 99901. Weekly. Free.

Marine Highway News, 3100 Channel Drive, Juneau 99801. Annually. Free.

Marine Yellow Pages, 15311 NE 90th St., Redmond, WA 98052. Annually. Free.

The MILEPOST, Morris Communications, 619 E. Ship Creek Ave., Suite 329, Anchorage 99501. Annually. 2000–01 edition: $24.95.

Mukluk News, P.O. Box 90, Tok 99780. Bimonthly. Annual rate: $20.

Mushing, P.O. Box 149, Ester 99725; www.mushing.com. Bimonthly. Annual rate: $24.

The Nickelsaver, 500 Main St., Unit C, Wasilla 99687. Weekly. Free.

The Nome Nugget, P.O. Box 610, Nome 99762. Weekly. Annual rates: $55; outside Alaska $60.

Nome Visitors Guide, 301 Calista Court, Suite B, Anchorage 99518. Annually. Free.

Northcountry Companion Traveler's Guides, P.O. Box 336, Glennallen 99588. Annually. Free.

North View, P.O. Box 200070,

Anchorage 99520-0070. Monthly. Annual rate: $25.

Northern Light, 3211 Providence Drive, Anchorage 99508. Weekly. Free.

On Board, 411 W. First Ave., Anchorage 99501. Annually. Free.

Peninsula Clarion, P.O. Box 3009, Kenai 99611. Sunday through Friday. Annual rate: $78.

Pennysaver, 1001 Northway Drive, Anchorage 99508. Weekly. Free.

Petersburg Pilot, P.O. Box 930, Petersburg 99833. Weekly. Annual rate: $40.

Petroleum News, P.O. Box 231651, Anchorage 99523-1651. Monthly. Annual rate: $35.95.

Prince William Sound Visitor's Guide, 301 Calista Court, Suite B, Anchorage 99518. Annually. Free.

Real Estate Now, 702 W. 32nd Ave., Suite 203, Anchorage 99503. Biweekly. Free.

Real Estate This Week, 741 Sesame St., Suite 100, Anchorage 99503. Weekly. Free.

Sealaska Shareholder, 1 Sealaska Plaza, Suite 400, Juneau 99801-1276. Five times a year. Free to shareholders.

Senior Voice, 325 E. Third Ave., Suite 300, Anchorage 99501. Monthly. Annual rate: $12.

Seward Phoenix-Log, P.O. Box 89, Seward 99664. Weekly. Annual rates: second-class mail $45; first class $90.

Seward Visitor's Guide, P.O. Box 89, Seward 99664. Annually. Free.

Skagway News, P.O. Box 498, Skagway 99840-0498. Biweekly. Annual rate: $30.

Sourdough Sentinel, Third Wing, Public Affairs, 6920 12th St., Elmendorf Air Force Base 99506. Weekly. Free.

Southeast Empire, 3100 Channel Drive, Juneau 99801-7814. Monthly. Free.

Sun Star, P.O. Box 756640, Fairbanks 99775-6640. Weekly. Annual rate: $20.

Trade Winds, 401 W. International Airport Road, Suite 11, Anchorage 99518. Quarterly. Free.

True North, Journalism and Public Communications Department, Bldg. K, University of Alaska Anchorage, 3211 Providence Drive, Anchorage 99508. Annually. Free.

Tundra Drums, Box 868, Bethel 99559. Weekly. Annual rate: $45.

Turnagain Times, P.O. Box 1044, Girdwood 99587. Semimonthly. Annual rates: $18 in state; $24 out of state; $30 international.

Unalaska/Dutch Harbor Visitor's Guide, 301 Calista Court, Suite B, Anchorage 99518. Annually. Free.

Valdez Star, P.O. Box 2949, Valdez 99686. Weekly. Annual rate: $45.

Valdez Vanguard, P.O. Box 98, Valdez 99686-0098. Weekly. Annual rates: second-class mail $45; first class $90.

Valley Sun, 5751 E. Mayflower Court, Wasilla 99654. Weekly. Free to Matanuska–Susitna Borough box holders.

Welcome to Alaska and the Mat-Su Valley, 401 W. International Airport Road, Suite 11, Anchorage 99518. Annually. Free.

Wrangell Sentinel and **Wrangell Guide,** P.O. Box 798, Wrangell 99929. Weekly. Annual rate: $32.

Wrangell–St. Elias News, McCarthy, Box MXY, Glennallen 99588. Bimonthly. Annual rate: $10.

NOME Located on the shores of Norton Sound on the Seward Peninsula's south coast, Nome, with a population of just over 3,500, is the transportation and commercial center for northwestern Alaska.

Nome owes its name to a misinterpretation of the notation "? name" on a chart in 1850. The question mark was taken as a

The Headline of the Year award goes to the *Kodiak Daily Mirror*, which proclaimed: "Senate passes bill that would set up hunting seasons for children."

"C" standing for Cape, and the letter "a" in "name" was read as an "o." Originally the settlement was named Anvil City when gold was found in the Anvil Creek area in the summer of 1898.

The real gold stampede to Nome began in June 1899, when an estimated 30,000 miners rushed to Nome to stake claims and pitch their tents along the beaches of the Bering Sea Coast. That year, Nome was the largest city in the Alaska Territory. Miners quickly fled when their claims didn't pay, and by 1906 most of the gold and the prospectors were gone.

The mean average daily temperature in winter is –8°F and summer temperatures range from 40°F to 50°F. Mean annual snowfall, occurring from late September through early June, is 53 inches.

A 3,350-foot-long granite wall built by the U.S. Army Corps of Engineers protects Nome from the sea. It is 65 feet wide at the base, 16 feet wide at its top and 18 feet above mean low water.

Although not connected by road to the rest of the state, Nome boasts more than 300 miles of road in the area—the second-largest city road system in the state. There is no winter maintenance of the roads.

The city of Nome has several schools, including the Northwest College, and the distinction of having the state's oldest first-class school district. It also offers many churches; a library and museum containing more than 6,000 photographs of the gold rush, Eskimo history and the Bering Land Bridge; and a historical park with a nonworking gold dredge and mining equipment from the gold-rush days. For a fee, visitors may still try their luck panning the sands of the Nome beaches.

Throughout the year Nome offers many festivals and celebrations including its most famous event—the finish of the Iditarod Trail Sled Dog Race. There's the Bering Sea Ice Classic Golf Tournament played on the frozen Bering Sea in March; a Polar Bear Swim on Memorial Day; a Midnight Sun Festival in June, featuring a raft race on the Nome River with many a strange craft taking part; a 12.5-mile run to the top of 1,977-foot Anvil Mountain on July 4; and a Labor Day Bathtub Race. Other events include snowmobile races, snowshoe, softball games and the largest state basketball tournament.

The city today is a jumping-off point for flights to Russia (only an hour-long flight away), surrounding Bush villages and tours of the Arctic. For details, consult www.nomealaska.org.

NO-SEE-UMS
The words describe a small, biting, two-winged midge. In its usual swarms this tiny, gray-black, silver-winged gnat is a most persistent pest and annoys all creatures. The insect is difficult to see when it's flying alone. While no-see-ums don't transmit disease, their bites are irritating. Protective clothing, netting and a good repellent are recommended while in dense brush or near still-water ponds. Tents and recreational vehicles should be well screened.

OIL AND GAS
(SEE ALSO National Petroleum Reserve; Pipeline) Alaska's first exploratory oil well was drilled in 1898 on the Iniskin Peninsula, Cook Inlet, by Alaska Petroleum Co. Oil was encountered in this first hole at about 700 feet but a water zone beneath the oil strata cut off the oil flow. Total depth of the well was approximately 1,000 feet.

The first commercial oil discovery was made in 1902 at Katalla, near the mouth of the Bering River east of Cordova. This field produced until 1933.

As early as 1921, oil companies surveyed land north of the Brooks Range for possible drilling sites. In 1923, the federal government created Naval Petroleum Reserve Number 4 (now known as National Petroleum Reserve Alaska; see National Petroleum Reserve), a 23 million-acre area of Alaska's North Slope. Wartime needs speeded up exploration.

In 1944, the Navy began drilling operations on the petroleum reserve and continued until 1953, but made no oil discoveries that were economic. Between 1981 and 1984, the U.S. Department of

Getting Alaska Oil to Market

How does a barrel of oil travel along the 800-mile trans-Alaska oil pipeline?

Oil from the Prudhoe fields is 145°F to 180°F when it is pumped to the surface of the North Slope. The oil is cooled to about 120°F before it enters the pipeline.

The pipeline is 48 inches in diameter; much of it is raised above the permafrost but at 21 spots it dives underground. Oil takes five to six days to travel the 800 miles from Prudhoe Bay to the terminal at the ice-free port of Valdez. Ten pump stations hustle the oil along. On the way, it crosses 834 rivers and streams, three major mountain ranges and an earthquake fault line. Caribou and other wildlife wander under raised parts of the pipeline. At Valdez, the crude is loaded onto oceangoing oil tankers.

Alyeska Pipeline Service Co. shipped its 13 billionth barrel of Alaska North Slope crude in August 2000.

the Interior leased oil and gas tracts in the reserve but oil companies were focusing most of their attention elsewhere.

In the mid-1990s, oil companies began developing smaller fields close to the eastern edge of the reserve, spurring new interest in what lay within NPRA. BP, Chevron and Phillips launched an aggressive exploration program in the reserve during 2001.

Today, virtually all of Alaska's oil is produced from two regions, the North Slope and Cook Inlet.

North Slope. Discovered in 1968, Prudhoe Bay was the first commercial North Slope oil field to produce oil. Commercial production began in 1977, when Alyeska Pipeline Service Co. completed the pipeline between Prudhoe Bay and the port at Valdez. North Slope fields had produced a total of about 13 billion barrels as of the end of 2000, 80 percent of it from Prudhoe Bay, 14 percent from Kuparuk and 6 percent from other fields.

Three North Slope satellite developments began production in 1993: Point McIntyre, by far the largest; North Prudhoe Bay State; and West Beach. The Niakuk pool began producing in 1994 and the Midnight Sun started in 1998. Milne Point, a Kuparuk River field development, increased production in late 1994 and 1995. Other new Kuparuk River developments are: the Aurora Pool, which started production in November 2000; Schrader Bluff, which began production in November 1999; Tarn, which started production in July 1998; Tabasco, in April 1998; and West Sak, in late 1997. These recent additions have somewhat offset the regional decline in oil production.

Recent exploration has resulted in several discoveries that should contribute to North Slope production. The Colville River field, discovered in 1994, is the largest of these and began production in November 2000. Various satellite developments are being evaluated throughout the North Slope. New additions can only partially limit the decline at Prudhoe Bay and the other larger oil fields.

Cook Inlet. Companies first discovered Cook Inlet oil at Swanson River on the Kenai Peninsula in 1957 and began production in 1959. In 1962, the first offshore oil in Cook Inlet was discovered, making the inlet one of three successful areas in the United States for offshore oil production. Currently there are 16 production platforms in Cook Inlet, one of which produces only natural gas. The Forest Oil Corp. Osprey Platform was set in 2000 and exploratory drilling is under way.

Regional production in Cook Inlet peaked in 1970 at 230,000 barrels daily (83 million barrels a year) and subsequently declined to 29,910 barrels a day in 2000. By the end of 2000 Cook Inlet fields had produced 1.3 billion barrels of oil, 47 percent of this from McArthur River, 18 percent from Swanson River and 35 percent from the other fields. Two fields, West McArthur River and Sunfish (Tyonek Deep), were discovered in 1991. West McArthur River began production in 1993 and has produced 6.7 million barrels by 2001.

Gas production from the Cook Inlet continues at significant levels with 181 billion cubic feet produced during 2000. Forest Oil Corp. is planning to develop the West Foreland gas reservoir and Redoubt Shoals Oil Field. Forest Oil installed its Osprey platform at Redoubt Shoals and drilled an exploration well during the winter of 2000–01. Several companies are exploring for coalbed methane in the Matanuska Valley.

Projected Reserves and Production. The Division of Oil and Gas estimates that Alaska's total reserves are: oil, 6.4 billion barrels; natural gas, 33 trillion cubic feet. North Slope fields hold 99 percent of the oil and 92 percent of the state's gas reserves. The balance is in Cook Inlet

Oil. Reserve estimates of oil for North Slope fields have increased through the years. In January 1986, Prudhoe Bay had produced 4.4 billion barrels and reserves were 5.8 billion barrels. By January 1998 the field had produced nearly 10.2 billion barrels and reserves were estimated at 3.2 billion barrels. Much of the increase in ultimate recovery was due to improved technology, such as increased horizontal drilling and enhanced oil recovery. Technology may further increase future reserve estimates, but the main variables in recovering oil will be the perceived oil prices and the cost of production.

North Slope oil production peaked in 1988 at 2 million barrels a day and subsequently declined to 1.1 million barrels a day by 1999. The Division of Oil and Gas estimates that combined production from operating fields and to-be-developed fields will decline to 408,000 barrels a day by the year 2021.

Cook Inlet fields will continue to produce well into the century, although production is estimated to decline to 20,440 barrels a day by 2004. Cumulative production between 2000 and 2004 will be an estimated 47 million barrels.

Since 1987, Alaska and Texas have alternated as the No. 1 state in oil production. The top five oil-producing states in 2000 were Texas, Alaska, California, Louisiana and Oklahoma. Alaska currently provides about 17 percent of the nation's domestic production of oil.

Natural Gas. All Alaska gas is produced from the North Slope, mostly from the Prudhoe Bay area, and from Cook Inlet, the same two regions that produce the state's oil. The production regimes of the two regions are very different because their markets are very different.

On the North Slope, most of the extracted gas is injected back into the reservoirs. That gas is available for sale if and when a market develops. North Slope fields had produced a cumulative net 3.7 trillion cubic feet by the end of 1999.

The Alaska Natural Gas Transportation System, a gas pipeline, was authorized by the federal government in 1977 but efforts to develop North Slope natural gas reserves were hampered by the high cost of bringing it to market. In 2000, a surge in demand for natural gas in the Lower 48, higher gas prices, advances in technology and regulatory changes spurred oil companies operating on the North Slope to launch a $75 million gas line feasibility study. Company officials say, if all goes smoothly, a gas pipeline could be completed by 2007.

In addition to a natural gas line, several companies, including Phillips, BP and Yukon Pacific Corp., are studying technology to convert gas to liquid fuel that could be sold to overseas markets.

Cook Inlet fields lie near two gas-processing plants and the Anchorage and Kenai commercial markets. Nearly all extracted gas has been consumed and very little has been injected. Regional production reached an all-time high of 215 billion cubic feet a year in 1998. It dipped to 210 billion cubic feet in 1999. Cook Inlet fields had produced a cumulative net 5.8 trillion cubic feet by the end of 1999.

Financial. In fiscal 2000, the state of Alaska received $1.03 billion in royalties (including previous revisions and settlements) from its oil and gas resources; approximately 76 percent of its unrestricted revenue comes from petroleum taxes and royalties. Since 1965, the state has collected more than $48 billion in unrestricted oil and gas revenues. When the price of oil dropped in early 1986, oil industry employment declined and state government was in a more tenuous fiscal situation.

Oil prices had improved by early 1990, but by then Prudhoe Bay production had begun to decline. In January 1994, crude oil prices sank to a 10-year low although they recovered at midyear. The state's oil and gas industry absorbed major layoffs in 1994 and 1995.

The oil industry received some good news in 1995 when the federal ban on exporting Alaska oil was lifted. Oil companies began exports in 1996. For the period from May 1996 to April 2000, when exports stopped, approximately 5 percent of total North Slope oil production was exported to the Far East.

In 2000, BP Amoco struck a $30 billion deal to acquire Atlantic Richfield Co., dramatically changing the playing field for Big Oil. To satisfy antitrust worries, BP agreed to sell Arco's Alaska assets to Phillips Petroleum.

The Department of Natural Resources, Division of Oil and Gas manages oil and gas leasing on state land in Alaska. The secretary of the interior is responsible for oil and gas leasing on federal lands in Alaska, including the outer continental shelf.

In 1986, Chevron, in partnership with a Native corporation, completed its well at Kaktovik on the coastal plain of the Arctic National Wildlife Refuge. The land was obtained in a swap with the U.S. Department of the Interior but Congress will have to approve any further development within the boundaries of the refuge.

Alaska Oil and Natural Gas Liquid Production

Year	Oil*	Natural Gas**
1988	738.1	400.415
1989	684.0	403.920
1990	647.3	412.121
1991	656.3	442.317
1992	627.3	449.126
1993	577.9	455.835
1994	568.9	469.041
1995	541.6	499.008
1996	544.2	490.591
1997	507.7	481.910
1998	450.8	473.650
1999	415.2	430.000

*Millions of barrels
**Billions of cubic feet
Source: Alaska Department of Natural Resources, Division of Oil & Gas

OIL SPILL Prince William Sound was the site of the largest oil spill in U.S. history when the 987-foot *Exxon Valdez* tanker, carrying a full cargo of 53 million gallons of crude oil, struck Bligh Reef on March 24, 1989. Before the tanker leak could be stopped, more than 270,000 barrels, or more than 11.3 million gallons, of crude oil oozed into Prince William Sound. The oil, which poured out of the tanker at a rate of 42,488 barrels an hour, contaminated more than 1,500 miles of coastline in Prince William Sound, the Gulf of Alaska and lower Cook Inlet.

Shortly before the collision, the captain had changed course, veering from the normal shipping lane to avoid icebergs. At the time the tanker hit the reef, however, the third mate was piloting the tanker.

Within 15 hours of the spill, skimmer ships began to vacuum oil off the water's surface; booms were set up strategically to prevent the oil spill from contaminating salmon fisheries. Other fishing vessels assisted in attempts to capture oiled and wounded wildlife and transport those animals to rehabilitation centers.

Four days after the spill, the oil slick covered a 300-square-mile area, hitting islands, beaches and fish hatcheries throughout the sound, an area known for its rich commercial herring and salmon hatcheries. Oil from the tanker also was found to have fouled beaches on the Alaska Peninsula, almost 600 miles from the spill site.

Cleanup involved armies of crews, who tried scrubbing rocks by hand to washing the shore rocks with highly pressurized hot water. Bioremediation was another cleanup technique; it involved applying fertilizer to oiled shorelines to accelerate oil-metabolizing bacteria. Winter storms scoured many beaches throughout the oil spill area. Cleanup efforts resumed in the spring of 1990 and continued into 1992.

Thousands of marine mammals, birds and other wildlife perished as a result of the oil spill. Carcasses of 1,011 sea otters were recovered from the sound in 1989, and estimates of the number of otters that died range from about 3,500 to 5,500. About 31,000 birds were reported to have been killed.

But scientists believe these figures represent only a fraction of the total loss, since many birds were thought to have floated out to sea; still others sank or simply have not been found. Preliminary figures fix the loss at between 350,000 and 390,000 birds, according to a report by federal agencies including the U.S. Department of Fish and Wildlife, in charge of damage assessment and restoration.

Exxon Corp. accepted responsibility, and more than 29,000 claims were filed for damages related to the oil spill. Many of the claims were from fishermen, canneries, Natives and business owners whose livelihood was curtailed by the spill. In 1989, the red salmon season was canceled in Prince William Sound.

The state sued Exxon and Alyeska Pipeline Service Co. in 1989; Exxon countersued, alleging that state officials had hampered cleanup efforts. In October 1991, the state and the federal government settled their suits with Exxon, splitting $1.25 billion. Of this amount, $900 million in civil damages was to be paid over a 10-year period.

In 1994, Exxon and 3,500 Alaska Natives reached an agreement in which Exxon agreed to pay $20 million for loss of subsistence hunting. Also that year a jury awarded commercial fishermen $286.8 million in damages. And a federal

Nearly 19,000 Anchorage homes and businesses lost power minutes before the kickoff of Super Bowl XXXV between the Baltimore Ravens and the New York Giants. Power was out for up to two hours and fans were irate. The outage was traced to a RAVEN that touched live wires and was zapped by 34,000 volts.

jury ordered Exxon to pay $5 billion in punitive damages. Litigation continues as Exxon appeals the punitive damage award.

It is estimated that Exxon spent about $2.5 billion on the cleanup. During its peak, 11,000 people worked on the cleanup, using 1,400 vessels and 85 aircraft. Environmental monitoring continues.

Exxon released its own scientific study on the oil spill in mid-1993, which concluded that no significant effects on the shoreline persist.

For further information, contact the Exxon Valdez Oil Spill Trustee Council, 645 G St., Anchorage 99501; (907) 278-8012. Other contacts: Alaska Resources Library and Information Services, 3150 C St., Suite 100, Anchorage 99503-3916, (907) 272-7547; Exxon Mobil, 5959 Las Colinas Blvd., Irving, TX 75039-2298, (972) 444-1000.

OOSIK An *oosik* is the baculum, or penis bone, of the male walrus. The *oosik* is a symbol of strength and potency in some Alaska Native cultures. It is also a novelty item found in shops selling Native crafts. Size matters: *Oosiks* generally measure from one to two feet long and are priced accordingly, with the longest costing upwards of $250.

PARKA Pronounced *PAR-kee* and sometimes spelled "parky," this over-the-head garment worn by Eskimos was one of their main pieces of clothing. Parka styles, materials used and ornamentation (such as pieced calfskin or beadwork trim) varied from village to village. The cut of parkas also changed from north to south.

The work parka was worn with the skin on the outside and the fur inside. Work parkas were meant to be serviceable, not beautiful. Often worn with pants made from skins, they provided excellent protection from the cold. These parkas usually used a secondhand worn ruff on the hood. Very poor persons did not have ruffs on their parkas at all, and if a person owned a parka without a ruff, he or she was given a ruff to use. When that person died, the

Warm and beautiful, the "fancy parka" showcases a skin-sewer's artistry. Photo by Roy Corral.

ruff was cut off the parka and returned to the original owner.

A fancy parka, reserved for special occasions, used the skin of the male ground squirrel, which produces large gray pelts. These decorated parkas had intricate fancywork with wolverine tassels and trims and were topped with a wide wolf ruff, made in layers so the ruff stood out from the face. The fancy parka had furs inside and out. Wealth was judged by the quality of a wearer's best parka.

The Aleut rain parka was made from *oogruk* (bearded seal) intestine. Instead of a fur ruff around the face of the hood, the rain parka had a folded *oogruk* piece which served as a sinew drawstring casing.

Eskimos used the skins of many different animals for parkas including seal, reindeer, caribou and ground squirrel. Wolf and wolverine were prized for ruffs. Also used to make parkas were skins from the wolf fish

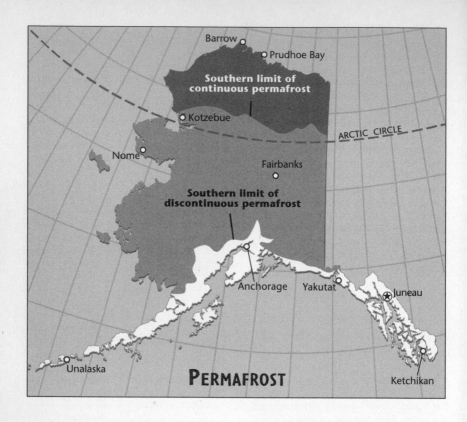

Barrow

Prudhoe Bay

**Southern limit of
continuous permafrost**

Kotzebue

ARCTIC CIRCLE

Nome

Fairbanks

**Southern limit of
discontinuous permafrost**

Anchorage   Yakutat   Juneau

Unalaska

PERMAFROST

Ketchikan

and bird skins—leaving the feathers on the outside—including those of murre, cormorants and diving fish ducks.

PERMAFROST Permafrost is defined as ground that remains frozen for two or more years. In its continuous form, permafrost underlies the entire Arctic region to depths of 2,000 feet. In broad terms, continuous permafrost occurs north of the Brooks Range and in the alpine region of mountains, including those of the Lower 48.

Discontinuous permafrost occurs south of the Brooks Range and north of the Alaska Range. Much of the Interior and parts of Southcentral Alaska are underlain by discontinuous permafrost.

Permafrost affects many buildings and natural bodies. It influences construction in the Arctic because building on it may cause the ground to thaw and if the ground is

ice-rich, structures will sink. Arctic and subarctic rivers typically carry 55 percent to 65 percent of the precipitation that falls onto their watersheds, roughly 30 percent to 40 percent more than rivers of more temperate climates. Consequently, northern streams are prone to flooding and carry high silt loads.

Permafrost is responsible for the thousands of shallow lakes dotting the arctic tundra because groundwater is held on the surface.

A tunnel excavated in permafrost near Fox, about 11 miles north of Fairbanks, during the early 1960s is maintained cooperatively by the University of Alaska Fairbanks and the U.S. Army Cold Regions Research and Engineering Laboratory. One of the few such tunnels in the world, it offers unique research opportunities on a 40,000-year-old accumulation of sediments and ice.

PERMANENT FUND

PERMANENT FUND In 1976 state voters approved a constitutional amendment to establish the Alaska Permanent Fund. This provides that a percentage of all mineral lease rentals, royalties, royalty sales proceeds, federal mineral revenue-sharing payments and bonuses be placed in a permanent fund. Essentially a trust fund for all Alaskans, money in the principal must be invested and cannot be spent without a vote of the people. Income from the permanent fund is available for appropriation by the legislature.

In 1980 the legislature established a permanent fund dividend payment program that provides distribution of approximately one-half of the fund's earnings (interest dividends and capital gains) among the people of Alaska. Eligible residents were to receive a $50 dividend for each year of residency since 1959. The U.S. Supreme Court declared the 1980 program unconstitutional on the grounds that it discriminated against short-term residents, and in 1982 a new state program was signed into law. Under that plan, an initial $1,000 dividend was paid to applicants who had lived in the state for at least six months prior to applying. Since then, dividends have been distributed each year to every resident who applies by March 31 and qualifies. The amount is decided by adding together the fund's net income for the last five years, multiplying that number by 21 percent, and dividing that number in half.

Since its first deposit of $734,000 in 1977, Alaska's Permanent Fund now ranks among the 50 largest pools of money in the country. As compared to the Fortune 500 list of America's largest businesses, the Permanent Fund would rank near the top 5 percent in terms of net income. In fiscal year 2000, the fund earned $2.2 billion, bringing its total market value to $28.1 billion and that year the fund generated a record dividend to each qualified Alaskan of $1,963.86.

The Fund's total rate of return for fiscal 2000 was 9.18 percent—below its total average annualized rate of return of 11.83 percent, but greater than the fund's projected long-term annualized rate of return of 8 percent.

PIONEERS' HOMES

PIONEERS' HOMES The first pioneers' home was established in Sitka in 1913 for "indigent prospectors and others who have spent their years in Alaska." Of the thousands of stampeders who came north between 1896 and 1900, 933 men and women submitted applications. However the home was not open to women until 1950; upon statehood in 1959, it was opened to Natives.

Currently six state-supported pioneers' homes offer assisted-living care for some 600 older Alaskans. The homes offer a range of service levels, providing assistance with activities of daily living, intermittent health care and recreation, with an emphasis on care of individuals with Alzheimer's disease and related disorders.

Applicants must be 65 years of age or older, must have lived continuously in Alaska for one year immediately preceding application, must have a need for the services provided in the homes and, if able, must pay rent established by the Department of Administration.

For additional information about pioneers' homes, contact the Director of the Division of Alaska Longevity Programs, P.O. Box 110211, Juneau 99811-0211; (907) 465-4400; fax (907) 465-4108; www.state.ak.us/admin/alp.

Anchorage Pioneers' Home, 923 W. 11th Ave., Anchorage 99501; (907) 276-3414.

Fairbanks Pioneers' Home, 2221 Eagan Ave., Fairbanks 99701; (907) 456-4372.

Juneau Pioneers' Home, 4675 Glacier Highway, Juneau 99801; (907) 780-6422.

Sitka Pioneers' Home.

Send-offs with a Salute

In 1988, brief obituaries presented in *The Alaska Almanac®* marked the passing of old-timers and prominent Alaskans. Among the notables:

Bessie Barnabus, 100, lifelong Alaskan and one of the last full-blooded Salcha Athabascans. She died April 6, 1986, at Salcha, where she was born.

Klondy Dufresne, 90, widow of Frank Dufresne, died Nov. 19, 1987. Named by her father, who followed the gold-rush trails through the Klondike to the beaches of Nome, she grew up in the Seward Peninsula gold country and wrote a book of her adventures, *Daughter of the Gold Rush.*

Henry O. Hanson, 91, 49-year Alaskan, died Nov. 29, 1986. A World War I veteran, deemed by the selection committee as too old to become a Matanuska Valley colonist in 1935, he came to the North on his own, homesteaded on the Fairview loop near Wasilla, and worked as a carpenter.

Alice Allen Killbear, 74, lifelong Alaskan, died May 30, 1987. A daughter of Arthur James Allen, whaler and trader, she was born in Point Hope, grew up in Wainwright, and returned there after college to teach. After her marriage she lived in Kaktovik and Barrow.

The Very Rev. Archpriest Nicholas Kompkoff, 54, born in Valdez, died June 19, 1987. A commercial fisherman, oil technician and postal worker, he was ordained in 1970 as a priest in the Russian Orthodox Church and served in Tyonek, Sitka, Cordova, Chenega Bay and Anchorage. He became an archpriest in 1987.

Dr. Lee McKinley, 80, Alaska's "Flying Dentist," died Nov. 12, 1986. He drove to Alaska the year the Alaska Highway opened, set up an office in the Polaris Hotel in Anchorage, then in 1947 opened the office at Fifth Avenue and D Street where he practiced until retirement in 1981. He settled on a farm near Palmer, leveled an airstrip, bought an Aeronca Sedan in 1948, and extended his practice to the Bush. Often he treated patients at an airstrip, using a wing of his plane as an instrument table.

Anne S. Purdy, 85, 59-year Alaskan, died April 16, 1987. She came north in 1928 with the Bureau of Indian Affairs and taught in Tetlin, Eagle and Chicken. She wrote an autobiographical novel, *Tisha,* and *Dark Boundary,* about the town of Eagle. As a free-lance journalist she wrote a column, "Chicken Pickin's," for the *Fairbanks Daily News-Miner.* She and her late husband, a gold miner, reared eleven adopted children. —1988 *The ALASKA ALMANAC®*

Ketchikan Pioneers' Home, 141 Bryant, Ketchikan 99901; (907) 225-4111.

Palmer Pioneers' Home, 250 E. Fireweed, Palmer 99645; (907) 745-4241.

Sitka Pioneers' Home, 120 Katlian St., Sitka 99835; (907) 747-3213.

PIPELINE Alyeska Pipeline Service Co., builder and operator of the trans-Alaska oil pipeline, is a consortium of seven oil companies:

BP Pipelines (Alaska), Inc., 50.01 percent

Phillips Transportation Alaska, Inc., 22.3 percent

Exxon Mobil Pipeline Co., 20.34 percent

Williams Alaska Pipeline Company LLC, 3.08 percent

Amerada Hess Pipeline Corp., 1.5 percent

Phillips Alaska Pipeline Corp., 1.42 percent

Unocal Pipeline Co., 1.36 percent

Pipeline length: 800 miles; slightly less than half that length is buried, the remainder is on 78,000 above-ground supports, located 60 feet apart and built in a flexible zigzag pattern. There are more than 800 river and stream crossings. Normal burial of pipe was used in stable soils and rock; above-ground pipe—insulated and jacketed—was used in thaw-unstable permafrost areas. Thermal devices prevent thawing around vertical supports. The pipeline has 151 stop-flow valves.

Pipe: Specially manufactured coated pipe with zinc anodes installed to prevent corrosion. Size is 48 inches in diameter, with thickness from 0.462 to 0.562 inch.

Cost: $8 billion, which includes terminal at Valdez but excludes interest on money raised for construction.

Amount of oil pumped through pipeline: As of the end of 2000, a total of more than 13 billion barrels of oil had been pumped through the pipeline. The current flow represents about 15 percent of total U.S. oil production. At any one moment, there are about 9 million barrels of oil in the line.

Operations: Control center at Valdez terminal and pump stations along the line monitor and control pipeline.

Terminal: 1,000-acre site at Port Valdez, northernmost ice-free harbor in the United States, with 18 tanks providing storage capacity of 9.2 million barrels of oil.

Valdez ship-loading capacity: 110,000 barrels an hour for each of three berths; 80,000 barrels per hour for one berth.

Length and cost of pipeline haul road built by Alyeska: 360 miles, from the Yukon River to Prudhoe Bay; $150 million.

Yukon River bridge: First bridge (2,290 feet long) to span the Yukon in Alaska.

Important dates: July 1968, Prudhoe Bay oil field discovery confirmed; **1970,** lawsuits filed to halt construction, Alyeska Pipeline Service Co. formed; **Nov. 16, 1973,** presidential approval of pipeline legislation; **April 29, 1974,** construction begins on North Slope Haul Road (now the Dalton Highway) and is completed 154 days later; **March 27, 1975,** first pipe

The trans-Alaska oil pipeline 15 miles south of Livengood in the late 1970s. Special Collections Division, UW Libraries. From *Alaska's History* by Harry Ritter.

installed at Tonsina River; **June 20, 1977,** first oil leaves Prudhoe Bay, reaches Valdez terminal July 28; **Aug. 1, 1977,** first tanker load of oil shipped aboard the SS *ARCO Juneau;* **June 13, 1979,** tanker number 1,000 (SS *ARCO Heritage*) sails; **July 15, 1983,** 3 billionth barrel of oil leaves pump station; **Sept. 15, 1986,** 5 billionth barrel of oil leaves pump station; **Feb. 16, 1988,** 6 billionth barrel arrives at the marine terminal; **May 2, 1988,** *Chevron Mississippi* is 8,000th tanker to load crude oil at marine terminal; **March 24, 1989,** *Exxon Valdez* tanker runs aground after departing the marine terminal and spills more than 11 million gallons of North Slope crude into Prince William Sound; **Dec. 28, 1992,** *ARCO California,* 12,000th tanker to load; **March 1994,** 10 billionth barrel is pumped from the North Slope into the pipeline; **April 1996,** 22,000-gallon spill from defective valve; **June 20, 1997,** 20th anniversary of the pipeline system; **Aug. 8, 1997,** Pump Station 6 placed in standby status, the fourth station to be idled due to declining oil output; **Aug. 27, 2000,** the 13 billionth barrel of North Slope crude is delivered through the pipeline to Valdez.

Joint Pipeline Office: The Joint

Pipeline Office, established in 1990, is composed of nine state and federal regulatory and management agencies. Each agency has responsibilities either for issuing permits or for monitoring the operation and environmental safety of pipelines in Alaska.

State agencies include the Department of Natural Resources, Department of Environmental Conservation, Department of Fish and Game, and the Office of the Governor.

PLACE NAMES Alaska has a rich international heritage of place names. Throughout the state, names of British (Barrow), Spanish (Valdez), Russian (Kotzebue), French (La Perouse), American (Fairbanks) and Native Alaskan (Sitka) origin dot the map.

Some Alaska place names are quite common. There are about 70 streams called Bear Creek in Alaska (not to mention Bear Bay, Bear Bluff, Bear Canyon, Bear Cove and Bear Draw) and about 50 called Moose Creek.

Many place names have an unusual history. Moose Pass is said to derive its name from a 1903 incident when a mail carrier driving a dog team had difficulty gaining the right-of-way from a large moose.

POISONOUS PLANTS (SEE ALSO Mushrooms) Alaska has few poisonous plants, compared to the number of species growing here. Nonetheless, some extremely poisonous plants thrive. Baneberry (*Actaea rubra*), water hemlock

According to groundskeepers, approximately 50 percent of all new ornamental trees planted on the University of Alaska Anchorage campus are eaten by moose during the following winter.

Deadly Monkshood

They're so beautiful a flower, so innocent in appearance, that it seems unkind to bandy about the nefarious ways these flowers have been used. But monkshood in particular is so deadly poisonous that it is essential foragers be aware. . . . In medieval times, monkshood was called "thung" (a name for any deadly plant) and was used for warfare; the root was placed in water holes and wells to poison water supplies of pursuing armies. *The Herb Book* says that witches smeared the root on their broomsticks and bodies, took a dose of delirium-producing belladonna, and then went "flying." On a more mundane plane, the roots were mixed with toasted cheese to kill rats.

—Janice Schofield,
Discovering Wild Plants

(*Cicuta douglasii* and *C. mackenzieana*), fly agaric mushroom (*Amanita muscaria*), monkshood (*Aconitum* species) and false hellebore (*Veratrum* species) are the most dangerous. Be sure you have properly identified plants before harvesting for food.

Alaska has no poison ivy or poison oak, found in almost all other states, but Alaska's cow parsnip produces a photoreactive chemical that can cause blisters and burns.

POLITICAL PARTIES A recognized political party in Alaska is an organized group that represents a political program and either nominates a candidate for governor who received at least 3 percent of the total votes cast for governor in the preceding general election, or has registered enough voters to equal 3 percent of the votes cast for governor in the last election. Until it qualifies as a political party under this definition, an independent political group may field candidates for statewide and districtwide offices by filing nominating petitions.

Alaska's six political parties are:

Alaskan Independence Party, Chairman Mark Chryson, P.O. Box 70007, Fairbanks 99707; (907) 376-8285.

Democratic Party, State Chair Christopher Cook, P.O. Box 200445, Anchorage 99520; (907) 344-9888.

Green Party, Chairman Soren Wuerth, 3180 Amber Bay Loop, Anchorage 99515; (907) 274-7336.

Libertarian Party, Chairman Len Karpinski, (907) 248-4367.

Republican Moderate Party, Chairman Ray Metcalfe, (907) 344-4514.

Republican Party, Chairman Tom McKay, 1001 W. Fireweed Lane, Anchorage 99503; (907) 276-4467.

POPULATIONS AND ZIP CODES

According to the Alaska Department of Labor and Workforce Development, many areas of Alaska gained population in the past decade. Between 1990 and 2000, Alaska's population increased by 14 percent, compared with a 13 percent increase in the U.S.

NUGGETS

Gov. Jay Hammond okayed a plan in July 1981, designed by the State Reapportionment Board, dividing Alaska into new election districts based on the 1980 census figures. Under the plan, Juneau and Anchorage each gained a new state Senate seat, while the city of Fairbanks lost a seat to the surrounding area.

—1982 The ALASKA ALMANAC®

population. The greatest overall growth occurred in Anchorage, which accounted for 42 percent of the state's population in 2000.

Populations for cities and communities in the following lists are taken from the Alaska Department of Labor figures, based on the 2000 national census, for March 2001. The population numbers listed below will not equal the total state population, as CDP (Census Designated Places) are not included. Entries lacking zip codes are communities without a U.S. post office. Population numbers also are available online at www.labor.state.ak.us/research/research.htm.

(NA=Not Available)

Community	Year Incorporated	Population	Zip
Adak Station	1972	316	96546
Akhiok (AH-key-ok)	1972	80	99615
Akiachak (ACK-ee-a-chuck)	—	585	99551
Akiak (ACK-ee-ack)	1970	309	99552
Akutan (ACK-oo-tan)	1979	713	99553
Alakanuk (a-LACK-a-nuk)	1969	652	99554
Aleknagik (a-LECK-nuh-gik)	1973	221	99555
Alexander	—	39	99695
Allakaket (alla-KAK-it)	1975	97	99720
Ambler	1971	309	99786
Anaktuvuk Pass (an-ak-TOO-vuk)	1957	282	99721
Anchor Point	—	1,845	99556
Anchorage (municipality)*	1920	260,283**	99510

* Includes Eklutna.

** Population of Chugiak–Eagle River is counted as part of the Municipality of Anchorage.

Community	Year Incorporated	Population	Zip
Eastchester Station	—	—	99501
Fort Richardson	—	—	99505
Elmendorf Air Force Base	—	—	99506
Mountain View	—	—	99508
Spenard Station	—	—	99509
Downtown Station	—	—	99510
South Station	—	—	99511
Alyeska Pipeline Company	—	—	99512
Federal Building	—	—	99513
Anderson	1962	367	99744
Angoon	1963	572	99820
Aniak (AN-ee-ack)	1972	572	99557
Anvik	1969	152	99558
Arctic Village	—	138	99722
Atka	1988	92	99547
Atmautluak (at-MAUT-loo-ack)	1976; dissolved 1996	294	99559
Atqasuk	1983	228	99791
Attu Coast Guard Station	—	20	99619
Auke Bay	—	NA	99821
Barrow	1959	4,581	99723
Beaver	—	84	99724
Bethel	1957	5,471	99559
Bettles City	1985	43	99726
Big Delta	—	749	99737
Big Lake	—	2,635	99652
Birch Creek	—	28	99790
Brevig Mission	1969	276	99785
Buckland	1966	406	99727
Butte	—	2,561	NA
Cantwell	—	222	99729
Cape Yakataga	—	NA	99574
Central	—	134	99730
Chalkyitsik (chawl-KIT-sik)	—	83	99788
Chase	—	41	NA
Chefornak (cha-FOR-nack)	1974	394	99561
Chenega	—	86	99574
Chevak	1967	765	99563
Chickaloon	—	213	99674
Chicken	—	17	99732
Chignik	1983	79	99564
Chignik Lagoon	—	103	99565
Chignik Lake	—	145	99548
Chiniak	—	50	99615
Chistochina	—	93	99586
Chitina (CHIT-nah)	—	123	99566
Chuathbaluk (chew-ATH-ba-luck)	1975	119	99557
Chugiak (CHOO-gee-ack)	—	**	99567
Circle	—	100	99733
Circle Hot Springs	—	35	NA
Clam Gulch	—	173	99568
Clarks Point	1971	75	99569

Community	Year Incorporated	Population	Zip
Clear	—	NA	99704
Coffman Cove	1989	199	99918
Cohoe	—	1,168	99669
Cold Bay	1982	88	99571
Coldfoot	—	13	99701
College	—	11,402	99708
Cooper Landing	—	369	99572
Copper Center	—	362	99573
Copperville	—	179	NA
Cordova***	1909	2,454	99574
Covenant Life	—	102	NA
Craig	1922	1,397	99921
Crooked Creek	—	137	99575
Crown Point	—	75	NA
Cube Cove	—	72	99850
Deadhorse	—	2	99734
Deering	1970	136	99736
Delta Junction	1960	840	99737
Denali National Park	—	NA	99755
Dillingham	1963	2,466	99576
Diomede (DY-o-mede)	1970	146	99762
Dot Lake	—	19	99737
Douglas	1902	NA	99824
Dry Creek	—	128	NA
Dutch Harbor	1942	NA	99692
Eagle	1901	129	99738
Eagle River	—	**	99577
Eagle Village	—	68	NA
Edna Bay	—	49	99950
Eek	1970	280	99578
Egegik (EEG-gah-gik)	1985	116	99579
Eielson Air Force Base	—	5,400	99702
Ekwok (ECK-wok)	1974	130	99580
Elfin Cove	—	32	99825
Elim (EE-lum)	1970	313	99739
Emmonak (ee-MON-nuk)	1964	767	99581
Ester	—	1,680	99725
Evansville	—	28	99726
Fairbanks (city)	1903	30,224	9970–
Main Office	—	—	99701
Eielson Air Force Base	—	5,400	99702
Fort Wainwright	—	—	99703
Main Office Boxes	—	—	99706
Downtown Station	—	—	99707
College Branch	—	—	99708
Salcha	—	—	99714
False Pass	1990	64	99583
Ferry	—	29	NA
Flat	—	4	99584

** Population of Chugiak–Eagle River is counted as part of the Municipality of Anchorage.

*** Includes Eyak since 1993.

Community	Year Incorporated	Population	Zip
Fort Greely	—	461	99790
Fort Wainwright	—	—	99703
Fort Yukon	1959	595	99740
Fox	—	300	99712
Fox River	—	616	NA
Fritz Creek	—	1,603	99603
Gakona (ga-KOH-na)	—	215	99586
Galena (ga-LEE-na)	1971	675	99741
Gambell	1963	649	99742
Game Creek	—	35	NA
Girdwood	—	NA	99587
Glennallen	—	554	99588
Gold Creek	—	NA	99695
Golovin (GAWL-uh-vin)	1971	144	99762
Goodnews Bay	1970	230	99589
Grayling	1969	194	99590
Gulkana	—	88	99586
Gustavus (ga-STAY-vus)	—	429	99826
Haines	1910	1,811	99827
Halibut Cove	—	35	99603
Hamilton	—	0	NA
Happy Valley	—	489	99603
Harding–Birch Lakes	—	216	99714
Healy	—	1000	99743
Healy Lake	—	37	NA
Hobart Bay	—	3	99850
Hollis	—	139	99950
Holy Cross	1968	227	99602
Homer	1964	3,946	99603
Hoonah	1946	860	99829
Hooper Bay	1966	1,014	99604
Hope	—	137	99605
Houston	1966	1,202	99694
Hughes	1973	78	99745
Huslia (HOOS-lee-a)	1969	293	99746
Hydaburg	1927	382	99922
Hyder	—	97	99923
Icy Bay	—	NA	99695
Iguigig (ig-ee-AH-gig)	—	53	99613
Iliamna (ill-ee-YAM-nuh)	—	102	99606
Indian	—	NA	99540
Ivanof Bay	—	22	99695
Jakolof Bay (Red Mountain)	—	40	99603
Juneau (city/borough)	1900	30,711	99801
Main Office	—	—	99801
Main Office Boxes	—	—	99802
Mendenhall Station	—	—	99803
State Government Offices	—	—	99811
Kachemak (CATCH-a-mack)	1961	431	99603
Kake	1952	710	99830
Kaktovik (kack-TOE-vik)	1971	293	99747

Community	Year Incorporated	Population	Zip
Kalifonsky	—	5,846	99669
Kalskag	1975	NA	99607
Kaltag	1969	230	99748
Karluk	—	27	99608
Kasaan (Ka-SAN)	1976	39	99950
Kasigluk (ka-SEEG-luk)	1982; dissolved 1996	543	99609
Kasilof (ka-SEE-loff)	—	471	99610
Kasitsna Bay	—	NA	99695
Kenai (KEEN-eye)	1960	6,942	99611
Kenny Lake	—	410	99573
Ketchikan	1900	7,922	99901
Kiana (Ky-AN-a)	1964	388	99749
King Cove City	1947	792	99612
King Salmon	—	442	99613
Kipnuk (KIP-nuck)	—	644	99614
Kivalina	1969	377	99750
Klawock (kla-WOCK)	1929	854	99925
Klukwan	—	139	99827
Knik	—	582	99687
Kobuk	1973	109	99751
Kodiak	1940	6,334	99615
U.S. Coast Guard Station	—	1,831	99619
Kokhanok (KO-ghan-ock)	—	174	99606
Koliganek (ko-LIG-a-neck)	—	182	99576
Kongiganak (kon-GIG-a-nuck)	—	359	99559
Kotlik	1970	591	99620
Kotzebue (KOT-sa-bue)	1958	3,082	99752
Koyuk	1970	297	99753
Koyukuk (KOY-yuh-kuck)	1973	101	99754
Kupreanof (ku-pree-AN-off)	1975	23	99833
Kwethluk (KWEETH-luck)	1975	713	99621
Kwigillingok (kwi-GILL-in-gock)	—	338	99622
Lake Minchumina (min-CHOO-min-a)	—	32	99757
Larsen Bay	1974	115	99624
Lazy Mountain	—	1,158	NA
Levelock (LEH-vuh-lock)	—	122	99625
Lignite	—	131	NA
Lime Village	—	6	99627
Loring	—	NA	99950
Lower Kalskag	1969	267	99626
Lutak	—	39	NA
Manley Hot Springs	—	72	99756
Manokotak (man-a-KO-tack)	1970	399	99628
Marshall	1970	349	99585
McCarthy	—	42	99588
McGrath	1975	401	99627
McKinley Park	—	142	99755
Meadow Lakes	—	4,819	NA
Mekoryuk (ma-KOR-ee-yuk)	1969	210	99630
Mendeltna	—	63	NA
Mentasta Lake	—	142	99780

Community	Year Incorporated	Population	Zip
Metlakatla	1944	1,375	99926
Meyers Chuck	—	21	99903
Minto	—	258	99758
Moose Creek	—	542	99705
Moose Pass	—	206	99631
Mosquito Lake	—	221	NA
Mountain Village	1967	755	99632
Naknek (NACK-neck)	—	678	99633
Nanwalek (formerly English Bay)	—	177	99603
Napakiak (NAP-uh-keey-ack)	1970	353	99634
Napaskiak (na-PASS-kee-ack)	1971	390	99559
Naukati Bay	—	135	99950
Nelson Lagoon	—	83	99571
Nenana (nee-NA-na)	1921	402	99760
New Stuyahok (STU-ya-hock)	1972	471	99636
Newhalen	1971	160	99606
Newtok	1976; dissolved 1997	321	99559
Nightmute	1974	208	99690
Nikiski	—	4,327	99635
Nikolaevsk	—	345	99556
Nikolai	1970	100	99691
Nikolski	—	39	99638
Ninilchik (Nin-ILL-chick)	—	772	99639
Noatak (NO-uh-tack)	—	428	99761
Nome	1901	3,505	99762
Nondalton	1971	221	99640
Noorvik	1964	634	99763
North Pole	1953	1,570	99705
Northway	—	95	99764
Northway Junction	—	72	NA
Northway Village	—	107	NA
Nuiqsut (noo-IK-sut)	1975	433	99789
Nulato	1963	336	99765
Nunapitchuk (NU-nuh-pit-CHUCK)	1982	466	99641
Old Harbor	1966	237	99643
Olga Bay	—	NA	99697
Ophir	—	NA	99695
Oscarville	—	61	99695
Ouzinkie (oo-ZINK-ee)	1967	225	99644
Palmer	1951	4,533	99645
Paxson	—	43	99737
Pedro Bay	—	50	99647
Pelican	1943	163	99832
Perryville	—	107	99648
Petersburg	1910	3,224	99833
Pilot Point	1992	100	99649
Pilot Station	1969	550	99650
Pitkas Point	—	125	99658
Platinum	1975	41	99651
Pleasant Valley	—	623	NA
Point Baker	—	35	99927

Community	Year Incorporated	Population	Zip
Point Hope	1966	757	99766
Point Lay	—	247	99759
Port Alexander	1974	81	99836
Port Alice	—	4	99950
Port Alsworth	—	104	99653
Port Clarence	—	21	99762
Port Graham	—	171	99603
Port Heiden	1972	119	99549
Port Lions	1966	256	99550
Port Protection	—	63	99950
Portage Creek	—	36	NA
Primrose	—	93	NA
Prudhoe Bay	—	5	99734
Quinhagak (QUIN-a-gak)	1975	555	99655
Rampart	—	45	99767
Red Devil	—	48	99656
Red Dog Mine	—	32	NA
Ridgeway	—	1,932	NA
Ruby	1973	188	99768
Russian Mission	1970	296	99657
St. George	1983	152	99591
St. Marys/Andreafsky	1967	500	99658
St. Michael	1969	368	99659
St. Paul	1971	532	99660
Salamatof	—	954	99611
Salcha	—	854	99714
Sand Point	1966	952	99661
Savoonga (suh-VOON-guh)	1969	643	99769
Saxman	1930	431	99901
Scammon Bay	1967	465	99662
Selawik (SELL-a-wick)	1977	772	99770
Seldovia	1945	286	99663
Seward	1912	2,830	99664
Shageluk (SHAG-a-look)	1970	129	99665
Shaktoolik (shack-TOO-lick)	1969	230	99771
Sheldon Point	1974	64	99666
Shishmaref (SHISH-muh-reff)	1969	562	99772
Shungnak (SHOONG-nack)	1967	256	99773
Sitka	1963/1971	8,835	99835
Skagway	1900	862	99840
Skwentna	—	111	99667
Slana	—	124	99586
Sleetmute	—	100	99668
Soldotna	1967	3,759	99669
South Naknek	—	137	99670
Stebbins	1969	547	99671
Sterling	—	4,705	99672
Stevens Village	—	87	99774
Stony River	—	61	99557
Sutton–Alpine	—	1,080	99674
Takotna (Tah-KOT-nuh)	—	50	99675

Community	Year Incorporated	Population	Zip
Talkeetna (Tal-KEET-na)	—	772	99676
Tanacross	—	140	99776
Tanana (TAN-a-nah)	1961	308	99777
Tatitlek	—	107	99677
Telida	—	2	99695
Teller	1963	268	99778
Tenakee Springs	1971	104	99841
Tetlin	—	117	99779
Thorne Bay	1982	557	99919
Togiak (TOE-gee-yack)	1969	809	99678
Tok (TOKE)	—	1,393	99780
Toksook Bay	1972	532	99637
Tonsina	—	92	99573
Trapper Creek	—	423	99683
Tuluksak (tu-LOOK-sack)	1970; dissolved 1997	428	99679
Tuntutuliak (TUN-too-TOO-li-ack)	—	370	99680
Tununak	1975; dissolved 1997	325	99681
Twin Hills	—	69	99576
Two Rivers	—	482	99716
Tyonek (ty-O-neck)	—	193	99682
Ugashik	—	11	99695
Unalakleet (YOU-na-la-kleet)	1974	747	99684
Unalaska (UN-a-LAS-ka)	1942	4,283	99685
Upper Kalskag/Kalskag	1975	230	99607
Valdez (val-DEEZ)	1901	4,036	99686
Venetie (VEEN-a-tie)	—	202	99781
Wainwright	1962	546	99782
Wales	1964	152	99783
Wasilla (wah-SIL-luh)	1974	5,469	99687
Whale Pass	—	58	99950
White Mountain	1969	203	99784
Whitestone Logging Camp	—	116	NA
Whittier	1969	182	99693
Willow	—	1,658	99688
Wiseman	—	21	99790
Womens Bay	—	690	NA
Wrangell	1903	2,308	99929
Yakutat (YAK-a-tat)	1948/1992	680	99689

Population by Census Areas

Key	Census Area	1970	1980	1990	2000
	Alaska	302,583	401,851	550,043	626,932
1	North Slope Borough	3,451	4,199	5,979	7,385
2	Northwest Arctic Borough	4,048	4,831	6,113	7,208
3	Nome	5,749	6,537	8,288	9,196
4	Yukon–Koyukuk	7,045	6,471	6,681	6,551
5	Fairbanks North Star Borough	45,864	53,983	77,720	82,840

(Continued on page 184)

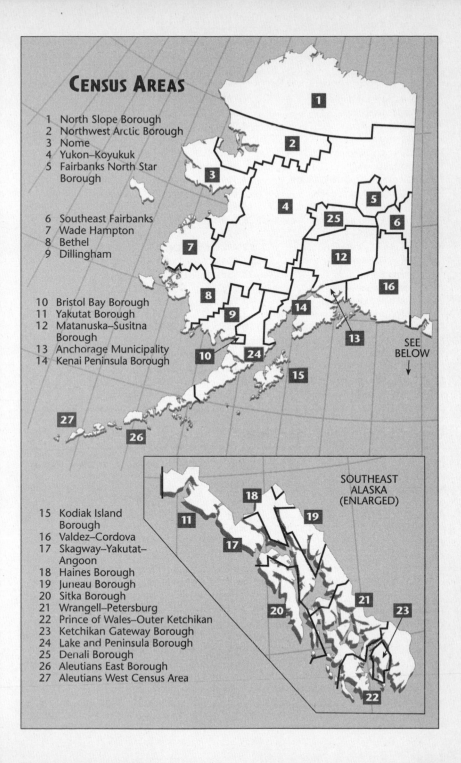

CENSUS AREAS

1 North Slope Borough
2 Northwest Arctic Borough
3 Nome
4 Yukon–Koyukuk
5 Fairbanks North Star
   Borough

6 Southeast Fairbanks
7 Wade Hampton
8 Bethel
9 Dillingham

10 Bristol Bay Borough
11 Yakutat Borough
12 Matanuska–Susitna
    Borough
13 Anchorage Municipality
14 Kenai Peninsula Borough

15 Kodiak Island
    Borough
16 Valdez–Cordova
17 Skagway–Yakutat–
    Angoon
18 Haines Borough
19 Juneau Borough
20 Sitka Borough
21 Wrangell–Petersburg
22 Prince of Wales–Outer Ketchikan
23 Ketchikan Gateway Borough
24 Lake and Peninsula Borough
25 Denali Borough
26 Aleutians East Borough
27 Aleutians West Census Area

SEE
BELOW
↓

SOUTHEAST
ALASKA
(ENLARGED)

Populations by Census Areas *(continued)*

Key	Census Area	1970	1980	1990	2000
6	Southeast Fairbanks	4,308	5,676	5,913	6,194
7	Wade Hampton	3,917	4,665	5,791	7,028
8	Bethel	8,917	10,999	13,656	16,006
9	Dillingham	2,510	3,232	4,012	4,922
10	Bristol Bay Borough	1,147	1,094	1,410	1,258
11	Yakutat Borough	385	563	705	808
12	Matanuska–Susitna Borough	6,509	17,816	39,683	59,322
13	Anchorage Municipality	126,385	174,431	226,338	260,283
14	Kenai Peninsula Borough	16,586	25,282	40,802	49,691
15	Kodiak Island Borough	9,409	9,939	13,309	13,913
16	Valdez–Cordova	4,979	8,348	9,952	10,195
17	Skagway–Yakutat–Angoon	2,792	3,478	4,385	3,436
18	Haines Borough	1,401	1,680	2,117	2,392
19	Juneau Borough	13,556	19,528	26,751	30,711
20	Sitka Borough	6,073	7,803	8,588	8,835
21	Wrangell–Petersburg	4,920	6,167	7,042	6,684
22	Prince of Wales–Outer Ketchikan	3,782	3,822	6,278	6,146
23	Ketchikan Gateway Borough	10,041	11,316	13,828	14,070
24	Lake and Peninsula Borough	1,362	1,384	1,668	1,823
25	Denali Borough	NA	1,402	1,792	1,893
26	Aleutians East Borough	1,301	1,643	2,464	2,697
27	Aleutians West Census Area	6,533	6,125	9,478	5,465

Source: Alaska Department of Labor, Census 2000

Growth of Alaska's Major Cities

City	1900	1920	1940	1950	1970	1980	2000**
Anchorage*	NA	1,856	4,229	11,254	48,081	174,431	260,283
Barrow	NA	NA	NA	NA	2,104	2,207	4,581
Cordova	NA	955	938	1,165	1,164	1,879	2,454
Fairbanks	NA	1,155	3,455	5,771	14,771	22,645	30,224
Juneau	1,864	3,058	5,729	5,956	6,050	19,528	30,711
Kenai	290	332	303	321	3,533	4,324	6,942
Ketchikan	459	2,458	4,695	5,305	6,994	7,198	7,922
Kodiak	341	374	864	1,710	3,798	4,756	6,334
Nome	12,488	852	1,559	1,876	2,357	2,301	3,505
Petersburg	NA	879	1,323	1,619	2,042	2,821	3,224
Seward	NA	652	949	2,114	1,587	1,843	2,830
Sitka	1,396	1,175	1,987	1,985	6,075	7,803	8,835
Valdez	315	466	529	554	1,005	3,079	4,036
Wrangell	868	821	1,162	1,263	2,029	2,184	2,308

*Includes Eklutna

Source: Alaska Department of Labor, Census 2000

POTLATCH This Native gathering, primarily an Indian custom, is held to commemorate major life events.

Traditional Native foods are served, songs and dances are performed and gifts are distributed to attendees. A funeral potlatch might include the giving away of the deceased's possessions to relatives or to those who had shown kindness to the deceased.

Before the U.S. and Canadian governments outlawed the practice in the 1880s, potlatches were a focal point of Native society. The host family might give away all its possessions to demonstrate its wealth to the guests. Each guest in turn would feel obliged to hold an even more sumptuous potlatch. The outlawing of potlatches resulted in the disintegration of many aspects of Native culture. Potlatch restrictions were repealed in 1951.

QIVIUT This material is the downy soft undercoat of the musk ox. Qiviut (KIV-ee-ute) is prized for its light weight and exceptional warmth. It is said to be eight times warmer than sheep's wool. It is knitted by hand into hats, scarves and other garments by members of the Oomingmak Musk Ox Producers' Co-operative. The cooperative is made up of approximately 250 Native women from Western Alaska villages. Each garment bears the distinctive traditional pattern of the village where it was made.

RADIO STATIONS Alaska's radio stations broadcast a variety of music, talk shows, and religious and educational programs. Many radio stations in Alaska also broadcast personal messages, long a popular and necessary form of communication in Alaska—especially in the Bush.

To accommodate these messages—and radio's unique role in providing vital weather information to fishermen and hunters—the United States and Canada agreed to grant some Alaska radio stations international communication status. The "clear channel" status provides protection against interference from foreign broadcasters. Personal messages are heard on:

Anchorage, KYAK's Bush Pipeline
Barrow, KBRW's Tundra Drum
Bethel, KYUK's Tundra Drums
Dillingham, KDLG's Bristol Bay Messenger
Fairbanks, KIAK's Pipeline of the North
Galena, KIYU's Yukon Wireless
Glennallen, KCAM's Caribou Clatter
Haines, KHNS's Listener Personals
Homer, KBBI's Bay Bush Lines
Ketchikan, KRBD's Muskeg Messenger; KTKN's Public Service Announcements
Kodiak, KVOK's Highliner Crabbers
Kotzebue, KOTZ's Messages
McGrath, KSKO's Messages
Nome, KICY's Ptarmigan Telegraph; KNOM's Hot Lines
North Pole, KJNP's Trapline Chatter
Petersburg, KFSK's Muskeg Messages; KRSA's Channel Chatters
Sitka, KCAW-FM's Muskeg Messages
Soldotna, KSRM's Tundra Tom Tom
Valdez, KCHU's Billboard Service
Wrangell, KSTK-FM's Radiograms

Statewide. APRN, 810 E. Ninth Ave., Anchorage 99501.
Bush Radio Network, Box 91941, Anchorage 99509.

Anchorage. KADX-FM 94.7 MHz; 2509 Ide St., 99503.

6KAFC-FM 93.7 MHz; 6401 E. Northern Lights, 99504.

KASH 1080 kHz; 3601 C St., Suite 290, 994503.

KASH-FM 107.5 MHz; 800 E. Dimond Blvd., Suite 3-370, 99515.

KATB-FM 89.3 MHz; 6401 E. Northern Lights, 99504.

KAXX 1020 kHz; 2509 Ide St., 99503.

KBFX-FM 100.5 MHz; 800 E. Dimond Blvd., Suite 3-320, 99515.

KBRJ-FM 104.1 MHz; 9200 Lake Otis Pkwy., 99507.

KBYR 700 kHz; 1007 W. 32nd Ave., 99503.

KEAG-FM; KOOL-FM 97.3 MHz; 9200 Lake Otis Pkwy., 99507.

KENI 650 kHz; 800 E. Dimond Blvd., Suite 3-320, 99515.

KFAT-FM 92.9 MHz; 11259 Tower Road, 99515.

KFQD 750 kHz; KWHL-FM 106.5 MHz; 9200 Lake Otis Pkwy., 99507.

KGOT-FM 101.3 MHz; 800 E. Dimond Blvd., Suite 3-370, 99515.

KHAR 590 kHz; 9200 Lake Otis Pkwy., 99507.

KKIS-FM 96.5 MHz; 2509 Eide St., 99503-2634.

KKRO-FM 102.1 MHz; 11259 Tower Road, 99515.

KLEF-FM 98.1 MHz; 3601 C St., Suite 290, 99503.

KMXS-FM 103.1 MHz; 9200 Lake Otis Pkwy., 99507.

KNBA-FM 90.3 MHz; 818 E. Ninth Ave., 99501-3826.

KNIK-FM 105.3 MHz; 907 E. Dowling Road, Suite 24, 99518.

KQEZ-FM 92.1 MHz; 11259 Tower Road, 99515.

KRPM-FM 96.3 MHz; 11259 Tower Road, 99515.

KRUA-FM 88.1 MHz; 3211 Providence Drive, 99508.

KSKA-FM 91.1 MHz; 3877 University Drive, 99508.

KTZN 550 kHz; 800 E. Dimond Blvd., Suite 3-370, 99515.

KWHL-FM 106.5 MHz; 9200 Lake Otis Pkwy., 99507-4228.

KYMG-FM 98.9 MHz; 800 E. Dimond Blvd., Suite 3-370, 99515.

Barrow. KBRW 680 kHz; **KBRW-FM** 91.9 MHz; P.O. Box 109, 99723.

Bethel. KYKD-FM 100.1 MHz; 406 Ptarmigan St., 99559.

KYUK 640 kHz; 640 Radio St., 99559.

Chevak. KCUK 88.1 kHz; 985 KSD Way, 99563.

Cordova. KCDV-FM 100.9 MHz; **KLAM** 1450 kHz; 1 Forestry Way, 99574.

Dillingham. KDLG 670 kHz; 670 Seward St., 99576.

KRUP-FM 99.1 MHz; 301 Airport Road, 99576.

Fairbanks. KAKQ-FM 101.1 MHz; 546 Ninth Ave. No. 200, 99701.

KCBF 820 kHz; **KXLR-FM** 95.9 MHz; 1060 Aspen St., 99709.

KFAR 660 kHz; **KWLF-FM** 98.1 MHz; 1060 Aspen St., 99709.

KIAK 970 kHz; **KIAK-FM** 1025 MHz; **KKED-FM** 104.7 MHz; 546 Ninth Ave., Suite 200, 99701.

KSUA-FM 91.5 MHz; 307 Constitution Hall, University of Alaska, 99775.

KUAC-FM 89.9 MHz; University of Alaska, P.O. Box 755620, 99775-5620.

KUWL-FM 103.9 MHz; 1060 Aspen St., 99707.

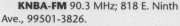

A national publication claimed it's against the law in Anchorage to stop a person on the street, hold them at gunpoint and make them whistle "Hail, Hail, the Gang's All Here." We tried to verify this with law enforcement officials, but every call we made was met with an extremely snotty reply.

KWLF-FM 98.1 MHz; **KXLR-FM** 95.9 MHz; 1060 Aspen St., 99707.

Fort Yukon. KZPA-FM 900 MHz; 1936 E. Third Ave., 99740.

Galena. KIYU 910 kHz; P.O. Box 165, 99741.

Glennallen. KCAM 790 kHz; P.O. Box 249, 99588.

Haines/Klukwan/Skagway. KHNS-FM 102.3 MHz; P.O. Box 1109, Haines 99827.

Homer. KBBI 890 kHz; 3913 Kachemak Way, 99603.
    KGTL 620 kHz; **KWVV-FM,** 103.5 MHz; P.O. Box 109, 99603.
    KPEN-FM 101.7 MHz; P.O. Box 109, 99603.
    KWVV-FM 103.5 MHz; P.O. Box 109, 99603.

Juneau. KINY 800 kHz; 1107 W. Eighth St., Suite 2, 99801.
    KJNO 630 kHz; 3161 Channel Drive, Suite 2, 99801.
    KSUP-FM 106.3 MHz; 107.9 kHz; 1107 W. Eighth St., Suite 2, 99801.
    KTKU-FM 105.1 MHz; 3161 Channel Drive, Suite 2, 99801.
    KTOO-FM 104.3 MHz; 360 Egan Drive, 99801.

Kenai. KDLL 91.9 kHz; Box 2111, 99611.
    KSRM 920 kHz; **KWHQ-FM** 100.1 MHz; 36935 K–Beach Road, 99611.
    KZXX 980 kHz; 6672 Kenai Spur Road, 99611.

Ketchikan. KFMJ 99.9 kHz; 516 Stedman St., 99901.
    KGTW-FM 106.7 MHz; 526 Stedman St., 99901.
    KRBD-FM 105.9 MHz; 123 Stedman St., 99901.
    KTKN 930 kHz; 526 Stedman St., 99901.

Kodiak. KMXT-FM 100.1 MHz; 620 Egan Way, 99615.
    KRXX-FM 101.1 MHz; 1315 Mill Bay Road, 99615.
    KVOK 560 kHz; 1315 Mill Bay Road, 99615.

Kotzebue. KOTZ 720 kHz; P.O. Box 78, 99752.

McCarthy. KXKM-FM 89.7 MHz; P.O. Box 467, Valdez 99686.

McGrath. KSKO 870 kHz; P.O. Box 70, 99627.

Naknek. KAKN-FM 100.9 MHz; P.O. Box 214, 99633.

Nenana. KIAM 630 kHz; P.O. Box 474, 99760.

Nome. KICY 850 kHz; **KICY-FM** 100.3 MHz; P.O. Box 820, 99762-0820.
    KNOM 780 kHz; **KNOM-FM** 96.1 MHz; P.O. Box 988, 99762.

North Pole. KJNP 1170 kHz; **KJNP-FM** 100.3 MHz; P.O. Box 56359, 99705.

Petersburg. KFSK-FM 100.9 MHz; P.O. Box 149, 99833.
    KRSA 580 kHz; P.O. Box 650, 99833.

St. Paul. KUHB-FM 91.9 MHz; P.O. Box 905, 99660.

Sand Point. KSDP 830 kHz; P.O. Box 328, 99661.

Seward. KSWD 950 kHz; **KPFN-FM** 105.9 MHz; 222 Fourth Ave., 99664.

Sitka. KCAW-FM 104.7 MHz; 2-B Lincoln St., 99835-7538.
    KIFW 1230 kHz; **KSBZ-FM** 103.1 MHz; 611 Lake St., 99835-7402.

Soldotna. KKIS-FM, 96.5 MHz; HC2, P.O. Box 852, 99669.
    KSLD 1140 kHz; HC2, P.O. Box 852, 99669.

Talkeetna. KTNA-FM, 88.5 MHz; P.O. Box 300, 99676.

Tok. KUDU-FM 91.9 MHz; P.O. Box 719, 99780.

Unalakleet. KNSA 930 kHz; P.O. Box 178, 99684.

Unalaska. KIAL 1450 kHz; Fifth and Broadway, 99685-9999.

Valdez. KCHU 770 kHz; **KCHU-FM** 88.1 MHz; P.O. Box 467, 99686.
    KVAK 1230 kHz; P.O. Box 367, 99686.
    KXGA-FM 90.5 MHz; P.O. Box 467, 99686.

Wasilla. KMBQ-FM 99.7 MHz; 2200 E. Parks Hwy., 99654.

Wrangell. KSTK-FM 101.7 MHz; P.O. Box 1141, 99929.

RAILROADS (SEE ALSO Skagway)

The Alaska Railroad is the northernmost railroad in North America and was for many years the only one owned by the federal government. Ownership has been transferred to the state. The Alaska Railroad rolls on 470 miles of mainline track from the ports of Seward and Whittier to Anchorage, Cook Inlet and Fairbanks in the Interior.

The Alaska Railroad began in 1912 when Congress appointed a commission to study transportation problems in Alaska. In March 1914, President Woodrow Wilson authorized railroad lines in the Territory of Alaska to connect open harbors on the southern coast of Alaska with the Interior. The Alaska Engineering Commission surveyed railroad routes in 1914 and, in April 1915, the president announced the selection of a route from Seward north 412 miles to the Tanana River (where Nenana is now located), with branch lines to Matanuska coal fields. The main line was later extended to Fairbanks. Construction of the railroad began in 1915 from a wilderness construction camp on Cook Inlet. Almost overnight, a tent city of 2,000 sprang up and Anchorage was born.

On July 15, 1923, President Warren G. Harding drove in the golden spike at Nenana, signifying completion of the railroad.

The Alaska Railroad offers year-round passenger and freight service. The railroad features flag-stop service along the Anchorage-to-Fairbanks corridor, as well as summer express trains to Denali National Park and Preserve and beyond to Fairbanks. Passenger service is daily between mid-May and mid-September, and in winter weekly service is available between Anchorage and Fairbanks. One-day excursions between Anchorage, Seward and Whittier are provided daily, mid-May to early September. In 2000, a total of 501,138 passengers rode the Alaska Railroad. For more information contact the Alaska Railroad, P.O. Box 107500, Anchorage 99510; (800) 544-0552; www.alaskarailroad.com.

The privately owned White Pass & Yukon Route provided a narrow-gauge link between Skagway, Alaska, and Whitehorse, Yukon Territory. When it was built—1898 to 1900—it was the farthest north any railroad had operated in North America. The railway maintains one of the steepest railroad grades in North America, climbing to 2,885 feet at White Pass in only 20 miles of track.

The White Pass & Yukon Route provided both passenger and freight service until 1982, when it suspended service until 1988. Currently, the route provides daily passenger service only. Contact the White

The White Pass & Yukon Route railway still operates its historic steam engine.
Photo by Tricia Brown.

Pass & Yukon Route, P.O. Box 435, Skagway 99840; (800) 343-7373; fax (907) 983-2743; www.whitepassrailroad.com.

REGIONS OF ALASKA
The state of Alaska is organized by geography and climate into six general regions. (SEE MAP, pages 6–7)

Southeast. Southeast, Alaska's panhandle, stretches approximately 500 miles from Icy Bay, northwest of Yakutat, south to Dixon Entrance at the U.S.–Canada border beyond the southern tip of Prince of Wales Island. Massive ice fields, glacier-scoured peaks and steep valleys, more than a thousand named islands and numerous unnamed islets and reefs characterize this world where few flat expanses break the steepness. Spruce, hemlock and cedar cover many mountainsides and are harvested as timber.

Average temperatures range from 50°F to 60°F in July and from 20°F to 40°F in January. Average annual precipitation varies from 80 inches to more than 200 inches. The area receives from 30 inches to 200 inches of snow in the lowlands and more than 400 inches in the high mountains.

The region's economy revolves around fishing and fish processing, timber and tourism. Mining has increased with development of a world-class molybdenum mine near Ketchikan.

Airplanes and boats are principal means of transportation. Only three communities in Southeast are connected to the road system: Haines, via the Haines Highway to the Alaska Highway at Haines Junction; Skagway, via Klondike Highway 2 to the Alaska Highway; and Hyder, to the continental road system via the Cassiar Highway in British Columbia. Juneau, on the Southeast mainland, is the state capital; Sitka, on Baranof Island, was the capital of Russian America.

Southcentral/Gulf Coast. The Southcentral/Gulf Coast region curves 650 miles north and west of Southeast Alaska and includes Kodiak Island. About two-thirds of the state's residents live in the arc between the Gulf of Alaska on the south and the Alaska Range on the north, the region commonly called Southcentral. On the region's eastern boundary, only the Copper River valley breaches the mountainous barrier of the Chugach and St. Elias mountains. On the west rise lofty peaks of the Aleutian Range. Within this mountainous perimeter course the Susitna and Matanuska Rivers.

The irregular plain of the Copper River lowland has a colder climate than the other major valley areas. The January average for Kenny Lake is –2°F. The January average for the Talkeetna airport is 10°F. July temperatures average 50°F to 60°F in the region.

NUGGETS

For the first time since October 1982, the White Pass & Yukon Route railway was back on track as a tourist attraction in May 1988, transporting visitors from Skagway to the top of the White Pass, a trip of 20.4 miles and 2,885 vertical feet. The train has hauled gold seekers and freight, as well as running as an excursion train, since 1898.—1989 *The ALASKA ALMANAC®*

189

Regional precipitation ranges from a scant 17 inches annually in drier areas to more than 76 inches a year at Thompson Pass in the coastal mountains.

Vegetation varies from the spruce-hemlock forests of Prince William Sound to mixed spruce and birch forests in the Susitna Valley to tundra in the highlands of the Copper River–Nelchina Basin.

Alaska agriculture historically has been most thoroughly developed in the Matanuska Valley. The state's dairy industry is centered there and at a project at Point MacKenzie, across Knik Arm from Anchorage. Vegetables thrive in the area, which is well known for its giant cabbages. Hub of the state's commerce, transportation and communications is Anchorage, on a narrow plain at the foot of the Chugach Mountains, and bounded by Knik Arm and Turnagain Arm, offshoots of Cook Inlet. The population of Alaska's largest city is closely tied to shifts in the state's economy.

Alaska's major banks, oil companies and the Alaska Railroad have headquarters in Anchorage. The city's port handles most of the shipping in and out of the state. Valdez, to the east of Anchorage on Prince William Sound, is the southern terminal of the trans-Alaska oil pipeline, which transports oil from Prudhoe Bay on the North Slope.

Interior. Great rivers have forged a broad lowland, known as the Interior, in the central part of the state between the Alaska Range on the south and the Brooks Range on the north. The Yukon River carves a swath across the entire state. In the Interior, the Tanana, Porcupine, Koyukuk and several other rivers join with the Yukon to create summer and winter highways. South of the Yukon, the Kuskokwim River rises in the hills of the western Interior before beginning its meandering course across the Bering Sea coast region.

Winter temperatures in the Interior commonly drop to –50°F or colder. Ice fog sometimes hovers over Fairbanks and other low-lying communities when the temperature falls below zero. Controlled by the extremes of a continental climate, summers usually are warmer than in any other region; high temperatures can climb to 90°F. The climate is semiarid, with about 12 inches of precipitation recorded annually.

Immense forests of birch and aspen bring vibrant green and gold to the Interior's landscape. Spruce covers many of the slopes and cottonwoods thrive near river lowlands. But in northern and western reaches of the Interior, the North American taiga gives way to tundra. In highlands above tree line and in marshy lowlands, grasses and shrubs replace trees.

Gold lured the first large influx of non-Natives to Alaska's Interior. From 1903 to 1910, the largest community in the region was the booming gold-mining camp of Fairbanks. Now the city on the banks of the Chena River is a transportation and supply center for eastern and northern Alaska. The main campus of the University of Alaska overlooks the city.

About 100 miles east of Fairbanks, farmers at the Delta project work to build a foundation for agriculture based on barley. At Healy, southwest of Fairbanks, the state's only operating coal mine produces coal used to generate electricity for the Interior. The rest of the Interior relies primarily on a subsistence economy, sometimes combined with a cash economy where fishing or seasonal government jobs are available.

Northern/Arctic. Beyond the Brooks Range, more than 80,000 square miles of tundra interlaced with meandering rivers and countless ponds spread out along the North Slope. In far northwestern Alaska, the Arctic curves south to take in Kotzebue and other villages of the Kobuk and Noatak river drainages.

Short, cool summers and temperatures between only 30°F and 40°F allow the permanently frozen soil to thaw just a few inches. Winter temperatures range well below zero but the Arctic Ocean moderates temperatures in coastal areas. Severe winds sweep along the coast and through mountain passes. Cold and wind often drop the windchill-factor temperature far below the actual temperature. Most areas receive less than 10 inches of precipitation a year but the terrain is wet in summer because of little evaporation and frozen ground.

Traditionally the home of Inupiat Eskimos, the Arctic was inhabited by few non-Natives until oil was discovered at Prudhoe Bay in the 1960s. Today the region's economy is focused on Prudhoe Bay and neighboring Kuparuk oil fields. Petroleum-related jobs support most of the region's residents. Subsistence hunting and fishing fill any economic holes left by the oil industry.

The largest Inupiat Eskimo community in the world, Barrow is the center of commerce and government activity for the region. Airplanes, the major means of transportation, fan out from there to the region's far-flung villages.

The Dalton Highway, formerly called the North Slope Haul Road, connects the Arctic with the Interior. The 416-mile road is open to the public all the way to Deadhorse. Permits are no longer required to drive the highway. (SEE Dalton Highway)

Western/Bering Sea Coast.
Western Alaska extends along the Bering Sea coast from the Arctic Circle south to where the Alaska Peninsula joins the mainland near Naknek on Bristol Bay. Home of Inupiat and Yup'ik Eskimos, the region centers around the immense Yukon–Kuskokwim River Delta, the Seward Peninsula to the north and Bristol Bay to the south.

Summer temperatures range from about 30°F to about 60°F. Winter readings generally range from just above zero to near 30°F. Wind chill lowers temperatures considerably. Total annual precipitation is about 20 inches; northern regions are drier.

Much of the region is covered with tundra, although a band of forest covers the hills on the eastern end of the Seward Peninsula and Norton Sound. In the south near Bristol Bay the tundra once again gives way to forests. In between, the marshy flatland of the great Yukon–Kuskokwim Delta spreads out for more than 200 miles.

Gold first attracted non-Natives to the hills and creeks of the Seward Peninsula.

To the south, only a few anthropologists and wildlife biologists entered the world of the Yup'ik Eskimos of the delta. At the extreme south, the world's largest sockeye salmon run drew fishermen to the riches of Bristol Bay.

The villages of Western Alaska are linked by air and water, dogsled and snow machine. Commerce on the delta radiates from Bethel, largest community in Western Alaska. To the north, Nome dominates commerce on the Seward Peninsula, while several fishing communities rely on the riches of Bristol Bay.

Southwestern/Alaska Peninsula and Aleutians.
Southwestern Alaska includes the Alaska Peninsula and Aleutian Islands. From Naknek Lake, the peninsula curves southwest about 500 miles to the first of the Aleutian Islands; the Aleutians continue south and west more than 1,000 miles. Primarily a mountainous region with about 50 volcanic peaks, only on the Bering Sea side of the peninsula does the terrain flatten out.

More than 200 islands, roughly 5,500 square miles in area, form the narrow arc of the Aleutians, which separate the Pacific Ocean from the Bering Sea. Nearly the entire chain is in the Alaska Maritime National Wildlife Refuge. Unimak Island, closest to the Alaska Peninsula mainland, is

> A tourist from Hawaii was quoted as saying: "Nobody gets very dressed up in Alaska. We're pretty casual in Hawaii, but at least we comb our hair before we go out. And I noticed that the closer you get to Homer, the more casual it gets."

1,000 miles from Attu, the most distant island. Five major island groups make up the Aleutians, all of which are treeless except for a few scattered stands that have been transplanted.

The Aleutian climate is cool. Summer temperatures range to about 50°F and winter readings reach 20°F or colder. Winds are almost constant and fog is common. Precipitation ranges from 21 inches to more than 80 inches annually. The peninsula's climate is somewhat warmer than the islands' in summer and cooler in winter.

Aleuts, original inhabitants of the chain, still live at Atka, Atka Island; Nikolski, Umnak Island; Unalaska, Unalaska Island; Akutan, Akutan Island; and False Pass, Unimak Island.

The quest for furs first drew Russians to the islands and peninsula in the 1700s. The traders conquered the Aleuts and forced them to hunt marine mammals. After the United States purchased Alaska in 1867, fur traders switched their efforts to fox farming. Many foxes were turned loose on the islands, where they flourished and destroyed native wildlife.

With the collapse of the fur market in the 1920s and 1930s, the islands were left to themselves. This relative isolation was broken during World War II when Japanese military forces bombed Dutch Harbor and landed on Attu and Kiska Islands. The United States military retook the islands, and after the war the government resettled Aleuts living in the western Aleutians to villages in the eastern Aleutians, closer to the mainland.

Today fishing provides the main economic base for the islands and the peninsula. Many Aleuts go to Bristol Bay or Unalaska to fish commercially in summer.

RELIGION Nearly every religion

practiced in American society is found in Alaska. Anchorage alone has nearly 200 churches and temples. Following is a list of addresses for some of the major ones:

Alaska Baptist Convention, 1750 O'Malley Road, Anchorage 99516.

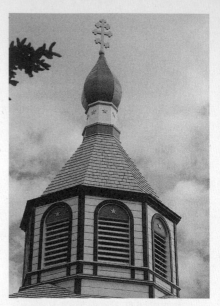

The Russian Orthodox church at Kenai is among the oldest buildings in the state. Photo by Tricia Brown.

Alaska Moravian Church, Bethel 99559.

Anchorage Friends Church (Native), 1227 E. 75th Ave., Anchorage 99503.

Assemblies of God District Council, 1048 W. International Airport Road, Anchorage 99502.

Baha'i Faith, 13501 Brayton Drive, Anchorage 99516.

Chapel by the Sea, 14730 Turnagain Bluff Way, Anchorage 99515-4153.

Christian Church of Anchorage, 10800 Lake Otis Pkwy., Anchorage 99516.

Christian House of Prayer Alaska, 3721 E. 84th Ave., Anchorage 99502.

Christian Science Church, 1347 L St., Anchorage 99501.

Church of God, 1711 S. Bragaw St., Anchorage 99508.

Church of Jesus Christ of Latter-day Saints, 13111 Brayton Drive, Anchorage 99516.

Congregation Beth Sholom, 7525 E. Northern Lights Blvd., Anchorage 99504.

Episcopal Diocese of Alaska, 1205 Denali Way, Fairbanks 99701.

Evangelical Lutheran Church of America, 1847 W. Northern Lights Blvd., Anchorage 99502.

Islamic Center of Alaska, 5630 Silverado Way, Anchorage 99518.

Jehovah's Witnesses, 2301 Strawberry Road, Anchorage 99507.

Lubavitch Jewish Center of Alaska, Congregation Shomrei Ohr, 1210 E. 26th Ave., Anchorage 99508.

Orthodox Church, Diocese of Alaska, Chancery, 513 E. 24th Ave., Anchorage 99504.

Presbyterian Church, 616 W. 10th Ave., Anchorage 99501.

Roman Catholic Archdiocese of Anchorage, 225 Cordova, Anchorage 99501.

Salvation Army, 143 E. Ninth Ave., Anchorage 99501.

Trinity Christian Reformed Church, 3000 E. 16th Ave., Anchorage 99508.

United Methodist Church, Alaska Missionary Conference, 3402 Wesleyan Drive, Anchorage 99508.

Unity of Anchorage, 2610 E. Northern Lights Blvd., Anchorage 99508.

REPTILES For all practical purposes,
reptiles are not found in Alaska outside of captivity. The northern limits of North American reptilian species may be the latitude at which their embryos fail to develop during the summer. Three sightings of a species of garter snake, *Thamnophis sirtalis,* have been reported on the banks of the Taku River and Stikine River.

RIVERS (See also National Wild and Scenic
Rivers; Yukon River) There are more than 3,000 rivers in Alaska. The 10 longest are:

Yukon River—1,400 miles in Alaska; the remainder is in Canada.

Porcupine River—555 miles. The Porcupine is a major tributary of the Yukon River.

Koyukuk—554 miles
Kuskokwim—540 miles
Tanana—531 miles
Innoko—463 miles
Colville—428 miles

Noatak—396 miles
Kobuk—396 miles
Birch Creek—314 miles

The major navigable Alaska inland waterways are:

Chilkat. Navigable by shallow-draft vessels to village of Klukwan, 25 miles above mouth.

Kobuk. Controlling channel depth is about 5 feet through Hotham Inlet, 3 feet to Ambler and 2 feet to Kobuk Village, about 210 river miles.

Koyukuk. Navigable to Allakaket by vessels drawing up to 3 feet during normally high river flow and to Bettles during occasional higher flows.

Kuskokwim. Navigable (June 1 to Sept. 30) by 18-foot-draft oceangoing vessels from mouth upriver 65 miles to Bethel. Shallow-draft (4-foot) vessels can ascend river to mile 465. McGrath is at mile 400.

Kvichak. The river is navigable for vessels of 10-foot draft to Alaganak River, 22 miles above the mouth of Kvichak River. Remainder of this river (28 miles) navigable by craft drawing 2 feet to 4 feet, depending on the stage of the river. Drains into Lake Iliamna, which is navigable an additional 70 miles.

Naknek. Navigable for vessels of 12-foot draft for 12 miles with adequate tide. Vessels with 3-foot draft can continue an additional 7.5 miles.

Noatak. Navigable (late May to mid-June) for shallow-draft barges to a point about 18 miles below Noatak village. Shallow-draft vessels can continue on to Noatak.

Nushagak. Navigable (June 1 to Aug. 31) by small vessels of 2½-foot draft to Nunachuak, about 100 miles above the mouth. Shallow-draft, oceangoing vessels can navigate to mouth of Wood River at mile 84.

Porcupine. Navigable to Old Crow, Yukon Territory, by vessels drawing 3 feet, during spring runoff and fall rain floods.

Stikine. Navigable (May 1 to Oct. 15) from mouth 165 miles to Telegraph

Rafting on Tatshenshini–Alsek River, Glacier Bay National Park and Preserve. From T*he Alaska River Guide* by Karen Jettmar.

Creek, British Columbia, by shallow-draft, flat-bottom riverboats.

Susitna. Navigable by stern-wheelers and shallow-draft, flat-bottom riverboats to confluence of Talkeetna River, 75 miles upstream, but boats cannot cross bars at mouth of river. Not navigable by oceangoing vessels.

Tanana. Navigable by shallow-draft (4-foot), flat-bottom vessels and barges from the mouth to Nenana and by smaller river craft to the Chena River 201 miles above the mouth. Craft of 4-foot draft can navigate to Chena River on high water to University Avenue Bridge in Fairbanks.

Yukon. Navigable (June 1 to Sept. 30) by shallow-draft, flat-bottom riverboats from the mouth to near the head of Lake Bennett. It cannot be entered or navigated by oceangoing vessels. Controlling depths are 7 feet to Stevens Village and 3 feet to 5 feet from there to Fort Yukon.

ROADHOUSES An important part

of Alaska history, roadhouses were modest quarters that offered bed and board to travelers along early-day Alaska trails. Because most travel was done in winter, many roadhouses provided accommodations for sled dog teams.

By 1920, there were roadhouses along every major transportation route in Alaska. Most roadhouses have vanished though a few of the historic roadhouses survive, including Gakona Lodge on the Glenn Highway, Paxson Lodge at the junction of the Richardson and Denali highways, and Talkeetna Roadhouse.

The Cape Nome Roadhouse was a major stopover for dog teams and also served as a temporary orphanage. Several roadhouses are included in the National Register of Historic Places. Some historic roadhouses are now museums or occupied by businesses.

ROCKS AND GEMS (SEE ALSO Gold; Jade; Minerals and Mining) Gemstones are

not easy to find in Alaska. Rockhounds must hunt for them and often walk quite a distance. The easiest specimens to collect are float-rocks scattered by glaciation. These rocks are found on ocean beaches and railroad beds, and in creeks and rivers all over Alaska. In most rock-hunting areas, every instance of high water, wind, heavy rain and a melting patch of snow and ice uncovers a new layer, so you can hunt repeatedly in the same area and make new finds.

The easiest gemstones to search out are in the crypto-crystalline group of quartz minerals. These gems have crystals not visible to the naked eye. They are the jaspers, agates, cherts and flints.

Thunder eggs, geodes and agatized wood (all in the chalcedony classification) occur in Alaska. Thunder eggs have a jasper rind enclosing an agate core. Harder-to-find geodes usually have an agate rind with a hollow core filled with crystals. Agatized and petrified woods come in various colors and often show the plant's growth rings. Sometimes even the bark or limb structure is visible on agatized and petrified woods.

Crystalline varieties of quartz can also be found: amethyst (purple), citrine (yellow), rose quartz (pink), rock crystal (clear) and smoky quartz (brown).

Other gems to search for in Alaska are onyx, feldspar, porphyry, jade, serpentine, soapstone, garnet, rhodonite, sapphire, marble, staurolite, malachite and covelite (blue copper).

RUSSIAN ALASKA (See also

Baranov, Alexander; Bering, Vitus; History; Seward, William H.; Veniaminov, Ioann) Russian presence in Alaska began with the 1741 voyages of Vitus Bering and Alexei Chirikov. Their exploration of the Aleutian Islands and the Alaska mainland spurred dozens of voyages by Russian fur entrepreneurs, or *promyshlenniki*.

By the mid-1800s, Russians had explored most of the coast of southern and southwestern Alaska and some of the Interior. Their interest in Alaska lay primarily in exploiting the rich fur resources of the region, especially sea otters and fur seals. In 1799, the Russian post known today as Old Sitka was established. That same year, a trade charter was granted to the Russian-American Company, a monopoly authorized by the czar in 1790 to control activities in Alaska.

During the entire Russian period, from 1741 to 1867, there were rarely more than about 500 Russians in Alaska at any one time. Nevertheless, the Aleuts, Eskimos and Indians whom the Russians encountered felt the devastating effects of foreign contact. Native populations declined drastically from introduced diseases. The population of the Aleut people, the first to succumb to Russian occupation, was reduced to less than 20 percent of the precontact level through warfare, disease and starvation. The Tlingit, Haida and Chugach may have been reduced by 50 percent.

The Russians also brought to the new land their customs, religion and language, which, through subjugation and the efforts of Orthodox missionaries, brought great changes in traditional technologies, social patterns and religious beliefs.

In 1867, facing increasing competition and frustrated in its efforts to expand, the Russians sold Alaska to the United States for $7.2 million.

One of the foremost legacies of the

Boalotchkee (Russian Buns)

1 pound butter	2 pounds flour
5 eggs	1 pound sugar
2 cups sour cream	Nuts
3/4 teaspoon baking soda	Beaten egg yolk

Combine butter and eggs. Mix sour cream and soda; combine with butter-egg mixture. Sift flour on board and mix with sugar. Make a hole in the middle and add the egg mixture. Knead the dough with hands, constantly sprinkling the board with flour. Shape into round buns, place in lightly oiled shallow pan, brush with beaten egg yolk and sprinkle with any kind of chopped nuts. Bake at 350° F until done, about 18 to 25 minutes. —Ann Lewis, St. Herman's Sisterhood Club, Kodiak, *Cooking Alaskan*

Russian period is the Russian Orthodox Church, still a vital aspect of Native culture in Southwestern, Southcentral and Southeast Alaska. Visitors to Kenai, Kodiak, Sitka and smaller Native communities will see the familiar onion-shaped domes of the Russian Orthodox churches.

RUSSIAN CHRISTMAS
Russian Christmas is the Russian Orthodox observance of the birth of Christ. It begins on Jan. 7—Twelfth Night, 12 days after Dec. 25.

The holiday, called *Selavi,* is celebrated for seven days, with church services including songs in Slavonic, fireworks and special foods. Part of the tradition involves carrying a star from house to house, caroling, and sharing food and small gifts.

Russian Christmas is observed in cities and towns with Orthodox parishes, such as Akutan, Anchorage, Dillingham, Eklutna, Juneau, Kenai, Kodiak, Lower Kalskag, Naknek, New Stuyahok, Newhalen, Ninilchik, Nushagak, Pedro Bay, St. Paul, St. George, Seldovia and Sitka.

SALMON STRIPS
These strips are salmon that has been dried or smoked for a long time until it's very chewy. The food is a staple in winter for rural Alaskans and their dogs. Other terms for this food are salmon jerky, strips, salmon candy or squaw candy.

SCHOOL DISTRICTS (SEE ALSO
Education) Alaska's 53 public school districts served 133,351 pre-elementary through 12th grade students in the 2000–2001 school year. There are two types of districts: city and borough school districts and Regional Educational Attendance Areas (REAA).

The 34 city and borough school districts are located in municipalities, each contributing funds for the operation of its local schools. City and borough school districts are supported by 61.9 percent state, 31.2 percent local and 6.9 percent federal funding.

The 19 REAAs are in the unorganized boroughs and have no local government to contribute funds to their schools. The REAAs are almost solely dependent upon state funds for school support.

Alaska's total education payroll for 2000 was $804 million—rivaling oil as the state's payroll leader.

The statewide average annual wage for classroom teachers was $48,165.

The Alyeska Central School provides courses by correspondence to students in grades K–12. The school can be contacted through Alaska Department of Education, 3134 Channel Drive, No. 100, Juneau 99801-7897. The Department of Education in Juneau can also provide information on Alaska's public school districts.

SEWARD
Located on Resurrection Bay, on the east coast of the Kenai Peninsula, Seward lies 127 miles south of Anchorage by road or 35 minutes by plane. Population is just over 2,800.

The city is named for U.S. Secretary of State William H. Seward, who was instrumental in negotiating the purchase of Alaska from Russia. The city of Seward was founded in 1902 by surveyors for the Alaska Railroad as the ocean terminus of the railroad.

Resurrection Bay is a year-round ice-free harbor, and Seward is an important cargo and fishing port. The Alaska state ferry and many cruise ships call here. The economy of the town is based on tourism, a coal terminal, fisheries and government offices. Visitors enjoy wildlife and glacier tours, sportfishing expeditions, kayaking, photography safaris, nature cruises, RV facilities, hotels, dozens of bed-and-breakfast establishments, art galleries, coffeehouses, dogsled tours and hiking.

The Alaska SeaLife Center and the Chugach Heritage Center were unveiled in 1988. Other attractions in the area include Exit Glacier (accessible by trail), Kenai Fjords National Park and Chugach National

Forest. From puffins to oystercatchers to bald eagles, more than 100 species of birds abound. Substantial numbers of marine mammals inhabit or migrate through Seward's coastal waters, including sea otters, Steller sea lions, dolphins and Pacific gray whales.

For information about Kenai Fjords National Park, call (907) 224-3175. For information about Seward, contact the Chamber of Commerce at (907) 224-8051; www.seward.org.

SEWARD, WILLIAM H. (SEE ALSO Russian Alaska)

William H. Seward, the man who negotiated the purchase of Alaska from Russia, was born in New York in 1801. He was admitted to the bar in 1822 and eventually became governor of New York for two terms (declining a third). Seward returned to his law practice until 1849, when he was elected to the United States Senate and served for two terms. In 1860 Seward was a candidate for the presidential nomination, but failing to receive it, he then supported Lincoln, whose cabinet he entered as secretary of state, a position he held from 1861 to 1869.

Due to the rapidly declining fur trade and the economizing and streamlining of the St. Petersburg regime in Russia, operations such as the Russian-American Company were deemed expendable. The Grand Duke Constantine urged the sale of Alaska to the United States in 1857, but the American Civil War in 1861 forestalled talks.

At the conclusion of the war, the czar's representative began immediate negotiations with Secretary of State Seward, who was eager to buy, and a selling price of $7.2 million was agreed upon—about 2 cents an acre. The treaty was signed on March 30, 1867, and ratified by the Senate on June 20. Formal handover did not occur until Oct. 18.

Newspaper editorials denounced the acquisition of the apparently worthless real estate, ridiculed the agreement as "Seward's folly" and caricatured Alaska as "Walrussia" and "Seward's icebox."

After leaving office in 1869, Seward traveled around the world; he visited Alaska in 1869. He died in 1872.

SHIPPING

Vehicles. Persons shipping vehicles between Washington and Anchorage are advised to shop around for the carrier that offers the services and rates most suited to the shipper's needs. Not all carriers offer year-round service, and freight charges vary greatly depending upon the carrier and the weight and height of the vehicle. Rates quoted here are only approximate. Sample fares per unit: northbound, Washington to Anchorage, under 66 inches in height, $1,030; over 66 inches and under 87 inches, $1,318. Southbound, Anchorage to Washington, any unit under 84 inches, $730. Fuel surcharges and terminal handling charges may be applied.

Not all carriers accept rented moving trucks and trailers, and a few of those that do accept them require authorization from the rental company to carry its equipment to Alaska. Check with the carrier and your rental company before booking service.

Make your reservation at least two weeks in advance, and prepare to have the vehicle at the carrier's loading facility two days prior to sailing. Carriers differ on what items they allow to travel inside the vehicle, from nothing at all to goods packaged and addressed separately. Coast Guard regulations forbid the transport of vehicles holding more than one-quarter tank of

From the police blotter of the *Seward Phoenix-Log:* At 4:50 A.M., a 29-year-old male was "placed into protective custody after banging on the city jail door demanding to come in since he had nowhere to go and was intoxicated."

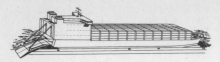

gas, and none of the carriers listed allows owners to accompany their vehicles in transit. *Remember to have fresh antifreeze installed in your car or truck prior to sailing.*

At a lesser rate, you can ship your vehicle aboard a state ferry to southeastern ports. However you must accompany your vehicle or arrange for someone to drive it on and off the ferry at departure and arrival ports.

Carriers that will ship cars, truck campers, house trailers and motor homes from Anchorage to Seattle/Tacoma include:

The Alaska Railroad, P.O. Box 107500, Anchorage 99510; (800) 478-2442.

CSX Lines, 1717 Tidewater Road, Anchorage 99501; (907) 274-2671; (907) 263-5900.

Totem Ocean Trailer Express, 2511 Tidewater Ave., Anchorage 99501; (800) 234-8683; (907) 276-5868.

In the Seattle/Tacoma area, contact:

A.A.D.A. Systems, P.O. Box 2323, Auburn, WA 98071; (206) 762-7840.

The Alaska Railroad, 2203 Airport Way S., Suite 215, Seattle, WA 98134; (206) 624-4234.

CSX Lines, 3600 Port of Tacoma Road, Tacoma, WA 98424; (253) 593-1504.

Totem Ocean Trailer Express, P.O. Box 24908, Seattle, WA 98124; (206) 628-4343 or (800) 426-7617 (outside Washington, Alaska and Hawaii).

Vehicle shipment between southeastern Alaska ports and Seattle is provided by:

Alaska Marine Lines, 5615 W. Marginal Way SW, Seattle, WA 98106; (206) 764-8346 or (800) 443-4343 (serves Ketchikan, Wrangell, Petersburg, Sitka, Juneau, Haines, Skagway, Yakutat, Excursion Inlet and Hawk Inlet).

Boyer Alaska Barge Line, 7318 Fourth Ave. S., Seattle, WA 98108; (206) 763-8575 (serves Ketchikan and Wrangell).

For shipping to Bush areas:

Alaska Bush Service, P.O. Box

190827, Anchorage 99519; (907) 344-6690.

Household Goods and Personal Effects. Many moving van lines have service to and from Alaska through their agency connections in most Alaska and Lower 48 cities. To initiate service, contact the van line agents nearest your starting point.

Northbound goods are shipped to Seattle and transferred through a port agent to a waterborne vessel for transportation to Alaska. Few shipments go overland to Alaska. Southbound shipments are processed in a like manner through Alaska ports to Seattle, then on to the destination.

Haul-it-yourself companies provide service to Alaska. It is possible to ship a rented truck or trailer into southeastern Alaska aboard the carriers that accept privately owned vehicles. A few of the carriers sailing between Seattle and Anchorage also carry rented equipment. However shop around for this service because it has not been common practice in the past—rates can be very high if the carrier does not yet have a specific tariff established for this type of shipment. *You will not be allowed to accompany the rented equipment.*

SITKA
The town of Sitka (population 8,835), one of the most scenic of Southeast Alaska's cities, is located on the west side of Baranof Island in the shadow of Mount Edgecumbe, about 95 miles southwest of Juneau.

Tlingit Indians originally occupied the townsite until Alexander Baranov, chief manager of the Russian–American Co., built a trading post and fort in 1799 just north of their settlement. The Indians burned down the fort, and in 1804 Baranov defeated the alliance of local Tlingits, driving them from their settlement and naming the site New Archangel Bay. By 1810, New Archangel was thriving as the capital of Russian Alaska. New Archangel was later renamed Sitka, meaning "by the sea" in the Tlingit language.

Today, tourism and commercial fishing are the mainstays of the town's economy.

The climate of Sitka is mild and wet, with an annual precipitation of 95 inches and an average daily temperature of 33°F in January and 55°F in July.

Among the many sights in Sitka are Castle Hill, where Russia turned Alaska over to the United States in 1867; the Sitka Pioneers' Home (the first of six pioneers' homes built in Alaska); and Sitka National Historical Park, which reflects both the community's Tlingit heritage and its Russian past with two units: the Fort Site and the Russian Bishop's House. A replica of the old Russian Blockhouse, the original Russian Bishop's House (built in 1842) and the Indian Fort Site are preserved as part of the Sitka National Historical Park.

Visitors can see Sitka's historical roots in St. Michael's Cathedral, which contains priceless icons saved from fire that destroyed the cathedral in 1966. The existing structure was rebuilt from the original plans. The Sheldon Jackson Museum boasts one of the finest collections of Native arts and crafts in Alaska.

Located within walking distance from downtown Sitka is the Alaska Raptor Center, offering self-guided or guided interpretive tours. The facility treats injured birds of prey so they can return to the wild.

Annual events include the Sitka Summer Music Festival, featuring world renowned chamber music, and the Island Institute Writers' Conference in June. Alaska Day Celebration in October celebrates the transfer of Alaska from the Russians. Whale Fest, an annual celebration of Sitka's marine life, takes place the first weekend in November.

For more information, contact the Sitka Convention and Visitors Bureau, Box 1226, Sitka 99835; (907) 747-5940; www.sitka.org.

SITKA SLIPPERS Also known as Alaska tennis shoes, Wrangell sneakers or Petersburg sneakers, Sitka slippers are heavy-duty rubber boots worn by residents of rainy southeastern Alaska.

The historic Slide Cemetery, near Skagway, holds the remains of avalanche victims on the Trail of '98. Photo by Tricia Brown.

SKAGWAY (See also Chilkoot Trail)
Skagway, population 862, is found at the north end of Taiya Inlet on Lynn Canal in Southeast Alaska, about 90 air miles north of Juneau. The climate at Skagway averages 57°F in summer, 23°F in winter and the city has an annual precipitation of about 30 inches. Skagway serves as a gateway to the Alaska Highway in Southeast Alaska.

Skagway began as a gold-rush town, springing up overnight as fortune-seekers made their way from Skagway, up the White Pass and Chilkoot Trails, to the Yukon goldfields.

In July 1897, Skagway was little more than a tent town. Within months the town swelled to more than 20,000, with dance halls and gambling houses, saloons and residences. Frontier Skagway was once described as "hell on earth." Two years later the Klondike gold rush was over, and by 1903 Skagway's population had dwindled to 500.

Today, tourism is Skagway's main economic activity. The town serves the Alaska State Ferry and many cruise ships. More than 690,000 visitors came to Skagway during the summer of 1999. A favorite tourist attraction, the White Pass & Yukon Route railway, has added a new steam engine, No. 40, from Colorado. (See also Railroads)

Visitors may walk Skagway's historical district, featuring false-fronted buildings and boardwalks of the Klondike Gold Rush National Historical Park. Other attractions include the Trail of '98 Museum and *The Days of 1898 Show with Soapy Smith,* a play that relates the history of the town in the days of one of its most notorious con men.

Prepared hikers can climb the 33-mile Chilkoot Trail, the historic route of the gold seekers over 3,739-foot Chilkoot Pass to Lake Bennett. Relics are still visible along the trail.

For more information on Skagway, consult the Skagway Convention and Visitors Bureau, P.O. Box 1025, Skagway 99840; (907) 983-2854; fax (907) 983-3854; www.skagway.org.

SKIING Both cross-country and

downhill skiing are popular forms of outdoor recreation in Alaska from November through May. There are developed ski facilities in several Alaska communities, backcountry powder skiing is available by charter helicopter or ski-equipped aircraft, and cross-country skiing opportunities are virtually limitless. It is also possible to ski during the summer months by chartering a plane to reach glacier skiing spots.

Several cross-country ski races are held each year. The largest, the Alaska Nordic Ski Cup Series, determines contestants for the Arctic Winter Games and Junior Olympic competitions. The series of five races is held in Anchorage, Homer, Salcha and Fairbanks. The World Masters Cross Country Ski Championships were held in Anchorage in February 1992, and Valdez is now home to the World Extreme Ski Championships in April.

In the 1992 Winter Olympics, Hilary Lindh of Juneau turned all eyes to Alaska when she won the silver medal for the downhill. Lindh's was the first individual-merit Olympic medal ever won by an Alaskan.

"Moe-mania" struck when Alaskan Tommy Moe captured the gold medal in the downhill and silver in the supergiant slalom at the 1994 Olympics in Lillehammer, Norway.

Anchorage. There are two major downhill ski areas in the Anchorage area: Alyeska Resort and Alpenglow at Arctic Valley.

Alyeska Resort, 40 miles southeast of Anchorage, is the state's largest ski resort, offering nine chair lifts with runs up to 2 miles long. Nearly half of the mountain is equipped for night skiing, and one chair lift is reserved for racer training. The resort also offers snowshoeing and cross-country skiing.

The Alyeska Prince Hotel, a seven-story, 307-room inn opened in 1994, includes six restaurants, an indoor pool, exercise and health facilities, and meeting rooms.

The resort features a high-speed gondola capable of carrying 60 passengers at a time to two restaurants high on the slopes.

Alyeska is open year-round, offering skiing from November through April and sightseeing in the summer. Hours of operation are 10:30 A.M. to 5:30 P.M. in winter, with Friday and Saturday night skiing until 9:30; summer hours are 10:30 A.M. to 9:30 P.M. daily.

Alpenglow, a few miles from Anchorage, is owned and operated by the Anchorage Ski Club, a nonprofit corporation. Arctic Valley is open on winter weekends and holidays. Facilities include two double chair lifts, a T-bar/Poma lift combination and three rope tows on beginner slopes.

Several smaller alpine slopes maintained by the municipality of Anchorage include Far North Bicentennial Park; Russian Jack Springs Park, with rope tows; and Hilltop, south of town, featuring the closest chair lift to the Anchorage area.

There are several popular cross-country ski trails in the Anchorage area in city parks. These include Russian Jack Springs, with nearly 5 miles of trails, all lighted; Kincaid Park, site of the first World Cup and U.S. National races in Alaska and the United States in March 1983, with 24 miles of trails, 6 miles lighted, and a warm-up chalet; Far North Bicentennial Park, with

3 miles of trails, about 2 miles lighted; Hillside Park, with 10.8 miles of trails, 1.5 miles lighted; Tony Knowles Coastal Trail, with 9 miles of trails, none lighted; and Chester Creek Greenbelt, with 6.2 miles of trails, none lighted.

Cross-country skiers also can find trails in Chugach State Park; in Hatcher Pass north of Anchorage and in the Turnagain Pass area; in Chugach National Forest, about 57 miles south of Anchorage; and at Sheep Mountain Lodge along the Glenn Highway. Call the Nordic Skiing Association, (907) 561-0949.

Cordova. The Sheridan Ski Club operates the Mount Eyak Ski Hill about seven blocks from downtown Cordova. The season starts in December and extends until April, depending on snow.

Fairbanks. Cleary Summit and Skiland, about 20 miles from town on the Steese Highway, both privately owned and operated, have rope tows, with a chair lift at Cleary Summit; Birch Hill, located on Fort Wainwright, is mainly for military use; the University of Alaska has a small slope and rope tow; and Chena Hot Springs Resort at Mile 57 on the Chena Hot Springs Road has a small alpine ski area that uses a tractor to transport skiers to the top of the hill.

Popular cross-country ski trails in the Fairbanks area include Birch Hill recreation area, about 3 miles north of town on the Steese Expressway to a well-marked turnoff, then 2 miles in; the University of Alaska Fairbanks, with 26 miles of trails that lead to Ester Dome; Creamers Field trail near downtown; Salcha cross-country ski area, about 40 miles south of town on the Richardson Highway, with a trail system also used for ski races; Two Rivers trail area, near the elementary school at Mile 10 on the Chena Hot Springs Road; and Chena Hot Springs Resort, offering cross-country ski trails for both novice and more experienced skiers.

Kenai Peninsula. Most communities on the lower Kenai have trails or areas for skiing, including Anchor Point, Seldovia

A pair of backcountry skiers heads into Turnagain Pass in the Chugach National Forest. Photo by Roy Corral.

and Ninilchik. The best concentration of trails and slopes for Nordic, backcountry and downhill skiing is in the Homer area. Among them are Baycrest–Diamond Ridge, Homestead Trail, Ohlson Mountain and McNeil Canyon. Skiing on glaciers (accessible by helicopter) is possible in the Kenai Mountains across Kachemak Bay from Homer. Ski-joring (cross-country with a dog towing you) is increasingly popular in Homer.

Palmer. Hatcher Pass, site of the Independence Mine State Park, north of Palmer, is an excellent cross-country ski area with several maintained trails. The lodge has a coffee shop and warm-up area. The ski area is open from October through May.

Southeast. Eaglecrest Ski Area on Douglas Island, 12 miles from Juneau, has a 4,800-foot-long chair lift, a Platter Pull lift, a 3,000-foot-long chair lift and a day lodge. Cross-country ski trails are also available. Eaglecrest is open from November to May. A few smaller alpine ski areas are located at Cordova, Valdez, Ketchikan and Homer. All have rope tows.

SKIN SEWING (SEE ALSO Beadwork; Mukluks; Parka)

The craft of sewing tanned hides and furs was highly developed among Alaska Natives. Although commercially made garments are now often worn by Eskimo villagers, women who are exceptional skin sewers still not only ensure the safety of family members who must face the harsh outdoors, but are regarded as a source of pride for the entire community.

Sewers place great importance on the use of specific materials, some of which are only available seasonally.

Winter-bleached sealskin can only be tanned during certain seasons. Blood, alder bark and red ochre are traditionally used for dyeing garments and footgear. Most sewers prefer sinew (animal tendon) as thread, although in some areas sinew cannot be obtained and waxed thread or dental floss is substituted. Skins commonly used for making parkas and mukluks include seal, reindeer, caribou and ground squirrel. Wolf and wolverine are prized for ruffs.

Parka styles, materials and ornamentation (such as pieced calfskin or beadwork trim) vary from village to village, and among Athabascan, Yup'ik, Inupiat and Siberian Yup'ik sewers. The cut of parkas changes from north to south.

In most regions, mukluk styles and material vary with changes in season and weather conditions. Mukluks advertise the skill of their makers and the villages where they were made.

The manufacture of moccasins and children's toys, primarily clothed dolls and intricately sewn balls, still reflects the traditional ingenuity of skin sewers.

SKOOKUM

Skookum means strong or serviceable. The word originated with the Chehalis Indians of western Washington and was incorporated into the Chinook jargon, a trade language dating from the early 1800s.

A *skookum chuck* is a narrow passage between a saltwater lagoon and the open sea. In many areas of Alaska, because of extreme tides, *skookum chucks* may resemble fast-flowing river rapids during changes of the tide.

SOAPSTONE

This soft, easily worked stone is often carved into art objects by Alaskans. Most of the stone is imported. Alaska soapstone is mined in the Matanuska Valley by blasting, a process that leaves the stone susceptible to fracture when carved.

SOLDOTNA

Located 150 highway miles south of Anchorage, Soldotna is a hub city on the Kenai Peninsula. The Kenai River runs through Soldotna, and the town's fate and fortune is closely tied to the river, which is famous for its trophy-size king salmon. It's here that anglers meet up with guides and stock up on food and supplies for a day of fishing.

The city was named for nearby Soldotna Creek. Soldotna's first homesteaders were World War II veterans who were given a preference in selecting property in 1947. Today the city has about 3,800 residents, who make their living from commercial fishing, tourism, and the oil and gas industry.

Soldotna is home of the Tustumena 200 Sled Dog Race, held in January, and the Progress Days Festival in July, which

Basic Recipe for Sourdough Hotcakes

2 cups sourdough starter
2 tablespoons sugar
4 tablespoons oil
1 egg
$^1/_2$ teaspoon salt
1 scant teaspoon soda; full teaspoon if
   starter is real sour

Into the sourdough, dump sugar, salt, egg and oil. Mix well. Add soda the last thing, when ready for batter to hit the griddle. Dilute soda in 1 tablespoon of warm water. Fold gently into sourdough. *Do not beat.* Notice deep, hollow tone as sourdough fills with bubbles and doubles bulk. Bake on hot griddle to seal brown. Serve on hot plates.

—Ruth Allman, *Alaska Sourdough*

commemorates the completion of a gas pipeline in 1960.

The visitor center for the Kenai National Wildlife Refuge can be found in Soldotna. The sprawling refuge surrounds the town and offers fishing, canoeing and prime wildlife viewing. Information on the town is available from the Soldotna Chamber of Commerce, 44790 Sterling Highway, Soldotna 99669; (907) 262-9814; www.soldotnachamber.com.

SOURDOUGH
Carried by many early-day pioneers, this versatile, yeasty starter was used to make bread, doughnuts and hotcakes. Sourdough cookery remains popular in Alaska today. Because the sourdough supply is replenished after each use, it can remain active and fresh indefinitely.

A popular claim of sourdough cooks is that their batches trace back to pioneers at the turn of the century.

The name "sourdough" also came to be applied to any Alaska or Yukon old-timer.

SPEED LIMITS
The basic speed law in Alaska states the speed limit is "no speed more than is prudent and reasonable." The maximum speeds are 15 miles per hour in an alley, 20 miles per hour in a business district or school zone, 25 miles per hour in a residential area and 55 miles per hour on most roadways. The speed limit on portions of the Parks and Glenn highways is 65 miles per hour.

Locally, municipalities and the state may, and often do, reduce or alter maximums as long as no maximum exceeds 55 miles per hour.

SPRUCE BARK BEETLE
Spruce bark beetles are cold-blooded insect pests that feed on the trees' phloem, a thin layer of nutrient tissue just under the bark. Adults are blackish brown cylinders, about 1/4-inch long, bearing reddish or black wing covers. The range of *Dendroctonus rufipennis Kirby* extends from Alaska through British Columbia to the Pacific Northwest, into areas of Montana, Idaho and Utah, and across the northern Great Lakes states and Canada's Maritime Provinces. The beetle has a one- to three-year life cycle and will infest all spruce species.

After the mosquito, the spruce bark beetle is the most notorious insect of the north. Over the past decade the boreal forests of Alaska have endured a widespread spruce beetle outbreak. Up to 3 million acres of spruce forest show the unsightly results of beetle activity, and billions of board feet of potential lumber have been lost in Alaska during the current beetle epidemic.

Within the Municipality of Anchorage, for example, more than 80,000 acres of spruce forest have seen up to 90 percent spruce mortality blamed on beetles. On the Kenai Peninsula, cumulative spruce beetle damage has been documented from aerial surveys on more than 1.4 million acres across multiple ownership since 1990.

Because warmer, drier springs encourage beetles while simultaneously placing trees under moisture stress, the meteorological effects of El Niño and a general warming trend since the early 1990s are considered contributing factors. In turn, beetle-killed trees create a fire hazard as well as a windstorm hazard.

STATE FORESTS Created in 1983,
the 1.81-million-acre **Tanana Valley State Forest** is located almost entirely within the Tanana River basin and includes 200 miles of the Tanana River.

Principal tree species are paper birch, quaking aspen, balsam poplar, black spruce, white spruce and tamarack. There are many rivers, streams and lakes with significant fish, wildlife, recreation and water values. Nearly all of the land is open for mineral development. Rivers and trails throughout the river basin provide additional access. The Eagle Trail State Recreation Site is the only developed facility and has 40 campsites. Contact the Regional Forester, Northern Region, 3700 Airport Way, Fairbanks 99709; (907) 451-2600.

The **Haines State Forest** was created in 1982 and contains 270,410 acres, including the watersheds of several major rivers. Topography ranges from sea level to more than 7,000 feet. Forest growth is diverse, but is dominated by western

hemlock, Sitka spruce, black cottonwood and willow.

About 18 percent of the forest is dedicated to timber harvest with an annual allowable harvest of 6.96 million board feet. All logged areas have been replanted since the 1970s.

The Haines State Forest also offers recreation such as hiking, hunting, fishing, skiing and camping. Contact the Division of Forestry's Haines Area Office, P.O. Box 263, Haines 99827; (907) 766-2120.

STATE PARK SYSTEM (SEE MAP,
page 206–207) The Alaska State Park system began in July 1959 with the transfer of federally managed campgrounds and recreation sites from the Bureau of Land Management to the new state. Since October 1970, these sites have been managed by the Division of Parks and Outdoor Recreation.

The Alaska State Park system consists of a wide variety of individual units divided into seven park management areas. Included are recreation sites, recreation areas, historical parks, historic sites, state trails, state parks (Afognak Island, Chilkat, Chugach, Denali, Kachemak Bay, Point Bridget, Shuyak Island and Wood–Tikchik), marine parks, a wilderness park, special management area and a preserve.

The Kenai River Special Management Area is renowned for its salmon fishing. The 49,000-acre Alaska Chilkat Bald Eagle Preserve has the world's largest concentration of bald eagles. Wood–Tikchik State Park is Alaska's most remote state park and, with 1.6 million acres of wilderness, is the largest contiguous state park in the United States. All told, Alaska's State Park system embraces more than 3 million acres and hosts 3 million visitors a year.

Campsites are available on a first-come, first-served basis usually for $5 or $10 nightly. Fee exceptions are Eagle River Campground (Chugach State Park) and Chena River State Recreation Site for $15. Daily use of improved boat launches is $5 to $10, depending on location. Use of sanitary dump stations

Alaska ranks number three in gun-related deaths. In May, a couple called 911 in Seward to report they found a gun in a sofa they had bought TWO YEARS AGO in Anchorage. We don't have the current U.S. rankings for IQ, but we could make a pretty good guess.

is $5. These are located at Big Delta State Historical Park, Chena River State Recreation Site, Eagle River Campground (Chugach State Park), Harding Lake State Recreation Area and Ninilchick State Recreation Area. There is free use of the dump station at Buskin River State Recreation Site. A daily parking fee of $3 to $5 is charged at selected park units.

A yearly camping pass is available for $100 for residents; a yearly boat launch pass is $75; a yearly parking pass is $30. An Alaska resident may purchase all three passes for $190. A second pass of any kind may be purchased for a discount to the same resident family living at the same address. Second-pass prices are: camping, $50; boat launch, $40; daily parking, $15.

In addition to camping and picnicking, many units offer hiking trails, boating and fishing, as well as winter activities. Most developed campgrounds have picnic tables, firepits, water and latrines. General information on the state park system is available from Alaska State Park Information, 550 W. Seventh Ave., Anchorage 99501-3561.

State park units (SEE MAP on pages 206–207) are managed by seven area offices:

Chugach Area, HC 52, P.O. Box 8999, Indian 99540.

Kenai Peninsula and Prince William Sound Area, P.O. Box 1247, Soldotna 99669.

Kodiak Area, 1400 Abercrombie Drive, Kodiak 99615.

Mat–Su/Valdez–Copper River Area, HC 32, Box 6706, Wasilla 99687.

Northern Area, 3700 Airport Way, Fairbanks 99709.

Southeast Area, 400 Willoughby Building, Juneau 99801.

Southwest Area, Wood–Tikchik State Park, 550 W. Seventh Ave., Suite 1380, Anchorage 99501-3561.

STATE SYMBOLS

Flag—Alaska's state flag was designed in 1926 by Benny Benson, a seventh-grade Aleut boy who entered his design in a territorial flag contest. The Alaska Legislature adopted his design as the official flag of the Territory of Alaska on May 2, 1927.

The flag consists of eight gold stars— the Big Dipper and the North Star—on a field of blue. In Benny Benson's words, "The blue field is for the Alaska sky and the forget-me-not, an Alaska flower. The North Star is for the future state of Alaska, the most northerly of the Union. The Great Bear—symbolizing strength."

Alaska was proclaimed the 49th state of the Union on Jan. 3, 1959. The drafters of the constitution for Alaska stipulated that the flag of the territory would be the official flag of the state of Alaska. When the flag was first flown over the capital city on July 4, 1959, Benny Benson led the parade that preceded the ceremony, carrying the flag of eight stars on a field of blue, which he had designed 33 years before.

Seal—The first governor of Alaska designed a seal for the then-District of Alaska in 1884. In 1910, Gov. Walter E. Clark redesigned the original seal, which became a symbol for the new Territory of Alaska in 1912. The constitution of Alaska adopted the territorial seal as the seal for the state of Alaska in 1959.

Represented in the state seal are icebergs, northern lights, mining, agriculture, fisheries, fur seal rookeries and a railroad.

Song—
Alaska's Flag
Eight stars of gold on a field of blue—
Alaska's flag.
May it mean to you the blue of the sea, the evening sky,
The mountain lakes, and the flow'rs nearby;
The gold of the early sourdough's dreams,
The precious gold of the hills and streams;
The brilliant stars in the northern sky,
The "Bear"—the "Dipper"—and, shining high,

(Continued on page 208)

STATE PARK SYSTEM

KEY

P = Preserve
SHP = State Historical Park
SHS = State Historical Site
SMA = Special Management Area
SMP = State Marine Park
SP = State Park
SRA = State Recreation Area
SRS = State Recreation Site
ST = State Trail
WP = Wilderness Park

Bold type indicates parks with camping and/or cabins

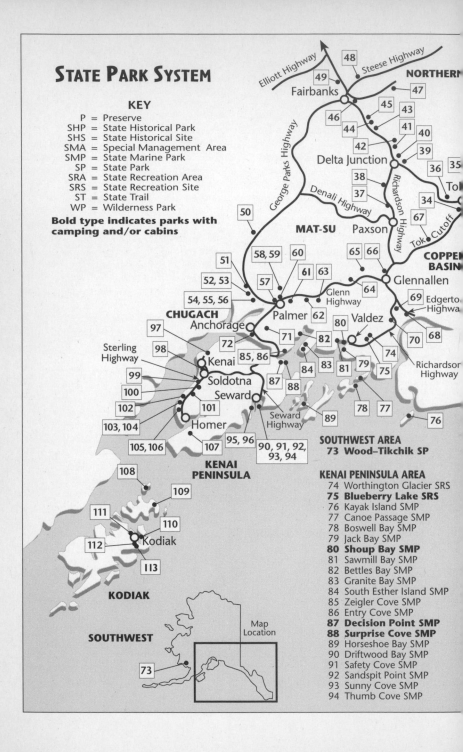

NORTHERN

Elliott Highway

48
49 Steese Highway
Fairbanks
47
45 43
46
44 41 40
42 39 36 35
Delta Junction Tol

George Parks Highway
Richardson Highway

50
38
Denali Highway 37 34
67

MAT-SU Paxson

58, 59 60
51 61 63
52, 53 57
54, 55, 56 Glenn Highway
CHUGACH
Anchorage Palmer 62
97 72
98 85, 86 71
Sterling Highway Kenai
99 Soldotna 87 88
100 Seward
102 101
103, 104 Homer Seward Highway
105, 106 107 95, 96 90, 91, 92, 93, 94

KENAI PENINSULA

108
109
111
110
112 Kodiak
113

KODIAK

65 66
64 Glennallen
80 Valdez 69 Edgerto Highwa
82 70 68
83 81 79 74
84 75 Richardson Highway
78 77
89 76

COPPER BASIN

SOUTHWEST

Map Location

73

SOUTHWEST AREA
73 **Wood–Tikchik SP**

KENAI PENINSULA AREA
74 Worthington Glacier SRS
75 **Blueberry Lake SRS**
76 Kayak Island SMP
77 Canoe Passage SMP
78 Boswell Bay SMP
79 Jack Bay SMP
80 **Shoup Bay SMP**
81 Sawmill Bay SMP
82 Bettles Bay SMP
83 Granite Bay SMP
84 South Esther Island SMP
85 Zeigler Cove SMP
86 Entry Cove SMP
87 **Decision Point SMP**
88 **Surprise Cove SMP**
89 Horseshoe Bay SMP
90 Driftwood Bay SMP
91 Safety Cove SMP
92 Sandspit Point SMP
93 Sunny Cove SMP
94 Thumb Cove SMP

SOUTHEAST AREA
1 Dall Bay SMP
2 Black Sands Beach SMP
3 Totem Bight SHP
4 Refuge Cove SRS
5 Settlers Cove SRS
6 Grindall Island SMP
7 Thom's Place SMP
8 Joe Mace Island SMP
9 Beecher Pass SMP
10 Security Bay SMP
11 Magoun Islands SMP
12 Baranof Castle SHS
13 Halibut Point SRS
14 Old Sitka SHP
15 Big Bear/Baby Bear SMP

16 Taku Harbor SMP
17 Oliver Inlet SMP
18 Funter Bay SMP
19 Shelter Island SMP
20 Juneau Trail Sys. ST
21 Johnson Creek SRS
22 Wickersham SHS
23 Gruening SHP
24 Eagle Beach SRA
25 Point Bridget SP
26 St. James Bay SMP
27 Sullivan Island SMP
28 Chilkat Islands SMP
29 Chilkat SP
30 Portage Cove SRS
31 Chilkoot Lake SRS
32 Mosquito Lake SRS
33 Chilkat Bald Eagle P

NORTHERN AREA
34 Eagle Trail SRS
35 Tok River SRS
36 Moon Lake SRS
37 Fielding Lake SRS
38 Donnelly Creek SRS
39 Clearwater SRS

40 Delta SRS
41 Big Delta SHP
42 Quartz Lake SRA
43 Birch Lake SRS
44 Harding Lake SRA
45 Salcha River SRS
46 Chena River SRS
47 Chena River SRA
48 Upper Chatanika River SRS
49 Lower Chatanika River SRA

MAT-SU/COPPER BASIN AREA
50 Denali SP
51 Willow Creek SRA
52 Nancy Lake SRA
53 Nancy Lake SRS
54 Rocky Lake SRS
55 Big Lake North SRS
56 Big Lake South SRS
57 Finger Lake SRS
58 Independence Mine SHP
59 Summit Lake SRS
60 Kepler-Bradley Lakes SRA
61 King Mountain SRS
62 Long Lake SRS
63 Matanuska Glacier SRS
64 Little Nelchina SRS
65 Lake Louise SRA
66 Dry Creek SRS
67 Porcupine Creek SRS
68 Liberty Falls SRS
69 Squirrel Creek SRS
70 Little Tonsina SRS

CHUGACH AREA
71 Chugach SP
72 Potter Section House SHS

95 **Caines Head SRA**
96 Lowell Point SRS
97 **Captain Cook SRA**
98 **Kenai River SMA**
99 **Crooked Creek SRA**
100 **Kasilof River SRS**
101 **Johnson Lake SRA**
102 **Clam Gulch SRA**
103 **Ninilchik SRA**
104 **Deep Creek SRA**
105 **Stariski SRS**
106 **Anchor River SRA**
107 **Kachemak Bay SP&WP**

KODIAK AREA
108 **Shuyak Island SP**
109 **Afognak Island SP**
110 Woody Island SRS
111 **Fort Abercrombie SHP**
112 **Buskin River SRS**
113 **Pasagshak SRS**

Alaska Highway

UNITED STATES
CANADA

Klondike Highway 2

Haines Highway

Skagway

33 32 31 30 25 24

Haines

29 28 27 26

20, 21, 22, 23

19 18 17

Juneau

16

12, 13, 14
Sitka

15

11

10

9

Wrangell

7 3, 4, 5

8

SOUTHEAST

6 2

Ketchikan

1

(Continued from page 205)

The great North Star with its steady light,
Over land and sea a beacon bright.
Alaska's flag—to Alaskans dear,
The simple flag of a last frontier.

© University of Alaska

The lyrics were written by Marie Drake as a poem that first appeared on the cover of the October 1935 *School Bulletin,* a territorial Department of Education publication that she edited while assistant commissioner of education.

The music was written by Elinor Dusenbury, whose husband, Col. Ralph Wayne Dusenbury, was commander of Chilkoot Barracks at Haines from 1933 to 1936. Elinor Dusenbury wrote the music several years after leaving Alaska because, she later said, "I got so homesick for Alaska I couldn't stand it."

The Territorial Legislature adopted "Alaska's Flag" as the official song in 1955.

Other State Symbols

Bird—Willow ptarmigan, *Lagopus lagopus,* a small arctic grouse that lives among willows and on open tundra and muskeg. Its plumage changes from brown in summer to white in winter; feathers develop in winter to cover the entire lower leg and foot. Common from Southwestern Alaska into the Arctic. Adopted in 1955.

Fish—King salmon, *Oncorhynchus tshawytscha,* an important part of the Native subsistence fisheries and a significant species to the state's commercial salmon fishery. This anadromous fish ranges from beyond the southern extremes of Alaska to as far north as Point Hope. Adopted in 1962.

Flower—Forget-me-not, *Myosotis alpestris.* Adopted in 1949.

Fossil—Woolly mammoth. Adopted in 1986.

Gem—Jade. Adopted in 1968. (See Jade)

Insect—Four-spot skimmer dragonfly. Adopted in 1995.

Land Mammal—Moose. Adopted in 1998.

Marine Mammal—Bowhead whale. Adopted in 1983. (See Whales; Whaling)

Mineral—Gold. Adopted in 1968. (See Gold)

Motto—North to the Future. Adopted in 1967.

Sport—Dog mushing. Adopted in 1972. (See Dog Mushing)

Tree—Sitka spruce, *Picea sitchensis,* the largest and one of the most valuable trees in Alaska. Sitka spruce grows to 160 feet in height and 3 feet to 5 feet in diameter. Its long, dark green needles surround twigs that bear cones. It is found throughout Southeast and the Kenai Peninsula, along the Gulf Coast, and along the west coast of Cook Inlet. Adopted in 1962. (See Timber)

SUBSISTENCE (See also Whaling)

Alaska is unique among states in that it has established the subsistence use of fish and game as the highest-priority consumptive use. Alaska's legislature passed subsistence priority laws in 1978, 1986 and 1992. In addition, Congress passed a priority subsistence law in 1980 for federal lands in Alaska. Studies by the Alaska Department of Fish and Game have shown that many rural communities in Alaska depend upon subsistence hunting and fishing for a large portion of their diets and raw materials.

Subsistence is defined by federal law as "the customary and traditional uses by rural Alaska residents of wild, renewable resources for direct personal or family consumption as food, shelter, fuel, clothing, tools or transportation; for the making and selling of handicraft articles out of nonedible by-products of fish and wildlife resources taken for personal or family consumption; and for the customary trade, barter or sharing for personal or family consumption."

About 44 million pounds of wild foods are harvested annually by residents of rural areas, and about 10 million pounds by urban residents. The wild food harvest is primarily fish (60 percent by weight), followed by land mammals (20 percent) and marine mammals (14 percent); birds, shellfish and plants each account for 2 percent of the annual harvest. On average, rural Alaskans eat about a pound of wild food per person daily.

Subsistence fishermen often dry fish along a river, then store it for winter. From *The Alaska River Guide* by Karen Jettmar.

Rural residents may hunt and fish for subsistence on federal public lands in Alaska under federal regulations. All state residents may hunt and fish for subsistence on state lands under state regulations.

State subsistence fishing regulations are available from the Alaska Department of Fish and Game, P.O. Box 25526, Juneau 99802-5526; (907) 465-4100; www.state. ak.us/adfg. State subsistence hunting regulations are included with the annually published state hunting regulations, also available from the Alaska Department of Fish and Game.

Federal subsistence hunting and fishing regulations are available as a pamphlet from U.S. Fish and Wildlife Service, Office of Subsistence Management, 1011 E. Tudor Road, Anchorage 99503; (800) 478-1456; (907) 786-3888.

SUNDOGS
Sundogs are "mock suns" (parhelia) usually seen as bright, rainbow-hued spots on opposite sides of the winter sun. This optical phenomenon is created by the refraction of sunlight through tiny ice crystals suspended in the air. The ice crystals are commonly called "diamond dust."

TAIGA
(SEE ALSO Tundra) Taiga (TIE-guh) is a moist coniferous forest that begins where the tundra ends. Taken from a Russian word that means "land of little sticks," this name is applied to the spindly white spruce and black spruce forests found in much of Southcentral and Interior Alaska.

TALKEETNA
A small town in the shadow of a very big mountain, Talkeetna is where climbers gather before making their assaults on Mount McKinley.

Located 120 miles north of Anchorage, Talkeetna sits at the confluence of the Susitna, Chulitna and Talkeetna rivers. It was established as a trading post for gold miners in 1896 and boomed during construction of the Alaska Railroad in the early 1900s.

Today many of its residents make their living by providing services to the more than 1,000 climbers who pass through the town each spring and from the fast-growing tourism industry. Local air taxis fly climbers and tourists into the Alaska Range, landing on glaciers amid the towering peaks. Guides cater to those who come for hunting, fishing and rafting.

Talkeetna's downtown is a mix of

The one-street town of Talkeetna is a favorite destination for Anchorage day-trippers. Photo by Tricia Brown.

rough-hewn log cabins and historic buildings and is listed on the National Register of Historic Places.

The town has a friendly, comfortable feel to it and residents have come up with some unusual forms of entertainment. In December, the Talkeetna Bachelor Society invites single women to prove their skills in frontier living and meet local men at the Bachelor Auction and Wilderness Woman Contest. In July the Talkeetna Historical Society holds its moose dropping festival. No, it doesn't involve dropping moose. Rather, it offers games and contests that center around the use of dried moose droppings.

> **The Central Peninsula Hospital in Soldotna rates the success of the local fishing season by how many hooks are removed from anglers' bodies in their emergency room. The 2000 season was slow—the 77 lures removed were 29 percent lower than the 1999 total of 109.**

TELECOMMUNICATIONS

History. Alaska's first telecommunications project, begun in the 1860s, was designed to serve New York, San Francisco and the capitals of Europe, not particularly the residents of Nome or Fairbanks. It was part of Western Union's ambitious plan to link California to Russian America (Alaska) with an intercontinental cable that would continue under the Bering Strait to Siberia and on to Europe. Men and material were brought together on both sides of the Bering Sea, but with the first successful Atlantic cable crossing in 1867, the trans-Siberian intercontinental line was abandoned.

The first operational telegraph link in Alaska was laid in September 1900, when 25 miles of line were stretched from military headquarters in Nome to an outpost at Port Safety. It was part of a $450,000 plan by the Army Signal Corps to connect scattered military posts in the territory with the United States. By the end of 1903, land lines linked Western Alaska, Prince William Sound, and Interior and Southeast Alaska, where underwater cable was used.

Plagued by ice floes that repeatedly tore loose the underwater cables laid across Norton Sound, the military developed wireless telegraphy to span the icy water in 1903. It was the world's first application of radio-telegraph technology and marked the completion of a fragile network connecting all military stations in Alaska with the United States. Sitka, Juneau, Haines and Valdez were connected by a line to Whitehorse, Yukon. Nome, Fort St. Michael, Fort Gibbon (Tanana) and Fort Egbert (Eagle) were linked with Dawson, Yukon. A line from Dawson to Whitehorse continued to Vancouver, British Columbia, and Seattle.

In 1905, the 1,500 miles of land lines, 2,000 miles of submarine cables and the 107-mile wireless link became the Washington–Alaska Military Cable and Telegraph System. This, in turn, became the Alaska Communications System in 1935, reflecting a shift to greater civilian use and a system relying more heavily on wireless stations than land lines. The Alaska Communications System operated under the Department of Defense until RCA Corp., through its division RCA Alascom, took control in 1971.

Alaska Communications Systems.

ACS was founded in 1998 by former telecommunications executives of Alascom and Pacific Telecom. ACS has a nearly 500-mile fiber-optic network. The company is the primary provider of both fixed-line and mobile telephone service in Alaska. It operates more than 325,000 access lines and has more than 75,000 cellular subscribers, providing business, government and residential subscribers with long distance, local, wireless, data, network and Internet services.

ACS companies provide communications services to three-fourths of the state's population, serving residents in 74 communities, including the population centers of Anchorage, Fairbanks, Juneau, Kenai/Soldotna, Kodiak and Sitka. It is a publicly traded company, with headquarters in Anchorage.

AT&T Alascom.
Headquartered in Anchorage, AT&T Alascom is a wholly owned subsidiary of AT&T and employs about 400 people statewide.

What is now AT&T Alascom evolved from the Washington–Alaska Military Cable and Telegraph System of the early years of the 20th century.

On Oct. 27, 1982, Alascom launched its own telecommunications satellite, *Aurora I*, into orbit from Cape Canaveral, Fla. It was the first telecommunications satellite dedicated to a single state, and it was the first completely solid-state satellite to be placed in orbit.

In 1991, Alascom launched *Aurora II* from Cape Canaveral to replace the original *Aurora*. The newer satellite uses similar design, updated with modern technology to increase life span. AT&T launched *Aurora III* on Dec. 19, 2000.

As a certified long lines carrier for the state of Alaska, AT&T Alascom provides interstate and intrastate long-distance

NUGGETS

As of 1984, a typical long-distance telephone call from Alaska to points in the Lower 49 states may travel more than 100,000 miles in what engineers call a "double-hop"—a signal from a village to the telecommunications satellite *Aurora*, back to toll facilities in Fairbanks, Juneau or Anchorage, again up to *Aurora*, and finally to Lower 49 receiving stations.
—1985 *The ALASKA ALMANAC®*

telephone service as well as local service in the Anchorage area. The services include AT&T WorldNet service, high-speed data services, and live radio and television broadcast transmissions. The company has installed more than 200 satellite earth stations throughout the state.

AT&T Alascom designed and built the Rapid Deployment Earth Station, an air-transportable, self-contained mobile earth station. The station was used for emergency communications in Puerto Rico in the aftermath of Hurricane Hugo, for operations Desert Shield and Desert Storm in Saudi Arabia and Kuwait, and in other critical situations.

General Communication Inc.

Founded in 1979, GCI is an Alaska-based company offering voice, video and data communication services to more than 180,000 residential, commercial and government customers statewide.

In 1999 the company took delivery of its $125 million, 2,331-mile fiber-optic cable connecting Anchorage, Fairbanks and Juneau with the Lower 48.

The company said that in spring 2000, it was Alaska's largest Internet service provider with more than 65,000 dial-up, cable modem and digital subscriber line customers.

GCI completed its first long-distance call on Thanksgiving Day 1982; two years later, it filed an antitrust lawsuit against the then-dominant long-distance carrier, Alascom (a precursor to today's AT&T Alascom.) Litigation was settled in 1988; GCI received a payment of $27.5 million and in 1991 purchased capacity on the only fiber-optic cable linking Alaska with foreign countries and the contiguous United States.

GCI allied with long-distance carrier MCI Communications in 1993 to access MCI's global network. In 1995, GCI purchased a license to provide personal communication services statewide. GCI, a publicly traded company, has been the official communication sponsor of the Iditarod Trail Sled Dog race since 1994.

TELEPHONE NUMBERS IN THE BUSH

Although most Alaska Bush communities now have full telephone service, a handful of villages still have only one telephone. For those villages, call the information number, 555-1212. The area code for all of Alaska is 907.

The situation today is quite different from 1979, when RCA Alaska Communications reported that of the 291 communities it then served, 140 had only a single phone monitored by an operator.

TELEVISION STATIONS

Television in Anchorage and Fairbanks was available years before satellites were sent into orbit. The first satellite broadcast to the state was Neil Armstrong's moon walk in July 1969. Television reached the Bush in the late 1970s with the construction of telephone earth stations that could receive television programming via satellite transmissions. The state funds Alaska Rural Communication Service (ARCS), which broadcasts general and educational programming to over 200 rural communities. For more information about ARCS, contact the Department of Administration, Information Services,

5900 E. Tudor Road, Anchorage 99507; (907) 269-5744.

Regular network programming (ABC, CBS, NBC and PBS) on a time-delayed basis is provided through the RATNet system. Most of the stations listed here carry a mixture of network programming, with local broadcasters specifying programming. Some stations, such as KJNP, carry locally produced programming. Cable television is available in areas throughout Alaska.

The following list shows the commercial and public television stations in Alaska:

Anchorage. KAKM Channel 7 (public television); 3877 University Drive, 99508.
KCFT (UHF 20/Cable 20); P.O. Box 210830, 99521.
KDMD (Prime Cable 33); 1310 E. 66th Ave., 99518.
KIMO Channel 13; 2700 E. Tudor Road, 99507.
KTBY Channel 4; 440 E. Benson, Suite 1, 99503.
KTUU Channel 2; 701 E. Tudor Road, Suite 220, 99503.
KTVA Channel 11; 1007 W. 32nd Ave., 99503.
KYES Channel 5; 3700 Woodland Park Drive, Suite 800, 99517.

Bethel. KYUK Channel 4 (public television); Pouch 468, 99559.

Fairbanks. KATN Channel 2; 516 Second Ave., Suite 400, 99701.
KDMD-LP Channel 18; 1010 College Road, 99701.
KFXF Channel 7; 3650 Braddock St., Suite 2, 99701.
KTVF Channel 11; 3528 International Way, 99701.
KUAC Channel 9 (public television); University of Alaska, P.O. Box 755620, 99775-5620.
KXD Channel 13; 3650 Braddock St., No. 2, 99701.

Juneau. KATH Channel 5; 1107 Eighth St., 99801.
KJUD Channel 8; 175 S. Franklin St., 99801.

KTOO Channel 3 (public television); 360 Egan Drive, 99801.

Ketchikan.
KJMW (Cable 3); 501 Dock St., 99901.
KUBD Channel 4; 516 Stedman St., 99901.

Kodiak. KMXT Channel 9 (independent); 620 Egan Way, 99615.

North Pole. KJNP Channel 4; P.O. Box 56359, 99705.

Sitka. KSCT Channel 5; 520 Lake St., 99835.
KTNL Channel 13; 520 Lake St., 99835.

Unalaska. KO8IW Channel 8 (independent); P.O. Box 181, 99685.

TIDES (See also Bore Tide)

In southeastern Alaska, Prince William Sound, Cook Inlet and Bristol Bay, salt water undergoes extreme daily fluctuations, creating powerful tidal currents. Some bays may go totally dry at low tide.

The second greatest tide range in North America occurs in upper Cook Inlet near Anchorage, where the maximum diurnal range during spring tides is 38.9 feet. (The greatest tide range in North America is at Nova Scotia's Bay of Fundy, with spring tides over 50 feet.)

Here are diurnal ranges for some coastal communities: Bethel, 4 feet; Cold Bay, 7.1 feet; Cordova, 12.4 feet; Haines, 16.8 feet; Herschel Island, 0.7 feet; Ketchikan, 15.4 feet; Kodiak, 8.5 feet; Naknek River entrance, 22.6 feet; Nikiski, 20.7 feet; Nome, 1.6 feet; Nushagak, 19.6 feet; Point Barrow, 0.4 feet; Port Heiden, 12.3 feet; Port Moller, 10.8 feet; Sand Point, 7.3 feet; Sitka, 9.9 feet; Valdez, 12 feet; Whittier, 12.3 feet; Wrangell, 15.7 feet; Yakutat, 10.1 feet.

TIMBER (See also Spruce Bark Beetle)

According to the U.S. Forest Service, 127 million acres of Alaska's 365 million acres of land surface are forested, 12 million acres of which are classified as timberland. Timberland is forest land capable of producing in excess of 20 cubic feet of industrial wood an acre a year in natural stands and not withdrawn from timber utilization.

Alaska has two distinct forest ecosystems: the Interior forest and the coastal rain forest. The vast Interior forest covers 114 million acres, extending from the south slope of the Brooks Range to the Kenai Peninsula, and from Canada to Norton Sound. More than 7 million acres of white spruce, paper birch, quaking aspen, black cottonwood and balsam poplar stands are considered timberland, comparing favorably in size and growth with forests of the lake states of Minnesota, Wisconsin and Michigan. There are an additional 2.8 million acres capable of producing as timberland but are unavailable for harvest because they are in parks or wilderness.

The Interior region's remoteness from large markets has limited timber use to approximately 20 sawmills, with most cutting less than 300,000 board feet a year. There are some exports of sawlogs, cants and chips.

The coastal rain forests extend from Cook Inlet to the Alaska–Canada border south of Ketchikan, and they continue to provide the bulk of commercial timber volume in Alaska. Of the 13.9 million acres of forested land, 5 million acres are classified as timberland. Under the management plan for the Tongass National Forest in southeastern

Alaska, only 576,000 acres were available for harvest, and a federal roadless policy could reduce that to 311,000. An additional 2.6 million acres of timber stands are capable of producing more than 20 cubic feet an acre a year, but are in parks and wilderness.

Western hemlock and Sitka spruce provide most of the timber harvest for domestic and export lumber and pulp markets. Western red cedar and Alaska cedar make up most of the balance, along with mountain hemlock, lodgepole pine and other species.

Lands from which substantial volumes of timber are harvested are divided into two distinct categories: privately owned by Native corporations and villages under the 1971 Native Claims Settlement Act, and publicly owned and managed federal, state and borough lands. Timber harvests from publicly owned lands are carried through short-term open sales and Small Business Administration set-aside sales.

The forest products of Alaska are also divided somewhat along the same lines as land ownership. By federal law, timber harvested from federal lands cannot be exported without processing. While processors dependent on federal lands produce primarily rough-sawn lumber, pulpwood, veneer, railroad ties and chips, the Native corporations primarily produce round logs, which find more buyers along the Pacific Rim, especially Japan. The Alaska forest products industry is almost entirely dependent on the Japanese market, and the processing requirement has had considerable effect on some sections of the forest industry.

Small sawmills are scattered throughout Southeast Alaska. The larger mills in coastal Alaska are located at Hoonah, Klawock, Wrangell, Ketchikan, Ninilchik/Anchor Point and Metlakatla, all of which were operating at less than 50 percent of capacity.

In 2000, approximately 15.2 million board feet of timber were harvested from state lands. The harvest from federal lands totaled 136 million board feet in 2000. The Alaska Forest Association reports that at least 104 million board feet were harvested in Southeast Alaska that year off private lands. For additional timber information, see the Web site of the forest industry, www.akforest.org; the state, www.dnr.state.ak.us/forestry; and the federal government, www.fs.fed.us/r10.

TIME ZONES More than 90 percent of Alaska residents are on Alaska time, one hour behind the West Coast (Pacific time). The far reaches of the Aleutian Islands and St. Lawrence Island observe Hawaii–Aleutian time, two hours behind Pacific time.

Until 1983, Alaska had four time zones: Pacific time (in southeastern Alaska); Yukon time (in Yakutat); Alaska time (from just east of Cold Bay and west of Yakutat northward, including Nome); and Bering time (including Nome, far Western Alaska and the Aleutians). Consolidating these time zones aided business and improved communications.

TOTEMS (See also Native Arts and Crafts; Potlatch) In the prehistory of southeastern Alaska and the Pacific Northwest coast, the Native way of life was based on the rich natural resources of the land, respect for living things and a unique and complex social structure. Totemic art reflects this rich culture.

Carved from the huge cedar trees of the northern coast, totem poles are a traditional art form among the Natives of the Pacific Northwest and southeastern Alaska. Although the best-known type of

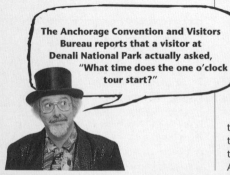

The Anchorage Convention and Visitors Bureau reports that a visitor at Denali National Park actually asked, "What time does the one o'clock tour start?"

totem pole is tall and freestanding, totemic art also is applied to house frontal poles, house posts and mortuary poles. Totem poles are bold statements that make public records of the lives and history of the people who had them carved; they represent pride in clans and ancestors.

Animals of the region are most often represented on the poles. Commonly depicted are eagles, ravens, frogs, bears, beavers, wolves and whales. Also represented are figures from Native mythology: monsters with animal features, humanlike spirits and legendary ancestors. Occasionally included are objects, devices, masks and charms and, more rarely, art illustrating plants and celestial phenomena.

The poles were traditionally painted with natural mineral and vegetable pigments. Salmon eggs were chewed with cedar bark to form the binder for the ground pigment. Traditional colors are black, white and red-brown; green, blue-green, blue and yellow are also used, depending on tribal convention. The range of colors broadened when modern paints became available. Totem art grew rapidly in the late 18th century, with the introduction of steel European tools acquired from

Tlingit totem pole, Sitka. Alaska Division of Tourism.

NUGGETS

Residents of Klawock, a tiny Southeast Alaska community, renewed their ancestral ways by raising the town's first totem pole in 50 years. More than 800 people and 17 Native dance groups, from Haines to Metlakatla, participated in the pole-raising ceremony in June 1991. The pole was carved by Israel Shotridge of Ketchikan through a $20,000 grant from the U.S. Forest Service.
—1991 *The ALASKA ALMANAC®*

explorers and through the fur trade. Large totem poles were a thriving cultural feature by the 1830s and signified social standing. For example, wealthy Tlingit often commissioned the Tsimshian to carve totems for them.

Totem pole carving almost died out between the 1880s and 1950s during the enforcement of a law forbidding the potlatch, the core of Northwest Coast Indian culture. The potlatch ceremony is held to observe events such as marriages; guests are invited from near and far, dancing and feasting take place, property is given away and often poles are raised to commemorate the event. Since the anti-potlatching law was repealed in 1951, a revival of Native culture and the arts has taken place, and many tribes are actively carving and raising poles again. (SEE Potlatch)

Totem poles were left to stand as long as nature would permit, usually about 50 to 60 years. Once a pole became so rotten that it fell, it was left to decay naturally or used for firewood. Some totem poles still standing in parks today are 40 to 50 years old. Heavy precipitation and acid muskeg soils hasten decomposition even though cedar is resistant to decay.

Collections of fine totem poles may be

Most Visited Tourist Attractions–2000

Indicates percentage of all state visitors to attractions.

1. Inside Passage		46%
2. Portage Glacier		44%
3. Mendenhall Glacier		40%
3. Ketchikan Totems		40%
4. Denali/McKinley		36%
5. Skagway Gold Rush District		35%
6. Glacier Bay		31%
7. Anchorage Museum		26%
8. Trans-Alaska Pipeline		24%
9. Sitka's Russian Church		22%
Tied:		
10. University of Alaska Museum		20%
10. Sitka National Historical Park		20%
10. Prince William Sound		20%
10. Kenai River		20%

—Ranked by the *Alaska Journal of Commerce, 2001 Book of Lists*

seen either outdoors or in museums in several Alaska communities including Ketchikan, Wrangell, Hydaburg and Sitka. Carvers practice their art at cultural centers in those towns as well as in Haines and Saxman.

TOURISM Although Alaska has been attracting tourists for more than 100 years, residents sometimes are surprised that the visitor industry has quietly become the state's second-largest primary employer. The visitor industry employs more than 20,000 Alaskans directly during peak seasons and affects some 10,000 other Alaskan jobs. More than 2,500 businesses in Alaska derive most of their income from visitor sales. Tourism is a renewable resource that brings dollars to all regions of Alaska. The visitor industry generates more than $2.6 billion in revenues each year and is expected to continue to grow.

The state of Alaska has long recognized the value of the visitor industry. For fiscal 2002, the Alaska Department of Community and Economic Development's projected tourism budget is $5.6 million. The department contracts with the Alaska Travel Industry Association to provide tourism marketing services. Of that $5.6 million, $4.5 million is budgeted to the association for domestic and international marketing. The legislature allocates these monies to promote Alaska as a visitor destination.

Alaska welcomed more than 1.4 million visitors between October 1998 and September 1999. Visitors spend nearly $1 billion annually in Alaska, or about $770 per person.

The largest portion of Alaska visitors in 1999, the most recent year for which statistics were available, came from the United States and Canada, while overseas travelers represented about 6 percent of visitors. The most popular modes of entry for visitors were domestic air (47.2 percent), cruise ships (38.1 percent), personal vehicles (8.9 percent) and the ferry system (1.7 percent). The remainder arrived by international air (1.8 percent), motor coach tours (.3 percent) and other means, such as private vessels, private aircraft or commercial trucks (2.0 percent).

Alaska's scenic beauty, trophy fish, abundant wildlife and unique history remain its biggest attractions. The adventure travel market is growing in Alaska; an increasing number of visitors participate in river rafting, kayaking, backcountry trekking and other wilderness experiences.

Further information is available from the Division of Tourism, www.dced.state.ak.us/tourism/sources/visinfo.htm; and from the Alaska Travel Industry Association, www.alaskatia.org.

TREES AND SHRUBS (SEE ALSO Spruce Bark Beetle) According to the U.S.

A Fallen 'Giant'

For more than 20 years, a single white spruce stood five miles from town in the treeless tundra of the Baldwin Peninsula. Rumored to have been planted by homesick Air Force personnel from a nearby base, the tree was surrounded by a white picket fence and a sign designating the tree the "Kotzebue National Forest."

In June 1993, the tree was pushed over after it had been partially cut by vandals, leaving only a stump.

A radio broadcast about the felling caught the attention of Matt Tyrala of Anchorage, executive director of Alaska TREES (Tree Recycling and Ecology Education Systems). Tyrala arranged to have a 10-year-old, 6-foot replacement white spruce shipped free from Nenana by Alaska Airlines—a gift worth $2,000 for pining Kotzebue residents. The previous "forest" had been just 3 feet tall.

—1994 *The ALASKA ALMANAC®*

Department of Agriculture, the number of native tree species in Alaska is less than in any other state. Species of trees and shrubs in Alaska fall under the following families: yew, pine, cypress, willow, bayberry, birch, mistletoe, gooseberry, rose, maple, elaeagnus, ginseng, dogwood, crowberry, pyrola, heath, dispensia, honeysuckle and composite.

Commercial timber species include white spruce, Sitka spruce, western hemlock, mountain hemlock, western red cedar, Alaska cedar, balsam poplar, black cottonwood, quaking aspen and paper birch.

Rare tree species include the Pacific yew, Pacific silver fir, subalpine fir, silver willow and Hooker willow.

TUNDRA Characteristic of arctic and subarctic regions, tundra is a treeless plain that consists of moisture-retaining soils and permanently frozen subsoil. Tundra climates, marked by frequent winds and low temperatures, are harsh on plants. Soils freeze around root systems and winds wear away portions exposed above rocks and snow. The three distinct types of Alaska tundra—wet, moist and alpine—support low-growing vegetation that includes a variety of delicate flowers, mosses and lichens.

According to *Alaska Science Nuggets,* every acre of arctic tundra contains more than 2 tons of live fungi that survive by feeding on dead organic matter. Since the recession of North Slope ice age glaciers 12,000 years ago, a vegetative residue has accumulated a layer of peat 3 feet to 6 feet thick overlying the tundra.

ULU A traditional Eskimo woman's knife designed for scraping and chopping, this fan-shaped tool was originally made of stone with a bone handle.

North of the Brooks Range, the tundra-covered land slopes gently toward the Arctic Ocean. Photo by Tricia Brown.

Today, an ulu is often shaped from an old saw blade and a wood handle is attached. The term derives from the Yup'ik word *uluaq* and the Siberian Yup'ik word *ulaaq*.

UMIAK (SEE ALSO Baidarka) The Eskimo
umiak is a traditional skin-covered boat whose design has changed little over the centuries. Although *umiaks* are mostly powered by outboard motors today, paddles are still used when stalking game and when ice might damage a propeller. Because *umiaks* must often be pulled long distances over pack ice, the boats are lightweight and easily repaired. The frames are wood, often driftwood found on beaches, and the covering can be sewn if punctured. The bottom is flat and the keel is bone, which prevents the skin from wearing out as it is pulled over the ice.

Female walrus skins are the preferred covering because they are the proper thickness when split (bull hides are too thick and often scarred) and because it takes only two skins to cover a boat. Sometimes female walrus skins are unavailable, so skins of the bearded seal, or *oogruk,* may be used. It may take six or seven skins to cover an *umiak.*

Umiak is the Inupiat word for skin boat and is commonly used by the coastal Eskimos throughout Alaska. St. Lawrence Islanders speak the Yup'ik dialect and their word for skin boat is *angyaq.*

UNALASKA/DUTCH HARBOR (SEE ALSO Military; World War II)
Located on Unalaska Island, the second-largest island in the Aleutian chain and 800 miles southwest of Anchorage, Ounalashka, or Unalaska, was the Russian-American Company's headquarters for the sea otter fur trade in the 1700s. At the turn of the century, Unalaska was a major stop for ships heading to and from the Nome goldfields.

The international port of Dutch Harbor is located across a bridge from Unalaska on Amaknak Island. The U.S. Army and Navy began building installations there in 1939; in June 1942 the area was bombed by the Japanese and most of the local Aleut people were evacuated. A memorial to those killed in the Aleutians in World War II is in Memorial Park near the cemetery.

Unalaska/Dutch Harbor is a significant port and gateway to the Bering Sea region. The climate is referred to as the "Cradle of the Storms." Here the warm Japan Current meets the colder air and water currents of the Bering Sea, creating an annual rainfall of 60.5 inches and colossal winds. Rare plants and birds and the historic Cathedral of the Holy Ascension of Christ draw visitors to the island. The Unalaska/Dutch Harbor area remains ice-free year-round and large canneries form the basis of the local economy, making it one of the most productive seafood processing ports in the United States.

UNIVERSITIES AND COLLEGES Higher education in Alaska
may be achieved through the University of Alaska system and private institutions. The university system includes three regional multicampus universities, one community college and a network of services for rural Alaska. The three regional institutions are the University of Alaska Anchorage (UAA), the University of Alaska Fairbanks (UAF) and the University of Alaska Southeast (UAS). University of Alaska institutions enrolled 30,249 students in 1999.

Campuses of the University of Alaska Southeast are located in Juneau, Sitka

The University of Alaska Anchorage campus has 16 acres of roof, 17 acres of lawn, 26 acres of interior floor space, 46 acres of pavement, and uses 80 acres of toilet paper each year.

and Ketchikan. The main University of Alaska Anchorage campus in that city is supplemented by a network of extended schools that includes Kenai Peninsula College, Kodiak College, Matanuska–Susitna College and Prince William Sound Community College, as well as the Chugiak–Eagle River Campus, a branch campus in Kachemak Bay and several military centers.

University of Alaska Anchorage units include the Center for Alcohol and Addiction Studies; Center for Economic Development; Center for Economic Education; Center for Human Development, University Affiliated Program; Environment and Natural Resources Institute, which includes the Alaska Natural Heritage Program, Alaska State Climate Center and the Arctic Environment and Natural Resources Institute; Institute for Circumpolar Health Studies; Institute of Social and Economic Research; and the Justice Center.

University of Alaska Fairbanks includes the main campus in Fairbanks; Bristol Bay Campus in Dillingham; Chukchi Campus in Kotzebue; Interior Campus with offices in Fairbanks and centers in Fort Yukon, McGrath, Tok and Unalaska; Kuskokwim Campus in Bethel; Northwest Campus in Nome; and Tanana Valley Campus in downtown Fairbanks.

University of Alaska Fairbanks research facilities include the Alaska Cooperative Fishery and Wildlife Research Unit; Alaska Native Language Center; Alaska Synthetic Aperture Radar Facility; Arctic Region Supercomputing Center; Center for Cross-Cultural Studies; Center for Global Change and Arctic Systems Research; Consortium for Research in Rural Alaska; Environmental Technology Laboratory; Fishery Industrial Technology Center; Forest Products Technology Center; Forest Soils Laboratory; Geophysical Institute; Georgeson Botanical Garden; Institute of Arctic Biology; Institute of Marine Science; Institute of Northern Engineering; Juneau Center for Fisheries and Ocean Sciences; Large Animal Research Station; Mineral Industry Resource Laboratory; Petroleum Development Laboratory; Poker Flat Research Range; Polar Ice Coring Office; Seismology Laboratory; Transportation Research Center; University of Alaska Museum; Water Research Center; and West Coast National Undersea Research Center.

The Alaska Cooperative Extension and the Alaska Sea Grant College Program interpret and report some of the university's research results to the residents of Alaska.

For more information:
University of Alaska Anchorage, 3211 Providence Drive, Anchorage 99508, www.uaa.alaska.edu; **Kenai Peninsula College,** 34820 College Drive, Soldotna 99669, www.uaa.alaska.edu/kenai; **Kodiak College,** 117 Benny Benson Drive, Kodiak 99615, www.koc.alaska.edu; **Matanuska–Susitna College,** P.O. Box 2889, Palmer 99645, www.matsu.alaska.edu/matsu; **Prince William Sound Community College,** P.O. Box 97, Valdez 99686, www.uaa.alaska.edu/pwscc.

University of Alaska Fairbanks, P.O. Box 757520, Fairbanks 99775, www.uaf.edu; **Bristol Bay Campus,** P.O. Box 1070, Dillingham 99576, www.uaf.edu/bbc; **Chukchi Campus,** P.O. Box 297, Kotzebue 99752-0297, www.beringia.chukchi.alaska.edu; **College of Rural Alaska,** P.O. Box 75672, University of Alaska Fairbanks, Fairbanks 99775-6720; www.uaf.edu/UAF/CRA.html; **Interior Aleutians Campus,** Box 248, Unalaska 99685,www.iac.uaf.edu; **Kuskokwim Campus,** P.O. Box 368, Bethel 99559, www.kuskokwim.bethel.alaska.edu; **Northwest Campus,** Pouch 400, Nome 99762, www.anvil.nome.alaska.edu; **Tanana Valley Campus,** P.O. Box 757495, Fairbanks 99775, www.uaf.edu/tvc/index.html.

University of Alaska Southeast, Juneau Campus, 11120 Glacier Highway, Juneau 99801, www.uas.alaska.edu; **Ketchikan Campus,** 2600 Seventh St., Ketchikan 99901, ketch.alaska.edu; **Sitka Campus,** 1332 Seward Ave., Sitka 99835, geocities.com/CollegePark/Campus/1909.

For information on private institutions of higher learning:

Alaska Bible College, P.O. Box 289, Glennallen 99588.

Alaska Pacific University, 4101 University Drive, Anchorage 99508.

Sheldon Jackson College, 801 Lincoln St., Sitka 99835.

Many other schools and institutes in Alaska offer religious, vocational and technical study. For a listing of these and other schools, write for the *Directory of Postsecondary Educational Institutions in Alaska,* Alaska Commission on Postsecondary Education, 3030 Vintage Blvd., Juneau 99801-7109.

VENIAMINOV, IOANN Father

Ioann (Ivan Popov) Veniaminov (1797–1879) often has been called "Paul Bunyan in a cassock." A figure of commanding height and proportions, a linguistic genius who could build furniture and clocks with his own hands, Veniaminov was a central figure in early efforts to convert Alaska's Native population to the Russian way of life through Orthodoxy.

Veniaminov was a Russian Orthodox priest who served as a missionary in the Aleutians and in Southeast Alaska. In each place, he learned the local language and devised a written alphabet for the local Native group, allowing him to translate some books of the Bible. In the Aleutians he traveled thousands of miles by kayak to visit his enormous parish. He rose to become Bishop of Russian America, with his headquarters at Sitka, and eventually was appointed Metropolitan of Moscow. His writings on Aleut language and ethnology are still standard references. A volcano on the Aleutian Peninsula is named after him. As Saint Innocent, Veniaminov is one of the four Orthodox saints of Alaska.

VOLCANOES (See map, pages

126–127) Volcanoes on the Aleutian Islands, on the Alaska Peninsula and in the Wrangell Mountains are part of the "Ring of Fire" that surrounds the Pacific Ocean basin. More than 80 potentially active volcanoes dot Alaska, about half of which have had at least one blast since 1760, the date of the earliest written record of eruptions.

Pavlof Volcano, in the Aleutian Range, is one of the most active of Alaska volcanoes, having had more than 40 reported eruptions since 1790. A spectacular eruption of Pavlof in April 1986 sent ash 10 miles high, causing black snow to fall on Cold Bay; it remained active through August 1988, producing lava and mud flows. The March 27, 1986, eruption of Augustine Volcano (4,025 feet) in lower Cook Inlet sent ash 8 miles high and disrupted air traffic in Southcentral Alaska for several days.

Southcentral's Mount Redoubt erupted Dec. 14, 1989, its first eruption since 1968. The biggest blasts sent ash throughout

Midnight at Midday

Anchorage received the brunt of ash fallout when Mount Spurr erupted for the second time in the summer of 1992, sending an ash plume 60,000 feet into the air, halting air traffic out of Anchorage and raining ash from the Matanuska Valley to Yakutat in Southeast Alaska. Visibility in Anchorage during the ashfall was almost zero, hampering traffic and burying the city in up to a quarter-inch of the stuff. Air filters and surgical masks were out of supply in a matter of hours. Three thousand weary travelers were stranded at Anchorage International Airport. Like Mount Spurr's earlier eruption on June 27, the event of Aug. 18 came with almost no warning.

—1992 *The ALASKA ALMANAC®*

most of Southcentral Alaska and disrupted air traffic. This eruption continued until April 1990. Mount Spurr erupted in June, August and September 1992. Anchorage received the brunt of ash fallout from the August eruption, which halted air traffic out of the city for several days. Flights were briefly interrupted again during the September eruption.

The most violent Alaska eruption recorded occurred over a 60-hour period in June 1912 from Novarupta Volcano. The eruption darkened the sky over much of the Northern Hemisphere for several days, deposited almost a foot of ash on Kodiak, 100 miles away, and filled the Valley of Ten Thousand Smokes (within Katmai National Park) with more than 2.5 cubic miles of ash during its brief but extremely explosive duration.

More than 10 percent of the world's known volcanoes are in Alaska. A chain of volcanoes arcing along the Aleutians contains at least 60 centers that have erupted in historic times; 40 of these volcanoes have been active since 1700.

About 1600 B.C.—Hayes Volcano destroys itself in seven eruptions within 100 years, each eruption producing as much ash as the 1980 eruption of Mount St. Helens.

1779—Bogoslof group begins to rise from the Bering Sea

1796—Bogoslof rises again

1812—Augustine Volcano; Peulik

1883—Fire Island, another member of the Bogoslofs, appears; Augustine Volcano

1908—Augustine Volcano

1909—Bogoslof group

1912—Katmai

1927—Mount Spurr

1929—Chiginagak

1931—The Bogoslof group; Aniakchak Caldera

1935—Augustine Volcano

1953—Mount Spurr

1963–64—Augustine Volcano

1975—Trident

1976—Augustine Volcano

1977—Ukinrek Maars

1980—Makushin

Mount Augustine's 1986 eruption halted air traffic. Photo by B. Young, USGS, courtesy Alaska Volcano Observatory. From *Alaska's Natural Wonders* by Robert H. Armstrong and Marge Hermans.

1986—Augustine Volcano

1986–88—Pavlof

1988—Shishaldin

1989–90—Mount Redoubt

1990—Kiska

1992—Mount Spurr

WAVES (See also Bore Tide; Earthquakes; Tides)

Alaska's recorded seismic history is very short yet extremely active. Alaska responds to movement in the Aleutian–Alaska megathrust zone, where the edge of the Pacific plate descends under the North American plate. These vertical movements of the earth's crust result in vertical motion of the seafloor, which can produce great seismic waves known as tsunamis. In fact, these crustal movements in the Alaska Peninsula, Aleutians and Gulf of Alaska can produce Pacific-wide tsunamis.

In southeastern Alaska, the Fairweather Fault lies inland. Though this fault has not triggered tectonic tsunamis as in other Alaska areas, it can unleash nearby underwater landslides, which may cause tsunamis.

According to the Alaska Tsunami Warning Center in Palmer, Alaska has had seven tsunamis that caused fatalities in recorded history. These were of local origin and occurred between 1788 and 1964. Tsunamis originating in Alaska Pacific waters have caused all of the fatalities reported on the West Coast and in Alaska, and most of those in Hawaii. The most recent damaging tsunami was in 1964 following the March 27 Good Friday earthquake. That wave destroyed three Alaska villages before reaching Washington, Oregon and California, and continued to cause damage as far away as Hawaii, Chile and Japan.

The word tsunami is taken from the Japanese words *tsu,* meaning "harbor," and *nami,* meaning "great wave." Often called tidal waves, tsunamis are not caused by tides. Generated by earthquakes occurring on or below the seafloor, tsunamis can race across the Pacific Ocean at speeds of up to 600 miles per hour. Tsunamis rarely cross the Atlantic. Traveling across the open ocean, the waves are only a few feet high and can be up to 100 miles from crest to crest. They cannot be seen from an airplane or felt in a ship at sea. Once they approach shore, however, shallower water causes the waves to grow taller by increasingly restricting their forward motion. Thus, a 2-foot wave traveling 500 miles per hour in deep water becomes a 100-foot killer at 30 miles per hour as it nears the shore. The wave action of a tsunami can repeat every 15 to 30 minutes, and the danger for a given area is generally not considered over until the area has been free from damaging waves for two hours.

Another type of wave action that occurs in Alaska is a seiche. A seiche is a long, rhythmic wave in a closed or partially closed body of water. Caused by earthquakes, winds, tidal currents or atmospheric pressure, the motion of a seiche resembles the back and forth movement of a tipped bowl of water. The water moves only up and down, and can remain active from a few minutes to several hours. The highest recorded wave in Alaska, 1,740 feet, was the result of a seiche that took place in Lituya Bay on July 9, 1958. This unusually high wave was caused by an earthquake-induced landslide that stripped trees from the opposite side of the bay.

More information about earthquakes and tsunamis is available from the Alaska Tsunami Warning Center at www.wcatwc.gov.

WEATHER (See Climate)

WHALES (See also Baleen; Whaling) Fifteen species of both toothed and baleen whales are found in Alaska waters.

Toothed whales include sperm, beluga, orca (or killer whale), pilot, beaked (three species), dolphins (two species) and porpoises (two species). Another toothed whale, the narwhal, a full-time resident of the arctic region, is almost never seen in Alaska waters. St. Lawrence Islanders call narwhals *bousucktugutalik,* or "beluga with tusk," due to a tusk that grows from the left side of the upper jaw on bulls only. Spiraling in a left-hand direction, the tusk can reach lengths up to 8 feet on an adult.

Baleen whales that inhabit Alaska waters include gray, bowhead, blue, northern right, fin (or finback), humpback, minke (or little piked) and sei. Baleen refers to the hundreds of strips of flexible fingernail-like material that hang from the gum of the upper jaw. The strips are fringed and act as strainers that capture krill—tiny shrimplike organisms—as well as other prey upon which whales feed. Once the baleen fills with prey, whales force water back out through the sides of their mouth, swallowing the food left behind. Baleen whale females are usually larger than males.

Gray Whales. According to the Alaska Department of Fish and Game, gray whales have the distinction of being the most primitive of the living *mysticete* ("moustached") or baleen whales. They can regularly be observed in large numbers from Alaska shores, and are found in the North Pacific Ocean and adjacent waters of the Arctic Ocean. There are two geographically isolated stocks: the Korean or western Pacific stock, and the California or eastern Pacific stock. The California stock migrates between Baja California and the Bering and Chukchi seas, a round-trip of 10,000 miles, the longest migration of any marine mammal.

Grays are mottled gray in color and covered with scars, abrasions and clusters of parasitic barnacles that are most abundant on their heads and backs, the parts exposed to air when the animals breathe.

The estimated daily consumption of an adult gray whale is about 2,600 pounds. In the approximately five months spent in Alaska waters, one whale eats about 396,000 pounds of food, primarily amphipod crustaceans. Gray whales feed on the bottom by sucking tube-dwelling amphipods out of the sandy sediment and leaving large oval feeding imprints behind. Scientists can study these imprints and gain knowledge about feeding habits. Muddy feeding trails are often seen when gray whales surface after feeding dives. Gray whales were called "devil fish" by early whalers because they were so aggressive and protective of their young when hunted.

Adult grays are about 36 to 50 feet long and weigh from 16 to 45 tons. Females are larger than males at any given age. They have been known to live up to 70 years, but the average life span is about 50 years.

Beluga Whales. The beluga, or white whale, belongs to the *odontocetes* ("toothed") group, which includes sperm and killer whales, dolphins and porpoises. Its closest relative is the narwhal. Belugas range widely in arctic and subarctic waters, and two populations occur in Alaska. The Cook Inlet population can be found in Turnagain Arm and in the Shelikof Straits region, although some belugas have been seen east to Yakutat Bay and west to Kodiak Island. Belugas of the western Arctic population range throughout the Bering, Chukchi and Beaufort seas. These

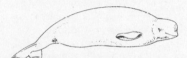

whales winter in the ice of the Bering Sea, moving in summer over 1,500 miles to concentration areas along the coast from Bristol Bay to the Mackenzie River delta in northwestern Canada.

In Alaska, large groupings occur in the Bristol Bay area, Norton Sound, Kotzebue Sound and Kasegaluk Lagoon. In Bristol Bay, belugas sometimes swim more than 100 miles a day.

Belugas are very vocal animals, producing a variety of grunts, clicks, chirps and whistles, which are used for navigating, finding prey and communicating. Because of their talkative nature, they are known as sea canaries. Belugas are also masters of echolocation, using their sophisticated sonar to detect fish and navigate in shallow waters or among gill nets without getting stranded. In some areas, they may dive more than 2,000 feet to feed on the bottom. At birth, belugas are dark blue-gray fading to white by the age of 5 or 6. Adult males are 11 to 16 feet long and weigh 1,000 to 2,000 pounds; adult females may reach 12 feet in length. Belugas can live up to 40 years.

Orcas. Also known as killer whales or blackfish, orcas are the largest member of the dolphin family. They range from the Beaufort Sea to Antarctica. In Alaska, two different stocks are designated resident and transient. A third stock offshore is being researched. It is thought that orcas migrate, riding currents south in the winter. The most unusual feature of the orca is the high dorsal fin, which has no muscle but may serve the whale as a keel would a boat. The fin on older males can grow to 6 feet in height.

Orcas are considered very intelligent and to possess all mammalian senses except smell. They take catnaps on the surface of the water and hunt in pods using complex, cooperative patterns of attack. Prey include sea lions, salmon, seals, porpoises, halibut, shark, squid, belugas and other whales. Male killer whales average 23 feet in length; females are smaller. Average life span is 30 to 40 years.

WHALING (See also Whales) Decimated
by commercial whaling in the late 1880s, the bowhead population today is growing. It is estimated that 199 whales are added to

the stock yearly; the 1999 population numbered 8,000 to 9,000.

Bowhead whales have been protected from commercial whaling for decades by a number of agreements, including the Convention for the Regulation of Whaling (1931), the International Convention for the Regulation of Whaling (1947), and by the Marine Mammal Protection Act (1972) and the Endangered Species Act (1973).

Blue, humpback, sei, fin, Northern right, bowhead and sperm whales are on the federal endangered species list.

Gray whales are also protected. Commercial whaling for grays has been banned by the International Convention for the Regulation of Whaling since 1947.

These conventions and regulations do allow for subsistence harvest by Natives. Since 1978, the International Whaling Commission (IWC) has regulated the Native taking of both bowheads and grays. The IWC reclassified the eastern stock of gray whales from a protected species to a sustained management stock with an annual catch limit of about 179 whales. The entire catch limit of grays and bowheads is reserved for Natives or by member governments on behalf of Natives. However, gray whales are not hunted in Alaska.

At a convention in 1994, the IWC revised the bowhead catch limit for Alaska, so that bowheads landed from 1995 to 1998 would not exceed 204. Hunters were forbidden to strike, land or kill calves or any bowhead accompanied by a calf.

Other species of large baleen whales, such as minke and fin whales, are occasionally taken by Alaska Eskimos for food. It is not necessary to report minke harvests. The only toothed whale taken by Eskimos is the beluga, and its harvest is monitored by the Alaska Beluga Whale Committee. Approximately 200 to 300 belugas are landed annually.

WILDFIRES Fire season starts in April or May, when winter's dead vegetation is vulnerable to any spark. Lightning is the leading cause of fires on wild land in Alaska. In June, thunderstorms bring as many as 3,000 lightning strikes a day to the Alaska Interior. By mid-July in a normal year, rainfall in Interior Alaska increases.

When wildfires threaten inhabited areas, the Bureau of Land Management (BLM) Alaska Fire Service (in the northern half of the state) and the State of Alaska Division of Forestry (in the southern half of the state) provide initial fire protection to lands managed by BLM, National Park Service, U.S. Fish and Wildlife Service, Native corporations and the state.

All land management agencies in Alaska have placed their lands in one of four protection categories—critical, full, modified and limited. These protection levels set priorities for fire fighting.

With its 570,374 square miles of land, Alaska is more than twice the size of Texas. Most of this vast area has no roads, and transportation for firefighters is usually by airplane. Fire camps are remote. Mosquito repellent is a necessity, but headlamps are often not required when the midnight sun shines all night. Aircraft bring in all supplies, even drinking water. Radios are the main means of communication with headquarters. Black spruce burns very quickly. Firefighters use chain saws to cut the trees and Pulaskis to cut through the underlying vegetation. It is nearly impossible to transport heavy equipment to fires in remote areas. Bulldozers are not used because they damage the delicate permafrost layer, leading to dramatic erosion.

Firefighters don't depend on lookout towers in the wilderness to spot wildfires. Today, computers detect the ionization from a lightning strike anywhere in the state, determine the latitude and longitude of the strike and display it on a computer screen. Detection specialists then fly to the areas of greatest risk.

When a fire is reported, computers tell

the dispatcher which agency manages the land and whether the fire should be aggressively attacked. Remote automatic weather stations report weather conditions all over Alaska, enabling weather forecasters to predict thunderstorms in any part of the state. Smoke jumpers and airplanes with fire-retardant chemicals are positioned close to the predicted thunderstorm activity.

The largest single fire ever reported in Alaska burned 5 million acres 74 miles northwest of Galena in 1957. Unusually dry weather in 1990 made it the most severe fire season on record in Alaska. Lightning was the primary cause of more than 900 fires, with an average of 2,000 strikes a day between June 26 and July 5.

In 1996, dryer than normal conditions made it difficult to control a wildfire that began near Big Lake, 60 miles northwest of Anchorage. Fire spread for more than a week, burning 37,500 acres and destroying 344 buildings. Smoke blanketed Anchorage and the Matanuska–Susitna Valley. Fire crews from the Lower 48 were brought in to help fight the blaze, which threatened populated areas. Alaska wildfires have destroyed more acreage in the past, but none have claimed more property.

Alaska Wildfires

Calendar Year	No. of Fires	Acres Burned
1991	760	1,667,965*
1992	474	150,057*
1993	869	713,116*
1994	643	265,722
1995	421	43,945
1996	724	599,267
1997	716	2,026,899
1998	413	176,000
1999	486	1,005,428
2000	369	756,296

* Combined AFS (federal) and state coverage

WILDFLOWERS
Wildflowers in Alaska usually are small, delicate and seldom showy. More than 1,500 plant species occur in the state including trees, shrubs, ferns, grasses and sedges, as well as flowering plants.

Alpine regions are particularly rich in flora and some of these species are rare. Anywhere there is tundra there is apt to be a bountiful population of flowers. The Steese Highway (Eagle Summit), Richardson Highway (Thompson Pass), Denali Highway (Maclaren Summit), Denali National Park and Preserve (Polychrome Pass), Seward Highway (Turnagain Pass), Glenn Highway just north of Anchorage (Eklutna Flats) and a locale near Wasilla (Hatcher Pass) are wonderful wildflower-viewing spots. All are readily accessible by car. Less easily accessible floral Edens are some of the Aleutian Islands, Point Hope, Anvil Mountain and the Nome–Teller Road (both near Nome), Pribilof Islands and other remote areas.

Alaska's official flower, the forget-me-not (Myosotis alpestris), is a diminutive beauty found throughout much of the state in alpine meadows and along streams. Growing to 18 inches tall, forget-me-nots are recognized by their bright blue petals surrounding a yellow eye. A northern "cousin," the arctic forget-me-not (Eritrichium aretioides), grows in sandy soil on the tundra, or in the mountains, and reaches only 4 inches in height.

Forget-me-not, Alaska's state flower.

WINDCHILL FACTOR
(SEE ALSO Hypothermia) The windchill factor can lower the effective temperature by many degrees. While Alaska's regions of lowest temperatures also generally have little wind, activities such as riding a snowmobile or even walking can produce the same effect on exposed skin.

The windchill factor, when severe, can lead to frostnip (the body's early-warning signal of potential damage from cold—a "nipping" feeling in the extremities), frostbite (formation of small ice crystals in the body tissues) or hypothermia (dangerous lowering of the body's core temperature). Other factors that combine with windchill and bring on these potentially damaging or fatal effects are exposure to wetness, exhaustion and lack of adequate clothing.

Calculating Windchill

Temperature (Fahrenheit)	Wind Speed (mph)			
	10	20	30	45
40	28	18	13	10
30	16	4	−2	−6
20	4	−10	−18	−22
10	−9	−25	−33	−38
0	−21	−39	−48	−54
−10	−33	−53	−63	−70
−20	−46	−67	−79	−85
−30	−58	−82	−94	−102
−40	−70	−96	−109	−117

WINDS (See also Climate; Windchill Factor)

Some of Alaska's windiest weather has been recorded on the western islands of the Aleutian chain. Causes are the same as elsewhere—planet rotation and the tendency of the atmosphere to equalize the difference between high and low pressure fronts. A few winds occur often and significantly enough to be given names: chinook, taku and williwaw.

Chinook. Old-timers describe chinook winds as unseasonably warm winds that can cause a thaw in the middle of winter. What they also cause are power failures and property damage, especially in the Anchorage bowl where in recent years hundreds of homes have sprung up on the sides of the Chugach Mountains, where chinook winds howl. One such wind occurred on April Fool's Day in 1980, causing $25 million in property damage. Parts of Anchorage were without power for 60 hours.

Until recently, it was not possible to predict chinook winds in Anchorage. Today, however, meteorologists can tell if the winds are gathering, when they will arrive and their relative strength. It was learned that such a warm wind could only originate in Prince William Sound and that its speed had to be at least 55 miles per hour or faster just to cross the 3,500-foot Chugach Mountains. Other factors include a storm near Bethel and relatively stable air over Anchorage. Meteorologists accurately predict chinook winds 55 percent of the time.

Taku. Taku winds are the sudden, fierce gales that sweep down from the ice cap behind Juneau and Douglas. Takus are shivering cold winds capable of reaching 100 miles per hour. They have been known to send a piece of two-by-four lumber flying through the wall of a frame house.

Williwaw. Williwaws are sudden gusts of wind that can reach more than 110 miles per hour after wind builds up on one side of a mountain and suddenly spills over into what may appear to be a relatively protected area. Williwaws are a bane of Alaska mariners. The term was originally applied to a strong wind in the Strait of Magellan.

WORLD ESKIMO–INDIAN OLYMPICS

Several hundred Native athletes from Alaska and the circumpolar nations compete each year in the World Eskimo–Indian Olympics, in Fairbanks. Held over four days in July, the games draw participants from all of Alaska's Native populations (Eskimo, Aleut, Athabascan, Tlingit, Haida and Tsimshian). Canadian, Greenlandic and Russian Eskimos are also invited to participate, as well as Native Americans from the Lower 48 states.

Feats may seem exotic—even painful—but they have roots in a hunting, fishing and gathering culture that rewards endurance, observation and cooperation. Spectators thrill to the knuckle hop and the ear-weight competition. Other traditional Native sports and competitions include the greased pole walk, fish cutting, stick pull, Indian and Eskimo dancing, men's and women's blanket toss, and the spectacular two-foot and one-foot high kicks. Some of the more boisterous games include a lively game of tug-of-war and the muktuk-eating contest.

Each year the judges choose a Native queen to reign over the Olympics. Over the next year she makes appearances throughout the state and represents the Olympics at the National Congress of American Indians.

For schedules and advance tickets, contact the World Eskimo–Indian Olympics, P.O. Box 72433, Fairbanks 99707; (907) 452-6646; www.weio.org.

2000 World Eskimo-Indian Olympic Games, First-Place Winners

Race of the Torch: *Men,* Stuart Grant 18:07; *Women,* Noel Gould 22:25

One-Hand Reach: *Men,* Garry Hull 5' 2"; *Women,* Noel Gould 4' 6"

Alaska High Kick: *Men,* George Melton 7' 2"; *Women,* Nicole Johnston 5' 6"

Indian Stick Pull: *Men,* Corey Katairoak; *Women,* Donna Rexford

Eskimo Stick Pull: *Men,* Eli Kagak; *Women,* Annette Donaldson

Ear Pull: *Men,* Robert Okpeaha; *Women,* Noel Gould

Toe Kick: *Men,* Phillip Blanchett 7' 0"; *Women,* Carol Pickett 3' 2"

Kneel Jump: *Men,* Phillip Blanchett 4' 1-1/16"; *Women,* Nicole Johnston 3' 2-1/2"

Scissors Broad Jump: *Men,* Phillip Blanchett 34' 9"; *Women,* Christina Long 25' 5-3/4"

The one-foot kick is among the ancient Native games featured at the World Eskimo-Indian Olympics. Photo by Roy Corral.

Two Foot High Kick: *Men,* Eltron Ipalook 7' 10"; *Women,* Nicole Johnston 6' 0"

One Foot High Kick: *Men,* George Melton 8' 10" (0 misses); *Women,* Nicole Johnston 6' 6"

Grease Pole Walk: *Men,* Samuel Nothstine 11' 4"; *Women,* Janet Ahlalook 7' 9"

Arm Pull: *Men,* Shawn Seetomona; *Women,* Annette Donaldson

Ear Weight: *Men,* Robert Okpeaha 876'; *Women,* Sheila Randazzo 82' 1"

Blanket Toss: *Men,* Othaniel Oomittuk; *Women,* Puyuk Joule

Drop the Bomb: *Men,* Ricko Dewilde 85' 7-1/4"; *Women,* Lily Tuzroyluke 24' 5-1/4"

Four Man Carry: *Men,* Eli Kagak 104'; *Women,* Annette Donaldson 11"

Knuckle Hop: *Men,* Rod Worl 124' 9"; *Women,* Janet Ahlalook 22' 7"

Dance Team: Eskimo, Anaktuvuk; **Indian,** St. Croix

Muktuk-Eating Contest: Donna Rexford

Native Dress Pageant: Eskimo Cloth

Parka, Claudia Tuzroyluke; **Eskimo Fur Parka,** Michelle Kalek; **Indian Cloth Dress,** Desiree Tallman; **Indian Skin Dress,** Rhodd Derendoff

Miss World Eskimo–Indian Olympics: Jessica Black, Fort Yukon/ Nenana

Howard Rock Outstanding Athlete Award: Phillip Blanchette

Olive Anderson Volunteer Award: Servant Team

WORLD WAR II (See also Military;

Unalaska/Dutch Harbor) World War II propelled development of modern Alaska. In 1940 Congress authorized the construction of Fort Richardson outside of Anchorage. After the bombing of Pearl Harbor, Alaska's strategic importance as a staging area for supplying forces in the North Pacific was apparent. The construction of the Alaska Canada Military Highway (the Alcan) began in March 1942, providing an overland route from the Lower 48 into Alaska.

The Japanese bombed a small military base at Dutch Harbor on June 3, 1942, in an attack that was designed to divert American forces north while engaging the American fleet in the central Pacific at Midway. The diversion failed and the battle at Midway became a turning point in the Pacific war.

On June 7, 1942, 1,200 Japanese troops landed on the Aleutian islands of Attu and Kiska, where they built an air base, bunkers

In a quick metropolitan area rundown: Fairbanks is the slowest-growing Alaskan city, Whittier ranks last in quality of life, and the Kodiak Coat Co. moved to Juneau. Those with a tendency to gloat at the misfortunes of others will enjoy a new T-shirt that reads, "He who laughs last, thinks slowest."

NUGGETS

The body of an American soldier was discovered in 1988, some 45 years after being listed as missing in action from World War II. The remains were found on Buldir Island, 50 miles from Shemya in the Aleutian chain.

—1989 *The ALASKA ALMANAC*®

and antiaircraft emplacements aimed at preventing the United States from using the Aleutians to launch an attack on Japan. Although the Japanese presence on the islands posed no real threat to the United States, foreign occupation was unthinkable. But the ensuing fight to drive the Japanese from the Aleutians was as much a battle against the bad weather as it was against enemy forces. More American aircraft were lost to the violent 120 mph winds, the dense fog and constant storms than to Japanese fire.

On May 11, 1943, after nearly a year of Japanese occupation, 11,000 American troops landed on Attu and engaged in a bloody battle with 2,600 Japanese troops. At the end of the month, 550 Americans were dead and 1,148 were wounded. Of the Japanese, only 28 prisoners were taken; American soldiers buried 2,351 Japanese troops killed in combat. Hundreds of others were presumed to have died and were buried in the hills or were thought to have committed suicide.

The battle for Kiska was different. On July 28, 1943, the 5,000-man Japanese garrison evacuated the island in dense fog. For three weeks, U.S. forces continued to bomb and shell the island, unaware that the island had been abandoned. In August, 35,000 Allied soldiers arrived on the island, but found only a few stray Japanese dogs.

YUKON QUEST INTERNATIONAL SLED DOG RACE

(SEE ALSO Dog Mushing; Iditarod Trail Sled Dog Race) The Yukon Quest International Sled Dog Race was begun by Roger Williams and LeRoy Shank in 1983 to foster a long-distance sled dog race between Fairbanks, Alaska, and Whitehorse, Yukon Territory. The first race took place in February 1984, when 26 teams competed, and had a purse of $50,000.

Named for the old-time winter "Highway of the North," the Yukon River, the 1,000-mile trek usually takes between 11 and 14 days to complete, depending on weather and trail. The Quest is held in February and is one of the toughest of sled dog races. During their journey between the two cities, teams retrace the footsteps of gold-rush trappers, miners, explorers and missionaries (SEE MAP, page 230). Mushers cross four major summits and diverse, challenging terrain. They travel 250 miles on the frozen Yukon River and cross the longest unguarded international border in the world.

The direction of the race alternates each year. Between the start and finish lines are a series of official checkpoints.

The longest distance between checkpoints is 290 miles, between Dawson City and Carmacks. The only checkpoint at which a musher may receive help is at Dawson City, where a 36-hour layover is mandatory. Rules allow for 8 dogs minimum and 14 dogs maximum at the start. Five dogs are the minimum allowed at the finish, and only four dogs can be dropped during the course of the race. Each musher may use only one sled throughout the race, and mandatory equipment includes a sleeping bag, hand ax, snowshoes, promotional material and eight booties per dog.

Information on the Yukon Quest is posted at www.yukonquest.org.

2001 Yukon Quest Results

	Musher	Days	Hrs.	Min.
1	Tim Osmar	11	15	10
2	Andrew Lesh	11	16	16
3	William Kleedehn	11	19	18
4	Joran Freeman	11	22	10
5	John Schandelmeier	12	0	4
6	Frank Turner	12	4	57
7	Cim Smyth	12	8	22
8	Carrie Farr	12	10	19
9	Ed Hopkins	12	11	13
10	Jerry Louden	12	12	11
11	Cor Guimond	12	14	46
12	Jim Hendrick	12	15	20
13	Dave Dalton	12	16	45
14	Bill Steyer	13	4	24
15	Bill Pinkham	14	5	8
16	Doug Grilliot	14	8	16
17	Jim Oehlschlaeger	4	19	24
18	Kyla Boivin	14	20	18
19	Bruce Milne	16	6	59

Winners and Times

Year	Musher	Days	Hrs.	Min.	Prize
1991	Charlie Boulding, Nenana	10	21	12	25,000
1992	John Schandelmeier, Paxson	11	21	40	29,837
1993	Charlie Boulding, Nenana	10	19	09	25,000
1994	Lavonne Barve	10	22	44	20,000
1995	Frank Turner, Whitehorse, YT	10	16	20	20,000
1996	John Schandelmeier, Paxson	12	16	47	20,000
1997	Rick Mackey, Nenana	12	05	55	20,000
1998	Bruce Lee, Denali Park	11	11	27	30,000
1999	Ramy Brooks	11	07	59	30,000
2000	Aliy Zirkle, Two River	10*	22	01	30,000
2001	Tim Osmar	11	15	10	30,000

*Due to poor trail conditions, the 2000 race ended at Takhini Hot Springs, near Whitehorse.

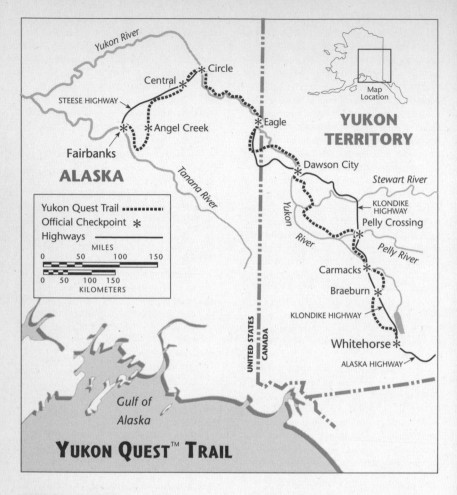

Yukon River

Circle

Central

STEESE HIGHWAY

Angel Creek

Eagle

Fairbanks

ALASKA

Tanana River

YUKON
TERRITORY

Dawson City

Stewart River

KLONDIKE
HIGHWAY

Pelly Crossing

Yukon

River

Pelly River

Carmacks

Braeburn

KLONDIKE HIGHWAY

Whitehorse

ALASKA HIGHWAY

Map
Location

Yukon Quest Trail ●●●●●●●●
Official Checkpoint ✳
Highways _____

MILES
0   50   100   150

0   50   100   150
KILOMETERS

UNITED STATES
CANADA

Gulf of
Alaska

YUKON QUEST™ TRAIL

YUKON RIVER (SEE ALSO Rivers) The
Yukon River is the longest river in Alaska,
flowing in a 2,000-mile arc (1,400 miles in
Alaska) from its British Columbia
headwaters across the Interior's forested
hills, narrow mountain valleys and vast
tundra flats to the Bering Sea. The fifth-
largest river in North America, the third
largest in the United States, the Yukon River
watershed drains 330,000 square miles—a
third of Alaska.

Archaeological evidence indicates that
humans may have lived along the river
more than 20,000 years ago. Historically,
two Native groups occupied the Yukon
valley: the Yup'ik Eskimos and the
Athabascans. Most Native villages were
established on the north bank of the river,
apparently the preferred side of the river,
to fish for the millions of migrating king,
coho and chum salmon that returned to
the river system to spawn. These fish return
to the Yukon today and fish traps and
summer fish camps can still be seen
along the river.

With the arrival of European trappers,
the Yukon became a well-used supply
route for the Interior. Travel was by
steamboat or canoe during the summer
and by dogsled from October to May,
when the river was frozen.

The Yukon has never been dammed

and is crossed by only one bridge, the Yukon River Bridge. It is on the Dalton Highway near Stevens Village, just south of the Arctic Circle.

The Yukon River attracts canoeists, kayakers and others for float trips. Many commercial guides offer excursions, and the popular jumping-off point is at Eagle. A summer float trip downriver through Yukon–Charley Rivers National Preserve to Circle is 154 river miles and averages 5 to 10 days. Also available are float trips from Dawson City, Yukon, to Circle that make a stop halfway at Eagle.

You can rent canoes in Eagle or choose a trip with a local commercial guide with gear supplied.

For information on proper clothing, weather conditions and best time to make a float, contact the National Park Service, Box 167, Eagle 99378; (907) 547-2233.

ZIP CODES (SEE Populations and Zip Codes)

Yearly Highlights, 2000–2001

Following are brief accounts of Alaska news from mid-2000 to mid-2001. Primary sources are the *Anchorage Daily News, Fairbanks Daily News-Miner* and The Associated Press.

Airport renamed for senator.
Anchorage International Airport was renamed in 2000 as Ted Stevens Anchorage International Airport to honor Alaska's senior senator.

Stevens, a Republican, has been in the Senate since 1968.

"There was a growing consensus among legislators and community leaders that something should be done to honor Sen. Stevens while he's still alive," said state Sen. Tim Kelly, one of the sponsors of the bill. "Renaming Anchorage's airport, the state's biggest and a hub for international air traffic, seemed an obvious choice."

About 5 million people a year pass through Alaska's largest airport, which is the No. 1 cargo hub in the nation.

As part of the renaming ceremonies, 1,200 people gathered at the airport's largest hangar for a banquet in Stevens' honor.

Stevens said he was grateful but a little dismayed by all the attention. He told the *Anchorage Daily News* he had no plans to slow down and would run for reelection in 2002.

Base Camp Annie comes down from the mountain. Annie Duquette, known as Base Camp Annie to the thousands of mountaineers who climb Mount McKinley, has called it quits after 10 years.

At the start of the climbing season each spring, Duquette would set up camp on the Kahiltna Glacier. From her perch at 7,200 feet she provided reports on the rapidly changing weather conditions for the pilots who flew tourists and climbers to the mountain. She also served as a messenger, helper and nurse to mountaineers during the 2 1/2-month climbing season.

Duquette said she wouldn't miss the middle-of-the-night trips to the outdoor bathroom in temperatures that dipped to 20 below zero. But she told The Associated Press it would be difficult to leave the job she loved.

"My whole life is on this mountain. You have to have some strong feelings," she said.

Alaskans join Gomez for Stanley Cup Party. Scott Gomez, the first National Hockey League player from Alaska, shared the New Jersey Devils 2000 Stanley Cup victory with Alaskans.

Each Devils player got a day of personal time with the cup, and Gomez, the NHL's rookie of the year, chose to bring the cup to Anchorage, where he grew up.

More than 8,000 hockey fans from across the state showed up in downtown Anchorage on July 14 to see, touch and pose with the cup.

"This is yours, too," Gomez told the crowd. "Kiss it, grab it, do whatever."

Chum salmon fail to return to Western Alaska. Gov. Tony Knowles declared a disaster emergency in 2000 for parts of Western Alaska, due to the collapse of salmon fisheries.

Chum and king salmon runs to the Yukon and Kuskokwim river drainages and the Norton Sound area were just a small fraction of their historic norms. On the Yukon, chum returns were the worst since statehood.

It marked the third time in four years that the governor declared a disaster for the region when salmon runs collapsed.

The reason for the collapse was not known. The dismal returns hurt both commercial fishermen and those who fish for subsistence.

"People are concerned and scared," said Tom Kron, regional supervisor for Fish and Game for the Western Alaska region. "The foundation has fallen out for them."

The disaster declaration opened the way for millions of dollars in state and federal disaster aid.

Alaska voters reject tax cap, marijuana initiatives. Alaskans overwhelmingly voted down ballot measures in 2000 that would have capped property taxes statewide and legalized marijuana and hemp products.

The marijuana initiative would have made Alaska's marijuana laws the most liberal in the country, doing away with civil and criminal penalties for those 18 or older who used marijuana or hemp products. People previously convicted of marijuana crimes would have been granted amnesty. The law also opened the door to the possibility that those fined or imprisoned for marijuana crimes could receive restitution payments.

Supporters argued that decriminalizing marijuana would free the state from a costly drug war. Opponents feared it would turn the state into a haven for potheads and drug dealers.

The tax cap proposal would have limited property taxes statewide to 1 percent of a property's assessed value. It would have cut about $150 million from local budgets across the state, raising fears of deep cuts in government services. Local officials throughout Alaska warned that schools would suffer, museums and libraries would see reduced hours, and streets would remain clogged with snow long after storms.

"Quality of life up here is important,"

said Gena Columbus of Anchorage after casting her ballot against the cap.

Steller sea lion ruling restricts pollock fishery. The Bering Sea and Gulf of Alaska pollock and cod fisheries faced tough new restrictions in 2000 after federal regulators found there could be a link between commercial fishing and the steep decline in Steller sea lions in Western Alaska.

U.S. Sen. Ted Stevens won a delay in full implementation of the restrictions while securing money for further study of the effects of fishing as well as changes in ocean temperatures, contaminants in the environment and the role of predators.

During the past three decades the Steller sea lion population in the Bering Sea and western Gulf of Alaska has declined by about 80 percent. The animals now number about 33,600.

Banker, philanthropist Rasmuson dies. Elmer E. Rasmuson, the son of missionary parents who grew up to become mayor of Anchorage and chairman of the state's largest bank, died Dec. 1, 2000. He was 91.

He left all of his personal fortune, estimated at more than $400 million, to charity. During his lifetime he gave generously to Alaska charities and institutions, most notably the University of Alaska.

"Elmer Rasmuson not only witnessed history, he helped make it as a businessman with an exceptional sense of civic pride, responsibility and dedication," Gov. Tony Knowles said.

Rasmuson was born in Yakutat and grew up in Skagway where his father operated the Bank of Alaska. As a boy, he started working at the bank as a janitor and, later, as a teller and bookkeeper.

Educated at the University of Washington and Harvard Business School, Rasmuson worked in banking, accounting and economics in New York, New Jersey and Texas before returning to Alaska in 1943 to take over for his father at National Bank of Alaska.

Rasmuson ran for mayor of Anchorage after the 1964 earthquake and served until 1967, overseeing much of the city's reconstruction.

He was a founder of the Anchorage Museum of History, the first chairman of the Alaska Permanent Fund and served on the University of Alaska board of regents.

Rasmuson retired from active management of the bank in 1974. Wells Fargo & Co. bought National Bank of Alaska in 1999.

Oil producers study gas line. The state's three biggest oil producers announced in December 2000 that they would spend $75 million to study construction of a gas pipeline to bring North Slope natural gas to markets in the Lower 48.

Alaska's North Slope is estimated to hold about 35 trillion cubic feet of natural gas—about 20 percent of known U.S. gas reserves. It has remained in the ground, due to the high costs and technological challenges involved in bringing it to market.

A surge in demand and rising prices in recent years have sparked renewed efforts to develop the reserves.

In announcing the joint study, officials with BP Exploration (Alaska) Inc., Phillips Alaska Inc. and Exxon Mobil Corp. said they would evaluate preliminary design and engineering work and permitting requirements as well as possible routes for a gas line.

Gov. Tony Knowles advocated construction of a line that would follow the Alaska Highway but producers were also studying a route along the Arctic coast that would go south through Canada's Mackenzie River valley.

Congressman Don Young said the announcement could be the start of what he called one of the most important economic projects in Alaska's history.

State's oldest regional airline cuts back. Reeve Aleutian Airways, the state's oldest regional air carrier, suspended its regularly scheduled flights and laid off about 250 workers in December.

Company President Dick Reeve said competition had eroded its business in recent years, to the point where the company didn't have enough customers on its scheduled flights to support operations. The company continued offering charter and contract flights. Reeve said the airline's bank, pilots and other creditors provided some financial relief, which helped the company avoid filing for bankruptcy.

The company provided scheduled service to Adak, Bethel, Cold Bay, Port Heiden, Sand Point, St. Paul and St. George.

Reeve Airways began operations in 1932 in Valdez when company founder Bob Reeve began flying gold miners and their supplies into remote areas.

When World War II broke out, Reeve moved to Anchorage and won a contract with the military to fly men and supplies to bases throughout the state, including the Aleutians.

ANWR takes center stage in national energy debate. Efforts to open the Arctic National Wildlife Refuge to oil exploration gained new momentum as President George Bush made development of the refuge a centerpiece of his national energy policy.

Alaska Sen. Frank Murkowski introduced a bill that would open the coastal plain of the refuge to drilling.

Environmentalists promised to fight any drilling proposals, and drilling opponents in Congress introduced bills that would set aside the coastal plain as wilderness, permanently protecting the area.

The coastal plain of the refuge is estimated to hold between 5.6 billion and 16 billion barrels of oil. It is also the calving grounds for thousands of caribou and attracts millions of migratory birds during summer.

Anchorage hosts Special Olympics. More than 2,400 athletes and coaches from 68 countries traveled to Anchorage as the city hosted the Special Olympics World Winter Games.

Organizers said the event was the largest sporting event ever held in Alaska. More than 7,000 Alaskans volunteered to help with everything from scorekeeping to serving on cheering squads. The athletes competed in alpine skiing, cross-country skiing, floor hockey, figure skating, speed skating, snowshoeing and snowboarding.

Founder of the games, Eunice Kennedy Shriver, had high praise for the city's efforts, saying the winter games were the best in the history of Special Olympics.

"This week here in beautiful Alaska, we have seen the best in sports, the best in volunteers, the best in families and the best in sponsors," Shriver said at the closing ceremonies.

Suggested Reading

Other Alaska books from Alaska Northwest Books™, WestWinds Press® and Graphic Arts Center Publishing®

Armstrong, Robert H. *Alaska's Birds.* Seattle: Alaska Northwest Books, 1994.

———. *Alaska's Fish.* Seattle: Alaska Northwest Books, 1996.

Amstrong, Robert H., and Marge Hermans. *Alaska's Natural Wonders.* Portland, Ore.: Alaska Northwest Books, 2000.

Billburg, Rudy, as told to Jim Rearden. *In the Shadow of Eagles: From Barnstormer to Bush Pilot, A Flyer's Story.* Seattle: Alaska Northwest Books, 1998.

Brown, Tricia (text) and Roy Corral (photographs). *Children of the Midnight Sun: Young Native Voices of Alaska.* Seattle: Alaska Northwest Books, 1998.

———. *Fairbanks: Alaska's Heart of Gold: A Traveler's Guide.* Portland, Ore.: Alaska Northwest Books, 2000.

Chandonnet, Ann. *The Alaska Heritage Seafood Cookbook.* Seattle: Alaska Northwest Books, 1999.

Field, Conrad, and Carmen Field. *Alaska's Seashore Creatures.* Seattle: Alaska Northwest Books, 1999.

Flowers, Pam, with Ann Dixon. *Alone across the Arctic.* Portland, Ore.: Alaska Northwest Books, 2001.

Grescoe, Paul and Audrey. *Alaska: The Cruise-Lover's Guide.* Seattle: Alaska Northwest Books, 1998.

Heacox, Kim. *Alaska's Inside Passage.* Portland, Ore.: Graphic Arts Center Publishing, 1997.

Hirschmann, Fred. *Alaska from the Air.* Portland, Ore.: Graphic Arts Center Publishing, 1999.

Hirschmann, Fred (photographs), and Kim Heacox (text). *Bush Pilots of Alaska.* Portland, Ore.: Graphic Arts Center Publishing, 1989.

Holleman, Marybeth. *Alaska's Prince William Sound: A Traveler's Guide.* Portland, Ore.: Alaska Northwest Books, 2000.

Jans, Nick. *A Place Beyond: Finding Home in Arctic Alaska.* Seattle: Alaska Northwest Books, 1996.

Jettmar, Karen. *Alaska's Glacier Bay.* Seattle: Alaska Northwest Books, 1997.

Keith, Sam, with Richard Proenneke. *One Man's Wilderness.* Seattle: Alaska Northwest Books, 1999.

Mergler, Wayne, ed. *The Last New Land: Stories of Alaska, Past and Present.* Seattle: Alaska Northwest Books, 1996.

Miller, Debbie. *Midnight Wilderness: Journeys in Alaska's Arctic National Wildlife Refuge.* Portland, Ore.: Alaska Northwest Books, 2000.

Mr. Whitekeys. *Mr. Whitekeys' Alaska Bizarre.* Seattle: Alaska Northwest Books, 1995.

Murie, Margaret. *Two in the Far North.* Seattle: Alaska Northwest Books, 1978; rev. 1997.

Murphy, Claire Rudolf, and Jane G. Haigh. *Gold Rush Women.* Seattle: Alaska Northwest Books, 1997.

———. *Children of the Gold Rush.* Portland, Ore.: Alaska Northwest Books, 2001.

———. *Gold Rush Dogs.* Portland, Ore.: Alaska Northwest Books, 2001.

Murphy, Claire Rudolf (text), and Charles Mason (photographs). *A Child's Alaska.* Seattle: Alaska Northwest Books, 1994.

Ritter, Harry. *Alaska's History.* Seattle: Alaska Northwest Books, 1993.

Rogers, Jean (text), and Rie Muñoz (illustrations). *Goodbye, My Island.* Portland, Ore.: Alaska Northwest Books, 2001.

Romano-Lax, Andromeda (text), and Greg Daniels and Bill Sherwonit (photographs). *Alaska's Kenai Peninsula: A Traveler's Guide.* Portland, Ore.: Alaska Northwest Books, 2001.

Sherwonit Bill. *To the Top of Denali: Climbing Adventures on North America's Highest Peak.* Seattle: Alaska Northwest Books, 1990; rev. 2000.

Troll, Ray (text and illustrations). *Sharkabet: A Sea of Sharks from A to Z.* Portland, Ore.: WestWinds Press, 2002.

Index

access to wilderness areas, 151
age of residents, 5
agriculture, 9–10, 33, 104
air travel, 10–12, 233; airport
  names, 231; flying fish and,
  30; hunting and, 100
aklaq (bears), 99. See also bears
akutak, 67
Akutan Volcano, 60
Alaska Army National Guard, 123
Alaska Aviation Heritage
  Museum, 130
Alaska-Canada boundary, 12–13,
  76
Alaska Communications Systems,
  211
Alaska Day, 94
Alaska Experience Center, 130
Alaska Highway, 13–14. See also
  highways
Alaska Homestead and Historical
  Museum, 132
Alaska Indian Arts, 134
Alaska Medal of Heroism,
  119–121
Alaska Museum of Natural
  History, 133
Alaska National Interest Lands
  Conservation Act (ANILCA),
  112, 142, 144, 148, 150
Alaska Native Claims Settlement
  Act, 111
Alaska Native Heritage Center,
  130–131
Alaska Natives. See Native
  Alaskans
Alaska Peninsula, 191–192
Alaska Permanent Fund, 171·
Alaska Public Lands Information
  Centers, 41, 131, 133, 135,
  138, 144
Alaska Public Radio Network,
  187
Alaska Railroad, 188
Alaska Resources Library and
  Information Services, 131
Alaska SeaLife Center, 137
Alaska State Archives, 135
Alaska State Museum, 135
Alaska State Troopers Museum,
  131
alcoholic beverages, 14–15, 99,
  121
Aleut people, 154–155, 192,
  195; arts and crafts, 22, 153;
  language, 113; masks, 118
Aleutian Islands, 191–192
Aleutian terns, 28
Alfred Starr Nenana Cultural
  Center, 136
Alpine Historical Park, 138
Alutiiq Museum and
  Archaeological Repository, 136
Alutiiq people, 155
Alyeska, 15
Alyeska Pipeline, 53, 138, 165,
  172–174
American Bald Eagle Foundation,
  134
amphibians, 15
Anaktuvuk Pass, 130, 175
Anchor Point, 36–39, 175

Anchorage, 15–16; events,
  36–39; growth, 184; historic
  sites, 143; museums,
  130–131; population, 175;
  "Scoop the Poop Day," 119;
  sewage problems, 142;
  skiing, 200–201; Special
  Olympics, 233; sunshine, 40;
  temperatures, 46; whistling
  laws, 186
Anchorage Museum of History
  and Art, 131
Anchorage Times, 161
Andrew Berg Cabin, 142–143
Aniakchak National Monument,
  145
ANILCA (Alaska National Interest
  Lands Conservation Act),
  112, 142, 144, 148, 150
annual events, 36–39
antiquities laws, 16
Anvik: Anvik Historical Society
  and Museum, 132;
  population, 176
ANWR (Arctic National Wildlife
  Refuge), 233
archaeology, 16–17
archives, 105, 130–139
Arctic Circle, 17–18
Arctic National Wildlife Refuge,
  233
Arctic region, 48, 190–191
Arctic terns, 28
Arctic warblers, 28
Arctic Winter Games, 18
arts and crafts, 152–153;
  basketry, 22–23; beadwork,
  23; Chilkat blankets, 43–44;
  ivory, 107–108; masks,
  117–118; skins, 202;
  soapstone, 202; totems,
  214–216
assisted living homes, 171–172
Athabascan Indians, 22, 23, 52,
  153–154. See also Native
  Alaskans
AT&T Alascom, 211
auctioning land, 112
auklets, 29
aurora borealis, 18–20
automobiles, shipping, 70,
  197–198

baidarkas, 20
baleen, 20, 22
baleen whales, 222, 224
Ballistic Missile Early Warning
  System stations, 123
barabaras, 20
Baranov, Alexander, 20–21.
  See also Sitka
Baranov Museum, 136
Barnette, E. T., 67
barometric pressure, 45
Barrow, 21; events, 37–39;
  growth, 184; museum, 132;
  population, 176;
  temperatures, 46
Base Camp Annie, 231
baseball, 21–22
basketry, 22–23
bats, 116

beach ivory, 108
beadwork, 23
bears, 23–25, 99, 110, 113;
  aklaq, 99; McNeil River State
  Game Sanctuary, 118–119;
  waking, 19
Beaton, Neil, 159
beavers, 115
beluga whales, 130, 222, 223,
  224
Bering, Vitus, 25–26
Bering Land Bridge, 26, 145
Bering Sea Coast region, 191
berries, 26–27
Bethel: events, 37–39;
  Kuskokwim Ice Classic, 160;
  museum, 132; population,
  176; temperatures, 46
bibliography, 234–235
bicycles, 102
Big Delta: Big Delta State
  Historical Park, 132;
  population, 176
Big Lake, 36–39, 176
billikens, 27
birds, 27–30; oil spill, 168;
  raven-caused power outages,
  168; skin usage in parkas,
  170; state bird, 208
birth and death rates, 185
bison, 99, 113–114
black bears, 24, 99, 113
Black Rapid Roadhouse, 144
black-tailed deer, 114
blanket toss, 30
blind resident hunters, 114
bluethroats, 29
BMEW (Ballistic Missile Early
  Warning System stations),
  123
boalotchkee, 195
boating, 30–32; baidarkas, 20;
  cruises, 55–56; ferries, 69–71;
  information sources, 104;
  kayaks, 20, 31, 104; umiaks,
  218
boom cycles, 62–63
boots, 32, 129–130, 199
bore tide, 32
boroughs, 82, 83–84, 182–184
bowhead whale, 130, 222, 224
breakup, 32; Nenana Ice Classic,
  158–160
breweries, 121
Bristol Bay Historical Museum,
  136
brown/grizzly bears, 24, 99,
  113, 118–119
buildings, mailing to building
  site, 60
bumper stickers, 14, 90
bunny boots, 32
bus lines, 32–33
Bush: community telephone
  numbers, 212; defined, 32;
  mail delivery rates, 60
business. See economy
bust cycles, 62–63

cabbage, 33
cabin fever, 33–34
cabins, 34–35, 93, 140, 150–151

flag, 205
flowers: state, 208; wildflowers, 225
food costs, 53
forest products industry, 213–214
forests: fires, 224–225; national forests, 140–142; spruce bark beetle, 203–204; state forests, 204; taiga, 209; timber, 213–214; trees and shrubs, 216–217
forget-me-nots, 225
Fort Richardson Fish and Wildlife Center, 131
fossils: mastodons, 17, 107; state, 208
Fourth Avenue Theater, 131
foxes, 115
frazil, 100
furs, 76, 169, 202

Gakona: Gakona Historic District, 143; population, 178
gas industry. SEE oil and gas industry
Gates of the Arctic National Park, 145
GCI (General Communication Inc.), 211–212
geese, 28, 29
gems, 194–195, 208
General Communication Inc., 211–212
geography, 76–77
George I. Ashby Memorial Museum, 132
geothermal hot springs, 96–97
Girdwood, 37–39, 134, 178
Glacier Bay National Park, 145
glaciers, 5, 77–80
Glennallen, 36–39, 143, 178
gold, 80–81, 105, 124, 208. SEE ALSO Chilkoot Trail
Gold Dredge No. 8, 134
gold strikes and rushes, 81, 91
golfing, 82
Gomez, Scott, 231
government, 82–88; courts, 54–55; legislature information, 105; officials, 84–88; political parties, 174–175
governors, 5, 86; territorial, 84–85
gray whales, 222–223, 224
grease ice, 100
grenades, 83
grizzly bears, 24, 99, 113, 118–119
groundfish, 73
guides and outfitters, 151
Gulf Coast Region, 189–190
guns, 83

Haida people, 22, 113, 153, 195
Haines, 37–39, 134–135, 178
Haines State Forest, 204
halibut, 72
harbors, 30–31, 71–72
hares, 116
Harry A. Johnson Trapline Cabin, 143
Haul Road, 191. SEE ALSO Dalton Highway
Headline of the Year award, 163

health facilities, 95–96, 105, 171–172
Heritage Library and Museum, 131
heroism, 119–121
herring, 72
hides, sewing, 202
highways, 5, 88–90; Alaska Highway, 13–14; Dalton Highway, 56–57; information sources, 105; Marine Highway System, 69–71; speed limits, 203
hiking, 44, 90
historic parks and sites, 16, 130–139, 142–144
historical archives, 105
historical societies, 130–139
history, 90–94
hoary marmots, 115
hockey, 231
holidays, 94, 196
Homer: casualness and, 191; events, 36–39; historic sites, 143; mud and dust, 109; museum, 135; population, 178; temperatures, 46
homesite program, 112
Homestead Acts, 112
homesteading, 94, 112
hooligan, 94–95
Hoonah: Hoonah Cultural Center, 135; population, 178
Hope: Hope and Sunrise Historical and Mining Museum, 135; population, 178
horned puffins, 29
hospitals, 95–96
hostels, 96
hot springs, 96–97
hotcakes, 203
hours of daylight, 57
House of Representatives, 87
House of Wickersham, 135
household goods, shipping, 198
housing: costs, 53; information sources, 105
Houston, 38–39, 178
hunting, 97–100, 105, 114, 208–209
Huslia: Huslia Cultural Center, 135; population, 178
Hyder/Stewart annual events, 37–39
hydroelectric power, 66
hypothermia, 100; windchill, 225–226

ice. SEE glaciers; ice fields; icebergs
ice breakup, 32, 158–160
ice cream, 67
ice fields, 77–80
ice fog, 101
icebergs, 100–101
iceworms, 101
Iditarod Trail Sled Dog Race, 101–104, 138
igloos, 104
Imaginarium Science Discovery Center, 131
income of residents, 5, 54
Independent Mine State Historic Park, 137

Indian peoples, 23, 118, 153–154. SEE ALSO Native Alaskans
inflation, 53
information centers, 50–51
information sources, 104–106
insects: mosquitoes, 125; no-see-ums, 164; spruce bark beetle, 203–204; state, 208
Inside Passage, 106
Interior and Arctic Alaska Aeronautical Museum, 134
Interior forest, 213
Interior region, 190
Internet service providers, 211–212
Internet usage, 10
Inuit Circumpolar Conference, 106–107
Inupiaq language, 113
Inupiat Heritage Center, 132
Inupiat people, 152, 154
Isabel Miller Museum, 137
islands, 77, 107
ivory, 107–108

jade, 108, 208
Japan, exports to, 67
jobs. SEE employment
judges, 54–55
Juneau, 108–109; events, 36–39; growth, 184; Juneau-Douglas City Museum, 135; museums, 135; population, 178; temperatures, 46
justices, 54–55

Kake Tribal Heritage Foundation, 135
Kasaan Totem Park, 137
Katmai National Park, 145
kayaks, 20, 31, 104
K'beq Kenaitze Indian Tribe archives, 135
Kenai: events, 36–39; growth, 184; Kenai Visitors and Cultural Center, 135; population, 179
Kenai Fjords National Park, 145
Kenai Peninsula skiing, 201
Kennecott Mine, 109, 136
Kennicott Glacier, 109
Ketchikan: events, 36–39; growth, 184; museums, 135–136; population, 179; temperatures, 47
killer whales (orcas), 222, 223
king salmon, 72, 208, 231–232
King Salmon (town), 47, 179
kittiwakes, 29
Klawock: Klawock Totem Park, 136; population, 179; totem pole, 215
Klondike Gold Rush National Historical Park, 44, 137–138, 145
Knik: Knik Museum, 138–139; population, 179
Kobuk Valley National Park, 145
Kodiak, 109; Coat Company loss, 228; events, 36–39; growth, 184; Kodiak Historical Society, 136; museums, 110, 136; population, 179; temperatures, 47